The Linguistics of Crime

Bringing together scholars from a range of disciplines, this book explores the analysis of crime-related language. Drawing on ideas from stylistics, pragmatics, cognitive linguistics, metaphor theory, critical discourse analysis, multimodality, corpus linguistics and intertextuality, it compares and contrasts the linguistic representation of crime across a range of genres, both fictitious (crime novels and crime in TV, film and music) and in real life (crime reporting, prison discourse and statements used in courts). It touches on current political topics like #BlackLivesMatter, human (child) trafficking and the genocide of the Kurds, among others, making it essential reading for linguists, criminologists and those with a general interest in crime-related topics alike. Covering a variety of text genres and methodological approaches, and united by the aim of deciphering how crime is portrayed ideologically, this book is the next step in developing research at the intersection of linguistics, criminology, literature and media studies.

JOHN DOUTHWAITE has a long-standing career as Professor of English Language. He was formerly Professor of English Language, Head of English Language at the Department of Foreign Languages and Head of Postgraduate Teacher Training Course in Foreign Languages, Literatures and Cultures at the University of Genoa, Italy. Recent publications include *The Stylistics of Landscapes, the Landscapes of Stylistics* (ed.) (2017).

ULRIKE TABBERT is a Senior Public Prosecutor (Oberamtsanwältin) at a German Prosecution Office and holds a PhD in Linguistics from the University of Huddersfield. She is a Member of the Poetics and Linguistics Association (PALA). Recent publications include *Language and Crime* (2016).

The Linguistics of Crime

Edited by
John Douthwaite
Università degli Studi di Genova

Ulrike Tabbert
University of Huddersfield

Shaftesbury Road, Cambridge CB2 8EA, United Kingdom

One Liberty Plaza, 20th Floor, New York, NY 10006, USA

477 Williamstown Road, Port Melbourne, VIC 3207, Australia

314–321, 3rd Floor, Plot 3, Splendor Forum, Jasola District Centre, New Delhi – 110025, India

103 Penang Road, #05–06/07, Visioncrest Commercial, Singapore 238467

Cambridge University Press is part of Cambridge University Press & Assessment, a department of the University of Cambridge.

We share the University's mission to contribute to society through the pursuit of education, learning and research at the highest international levels of excellence.

www.cambridge.org
Information on this title: www.cambridge.org/9781108456951

DOI: 10.1017/9781108581332

© Cambridge University Press & Assessment 2022

This publication is in copyright. Subject to statutory exception and to the provisions of relevant collective licensing agreements, no reproduction of any part may take place without the written permission of Cambridge University Press & Assessment.

First published 2022
First paperback edition 2025

A catalogue record for this publication is available from the British Library

Library of Congress Cataloging-in-Publication data
Names: Douthwaite, John, editor. | Tabbert, Ulrike, editor.
Title: The linguistics of crime / edited by John Douthwaite, Ulrike Tabbert.
Description: Cambridge, UK ; New York : Cambridge University Press, 2021. | Includes bibliographical references and index.
Identifiers: LCCN 2021040761 (print) | LCCN 2021040762 (ebook) | ISBN 9781108471008 (hardback) | ISBN 9781108456951 (paperback) | ISBN 9781108581332 (epub)
Subjects: LCSH: Crime in mass media | Crime in literature. | Language and culture. | Mass media and language. | BISAC: LANGUAGE ARTS & DISCIPLINES / Linguistics / General | LCGFT: Essays.
Classification: LCC P96.C74 L57 2021 (print) | LCC P96.C74 (ebook) | DDC 364.01/4–dc23/eng/20211120
LC record available at https://lccn.loc.gov/2021040761
LC ebook record available at https://lccn.loc.gov/2021040762

ISBN   978-1-108-47100-8   Hardback
ISBN   978-1-108-45695-1   Paperback

Cambridge University Press & Assessment has no responsibility for the persistence or accuracy of URLs for external or third-party internet websites referred to in this publication and does not guarantee that any content on such websites is, or will remain, accurate or appropriate.

Contents

List of Figures	*page*	vii
List of Tables		viii
List of Contributors		ix

1 Editorial Introduction   1
   JOHN DOUTHWAITE AND ULRIKE TABBERT

2 The Metaphoric and Metonymic Conceptualisation of the Other   16
   ZOLTÁN KÖVECSES AND JOHN DOUTHWAITE

3 Prison Metaphors: Conveying the Experience of Confinement   39
   MONIKA FLUDERNIK

4 Ideology in Mainstream Crime Fiction   57
   JOHN DOUTHWAITE

5 A Critical and Stylistic Analysis of the Depiction of the Transnational Human Trafficking Victim in Minette Walters' *The Cellar*   88
   CHRISTIANA GREGORIOU

6 The Linguistic Construction of Political Crimes in Kurdish-Iraqi Sherko Bekas' Poem *The Small Mirrors*   105
   MAHMOOD KADIR IBRAHIM AND ULRIKE TABBERT

7 Stylistic Aspects of Detective Fiction in Translation: The Case of 'The Murders in the Rue Morgue' in Slovenian   121
   SIMON ZUPAN

8 Transnational Adaptations of Sherlock Holmes: A Relevance-Theoretic Discussion   150
   ANNE FURLONG

9 The Ethical Effects of Voice-Over Narration on a Victim Testimonial: A Text-World Analysis of 'The Bed Intruder' Meme   174
   M'BALIA THOMAS

vi   Contents

10 Realising Betrayal: A Multimodal Stylistic Analysis of a Scene
    from the TV Series *The Sopranos*   194
    SIMON STATHAM

11 'Nossa Vida é Bandida': Reading Rio Prohibited Funk from
    a CDA Perspective   214
    ANDREA MAYR

12 Deviant Mind Style of a Schizophrenic Offender   253
    ULRIKE TABBERT

13 Narrower or Broader Ground? The Role and Function of
    Metaphors in Legal Discourse   282
    DOUGLAS MARK PONTON AND MARCO CANEPA

14 Condemning the Condemners: The Portrayal of Regulators in
    UK News about Corporate Crime   301
    ILSE A. RAS

15 Ideology in Critical Crime Fiction   330
    JOHN DOUTHWAITE

The full version of this chapter can be accessed online at www.cambridge.org/
LinguisticsOfCrime

Index   332

Figures

2.1	An image-schematic structure for the *Heart of Darkness*	*page* 26
3.1	Source terms for describing prisons (PRISON IS X metaphors)	41
9.1	Text-world architecture of 'The Bed Intruder'	185
14.1	Collocation of FSA and 'failed'	321

Tables

6.1	The tools of Critical Stylistics and their conceptual categories	*page* 110
12.1	Calculating statistical significance for first-person-singular pronoun use in JDC compared with LIWC 2015	265
13.1	The narrow ground versus the broad ground	295
14.1	Overview of articles and words per newspaper in corporate fraud corpus	304
14.2	Top twenty-five collocates of regulator|regulators, sorted by frequency	307
14.3	Top five n-grams for financial, authority, services, commission, securities, exchange and conduct	308
14.4	Top twenty-five collocates for FSA and Securities # Exchange Commission, sorted by frequency	309
14.5	Top twenty-five collocating verbs to regulator|regulators	318
14.6	Aggressive, fail*, flexing, overzealous, teeth, toothless and tough as collocates to regulator|regulators	319
14.7	Aggressive, fail*, flexing, overzealous, teeth, toothless and tough as collocates to Securities # Exchange Commission	322

Contributors

MARCO CANEPA is an Italian judge. From July 2018 to the present, he has been president of the penal section of the Court of Justice in Savona. Before then, he worked as a judge in Sicily (1999–2006), a public prosecutor in Sardinia (1996–1999) and a lawyer (1992). He writes papers and participates in legal conferences, giving talks about comparative law. In June 2016, he shadowed a judge at the English Crown Court.

JOHN DOUTHWAITE has a long-standing career as Professor of English Language and taught at several universities including Udine, Turin, Cagliari and at Scuola di Applicazione (the Italian Army Officer Training School) in Turin. He was Professor of English Language, Head of English Language at the Department of Foreign Languages and Head of Postgraduate Teacher Training Course in Foreign Languages, Literatures and Cultures at the University of Genoa, Italy.

MONIKA FLUDERNIK is Professor English Literature at the University of Freiburg/Germany. She is a narratologist by training but has also worked in postcolonial studies, aesthetics and Law and Literature. Her most recent book was published by Oxford University Press in 2019 (*Metaphors of Confinement*). She is currently directing a so-called Koselleck project (a specific type of project funded by the German Research Foundation) on diachronic narratology.

ANNE FURLONG is Associate Professor in the English Department at the University of Prince Edward Island. Her current research extends the application of relevance theory to adaptation studies.

CHRISTIANA GREGORIOU is an Associate Professor in English Language at the University of Leeds, specialising in the stylistics of crime writing. Most notable are her three monographs: *Crime Fiction Migration: Crossing Languages, Cultures, Media* (2017); *Language, Ideology and Identity in Serial Killer Narratives* (2011); and *Deviance in Contemporary Crime Fiction* (2007). Her edited collections include *Representations of Transnational Human Trafficking: Present-Day News Media, True Crime and Fiction* (2018) and *Constructing Crime: Discourse and Cultural Representations of Crime and 'Deviance'* (2012).

MAHMOOD KADIR IBRAHIM (known as Mahmood Baban) holds a PhD in Linguistics from the University of Huddersfield. His research interest is in the field of (Critical) Stylistics in English, Kurdish and Arabic, both literary and non-literary texts. He is a lecturer at Imam Ja'afar Al Sadiq University/ Kirkuk College of Arts, English Department. In 2010–2011, he was a linguist with Global Linguistic Solutions in Iraq. He was formerly an external lecturer at Kirkuk University (2011–2014) and an instructor at the University of Human Development in the Kurdistan region of Iraq in the same period. In July 2014, he joined the University of Huddersfield and worked as a student ambassador (2015–2016). In 2017, he worked as a lecturer (informant) in field linguistics at the same university. In 2018, he was a lecturer at The Islamic University/Al-Najaf Al-Ashraf/Iraq. During the Covid-19 pandemic, he also started to teach phonetics at Tishq International University.

ZOLTÁN KÖVECSES is Professor Emeritus at Eötvös Loránd University, Budapest. His main research interests include metaphor theory, the cognition-culture interface and the language of emotions.

ANDREA MAYR is Lecturer in Media and Communication at Zayed University, UAE, where she teaches and researches in the area of Critical Discourse Analysis and the semiotics of print, broadcast and new media with a particular focus on crime and deviance and social media activism.

DOUGLAS MARK PONTON is Associate Professor of English Language and Translation at the Department of Political and Social Sciences, University of Catania. His research interests include political discourse analysis, ecolinguistics, sociolinguistics, applied linguistics, pragmatics and critical discourse studies. He has dealt with a variety of social topics, including ecology, local dialect and folk traditions. His most recent book Understanding Political Persuasion: Linguistic and Rhetorical Aspects, was published by Vernon Press in 2019.

ILSE A. RAS is a Tutor in Criminology at Leiden University, the Netherlands. She completed her PhD in English Language at the University of Leeds. Her research and teaching often cross the boundaries between English Language and Criminology.

SIMON STATHAM is Lecturer in English Language in the School of Arts, English and Languages at Queen's University Belfast, where he teaches and researches in Stylistics, Critical Discourse Analysis, and Language and the Law. His most recent Stylistics research is in the area of crime fiction adaptation.

ULRIKE TABBERT is a Senior Public Prosecutor (Oberamtsanwältin) at a German prosecution office and a Visiting Research Fellow at the University of Huddersfield, UK. She holds a PhD in linguistics from Huddersfield and researches the construction of crime, criminals and victims across a variety of text types.

M'BALIA THOMAS is Assistant Professor at the University of Kansas, USA. She is a Critical Applied Linguist and TESOL teacher educator and writes on the everyday creativity of non-native and non-standard varieties of American English. Among her publications are *Rendering the Untellable, Tellable: The Cooperative Work of Negotiating Transgressive Talk* (2020) and *The Problematization of Racial/Ethnic Minority Student Participation in US Study Abroad* (2013).

SIMON ZUPAN is Assistant Professor at the Department of Translation Studies, University of Maribor, Slovenia, and holds a PhD in literary translation. He has taught courses in literary translation, stylistics, conference interpreting, American literature and style in translation. In recent years, his main research interests have included literary translation, stylistics and conference interpreting. He is an active translator and conference interpreter.

1 Editorial Introduction

John Douthwaite and Ulrike Tabbert

1.1 Crime, Social Structure, Values and the Linguistic Approach

Crime is an important societal phenomenon. It accounts for a significant proportion of a country's gross domestic product, it represents a serious threat to normal existence in many countries (Ras, Chapter 14), and it can at times constitute a challenge to the legitimacy of the extant order (Mayr, Chapter 11). Nevertheless, crime holds an enduring fascination for the general public, as is shown by the enormous sales figures for crime fiction (underscored by the vast amount of translation occurring in what has been a global market for some time now), and the huge amount of time devoted to crime fiction on television and in the cinema.

Much of this fascination stems from the fact that few people witness or fall victim to crime first hand. Despite direct encounters with criminal activity being rare, people manifest strong feelings about criminals and punishment. Two cogent reasons account for this phenomenon: (1) crime triggers reactions determined by people's deeply instilled values and (2) people's constant 'indirect' experience of crime can affect their lives quite radically, in at least two ways.

On the one hand, problems exist which touch their everyday lives (as well as triggering their values and consequent reactions): organised crime, drugs (of especial concern to parents with young children and of indirect concern to all caused by international drug trafficking), crimes of violence in certain areas, violent crimes against women everywhere,[1] corruption, effects of immigration,

---

[1] Currently, a woman is killed every three days in Italy, principally by her spouse or lover. In Germany 254 women were murdered in 2019. The problem is even more serious in those countries where the female is legally and/or culturally subordinated to the male. That this is ultimately a political problem worldwide is indicated by the culturally redolent diplomatic incident which took place at an official international meeting on 7 April 2021: Ursula von der Leyen, President of the European Commission, was left without a chair by Turkish President Recep Erdoğan. Perhaps even more significant was the fact that Charles Michel, President of the European Council, made no move to rectify the situation and offered no apology to von der Leyen following the meeting.

terrorism, war, state terrorism (Johnson 2019), all influence the day-to-day running of single individuals' lives and the global regulation of their lives. Consequences include higher taxation, greater state control over civil liberties, effects on international politics. To illustrate the latter, oil in the Middle East has produced a mix of war, terrorism and global politics which have worsened the situation, Saddam Hussein's supposed store of chemical weapons constituting a cogent exemplification. The current Russia-Ukraine war has detonated another world crisis. It is no coincidence that Chapter 6 by Ibrahim and Tabbert deals with Kurdistan. Indeed, over half of the chapters in this volume illustrate how daily lives are affected by crime: 4–6, 9, 11, 12, 14 and 15.

On the other hand, people experience crime from texts about criminality, whereby we understand the term 'text' in its widest sense, including, among others, newspaper and television reports as well as crime fiction novels, film, poetry, offenders' accounts of their own wrongdoings, legal documents, government and research institute studies and reports on crime and prisons. This point alone justifies extended research on crime in the media.

The key to understanding this enduring fascination that the phenomenon of crime holds therefore lies not only in studying real crime and criminals (as is the subject of criminology, sociology and economics) or in their detection and punishment (as falls within the realm of policing and the law), but principally in the study of the plethora of texts produced about crime, criminals and their punishment since this is where most people unwittingly acquire their knowledge about crime (Colbran 2014b), as well as gain enjoyment therefrom, another striking phenomenon requiring explanation.

Leaving crime actually occurring in the real world to be dealt with by legal, criminological and governmental agencies, there exists an immense parallel world of discourse on crime that we explore in this volume because this discourse constitutes a powerful component in determining human perception of the phenomenon itself (Colbran 2014a) and, consequently, subsequent behaviour concerning that phenomenon (such as one's attitude to punishment).

Crime is not an inbuilt, immanent, 'natural' phenomenon, but is socially defined. Thus, definitions of crime change as place, historical conditions and social structure change. Crime is thus a window on the world; it reflects the socioeconomic structure of society, its values, its attitudes and the social conflicts and social dysfunctions characterising any given society at a given time. Crime fiction is a privileged site in which society can be observed and analysed. One might object that crime fiction being fictitious, it cannot claim to constitute 'social' documentation. This is far from being the case since novels are taken from life and reflect life in some way. One crucial way in which they mirror, and so reveal, life is that texts present worldviews vying with each other to promote and buttress the value systems they champion: they are sites of struggle.[2] Our fundamental aim is to show how crime and the reaction to crime are portrayed in its various manifestations across individual texts, text types and genres, across cultures and different legal systems. An obligatory concomitant goal is, consequently, an investigation into how such portrayals affect or are intended to influence readers'/viewers' responses and how they react to the attempts made by texts to position them.

Since texts are conveyed basically through language, our aim is to show by means of a variety of linguistic methodologies how suasion actually works in those texts. Another fundamental reason why linguistics is our essential analytical tool is because language, or rather, any semiotic system, is not a neutral device which objectively describes 'the world out there', but one that has inbuilt values, one that creates a text world which necessarily conveys a worldview – as stated above, texts are sites of struggle in the battle for hegemony (Fairclough 1989). This is demonstrated either directly or indirectly in all of the chapters in this volume.

Exploring the textually constructed worldview accordingly entails dealing with ideological meaning in these texts, the major concern underlying the contents of this volume. Ideologies as 'a coherent and relatively stable set of beliefs and values' (Wodak & Meyer 2009, p. 8) can be understood as values attached to the text worlds (Jeffries 2000, p. 384) with language being 'the primary instrument through which ideology is transmitted, enacted and reproduced' (Teo 2000, p. 11). This ideological approach underlines the social, historical and critical aspects of the relationship between crime, socioeconomic structures and power relations in society which the present volume sets out to examine.

This volume illustrates the application of linguistic analysis to a range of crime-related text types, always positioning the text itself centre stage. Such an approach is extremely rare in crime studies. Linguistics allows hypothesising falsifiable assertions concerning what takes place in those texts linguistically and, consequently and primarily, about how the crime discourse world under scrutiny is constructed through language, as well as about how the mode of linguistic construction affects the reader. Although texts are created through language, as in any form of communication and comprehension, they necessarily deploy our knowledge of the world.[3] Hence, in addition to understanding how language works in crime texts, comprehending those texts concurrently requires the deployment of all our branches of knowledge. Some disciplines such as literary criticism are closely related to linguistics, while others such as music, forensic psychology, criminology or the law might at first appear to be extraneous to linguistics. As the various chapters in the

---

[2] Chapters 3–5 and 15 focus on this aspect.   [3] Chapter 15 illustrates this perfectly.

present volume will strive to show, all knowledge is interconnected. This accounts for our attempt to explore new routes of studying the societal phenomenon of crime, including the fascination it holds. Such fascination, we will try to demonstrate, is a product of the ideological functions of crime fiction, the reverse side of the coin being the psychological needs such fiction satisfies in the reader/viewer, the two functions being inextricably intertwined. Although the approach is multidisciplinary, the methodological starting point for each chapter, however, is always a linguistic one.

Among the various linguistic approaches deployed in this book, stylistics prevails. Stylistics understands itself as a 'systematic analysis of style in language' (Jeffries & McIntyre 2010, p. 1). By its very nature, stylistics embraces all domains of knowledge and deploys an extremely broad range of methodological tools. Above all, its crucial goal is not only that of identifying what a text means, but, even more vital, how a text means what it means, since attributing an effect to a linguistic construction is what makes stylistic hypotheses falsifiable.

While some critics argue that stylistics is a sub-discipline of linguistics, others claim that stylistics is much broader than linguistics, since it draws on other linguistic methodologies as well as subjects which are not specifically linguistic, such as sociology, psychology, anthropology and literature. Though stylistics began life investigating the language of literature, seen as a 'special' type of sub-language, stylisticians now analyse any form of communication, linguistic and non-, in all and every domain. The long-standing debate on whether language is a general phenomenon with general rules, or whether literature, economics, law, religion and so forth are 'special' languages, each with their own characteristic sub-rules, continues heatedly.

The present volume constitutes a cogent illustration of the breadth of approaches stylistics employs. Thus, from the 'traditional' stylistic toolkit employed in Chapters 4–6 by Douthwaite, Gregoriou and Ibrahim/Tabbert, and applied to translation studies by Zupan in Chapter 7, we move to Critical Discourse Analysis as covered by Ras in Chapter 14, Relevance Theory as dealt with by Furlong in Chapter 8, Text World Theory used by Thomas in Chapter 9 and Multimodal Analysis deployed by Statham in Chapter 10. Recent times have witnessed the 'cognitive turn' (Statham & Montoro 2019) in linguistic studies, which we endorse by opening this volume with an overarching cognitive metaphorical approach to the construction of the (deviant) Other (Chapter 2 by Kövecses and Douthwaite) and an investigation into metaphors used for prisons and prison-like everyday situations (Chapter 3 by Fludernik). Mayr (Chapter 11), employs the Appraisal framework to explore favela funk lyrics.

In order to shed full light onto the complexity of the crime and its textual representation, the present volume embraces the fields of criminology and sociology (Douthwaite in Chapters 2, 4 and 15), forensic psychology and criminology (Tabbert in Chapter 12), law and rhetoric (Ponton and Canepa in Chapter 13), thereby ensuring a wide-ranging interdisciplinary approach is brought to bear on our topic. Interdisciplinarity overrides the confines of the professions as well as those of knowledge domains in order to achieve depth and breadth so as to avoid, as far as possible, the limitations brought about by the blinkers of one's own and sometimes small area of expertise. Having forewarned the readers, it will come as no surprise to them to learn that Canepa is a judge, Tabbert is a public prosecutor, Ras is a criminologist and Douthwaite a criminologist by training.

Recent developments in linguistic studies of crime fiction have witnessed a significant broadening of the realms of investigation, including explorations of the cultural and social criticism inherent in important sectors of crime fiction novels, films and television series. The volume by Stougaard-Nielsen (2017) demonstrates that a great deal of recent Scandinavian crime-related texts deal with social concerns over globalisation, increasing poverty, concentration of power, and the crisis of the welfare state, issues which cause worldwide alarm, as our volume will bear out. Many of the articles in another collection entitled *Crime Fiction as World Literature* (Nilsson et al., 2017) show the same trend at work from Mexico to Thailand. We are in accordance with these approaches and pay attention to the social criticism that is inherent in discourse on crime (e.g., in Chapters 4–6, 9, 11, 14 and 15).

1.2   An Overview of the Volume

The lexemes 'crime' and 'criminal' of their essence suggest difference. Hence Kövecses and Douthwaite open the volume with a cognitive linguistic investigation of the concept of Otherness. Starting from the objective fact that people belong to different social and cultural groups, Kövecses notes that human beings distinguish people 'who belong to our group from people who do not in a rigid way'. This results in classifying people as either belonging or not belonging to a given category. Kövecses hypothesises that this 'container' logic of categorisation is a property of the human cognitive apparatus. Categorisation is a process of inclusion/exclusion. We include or exclude people from a given category on the basis of whether or not they possess certain defining features deemed essential. We thereby create the Other on the basis of difference, often stigmatising such difference.[4] We then metonymically take a typical representative of that category as standing for the entire category, despite the variations within a category. In this, the cognitive process

---

[4] Stigmatisation is generally related to dominance and exploitation, and is treated in several chapters in this volume: 4– 6, 11–13.

of metonymic thinking bolsters dichotomic categorisation and stigmatisation. Kövecses then identifies a number of cognitive or conceptual metaphors which typify Otherness, such as

> THE OTHER IS AN ENEMY
> THE OTHER IS A PRIMITIVE MAN/BARBARIAN/WILD ANIMAL

One crucial function of cognitive metaphors is that they perform ideological functions (Kövecses 2010). They do so by highlighting certain features and hiding others. Significantly, as Kövecses points out, the cognitive metaphors employed to 'refer' to Others generally underscore their supposed negative qualities, as in the previous example: THE OTHER IS A WILD ANIMAL. He then proceeds to apply his theoretical constructs to texts to demonstrate the validity of his argumentation.

Douthwaite continues the chapter by illustrating how the concepts work in a significant crime text where Otherness is the key variable, the material and ideological centre around which all the characters and events revolve.

The enormous importance of metaphor in communication (Douthwaite 2011; Kövecses 2010) is witnessed by the fact that the topic is taken up directly (i.e. as *the* object of investigation) by Fludernik (Chapter 3) and Ponton/Canepa (Chapter 13), and indirectly (i.e. as one of the analytical tools deployed) by Douthwaite (Chapters 4 and 15), Gregoriou (Chapter 5), Ibrahim/Tabbert (Chapter 6), Zupan (Chapter 7), Mayr (Chapter 11), Tabbert (Chapter 12) and Ras (Chapter 14).[5]

In Chapter 3, Fludernik goes directly to the key feature of metaphor in communication: metaphors express point of view, they have an ideological function. She demonstrates this quite neatly by pointing out that in these coronavirus-ridden days, out of the manifold possible ways of defining clinics, it is significant that they have often been labelled as 'prisons', rather than life-saving institutions, given the highly curtailed liberties reigning in those establishments. Fludernik illustrates how metaphors work (ideologically) by examining carceral metaphors, thus tackling a key component in crime – punishment – a topic which is heavily value-laden and consequently ridden with conflict. She takes up Foucault's view that prisons are heterotopias, parallel worlds, a variant of the binary dichotomy traditionally associated with prisons (prison is hell constituting the implicit opposite of the heaven of the outside world). Based on her previous study on English Middle Ages to

---

[5] Given its theoretical and practical importance, as witnessed by the number of contributions in this volume dealing with the topic, Otherness might be said to be one of the main, albeit indirect, topics of the volume. Kim (2010) has edited a volume of essays devoted to Otherness in crime fiction. What distinguishes our volume is the linguistic approach employed and the concurrent concentration on topics such as ideology, point of view and suasion.

contemporary Anglophone literature and on essays from newspapers from the last 150 years, Fludernik carries out a search in the LION (Literature Online) database for occurrences of key words such as 'prison', 'fetter', 'shackle', 'manacles', 'chains' which 'directly or metonymically invoke the prison scenario'. The metaphorical expressions obtained are then analysed and a complex classificatory system developed in order to identify social groups (such as (1) conservatives who view incarceration as retribution and (2) prisoners expressing their own viewpoints on the subject) in order to identify the precise worldviews and ideologies the metaphorical systems implicitly or explicitly propound, thereby linking ideology to social identity and historical situation.

Douthwaite's focal concern in Chapters 4 and 15 is also with the central topic of ideology. His underlying aim is to demonstrate that, like all texts, crime fiction texts are sites of struggle. Ideology and suasion are thus his two overarching themes. He divides crime texts into two main ideological camps, conservative and critical. He identifies the manifold linguistic features that are constitutive of each camp, showing how they are often diametrically opposed, reflecting their ideological opposition. Douthwaite also pinpoints the linguistic techniques deployed in the texts in order to position readers, demonstrating that such techniques are common to both camps, since suasion is a general category which is not directly dependent on specific content. He achieves his goals by examining a representative for each camp: *Midsomer Murders*, in the form of one of Caroline Graham's novels, *Written in Blood* (Chapter 4), to illustrate the position of the conservative camp, and the *Inspector George Gently* television series (based on Alan Hunter's eponymous novels, which, however, vie more towards the conservative camp), as a whole to elucidate the critical position (Chapter 15). Other novelists and television series are referred to when relevant to expanding the argument. A panorama is offered of the works produced in both the *Midsomer* works (Graham's novels and the TV series based on those novels) and the *Gently* artefacts in order to establish a general historical and contextual framework as well as furnishing production details for the products analysed relevant to identifying and accounting for their stances and their differences. This is followed by detailed close readings of selected excerpts to explicate the previously identified technical and linguistic differences in operation and to exemplify the suasive mechanisms at work. The methodology is stylistic, employing all the tools provided by that approach. Other scientific domains such as criminology are called on where necessary. The two chapters are thus complementary and meant to be read together. Given the limitations of space and in order to offer as wide a thematic and methodological panorama as possible, the chapter on *Gently* is provided online, which also accounts for its non-standard length.

Gregoriou (Chapter 5) analyses a novel about human (child) trafficking, an important crime involving global factors such as poverty, immigration, culture conflict and racism. A young African called Muna girl is kidnapped by an African family living in London and kept in a cellar as a domestic and sexual slave. She is regularly beaten and tortured, not simply as a means of subjugation, but also as a whipping horse for family members to work off their frustrations and jealousies. Four aspects are of especial importance to the cohesion of this volume. First, Gregoriou offers a stylistic analysis of the novel, employing speech presentation, naming strategies, metaphor, transitivity and (deontic) modality as her analytical tools. This enables her not simply to identify whose point of view is being propounded at various points in the text, but also, and crucially, to make the reader experience the events, thoughts and feelings of the characters, thereby positioning the reader. In addition, Gregoriou indicates the communicative effects achieved by the linguistic tools she identifies as having been deployed by the writer, making the results obtained reliable since falsifiable. Second, a social critique is offered by the chapter. Immigration is a topic of great relevance since in recent decades it has become a significant social phenomenon, not only because of the numerous wars creating refugees, but also because it is a rich source of organised criminal exploitation. The novel also deals with possible dire consequences of slavery, including the destruction of personality, with the extreme result, in this particular case, that in the end the victim becomes the persecutor wreaking terrible vengeance on her former oppressors, a phenomenon which is not new in human history. Third, Gregoriou points out that the novel deals with Africans exploiting Africans, totally ignoring the crucial role played by whites in trafficking. Finally, the ideology of the social groups involved is highlighted, relating each ideology to its culture of origin.

Chapter 6 (Ibrahim/Tabbert) continues on the topic of victims of crime introduced by Gregoriou and crosses cultural borders into Iraqi Kurdistan with an exploration of Iraqi Kurdish poet Sherko Bekas and his collection of poems known under the title *The Small Mirrors*. The selected passage under scrutiny has at its core the (Kurdish) victims of genocide but deliberately avoids naming explicitly those responsible for the atrocities. One effect of this strategy is to bestow upon the experience global significance, crucially so, since genocide and other 'political' crimes are given scant treatment, when not neglected completely, in crime fiction. By addressing this issue they draw attention to the sociopolitical situation worldwide and see this genocide in a row with fascism, the Balkan wars, the Rwandan genocide and many more. In the passage under scrutiny one highly significant aspect that receives critical attention is the fact that the linguistic construction of the victims automatically brings about the construction of the respective offenders even though the latter are not talked about, again bestowing global significance to the single instantiation. The authors employ the framework of Critical Stylistics (Jeffries 2010) that is particularly suited to detecting ideological meaning in texts and employ ten textual-conceptual functions of texts which, on the level of ideation as world creation in texts, unravel the world projected by the text and the values attached to this world, that is, the ideological meaning. Bekas' political statement and his tireless work to give a voice to the Kurdish people in their ongoing struggle against oppression emphasises the fact that victims of genocide might be numerous and anonymous but their suffering is as tragic as that of an individual victim of crime like (fictive) Muna in the previous chapter.

Translation might at first appear a strange component in a book on crime. Yet, as Zupan (Chapter 7) cogently demonstrates, translation of English crime fiction has played a fundamental role both in stimulating the development of crime fiction writing in non-English-speaking countries and in expanding the market for foreign as well as local crime fiction in those countries. More importantly for the main concerns of the present volume, as translation studies have demonstrated, translation raises issues regarding two interrelated levels: (1) the nature of equivalence and how equivalence may be achieved, given the diversity between languages, cultures and literary systems, and, indeed, if equivalence is a goal of translation, as classic theory would demand, and (2) how linguistic and social differences affect translators' decisions as to the type of translation to be effected and reader response to the translation and how the latter is affected by the receiving culture. Zupan thus deals with issues such as the market, the influence exerted by texts, how such influence is connected to culture and the social situation of the target audience/culture, all core questions addressed in various chapters in the volume, and further developed by Furlong in her discussion of adaptations in the next chapter.

Zupan tackles these questions by examining Slovenian translations of Edgar Allan Poe's short story *The Murders in the Rue Morgue*. After first tracing Poe's influence on market sales and on the development of world crime fiction and then providing an overview of stylistic theory on translating detective fiction, Zupan presents Poe's short story and its Slovenian translations. There follows the main part of the chapter, a meticulous stylistic analysis of an excerpt from the target text and two of its Slovenian translations. Zupan identifies differences between source and target texts and offers an account of the origin of those differences. He then links readerly response to the specific linguistic selections made by the author/translator, showing, where relevant, how such choices are related to the translator's attempt to nativise the text and how such choices are embedded in the target culture.

In Chapter 8, Furlong moves one step further than Zupan. If equivalence is impossible, and if, in addition, there are as many interpretations of a text as there are readings of that text, then adaptation necessarily produces a 'new' text, reflecting the adaptor's interpretation (or novel creation) of the original.

One reason accounting for novelty is that film and television adaptations invariably provide much richer visual signals than the original (written) text. Adaptations thus embody the intentions of the adaptor and not those of the original author. Furlong investigates the nature of such intentionality by examining adaptations in their historical and cultural target settings, taking crime texts as her subject matter. Due to the inherently ideological nature of the genre, it may be predicted to provide copious significant material. Furlong selects late nineteenth-century Russian and Japanese adaptations since at that time these countries were undergoing profound economic, social and political transformations, changes which also involved the issue of national identity (such as a reaction against British imperialist values). Furlong opts to scrutinise versions of Conan Doyle's works because of the range and variety of adaptations produced. She examines the 1981 Russian television production of *The Hound of the Baskervilles* because it was the acme of both exoticism (the life of the British bourgeoisie) and domestication (national culture). Furthermore, the investigation into intentionality is aided by director, producer and writer having outlined their goals and commented on the value of the film. Since the adapted texts vary little from the original, analytical attention is concentrated on the abundant visual signals. Setting, events, people, clothes and objects are carefully analysed to identify the relevant cultural behaviour they represent in the Russia of the time. Furlong underscores that the need to satisfy Russian censorship and protect the values of the status quo led to the lampooning of Doyle's original. However, Furlong demonstrates how domestication of Holmes to respect this political requirement produced contradictory effects in which national identity was both reinforced and destabilised. Furlong extends her analysis to present times by investigating the nature of British *Sherlock* and American *Elementary*, comparing the two works and then scrutinising the Japanese adaptations. Ideology, culture, goals are central topics in this chapter as they are in the entire volume.

Chapter 9 (Thomas) concludes the triad of Chapters 7–9 by adding the topic of parody to the previously examined topics of translation and adaptation. It develops Furlong's turn to multimodality. Thomas analyses an (American) YouTube video titled 'Bed Intruder', reporting on an attempted rape. The video has gone viral and inspired countless parodies. Thomas approaches the topic of race within US society that is a most pressing societal issue given the social unrests following the death of George Floyd and many other, mainly African Americans in police custody, inspiring a #BlackLivesMatter movement worldwide. Thomas employs Text World Theory (Gavins 2007; Werth 1999) to analyse the multimodal video sequence and three selected parodies. There ensues a highly detailed account which tracks processes, enactors, speech presentation modes in order to identify switches in text worlds and the nature of the text world that has been turned to so as to identify the functions each switch and each subsequent text world perform and how the presentation of the events reported affect viewer response. The chapter thus underlines the 'cognitive' turn which this volume pays particular attention to from the very beginning in Chapters 2 and 3.

Statham (Chapter 10) offers a methodological lesson in multimedia analysis by examining excerpts from an episode of the TV series *The Sopranos*. The episode is selected because it deals with an important and complex aspect of human communication – deceit – enabling analytical depth to be achieved. A mafioso betraying the boss by becoming an FBI informant and trying to get the boss to incriminate himself is thus a realistic instantiation of the communicative phenomenon under investigation, providing plentiful, non-superficial evidence of the behaviour in question. One key aspect of multimodal communication is the wide variety of informational sources (aural and visual) constituting the overall 'signal'. As the stylistic analyses provided by Chapters 4–7 show, texts are highly complicated artefacts, since a plethora of different types of signals interact, sometimes in contrasting or contradictory fashion, to build a highly complex whole, even at the level of sentence. Adding the wide variety of visual signals that are consciously or unconsciously employed in multimodal texts complicates matters *n*-fold. Statham first analyses three mini-texts employing Grice's theory of implicature to bring out the hidden (deceitful) meanings created verbally (reiterating its importance as discussed by Douthwaite in Chapter 4), followed by an examination of various cinematic techniques deployed to produce visual signals in order to show how those visual signals correlate with the verbal signals previously analysed. The result is a rich reading of the text, demonstrating what viewers are made to experience and the techniques employed to make them experience events in the fashion desired by the director.

Chapter 11 (Mayr) bridges the thematic gap between fictional and real criminals, the investigative domain of Chapters 11–14, as she takes us to the favelas of Rio de Janeiro, Brazil, and the glorification of gang leaders and gang activities in their funk songs (especially the sub-genre *proibidão*). Mayr provides a detailed examination of the historical, political, social and cultural context in order to bring out the full significance of the counterculture of funk in her subsequent linguistic analysis of the lyrics. Her analytical toolkit consists of Critical Discourse Analysis, Systemic Functional Grammar and Appraisal Theory. She combines this discourse-analytical approach with ethnographical insights from participant observation at funk events and informal interviews with funk insiders. One emblematic instance is Mayr's elucidation of the symbolic use of space. In funk, the favela is represented as an 'empire'. This metaphorical representation performs several ideological functions. It classifies, hence evaluates, this space as (1) a legitimate, legal institution, (2) a powerful institution (3) consequently inhabited by powerful people, hence people to be respected. Identity is thus inverted from powerless and disreputable ('demonised' by the ruling class, the police and the media, precluding any questioning of the harsh social realities underlying the funk phenomenon and the socioeconomic structure producing such poverty – Rio de Janeiro being classified as one of the most violent cities in the world) to powerful and 'respectable'. Such self-esteem is a necessary mental component if a person is to remain psychologically stable and functional, (4) a symbol of and spur to resistance, to protect space and identity from the onslaught of 'civil society'. In this sense, EMPIRE is connected to another central metaphor whose functions in funk are identified by Mayr: WAR. Gang leaders furnish underprivileged youth with opportunities to perform (hence to express their sense of honourable identity and articulate their criticism of their marginality through the 'poetics' of the 'antilanguage' of funk) by financing their equipment and providing protected space for their performances, in contrast to the repression carried out by the authorities. Funk thus performs crucial ideological functions, addressing and recontextualising the imbrications of state and criminal violence and expressing 'insurgent citizenship'.

Chapter 12 (Tabbert) follows Mayr's thematic lead and moves from the analysis of a group phenomenon to the analysis of a single individual, giving voice to one particular offender and his own account of his (criminal) action (and therefore his mind style). What is special about this offender is that he suffers from schizophrenia. He therefore perceives events taking place in the real world somewhat differently compared with the not mentally challenged person. This chapter bridges over to forensic psychology/psychiatry, providing an in-depth linguistic analysis of the language this offender uses to describe his perceptions and actions. Although his account comes across as bizarre at first glance, recurring linguistic patterns link with symptoms which people suffering from schizophrenia display. This study reveals the extreme loneliness and social isolation, in fact his 'otherness', this offender experiences due to schizophrenia and the vicious circle he finds himself in every time he wants to reach out for companionship, even leading, unfortunately, to a criminal act. One of the most striking linguistic features of this person's language is the 'ideological' use he makes of metaphors which have as their source domain the human body or body feelings, the psychological and communicative functions of which are to underline his inwardly directed focus. Linguistic analysis thus helps identify further social goals they can help to provide: a psychological portrait which could be used to provide care for persons in this type of situation.

Chapter 13 by Ponton and Canepa takes us into another real-world dimension: the legal domain. The interpretation of the law and hence language itself are at the core of every court decision. Ponton and Canepa's subject is the role played by metaphor in the legal sphere. While the two authors concur that the conceptual metaphor approach theorised by Kövecses and adopted by the majority of authors in this volume plays a fundamental part in legal language (by which they mean text production as well as textual interpretation), they return to Aristotle's rhetoric as constituting a fundamental analytical tool to investigate the importance of this figure of speech as a means of suasion in winning cases and as a linguistically constitutive tool 'through which laws are made and debated, commented on by legal specialists, revised, redrawn'. The ideological nature of both functions needs no clarification, especially given the fact that language is not neutral, as the authors confirm in this chapter.

After reviewing the theoretical issues involved regarding the nature and functions of metaphor, they analyse metaphor use in the British online *Cambridge Law Journal*. This source was selected because it is freely available and because it can also represent interactive courtroom discourse inasmuch as the articles share the same rhetorical/persuasive aims. Having identified those metaphors which perform a suasive function in the selected texts, they proceed with a qualitative analysis of those metaphors, identifying the argumentative structure implicit in the deployment of those metaphors. They then provide an in-depth case study (of what is termed 'the narrower ground'), in order to demonstrate how 'the development of such a metaphorical frame is a crucial resource in the business of negotiating, and shaping, the law itself'. The chapter thus helps unpack some of the complexity involved in legal language, shedding light on how it is exploited ideologically.

Chapter 14 closes the examination of real-world crime by dealing with the grave issue of corporate crime. Ras is in line with the central social concerns expressed by the present volume and the methodologies deployed. This type of crime is critical because it represents an important figure of the gross domestic income and because it is the 'crime of the powerful'.[6] One 'privilege' of belonging to the powerful is having greater access to the media. Ras reports studies demonstrating that the media exert great influence over public opinion, to the point of affecting de/legitimisation of law enforcement agencies. With regard to corporate crime, newspapers tend to deny corporate responsibility, resorting to tactics such as construing corporate misconduct as 'disasters'. Ras thus tackles the issue of the relationship between tax evaders, tax fraud investigators, and their relationship to the power structure and economic structure of the country.

Ras carries out a corpus analysis of articles in seven major British dailies on the UK-based Financial Services Authority (FSA) and US-focused Securities

---

[6] Although Ras studies Great Britain, the financial figures she provides and the analysis of the media she offers are equally valid for other parts of the world, including Italy, where Douthwaite lives, and Germany, Tabbert's abode. Although Italy, for instance, has the mafia to deal with, organised crime, including corporate crime, is a worldwide phenomenon.

and Exchange Commission (SEC), two leading regulatory agencies which should protect the interests of the nation. She examines the historical circumstances behind the founding of the agencies and the mandates entrusted to them. She applies Critical Discourse Analysis to the texts selected to eke out the social meaning conveyed by those texts and the linguistic devices by which those messages are conveyed. In order to do so, she also applies functional grammar, metaphor analysis and other relevant stylistics tools. On a global level she finds that the agencies are subjected to delegitimising media pressure by large companies, one major strategy adopted being to neg(oti)ate the legitimacy of condemning parties so as to shift blame to these parties. Another important finding is that such agencies succumb to pressures, for both 'legitimate' and illegitimate reasons. The printed volume thus concludes with the concern with ideology and where the foundations of a democratic society are necessarily to the fore.

The volume continues online with Chapter 15 by Douthwaite, commented on above, which deals with the topic of central interest to this volume: ideology in crime texts.

References

Colbran, M. (2014a). *Media Representations of Police and Crime: Shaping the Police Television Drama*. London: Palgrave.
   (2014b). Watching the Cops: Police Perceptions of Media Representations of Police Work in British Television Crime Drama. In V. Marinescu, S. Branea & B. Mitu, eds., *Contemporary Television Series: Narrative Structures and Audience Perception*. Newcastle upon Tyne: Cambridge Scholars Publishing, pp. 1–15.
Douthwaite, J. (2011). Conceptual Metaphor and Communication: An Austinian and Gricean Analysis of Brian Clark's *Whose Life Is It Anyway*? In M. Fludernik, ed., *Beyond Cognitive Metaphor Theory: Perspectives on Literary Metaphor*. London: Routledge, pp. 137–157.
Fairclough, N. (1989). *Language and Power*. London: Routledge.
Gavins, J. (2007). *Text World Theory: An Introduction*. Edinburgh: Edinburgh University Press.
Jeffries, L. (2010). *Critical Stylistics: The Power of English*. Basingstoke: Palgrave Macmillan.
Jeffries, L., & McIntyre, D. (2010). *Stylistics*. Cambridge: Cambridge University Press.
Johnson, P. (2019). The Crime and State Terrorism Nexus: How Organized Crime Appropriates Counterinsurgency Violence. *Perspectives on Terrorism*, 13(6), 16–26.
Kim, J. H., ed. (2010). *Race and Religion in the Postcolonial British Detective Story*. Jefferson: McFarland & Company.
Kövecses, Zoltán. 2010. *Metaphor: A Practical Introduction*. New York: Oxford University Press.
Nilsson, L., Damrosch, D., & D'haen, T. (2017). *Crime Fiction as World Literature*. London: Bloomsbury.

Statham, S., & Montoro, R. (2019). The Year's Work in Stylistics 2018. *Language and Literature*, 28(4), 354–374.

Stougaard-Nielsen, J. (2017). *Scandinavian Crime Fiction*. London: Bloomsbury.

Teo, P. (2000). Racism in the News: A Critical Discourse Analysis of News Reporting in Two Australian Newspapers. *Discourse & Society*, 11(1), 7–49.

Werth, P. (1999). *Text Worlds: Representing Conceptual Space in Discourse*. London: Longman.

Wodak, R., & Meyer, M., eds. (2009). *Methods of Critical Discourse Analysis*. London: Sage Publications.

2 The Metaphoric and Metonymic Conceptualisation of the Other

Zoltán Kövecses and John Douthwaite

In this chapter, I offer a cognitive linguistic analysis of the concept of the Other. In particular, I provide an answer to a set of questions that I take to be central to the understanding of this notion: (1) How can what can be called the 'we–other mentality' be explained in cognitive terms? (2) What could be a possible cognitivist explanation of the phenomenon of stereotyping the other? (3) Which constituents (persons, things) make up the category of the other? (4) How do we conceptualise the other metaphorically? (5) What is the conceptual relationship between the self and the other?

Introduction

My goal in this chapter is to construct a cognitive-linguistic framework for some of our existing body of knowledge concerning the Other. In particular, I propose that many of the concepts discussed in this large body of knowledge can be seen as arising from certain cognitive processes, such as categorisation, metaphor, and metonymy (on these, see, e.g., Kövecses 2006).

The chapter is divided into three sections. In Section 2.1, I will address the conceptual processes of categorisation, metonymy, and metaphor in the cognitive construction of Otherness. In Section 2.2, I will turn to the cognitive construction of the self, which is an obvious counterpart to the cognitive construction of the Other. In Section 2.3, I will consider the complex relationships

---

The Introduction and Sections 2.1–2.3 are written by ZK; Section 2.4 is written by JD; and the conclusions are jointly authored.

ZK is grateful to John Douthwaite for his continued interest in his work and providing him with important information in writing this essay. He also wants to thank several of his colleagues for generously offering their comments on various versions of this essay. He is especially indebted to Patrick Colm Hogan, Dieter Schulz, Vera Benczik, and Sonia Kleinke.

JD is also grateful to Zoltan. To avoid parallelism, he would like to stress that when Zoltan is invited to give plenaries, in addition to offering a polished, relevant talk, he does not then go off on a tourist hike, as some very famous names do, but participates actively providing helpful rather than destructive feedback. JD takes this opportunity to add that the same applies to another scholar of high stature in this volume, Monika Fludernik. To them both go his thanks.

between the self and the Other. I will illustrate these points with brief examples from *Othello*, *Moby Dick*, and *Heart of Darkness*.

I would like to stress that it is not the content of these claims that I take to be possibly interesting or novel to literary scholars, social scientists, and philosophers. Rather, it is the attempt to provide a cognitive background to the ideas that have been made that might be of interest and that can be seen as complementing our existing knowledge about the Other.

2.1 The Other

2.1.1 The I/We–Other Mentality

We belong to various social and cultural groups, and we tend to distinguish the people who belong to our group from people who do not in a rigid way. We tend to do this on the basis of the assumption that they are not like us, they are different from us. The person or persons that I perceive to be different from me or my group is the Other. The 'I' and the 'we' are clearly separated from the Other; where the former end, the latter begins. This is what I call the 'I/we–other mentality'. In order to begin to understand the mentality, we need to start with our folk theory of categorisation (see Lakoff 1987).

Nature of Categorisation

According to our folk theory of how we categorise things in the world, our conceptual categories have a container-like structure. What this means is that we take our conceptual categories to include certain things in the world, but exclude certain others. For example, certain things in the world will be included in the conceptual category of chair, while others will not be. The ones that are included will be members of the conceptual category of chair, while the ones that are not will be non-members. Things either belong to the category or they don't.

I believe this is the logic that underlies in part the I/we–other mentality. If I perceive you to be different from me or us, you do not belong to the category I belong to; you will be a non-member. I suggest that this follows in part from the general property of our conceptual categories: things are either included in a category and thus are members of the category or are not included and thus they are non-members. The container logic and the resulting I/we–other mentality are, in my view, a property of the human cognitive apparatus, which has a tendency to divide things in the world into rigid, exclusive categories, such as art and non-art, whites and non-whites, straights and non-straights, Americans and non-Americans, families and non-families, and many others.

2.1.2 Creating the Other as a Category

But there is an even deeper issue that needs to be clarified: on what basis is the category of the Other created? To say that the members of the category form the category also raises the question of why those members are in the category to begin with. This is a major concern in theories of the Other. The inclusion or exclusion of certain elements in a category can be a hotly debated social, cultural, and political issue.

Essential Features and Exclusion

Probably the first definitive answer to the question was provided by Aristotle, who suggested that what holds members of a category together is that they all share a set of essential features. In other words, the claim is that things in the world become members of a category on the basis of whether they share or do not share certain essential features: if they do, they become members of the same category, if they don't, they are outside the category, i.e., they are non-members.

As is apparent from this, the category of the Other is created by way of the process of exclusion: people or things that do not have the essential features required or expected by members of the we-group will be categorised as being non-members. The we-group defined by its assumed essential features functions as a reference group with respect to which people or things that do not have those essential features will be seen by members of the we-group as being outside the category. In my view, then, the group, that is, the category, of the Other is first formed as a result of exclusion. However, the excluded non-members may, in turn, also be defined in terms of their own essential features, and thus form a 'classical' category (i.e., one based on essential features).

2.1.3 Stereotyping the Other

So far I have suggested that the category of the Other has a 'container-like' structure. Furthermore, it can be suggested that, given that structure, some members of the category can represent all the members of the category. The Other is often stereotyped (and stigmatised), and, less commonly, also idealised. This is a cognitive process that utilises metonymic thinking (see, e.g., Kövecses and Radden 1998). In addition, it is a major characteristic of stereotypes that, on the whole, the 'we' group is associated with positive (or neutral) features, while the 'other' with negative features, which leads to stigmatisation.

Metonymic Thinking

Categories include any number of members, and some of the members may become (i.e., may be seen as) representative of all members, that is, of the entire category. This is a general metonymic process, the metonymy involved being: A MEMBER OF A CATEGORY FOR THE WHOLE CATEGORY. As pointed out by Lakoff (1987), the members of a category that can be used for the whole category include those that are typical (common), stereotypical, ideal, paragons, and so on. In other words, a more specific version of the above generic metonymy can be the following: A STEREOTYPICAL MEMBER OF A CATEGORY FOR THE WHOLE CATEGORY. For example, the stereotypical husband is bumbling, hen-pecked, balding, overweight, and so on, as opposed, say, to the ideal one, and can represent the entire category of husbands in certain contexts (such as cartoons) (Lakoff 1987). In this and many other cases, since stereotypes involve negative features, the negative features of some category members will be used to stand for all members of the category.

It may also happen that a feature that is assumed to be neutral (and non-offensive) by the 'we' group is rejected as a negative feature by the 'other' group. This also involves metonymic thinking. The generic metonymy involved is A FEATURE OF THE GROUP FOR THE GROUP. The case in point is the use of skin colour for groups of people; hence the more specific metonymy SKIN COLOR FOR AN ETHNIC GROUP. The terms white, black, yellow, red are often used for certain ethnic groups. This seems to be a neutral way of referring to the groups. However, the use of the colour term can be rejected by the group as a general designation. This is what happened, for example, in the case of black, since it was assumed by the respective other group to have negative symbolic content (which is based on certain conceptual metaphors, such as IMMORAL IS BLACK/DARK and DEATH IS BLACK/DARK). Thus, the metaphorically generated symbolic content of a feature characterising a group may be interpreted by the Other as negative and may lead the group to reject it as the appropriate metonymy to designate the group.

Negative Features

Since the Other is typically associated with negative features in general, members with negative features will be selected as being representative of the whole group. And, conversely, the negative features of some members of the 'we' group will be suppressed.

What is less commonly noted is that the metonymy-based stereotyping and stigmatisation is not a one-way process from the we-group to the Other. From its perspective, the Other also functions as a we-group and thus can also create its own stereotyped Others. For example, Christians often stereotype and stigmatise atheists, but atheists just as often stereotype and stigmatise Christians. In other words, the Other's cognitive behaviour, such as categorisation, metonymic thought, and stereotyping, cannot and should not be thought to be different from that of the I/we.

Positive Features

In some cases, however, some members of the 'other' group will be regarded as having positive features – often features that members of the 'we' group are assumed to have. These are cases of idealisation; that is, some members are taken to be ideal members of the category of the Other. Often, these members are recommended by the 'we' group as ideals to be followed by other members of the other group. When the ideal member is a single, well-known individual, it is a paragon, and it is commonly set as an example before the other group. And finally, in another set of cases, the same features of the Other can be interpreted negatively or positively at the same time.

A good example of this is provided by literary scholar Patrick Colm Hogan (2001), who discusses the positive and negative evaluation of the other in literature.

Negative and Positive Features

In discussing the cognitive nature of racism in colonialist writings, Hogan (2001) argues that the Other can be conceived in both negative and positive ways. He suggests that there are two key source domains for understanding the Other. He calls them 'maturity' and 'animacy'. There is a norm or standard in each case, as well as positive and negative versions of deviations from the norm. The in-group always occupies the place of the norm. Thus in the maturity domain 'we' are 'adult', while others are young or old; specifically, prepubescent innocents (positive youth) or rough adolescents (negative youth), wise elders (positive aged) or senile decadents (negative aged). In animacy, 'we' are 'human', while Others are work animals, wild animals, angels, or devils. These metaphors bring us to the metaphorical comprehension of the Other.

2.1.4 Metaphors for the Other

Perhaps the most common source domain for the conceptualisation of the Other is that of a stranger. This makes sense since a chief characteristic of the Other is that they are unlike the 'me' or the 'us'. The difference between the 'me/us' and the Other serves as the experiential basis for the conceptual metaphor THE OTHER IS A STRANGER or, more generally, THE OTHER IS A MYSTERY. Since I do not know the Other, I cannot predict their behaviour. This causes anxiety or fear in me, which leads to viewing the Other as something dangerous. The dangerous nature of the other can be captured in the form of either people or animals; hence the further metaphors: THE OTHER IS AN ENEMY and THE OTHER IS A PRIMITIVE MAN/A BARBARIAN or even a WILD ANIMAL. In other words, the Other is often viewed as uncivilised or less than human.

A curious feature of these metaphors is that, on the one hand, these metaphorical source domains are completely familiar ones to us. After all, we all have an idea of strangers, mysteries, enemies, or wild animals, and we may even have had direct experiences involving these entities. But, on the other hand, the dominant element in the meaning or conceptual content of these source domains is that we have very little actual knowledge about them.

In the course of conceptualising them, this is what makes them unpredictable and, consequently, a potential cause of fear.

Defamiliarisation and Demonisation

Given this property of metaphors for the Other, a difference between metaphors for the Other as a target domain and metaphors for other target domains as usually provided in the conceptual metaphor literature (such as the well-known metaphors LOVE IS FIRE, LIFE IS A JOURNEY, and THEORIES ARE BUILDINGS) may be observed. I believe the difference has to do with the process of 'defamiliarisation' that is commonly used for the conceptualisation of the Other. In conceptual metaphor theory, one of the most general claims is that we understand a target domain in terms of a source domain that is experientially more concrete or physical, and thus more familiar to us. For example, the physical qualities of fire are more directly experienced than an emotion, journey has a clearer physical and observable structure than the concept of life, building provides us with a more concrete kind of experience than a theory, and so on, and for this reason we have the well-known conceptual metaphors LOVE IS FIRE, LIFE IS A JOURNEY, and THEORIES ARE BUILDINGS. However, in understanding the Other, it is conceptualised in terms of something *less* familiar and known, a process that makes use of the unknown character or the unknowability of the Other as a target. This is most evident in the case of the source domain of MYSTERY, where the whole point is that I do not have the kind of knowledge about it that I assume I have about the 'me/us'. And because this aspect of the Other can be combined with the aspect of its dangerousness, we can have such further metaphorical source domains for the Other as demons and the devil. Defamiliarisation often goes hand in hand with demonisation.

But the conceptualisation of the Other does not necessarily have to entail demonisation. Clearly, if the Other is a positively viewed entity, such as God, it is not demonised. But defamiliarisation does happen even in such cases. Take, for example, the statement from the New Testament: 'the ways of the Lord are infinite'. Here, a familiar conceptual metaphor, MANNER IS PATH (ways), is used together with the infinite potential, the omniscience, of God (infinite). While the PATH metaphor by its nature familiarises God, the INFINITE POWER metaphor defamiliarises it, since it is outside our experiences.

The familiar/unfamiliar distinction links metaphors for the Other with metaphors for the self. We assume that we know the self in ways in which we do not know the Other. This gives rise to metaphorical source domains for the self that are opposite to the source domains for the Other. They include THE SELF IS A FRIEND, THE SELF IS A CARETAKER, THE SELF IS A MASTER (see Lakoff and Johnson 1999). Not only are these familiar source domains as such, but they are also familiar persons, unlike the persons used for the comprehension of the Other, as we saw above.

2.2 The Self

2.2.1 How Is the Self Constructed?

Just as the construction of the Other is linked with Self, that is, the I/we-group, so is the construction of the Self is linked with the Other. This is, I assume, another major theme in a variety of disciplines, including literary theory, social psychology, and philosophy. Here I take up the issue of self-construction in existential philosophy on the basis of Hogan's (2000) comments on Sartre's existentialism.

In characterising Sartre's view of the Self (ego) and the Other, Hogan (2000, pp. 127–128) makes the following statement, partly commenting on, partly quoting Sartre:

> Specifically, for Sartre, the Ego is a 'hypostatiz[ation] ... of the for-itself which is reflected on' and made into an 'in-itself' (156). In other words, it is the human self made into a static thing – for instance, a list of dispositions and character traits ('irritable', 'gregarious', 'sharp-tongued', or, for that matter, 'good' or 'evil') attached to the person like visible properties attached to a physical object. This Ego is formed, first of all, in relation to the other.

Hogan argues, following Sartre, that in my experience of myself, I am not a thing, a static object with a list of features; instead, I am an acting, choosing, experiencing being – a 'continual being-in-the-world'. We can interpret this view of self-construction by Sartre in two ways: metonymically or metaphorically.

On the metonymic interpretation, we can see the process as the functioning of the generic metonymy PROPERTIES OF THE WHOLE FOR THE WHOLE, where the Other notices some properties of the ego who adopts or 'inherits' them. The assumption here is that each person is characterised by a set of properties that define the person and, in this sense, create or construct the person. This reduces personhood to a set of properties. In it, a being-for-itself becomes a being-in-itself – a static object.

Given the metaphoric interpretation, the source domain of OBJECT is used to conceptualise the target domain of the Self (or ego or person). This could be described as the A PERSON IS AN OBJECT (WITH PROPERTIES) metaphor. Thus, the metaphor turns the acting, choosing, experiencing Self into a static entity. Metaphorical conceptualisation of this kind is called an 'ontological metaphor' (Lakoff and Johnson 1980; Kövecses 2010) in the course of which there is a change in the ontological status of the target domain – in this case in that of the Self or ego.

Othello

Hogan exemplifies this process of self-construction with Shakespeare's *Othello*. Othello, as he stabs himself, recounts the story of killing himself as stabbing a 'malignant Turk'. Othello is, of course, the Other in Venetian society (the 'we/us', the Self), but the example shows how a person's identity (self) can be influenced by the external other (Venetian society). (In other words, the roles of the Other and the self are reversible and a matter of perspective.) By calling himself a (malignant) Turk, he turns himself from a 'being-for-itself' into a 'being-in-itself'. As a result of Venetian society's judgment, he loses his basic humanity, his status as a 'being-for-itself', and adopts as his mode of being that of a static object, a 'being-in-itself'. Hogan's example demonstrates the potential tragic consequences of constructing a new mode of being, a new Self or ego, for oneself.

2.2.2 *The Self Is Not Unitary*

The Self (i.e., the person or the group who opposes themself or itself to the Other) is not unitary. As, for example, Freud pointed out, what we take to be the person in ourselves is not a unitary entity. For Freud, it is composed of the ego, the id, and the superego. Linguistic usage also seems to indicate that the self actually consists of several distinguishable parts, as the use of various pronouns, such as I, me, and myself, shows. This has important consequences for the metaphorical conceptualisation of the Other.

Imagine that someone, after an outburst of anger, says: 'I'm sorry, I couldn't control myself.' In the sentence, there is the 'I' and the 'myself'. It is the same person, and yet the person speaks about themself as divided into two parts. Who is the I and who is the myself? Lakoff and Johnson (1999), in a cognitive linguistic framework, see the self, the unitary person, as a relational concept. They conceive of the self as having a bifurcated structure that consists of the 'subject-self' and another self or selves. Lakoff and Johnson (1999) define these two concepts as follows: 'The Subject is the locus of consciousness, subjective experience, reason, will, and our "essence", everything that makes us who we uniquely are. There is at least one Self and possibly more. The Selves consist of everything else about us – our bodies, our social roles, our histories, and so on.' And we might add, also our emotions.

2.2.3 *Externalising a Self*

As we saw, the subject-self is opposed to another Self or a set of selves. The selves that stand in opposition to the subject-self are typically negative. This is why they need to be controlled by the subject. In Freud's theory of the person, the id consists of all kinds of desires and instincts that must be kept in check by the ego. Jung calls this dark, negative aspect of the self 'shadow'. The shadow is the projection of the negative self onto an entity outside the person. The externalised self can take on symbolic significance. Many literary works can be interpreted within this framework.

Moby Dick

A well-known literary example is *Moby Dick* by Melville. The novel is based on several generic-level conceptual metaphors. In it, the world is portrayed as the sea, which can be thought of as THE WORLD IS THE SEA metaphor. This lends the novel a universal character as regards its message. In addition, human life is conceptualised by Melville as a sea journey that depicts Captain Ahab's search for the white whale. This conceptualisation goes back to one of the best-studied metaphors in the cognitive linguistic literature on metaphor: LIFE IS A JOURNEY. But since Ahab not only searches the sea for the whale but considers it as his major enemy, there is also the metaphor LIFE IS A STRUGGLE.

Finally, as suggested by several literary scholars, we can think of the whale as the externalised form of the dark side of the human psyche. Within the framework of conceptual metaphor theory, the construction of the Jungian 'shadow', this externalised self, is essentially a metaphorical process, in which the dark side of the Self is viewed as an external object; hence the conceptual metaphor THE SELF IS AN EXTERNAL OBJECT. Since in the book this metaphor co-occurs with the LIFE IS A STRUGGLE metaphor, where the entity to struggle with, to fight, is the whale, we know that Ahab is really struggling with himself in an effort to control the dark forces inside him. And we know that he fails, and that, given the universal message of the novel, there is the danger that we fail with him.

2.3   The Self–Other Relationship

2.3.1   *Constructing the Subject–Self Relationship*

We saw above that the subject and the self can be metaphorically comprehended as friends, as caretaker and child, as master and student, respectively. In most of these cases, the subject is in a dominant position in relation to the self, and it is the responsibility of the subject to control the self – be the self the body, an emotion, or whatever. As in our example 'I couldn't control myself' referring to a case of anger, the subject holds themself responsible for not controlling the emotional self. In general, the main or decisive relationship between the subject-self and the other selves appears to be that of control: the subject controlling (or attempting to control or being responsible for controlling) the self.

We can identify the 'I/we' that opposes the Other with the subject-self that distinguishes itself from the self or selves. As much of the literature on the Other, and alterity in general, tells us, the 'I/we' is in a strikingly similar relationship to the Other as the internal subject is to the internal self or selves. The parallel seems to be that the internal subject is in the same relationship to the external Other, as the internal subject is to the internal self (or selves): the relationship of control. Much of this literature suggests that the I/we (the internal subject) tries to control the external Other in a variety of ways, similar to the internal subject in relation to the internal selves. This seems to be a general characteristic of the relationship between men and women, whites and non-whites, straights and gays, west and east, and so on.

I propose that the relationship between the internal subject and the internal self, on the one hand, and that between the internal subject and the external Other, on the other, constitute a metaphorical relationship, standing in a 'source domain–to–target domain' relationship. The question is which one is the source and which one is the target. To use the terminology of conceptual metaphor theory, the question is whether it is the internal relationship that conceptually structures (or historically structured) the external relationship, or the other way around. In other words: Do we have the EXTERNAL (SOCIAL) RELATIONSHIPS ARE INTERNAL (PSYCHOLOGICAL) RELATIONSHIPS metaphor or the INTERNAL (PSYCHOLOGICAL) RELATIONSHIPS ARE EXTERNAL (SOCIAL) RELATIONSHIPS metaphor?

Judging the issue by the principles of conceptual metaphor theory, we should suppose the existence of the latter: INTERNAL (PSYCHOLOGICAL) RELATIONSHIPS ARE EXTERNAL (SOCIAL) RELATIONSHIPS. This is because more abstract and, hence, less familiar concepts typically function as target domains, whereas more concrete and, hence, more familiar concepts typically function as source domains. Our mental life and the entities and relationships that make it up are less observable and, thus, less known to us than our social life and the entities and relationships that make it up. This is why the 'internal', the mental, is commonly conceptualised as 'external', the social or something physical. As noted by several linguists, for example, the epistemic sense of the auxiliary verb must follow the root, or deontic, sense of the word: 'You must do it because I am your father' came before 'She must be at home since the lights are on in her room.' In general, our internal life is patterned after the external world: either the social or the physical, including the human body. This view of the mind is known as the 'embodied mind'.

Heart of Darkness

An especially well-studied case of the interplay between the internal subject and the internal self, on the one hand, and the internal subject and the external other, on the other, is Joseph Conrad's novel *Heart of Darkness*. In a paper that deals with how image schemas can facilitate remembering the plot of a novel, Michael Kimmel (2005) describes how the Other can exert opposing forces on the Self: a force of attraction and a driving force. In the novel, Marlow is both propelled and attracted to the Congo, where he is looking for the enigmatic Mr. Kurtz.

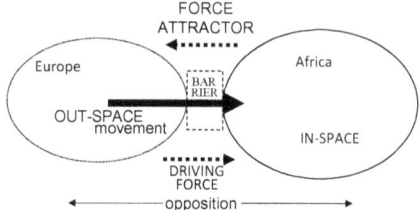

Figure 2.1 An image-schematic structure for the *Heart of Darkness* (from Kimmel 2005)

Figure 2.1 illustrates the workings of these contradictory forces. The heavy arrow schematically represents the literal journey into Africa. The ovals schematically represent Europe and Africa. Europe is an 'out-space' and Africa is an 'in-space'. Superimposed on the image schemas of container and source-path-goal, we find a force-dynamic schema represented by opposing dotted arrows. Marlow is both metaphorically driven and attracted by certain forces: the forces of intellectual curiosity and knowledge, on the one hand, and the forces of sensuality and passion, on the other. The 'push' and the 'pull', as Kimmel calls them, find actual linguistic expression in the text of the novel. The following examples are taken from Kimmel's paper:

> push attractor/drive
> 'driven toward the heat of fires'
> pull attractor
> 'smiling, ..., inviting, mute with an air of whispering, Come and find out';
>   'beguiled his unlawful soul'

As Kimmel's analysis makes clear, the Other is conceived as having a dual character: it is both the source of propulsion and attraction. We approach the ultimate unfamiliarity of the Other with both intellectual curiosity and the passions of the human soul.

2.4 Criminality as Otherness

In the preceding part of this chapter Kövecses has cogently demonstrated that Alterity is a dichotomic concept, one that is the result of cognitive processes such as categorisation and metaphor, and not hard-wired or handed down on Mount Sinai as the Eleventh Commandment. Crime, or 'the criminal', is an instantiation of Otherness, as criminologist Howard Becker (1963) clearly argues:

All social groups make rules and attempt, at some times and under some circumstances, to enforce them. Social rules define situations and the kinds of behaviour appropriate to them, specifying some actions as 'right' and forbidding others as 'wrong'. When a rule is enforced, the person who is supposed to have broken it may be seen as a special kind of person, one who cannot be trusted to live by the rules agreed on by the group. He is regarded as an *outsider*. (Becker 1963, pp. 1–2)

The processes identified by Kövecses are all present here: categorising (into two groups), labelling, negatively evaluating. Becker has identified the contraculture that Alterity may bring into being in the domain of crime:

But the person who is thus labelled as an outsider may have a different view of the matter. He may not accept the rule by which he is being judged and may not regard those who judge him as either competent or legitimately entitled to do so ... the rule-breaker may feel his judges are *outsiders*. (ibid.)

Since crime is defined by society, definitions of alterity are relative, as is confirmed by different laws and different applications of the 'same' laws by different societies and by changes in definitions within the same society over time. For instance, in Italy the 'crime of honour' (*delitto d'onore*) (see also note 2), whereby a husband who killed his wife if he discovered she had been unfaithful (hence, had become an Other) would obtain a reduced sentence (three to seven years' imprisonment), has been repealed, and this crime is now treated as first-degree murder.

Crime would thus seem a perfect instantiation of a dichotomic division. Dichotomic divisions, which were once a mainstay of both folk belief and 'science', have now lost ground to a far more complex vision of a stratified society.[1] However, crime, as would seem to emerge from Becker's words above, might seem to perpetuate dichotomy as a viable principle. Nevertheless, as Becker and Kövecses have pointed out and as the illustration of change in the definition of crime has demonstrated, different groups can have different opinions as to the identity of the outsider. One classic case is death ensuing from driving. Driving offences in general have long been considered by many people a minor crime committed by otherwise respectable citizens, if a crime at all. And murder by drunken driving is still punished in some countries by penalties which are far more lenient than those inflicted for other types of homicide.[2]

---

[1] Prototype theory (Rosch 1973) replaces either/or with gradation. A given real-world entity is a core or central instantiation of a category and other entities are less representative of the category. For example, a salmon is more prototypical of the category 'fish' than an eel since the latter breathes through the mouth and through gills. Kövecses theoretical account of the metonymic process of categorising in Section 2.1.3 is akin to prototype theorising. Another important feature of prototype theory is that it is cognitive in nature, since human evaluation is the basis for assigning entities to categories rather than objective features which may be machine-selected. See also note 8, Chapter 15.

[2] Those wishing to see this set of concepts connected to cultural relativity illustrated in a sociologically brilliant and concurrently hilarious manner can do no better than watch the crime-related film (which deals with a variant of the *delitto d'onore*) *Girl with a Gun*.

Demonstrating Alterity at work in crime is quite a straightforward matter. The stance of the prototypical 'good' citizen is expressed by the myriad of television news items and newspaper reports where offenders and supposed offenders are 'branded' as criminals and classified in debasingly negative terms and by CNN news broadcasts (to name but one television company). With regard to the presumed offenders, think of the number of social groups, both in the past and in the present, that openly challenge the status quo: terrorists and the mafia and similar organised crime, to name but two. Indeed, such groups have developed a fully-fledged ideology to justify their stances. Thus, Wolfgang and Ferracuti (1967; p. 166) have adopted the term 'contraculture' developed by Yinger (1960) to describe the phenomenon of a social group which embraces an ideology which is resistant and opposed to the dominant culture.

I will refer to two literary works and one film to illustrate crime as the expression of Otherness. All three represent Otherness as expressed by a minority contraculture 'answering back' (to borrow from Ashcroft, Tiffin, and Griffith's classic work, 1989) to the dominant group. Brendan Behan's novel *Borstal Boy* (1958) recounts the author's early rebelliousness, his involvement with the Irish Republican cause, and his consequent incarceration in an English Borstal. Age, religion, class, politics are some of the major contextual factors discussed in the book which thus provides an in-depth account of behaviour and ideology of the political contraculture of the time. The film *Nil by Mouth* (see Chapter 15) offers a dark representation of London's criminal contraculture in the 1990s. The film presents a literally and metaphorically dark picture of the ideology of crime as a way of life (IMMORAL IS BLACK/DARK, see Section 2.1.3), with drugs, alcohol, violence (to ensure success in carrying out the criminal venture, to gain allegiance from the 'rank and file' criminals and from family members, including the wife – hence depicting a strong patriarchal portrait) occupying centre stage in the criminals' lives. The third work I will refer to will also be subjected to brief analysis to illustrate the concepts identified by Kövecses applied to crime.

Alan Sillitoe's short story *The Loneliness of the Long-Distance Runner*, published in 1959, a year after Behan's novel, portrays the contraculture of a significant sector of the British working class of the time,[3] hence not simply that of the criminal subculture, as represented by *Nil by Mouth*. The main

---

[3] That Blairism put an end to class stratification has been questioned by many. Crime fiction has contributed to the debate, as this example from Ann Cleeves' novel *White Nights* (2007) shows: 'Becoming a cop had been seen as a betrayal. He'd joined up on the wrong side in the class war. Even now that the boundaries were blurred he didn't think that would ever be forgiven.' The debate on the so-called end of ideology (Bell 1960) has continued since the 1950s (Strand 2016).

character, a boy called Smith, the most common surname in England, hence metonymic, representing his social group, is sent to Borstal following being apprehended for robbery.

The story goes instantly to the heart of the matter, so to speak, by introducing the metaphorically generated framing symbol of running.

Text 1
As soon as I got to Borstal they made me a long-distance cross-country runner. I suppose they thought I was just the build for it because I was long and skinny for my age ... I didn't mind it much, to tell you the truth, because running had always been made much of in our family, especially running away from the police. I've always been a good runner ... the only trouble being that no matter how fast I run ... it didn't stop me getting caught by the cops after that bakery job. (opening paragraph, p. 7)

First, the thematic scene is set: crime constitutes oppositional ideological and social conflict, class conflict as we will learn shortly. Second, running, or 'running away', immediately emerges as a framing symbol. It conveys both the desire and the attempt to escape from repression and subjugation and to achieve freedom (escaping from 'Borstal', 'running away from the police'; conceptual metaphor [CM]: FREEDOM IS RUNNING AWAY). The symbol/metaphor thus divides the world into two distinct groups. The group-like nature of the phenomenon is underlined by the fact that it is not simply the single individual who engages in that (literal-cum-symbolic) activity, but the entire 'family'. The division is eminently social and untranscendable. Third, the dominated fail and will fail to escape subjugation, as demonstrated by the symbol/metaphor 'running away' constituting the only means available to achieve freedom. Fourth, and centrally, power is the key force in determining human relationships, since it is employed as a means of subjugation (erecting and maintaining class barriers). This is signalled by the lexical verb 'made', which acts as a metaphor (HUMANS ARE PHYSICAL OBJECTS) and as a (metaphorical) material process (Halliday & Matthiessen 2004) (the CM being CAUSATION IS MAKING) in which the hero is the object[4] acted upon ('me'). The concept of subordination and the feeling of being subordinated are also conveyed by the fact that 'no matter how fast I run ... it didn't stop me getting caught by the cops', expressing futility in the face of power. The feeling of objectification[5] is further reinforced by the temporal adverbial which starkly opens the story: 'as soon as'. Instantaneity implies strong, inevitable,

---

[4] Halliday and Matthiessen (2004) call what in classic structural grammar is known as the direct object the goal. The term is thus a metaphor indicating the depersonalised nature of the category. Gregoriou (Chapter 5) employs transitivity structure in her analysis, providing a brief explanation in note 1.

[5] Or of 'being-in-itself' as opposed to 'being-for-itself', in Hogan's (2001) terms – see Section 2.2.1.

unavoidable force being applied to impose the superior's will on the subordinate. 'I suppose they thought ...' confirms imposition since it implies 'they' in power did not explain to him why 'they' had taken that decision but had simply ordered him to do it. The modal construction 'suppose' and the lack of any explanation given to Smith confirm his powerlessness. The final point I wish to make about this opening paragraph of the many more that might be made is that 'they' is undefined.[6] Although it is a pronoun, no anaphoric referent precedes it as the rules of grammar lay down. Since this pronoun is devoid of a referent, in theory it is anonymous. Breaking this linguistic rule is an instantiation of foregrounding (Douthwaite 2000), namely, making a deliberate 'linguistic'[7] mistake to create some non-literal meaning. Clearly, employing knowledge of the world and what little information is textually available ('I got' and 'to Borstal') leads to the induction that 'they' refers to the prison authorities, and more generally to all those in authority, as the rest of the story will repeatedly underscore. Deploying an 'empty referent' produces important communicative effects. First, anonymity engenders depersonalisation. This in turn propagates further effects:

(1) a negative evaluation of the prison authorities through failing to recognise they have any identity, any specificity, any individuality, hence any humanity;
(2) a distancing effect which:
(2a) recalls the preceding point, and
(2b) recognises the subordinate's powerlessness with regard to the effects 'their' actions have over him. It resembles the powerlessness the 'ordinary' citizen feels when confronted by the bureaucratic machine of the state or of a large organisation;

---

[6] Communication is a highly complex affair. A multiplicity of symbolising devices go into the construction of even the simplest utterance, which may, moreover, perform a multiplicity of communicative functions or speech acts, at a variety of levels of meaning that such functions cover (ideational, emotional, psychological, social, textual [in the Hallidayan sense of the term]). On the other hand, communication is also characterised by reduction in explicitness. The verbal signal contains a very small amount of information, obliging the brain to reconstruct the meaning by adding the missing information and linking the various parts up into a coherent whole through a process of inferencing. For instance, the first sentence provides no information as to the identity of the 'I' referred to in the clause 'I got to Borstal', nor the vagueness of the lexical verb 'got', yet the reader reconstructs the meaning without experiencing any particular difficulty. (For an overview of the process of communication, see Douthwaite 2000, pp. 205–266.) The entire reconstructive process must be considered if the richness of an utterance is to be comprehended, especially when talking about the ideology conveyed by a metaphor. Since space obliges a concentration on metaphor, readers must themselves unravel the hidden complexities which cannot be explicated here.

[7] 'Linguistic' is here intended in the broadest sense possible to include all the dimensions of 'language as communication'. In addition to lexis, grammar, and phonology, this includes pragmatics, style, textual organisation, and behavioural and cultural rules (Douthwaite 2000).

(3) Smith is referring to the authorities as a category ('them', not 'us'), and not as single individuals with their own personal identities, a second form of depersonalisation (after [1] above), and one which implies that what is being represented through their actions is their ideology *in toto*.

This point regarding the dominant power structure subordinating the categories subjected to 'its' power is reiterated manifold times throughout the story. The second paragraph of the story expands on these aspects.

Text 2
You might think it a bit rare, having long-distance cross-country runners in Borstal, thinking that the first thing a long-distance cross-country runner would do when they set him loose at them fields and woods would be to run as far away from the place as he could get on a bellyful of Borstal slumgullion – but you're wrong, and I'll tell you why. The first thing is that them bastards over us aren't as daft as they most of the time look, and for another thing I'm not so daft as I would look if I tried to make a break for it on my long-distance running, because to abscond and then get caught is nothing but a mug's game, and I'm not falling for it. Cunning is what counts in this life, and even that you've got to use in the slyest way you can; I'm telling you straight: they're cunning, and I'm cunning. If only 'them' and 'us' had the same ideas we'd get on like a house on fire, but they don't see eye to eye with us and we don't see eye to eye with them, so that's how it stands and how it will always stand. The one fact is that all of us are cunning, and because of this there's no love lost between us. So the thing is that they know I won't try to get away from them: they sit there like spiders in that **crumbly** manor house, perched like jumped-up jackdaws on the roof, watching out over the drives and fields like German generals from the **tops** of tanks. (metaphorical linguistic expressions [MLEs] underlined, creative metaphors in bold) (pp. 7–8)

Text 2 (T2) represents just under half of the second paragraph of the story. It takes us further forward into the argument in several ways. First, there is an abundance of metaphors – thirty-four metaphorical linguistic expressions[8] (MLEs) (Kövecses 2010, p. 4) in all, in just 267 words, two of which may be classified as creative metaphors and the remaining ones as dead metaphors. The MLEs account for 96 of the 267 words (approximately 36% of the text), yielding a metaphor density of 120.[9] Stated differently, there is an abundance of metaphors.

Second, the key ideological point is made more explicitly than in T1 through the classificatory division "'them' and 'us'". This leads to a whole series of oppositions being set up linguistically, either directly (as in 'they don't see eye to eye with us and we don't see eye to eye with them') or indirectly (as in

---

[8] Purism has not been fully respected here since, to simplify argumentation, the figure quoted includes 'next of kin' figurative language such as similes. This does not significantly alter the analysis offered.
[9] On metaphor density, see Cameron (2008). On applications of metaphor density, see Douthwaite (2011, p. 270).

'they're cunning, and I'm cunning'). The latter example is oppositional despite the deployment of the coordinating conjunction 'and' since the two phrases are separated by a comma, indicating disunity as opposed to unity, the 'standard' function realised by this conjunction, thus creating the implicature that the hero's cunning will defeat 'their' cunning.

Third, there are a series of 'ideological metaphors'[10] that underscore the division and conflict between the haves and the have nots, singled out earlier by Kövecses. Prominent is THE OTHER IS AN ENEMY and the related conceptual metaphor (CM) LIFE IS WAR. The most blatant reference to war is the simile 'like German generals'. Alliteration ('g') makes the phrase stand out; hence it is a foregrounding mechanism indicating the linguistic expression requires critical attention. The reference to World War II implicitly characterises the Germans as Other and as the enemy. By extension, therefore, the authorities are also classified as the enemy or Other ('like'). Exploitation of the same metaphorical and semantic fields continues with 'from the tops of tanks'. This exploits the CM ABOVE IS GOOD/POWERFUL. Significantly, the rank selected is that of 'general', symbolising power, and equally significantly the generals are on the 'tops' of 'tanks' (instruments of violence) and not, for instance, on the roof of a high building. Note the parallel use of alliteration (the letter 't'). Power is being wielded directly and deliberately. That such effects are desired is shown by the fact that 'tops' is a strange collocation with 'tanks'. The other implicature set up by the simile is that Borstal is a prison camp and a battle field. Violence is suggested elsewhere in the paragraph, as in 'they set him loose at them fields and woods'. The standard MLE is 'let loose', as in 'they let loose the dogs at him'. By employing the lexeme 'set' in lieu of 'let', the degree of violence and agency (deliberateness) is increased.

Another CM signalled by Kövecses as characterising Otherness is THE OTHER IS A WILD ANIMAL (the category of animacy identified by Hogan – see Section 2.1.3). The MLEs realising the CMs here do not warrant the adjective 'wild', but they are equally denigratory. The clause 'they sit there like spiders' is actually a simile, a highly effective one, conveying war-related concepts such as aggression, speed of reaction, escape routes. The expression is reinforced by the creative metaphor (Douthwaite 2011) 'crumbly'. Again, this is deliberate foregrounding, since a more usual collocation with 'manor house' would have been 'crumbling'. The 'manor house' is a metonym for the ruling class, 'crumbly' signifying that the power structure is not solidly entrenched and could be resisted (through crime, for instance, that is to say, through a different life style). The spider (standing for the hero) is participating in the destruction of the said class. Negative labelling of the superior Other by

---

[10] On the ideological functions of metaphors, see Goatly (2007); Douthwaite (2009/2011).

the subordinate continues with the animal CM with (1) 'perched' and (2) 'like jumped-up jackdaws'.

Fourth, the irremediable inevitability of class conflict is confirmed, through another metaphor: 'that's how it stands and how it will always stand' – LIFE IS A BUILDING – representing solidity, hence long duration.

Text 3
I know who my enemies are and what war is. They can drop all the atom bombs they like for all I care: I'll never call it war and wear a soldier's uniform, because I'm in a different sort of war, that they think is child's play ... I got past that when I knew I already was in a war of my own, that I was born into one, that I grew up hearing the sound of 'old soldiers' who'd been over the top at Dartmoor, half-killed at Lincoln, trapped in no-man's-land at Borstal, that sounded louder than any Jerry bombs. Government wars aren't my wars; they've got nowt to do with me, because my own war's all that I'll ever be bothered about. I remember when I was fourteen and I went out into the country with three of my cousins, all about the same age, who later went to different Borstals, and then to different regiments, from which they soon deserted, and then to different gaols where they still are as far as I know. (pp. 17–18, MLEs underlined)

Indeed, in this short story WAR is a megametaphor, or extended metaphor (Kövecses 2010, p. 57) (the word 'war' appears forty-nine times), creatively used to great effect here. First, it continues the dichotomic view of society. Smith makes an absolute distinction between 'government wars', namely, those officially classified as wars by the superiors, such as World Wars I and II, which he classifies as 'suicide', in contrast to 'my own war', which Smith conducts through thieving. The expression 'nowt to do with me' underscores his total ideological dissent from the sense of national unity that the official propaganda championed during World War II (fighting for a better future for the people of Britain, which the person of Inspector George Gently represents; see Chapter 15). The social division is bolstered by the family reference (a constant in this story), which confirms the social rather than the individual level of the story: three cousins go 'the way of all flesh', so to speak, for that category of persons. Second, T3 praises the subordinates (1) by referring to them with an expression that is standardly deemed as emitting a positive evaluation: 'old soldiers', (2) by attributing to them bravery in the face of grave danger: 'over the top' and 'in no-man's land' (metaphorical creativity by invoking trench warfare in World War I where the death rate was incredibly high), 'half-killed'. Further creativity is achieved by substituting the place names of famous battles (such as the battle of Verdun, the Somme, the Marne) with those of prisons and prison types ('Dartmoor', 'Lincoln', and 'Borstal').

Text 4
They're training me up fine for the big sports day when all the pig-faced snotty-nosed dukes and ladies – who can't add two and two together and would mess themselves like

loonies if they didn't have slavies to beck-and-call – come and make speeches to us about sports being just the thing to get us leading an honest life and keep our itching finger-ends off them shop locks and safe handles and hairgrips to open gas meters. They give us a bit of blue ribbon and a cup for a prize after we've shagged ourselves out running or jumping, like race horses, only we don't get so well looked-after as race horses. (pp. 8–9)

The main theme of T4 is the objectification the human being, conveyed by the CM THE OTHER IS AN ANIMAL, in this case a 'race horse'. In itself, the race horse may be considered a noble animal. The negativity derives from the dehumanisation and objectification that the comparison involves. The horse is simply an object which the 'superior humans' use to gain pleasure, obliging the object to carry out their wishes and employing unpleasant means to exploit them to the full. Exploitation has two faces: making the subordinate work ('slavies to beck-and-call', 'shagged ourselves out running') and paying him very little for that work ('They give us a bit of blue ribbon and a cup for a prize', 'only we don't get so well looked-after as race horses'). The CM is reinforced in two ways. First, by (ironically) deploying another CM: UP IS GOOD: 'they're training me up'. Second by again using agency to suggest domination, since 'they' are deliberately and consciously performing the material process of 'training' on Smith, the non-consulted goal without a will being acted upon, thus a parallel to the CM CAUSATION IS MAKING encountered in 'they made me' (T1). The CAUSATION CM is further realised by 'get', in 'get us leading an honest life'.

As Kövecses and Becker have argued, the Other may not agree with the label attached to them, challenging the labeller's competence and legitimacy to do so, and may in their turn assign negative labels to the other group, as happens here: 'the pig-faced snotty-nosed dukes and ladies – who can't add two and two together and would mess themselves like loonies if they didn't have slavies to beck-and-call'. The ANIMAL CM is again deployed to disparage the superiors ('pig-faced ... dukes and ladies'), another manner of setting up oppositions. Their status as full, normal human beings is called into question with another two similes invoking different categories, 'like loonies' and 'slavies', traditionally highly derogatory appellations.

The superiors' justification for their labelling that given social group as Other is also provided: 'leading an honest life and keep our itching finger-ends off them shop locks and safe handles' – the protection of bourgeois property. Metonymy plays a major role in this example: 'itchy finger-ends' for the act of a person stealing and 'shop locks and safe handles' for the place of provenance of the stolen goods. The term 'finger-ends' is particularly interesting as a creative metaphor since the standard term is 'itchy fingers'. The lexeme 'ends' may be hypothesised as performing two functions: it calls up the goal in the criminal's behaviour (synonymity) and it refers to the most sensitive part of the hand which has to perform the act of theft. The latter also helps explain the choice of the two metonyms 'shop locks' and 'safe handles'.

Text 5
Be honest. It's like saying: Be dead, like me, and then you'll have no more pain of leaving your nice slummy house for Borstal or prison. Be honest and settle down in a cosy six pounds a week job. (p. 14)

Smith is remembering the Governor's speech when he first arrived at Borstal. The first sentence – 'be honest' – presents the Governor's words in Free Direct Speech. Smith then interprets the Governor's words into what being 'honest' would mean ('It's like saying') were he to adopt the Governor's value system. Recontextualisation is achieved through the CM HONESTY IS DEATH. The text is deeply ironic, since the Governor is obviously unaware that his worldview represents (metaphorical) death. The bleak picture continues with the CM LIFE IS PAIN ('the pain of leaving'). Local irony is also realised through the bizarre collocation 'nice slummy house'. One should also note the lexical and grammatical parallelism between 'slummy house' and 'crumbly manor house' in T2. Oppositions are drawn at all levels – conceptual and linguistic – throughout the story to underscore the conflict between the two groups. Irony is redoubled by the Governor 'inviting' Smith to exchange his 'nice' slummy house for 'Borstal or prison', implicitly accusing the Governor of stupidity and/or insanity.

The third sentence parallels the second sentence both conceptually and grammatically. It initiates with an imperative ('Be dead/honest') referring pragmatically to the same condition of life through the opposition drawn both in the previous sentence and in previous co-text. The most important linguistic parallel is that of 'cosy six pounds' with 'nice slummy house'. The first adjective in both noun phrases is positive, contradicting the second 'adjective' ('six' is technically a numeral, but performs an adjectival function) which expresses a negative value judgment ('six pounds' a week being a pittance) and the head noun is an object which constitutes a necessity in life. Oxymorons are employed to draw attention to the fact that the ideology represented by the Governor is a means of repression and exploitation, protecting the life of luxury of the haves. Ultimately, the story is a cry for liberty and social justice, expressing indirectly Lear's cry against his daughters' treatment:

> O, reason not the need! Our basest beggars
> Are in the poorest thing superfluous.
> Allow not nature more than nature needs,
> Man's life's as cheap as beast's.
>
> (*King Lear*, Act 2, Scene 4)

Where this chapter has concentrated principally on the role of metaphor in conceptualising and conveying Otherness, numerous chapters in this volume will examine the specific functions realised by metaphor, metonymy and simile in the texts they scrutinise, demonstrating the great signifying power of these cognitive linguistic devices. Further examples will emerge illustrating the metaphors of WAR and ANIMAL (Chapters 4, 5 11, 15). Fludernik, instead, offers a high-level theoretical analysis of one metaphor conveying Otherness: PRISONS.

2.5   Conclusions

In this chapter, we claimed that what we can call the 'we–other' mentality emerges in part from the way we think about our categories. We also suggested that the stereotyping and stigmatisation of the other has to do with metonymic thought. A further point we made is that the very creation of the Other as a category depends on thinking of categorisation in terms of 'essential features', as the chief way of creating categories. We additionally pointed out that the commonly recognised interdependence of the Self and the Other can be understood both metonymically and metaphorically. Moreover, we proposed that the nature of the metaphors for the Other is unlike the nature of most metaphors discussed in conceptual metaphor theory. And, finally, we claimed that the non-unitary conception of the Self as subject-self vs. other selves is brought about as a result of a metaphorical process that has its basis in the 'internal subject–external other' relationship, which serves as the source domain of the metaphor.

However, our general conclusion, based on the foregoing analyses, is that cognitive linguistics provides us with conceptual tools that help us to better understand the nature of some of the key notions in our mental life, and how they emerge as a result of certain basic cognitive processes, such as metonymy and metaphor. The analyses also throw some light on the deep interplay between our folk-theoretical and language-based understanding of SELF and OTHER, on the one hand, and the interpretation of literary works, on the other. Finally, they also equip us with tools that allow us to see literary, cultural, and philosophical frameworks of interpretation as being congruent with what we have recently discovered about the nature and functioning of the human mind.

The theoretical constructs developed in the first three sections of this chapter were verified by applying them to the domain of crime texts, focusing on one particular text where a key social factor constituted the essential feature creating Otherness: class. Many of the cognitive processes identified in the theoretical part of the chapter were shown to characterise the construction of Otherness in the selected text. Further confirmation will be obtained from a number of the subsequent chapters.

References

Ashcroft, B., Griffiths, G., & Tiffin, H. (1989). *The Empire Writes Back: Theory and Practice in Post-Colonial Literatures*. London: Routledge.

Becker, H. S. (1963) *Outsiders: Studies in the Sociology of Deviance*. New York: Free Press of Glencoe.

Behan, B. (1958/1965). *Borstal Boy*. London: Corgi Books.

Bell, D. (1960). *The End of Ideology: On the Exhaustion of Political Ideas in the Fifties*. Glencoe, IL: Free Press.

Cameron, L. (2008). Metaphor and Talk. In R. Gibbs, ed., *The Cambridge Handbook of Metaphor and Thought*. Cambridge: Cambridge University Press, pp. 197–211.

Cleeves, A. (2007). *White Nights*. London: Macmillan.

Douthwaite, J. (2000). *Towards a Linguistic Theory of Foregrounding*. Alessandria: Edizioni dell'Orso.

(2009/2011). Pragmatic Patterning in the Deployment of Conceptual Metaphor and Communication. In C. Marcato & V. Orioles, eds., *Studi plurilingui e interlinguistici in ricordo di Roberto Gusmani*. Udine: Forum, pp. 83–118.

(2011). Conceptual Metaphor and Communication: An Austinian and Gricean Analysis of Brian Clark's *Whose Life Is It Anyway?* In M. Fludernik, ed., *Beyond Cognitive Metaphor Theory: Perspectives on Literary Metaphor*. London: Routledge, pp. 137–157.

(2015). Cognitive Metaphor in *A Little Cloud*. In G. Cortese, G. Ferreccio, & M. T. Giaveri, eds., *James Joyce: Whence, Wither and How*. Alessandria: Edizioni dell'Orso, pp. 279–310.

Goatly, A. (2007). *Washing the Brain: Metaphor and Hidden Ideology*. Amsterdam: John Benjamins.

Halliday, M., & Matthiessen, C. (2004). *An Introduction to Functional Grammar*. London: Arnold.

Hogan, P. C. (2000). *Philosophical Approaches to the Study of Literature*. Gainesville: University Press of Florida.

(2001). *The Culture of Conformism: Understanding Social Consent*. Durham, NC: Duke University Press.

Kimmel, M. (2005). From Metaphor to the 'Mental Sketchpad': Literary Macrostructure and Compound Image Schemas in *Heart of Darkness*. *Metaphor and Symbol*, 20(3), 199–238.

Kövecses, Z. (2000). *American English: An Introduction*. Peterborough: Broadview Press.

(2006). *Language, Mind, and Culture: A Practical Introduction*. New York: Oxford University Press.

(2010). *Metaphor: A Practical Introduction*. New York: Oxford University Press.

(2015). *Where Metaphors Come From: Reconsidering Context in Metaphor*. New York: Oxford University Press.

Kövecses, Z., & Radden, G. (1998). Metonymy: Developing a Cognitive Linguistic View. *Cognitive Linguistics*, 9(7), 37–77.

Lakoff, G., & Johnson, M. (1980). *Metaphors We Live By*. Chicago: University of Chicago Press.

(1987). *Women, Fire, and Dangerous Things*. Chicago: University of Chicago Press.

(1999). *Philosophy in the Flesh*. New York: Basic Books.

Rosch, E. (1973). Natural Categories. *Cognitive Psychology*, 4, 328–350.
Sillitoe, A. (1959/2007). *The Loneliness of the Long-Distance Runner*. London: Harper.
Strand, D. (2016) *No Alternatives: The End of Ideology in the 1950s and the Post-Political World of the 1990s*. Malmö: Stockholm University.
Wolfgang, M., & Ferracuti, F. (1967) *The Subculture of Violence: Towards an Integrated Theory in Criminology*. London: Tavistock Publications.
Yinger M. (1960) Contraculture and Subculture. *American Sociological Review*, 25, 625–635.

3 Prison Metaphors
Conveying the Experience of Confinement

Monika Fludernik

3.1 Introduction

In *Metaphors of Confinement* (Fludernik 2019, pp. 42–52, 597–611) I presented a survey of what I called *carceral metaphors*, discussing two basic types of metaphoric transfer. On the one hand, I looked at metaphors attributing a number of qualities to prisons (e.g. PRISON IS ABATTOIR, PRISON IS JUNGLE); on the other hand, I examined the much longer, indeed limitless, number of metaphors in which a non-prison-related situation is being characterised as confining, hence prison-like (e.g. HATRED IS PRISON, SCHOOL IS PRISON, etc.). In the current coronavirus crisis, the second type of metaphor (X IS A PRISON) has become extremely common. For instance, not long ago I spent four weeks in a rehabilitation clinic after a hip operation, and patients kept joking about being in prison since there was an absolute ban on visitors and our food was handed to us on trays in prepackaged portions with no possibility of a choice between options. It is interesting to note that, due to the resulting waste (most people refused to eat what they did not like, sending back mountains of untouched dishes at each meal), one might have employed quite different metaphors such as CLINIC IS WASTE OF FOOD or HYGIENE AS ECOLOGICAL DISASTER or even CHOICE IS FREEDOM.

As researchers focusing on political rhetoric have long established (Mio 1997; Marks 2003; Musolff 2004, 2016; Charteris-Black 2009, 2011; Schoor 2015), the use of particular metaphors is often motivated by very concrete strategies of argument and by ideological preconceptions and prejudices. Thus, though the widespread existence of carceral metaphors in many cases is obviously unpremeditated, even 'natural', in other circumstances it follows a very specific intention and imposes a slanted or biased reading on the target domain. This is clearly the case with Brexit discourse characterising the EU as a prison from which the United Kingdom is keen to break out (Charteris-Black 2019, pp. 143–44)[1] – a metaphor that parallels the supposed invasions or

---

[1] 'The metaphorical framework of "exit" invites ideas like escaping prison, entering sunlit uplands, and so on – all of which are simple, easy, and quick' (Tapper 2019). This comment

floods of refugees that lend rightist political arguments leverage on exclusionary and xenophobic policies against asylum seekers. It is therefore necessary to ask for the intentional and unconscious purposes or the 'cultural work' of carceral metaphor.

In this essay, the emphasis will be on examining what prison metaphors imply about 'correctional facilities' (a US label) and their inmates. I will focus on literary texts (since I am a literary scholar), but my understanding of literary instances of these metaphors is that they are not peculiar to novels or poems but belong to a pool of conceptual metaphors shared across discourses and rooted in our conceptualisations of what confinement 'means' experientially. I have called this residue of images the *carceral imaginary* (Fludernik 2003, 2004, 2005, 2019). More concretely, I want to analyse two aspects or try to answer two questions. How are prisons imagined metaphorically? And when we attribute a prison-like quality to certain situations, why do we do so, and what features of incarceration are particularly being focused on? Looking at the first question will involve PRISON IS X metaphors, the second X IS A PRISON metaphors. In my conclusions I will consider the gap that exists between, on the one hand, conceptions of the prison as a site of suffering, despair and death-in-life and, on the other, the prevailing metaphorical representation of crime, offenders and prison inmates, which is predominantly derogatory.

3.2 Metaphorical Analogues of the Prison

In the material that I analysed for *Metaphors of Confinement* (literary texts from the English Middle Ages to contemporary Anglophone literature and essays from newspapers from the last 150 years), I found a number of recurring characterisations of prison which displayed a considerable variety of perspectives on penal institutions (compare Figure 3.1).

A number of these metaphors display what I have called a *global homology*; in other words, they acknowledge the pertinence of Foucault's categorisation of prisons as *heterotopias* (Foucault 1984 [1967]/2002). The prison is not merely a counterworld in the traditional conception as in the opposition of heaven and hell; it is a heterotopia to the extent that it can be observed to be a homological analogue of the world at large. In fact, the heaven versus hell dichotomy can be read as a homology, though in its customary model it primarily underlined the moral or evaluative opposition of the heavenly

---

alludes to the following utterance by Johnson: 'And hitting out at what he [Boris Johnson] described as the negative tactics of the Remain campaign, he said: "This is like the jailer has accidentally left the door of the jail open and people can see the sunlit land beyond"' (Withnall 2016). See also Islentyeva (2019, pp. 219, 225) and Daddow (2019) on the EU as prison trope. More recently, the metaphor has been used to describe Brexit itself as imprisoning, as in McGee (2019): 'Boris Johnson is trapped in a Brexit prison he helped build.'

I. (Global) HOMOLOGY METAPHORS

PRISON IS   WORLD
                BODY (Fennor)
                SCHOOL
                UNIVERSITY
                LIBRARY
                SHIP
                HOSPITAL

Partial Homology on basis of specific features

PRISON IS   LAW SCHOOL
                DICING HOUSE
                LABYRINTH
                BANQUETING HOUSE
                BROTHEL
                GARDEN

II. IDEOLOGICAL SLANT (external)

a) **Metaphors critical of prison**

PRISON IS   CRIME
                INJUSTICE

b) **Discourses of Law and Journalism**

PRISON IS   EXILE
                PUNISHMENT
                WORK
                SLAVERY
                FILTH, SEWER
                SURVEILLANCE?
                DISCIPLINE?
                PANOPTICON?
                DISHONOUR
                GUILT
                ZOO

c) **Symptomatic interpretations**

PRISON IS   COLONIALISM
                PATRIARCHY
                ancien régime
                SURVEILLANCE
                DISCIPLINE
                PANOPTICON

III. A. PRISONS OF EXPERIENCE (INTERNAL)

PRISON IS   POVERTY
                DEPRIVATION
                DISHONOUR
                GUILT

Figure 3.1 Source terms for describing prisons (PRISON IS X metaphors) (adapted from Fludernik 2019, pp. 608–9; see also p. 610)

B. a) Metaphors of Derogation and Praise

PRISON IS	**HELL**	
	DUNGEON	
	PURGATORY	positive:
		PARADISE
		PURIFICATION
		REFORMATION
		PILGRIMAGE
PRISON IS	**DEATH**	
	TOMB ('concrete womb')	
	LIVE BURIAL	
	SILENCE	
	LONELINESS	
	ICINESS	
PRISON IS	**ABATTOIR** (→ PRISONER IS ANIMAL)	
	SLAVERY	
	TORTURE	
	PUNISHMENT	
PRISON IS	**WILDERNESS** (→ PRISONER IS ANIMAL)	
	EXILE	
PRISON IS	**CAGE**	
	PEN	
	WAREHOUSE	
	BOREDOM	
PRISON IS	**MACHINE**	
	FACTORY (→ WORK IS PRISON)	
	FACTORY (→ PRISONERS AS OBJECTS)	
	INSANITY (overregulation)	
	ICINESS	

B. b) POSITIVE Metaphors

PRISON IS	HOME
	GARDEN
	REFUGE
	MONASTERY/HERMITAGE
	SCHOOL/SCOUTS' CAMP

Figure 3.1 (*cont.*)

paradise of eternal bliss versus the realm of eternal punishment. Yet those two kingdoms are conceived of in an extremely homologous fashion to the extent that they are ruled by God and Satan, respectively, with angels and devils as these rulers' ministers and the dead as their states' populations.

Among the global metaphors, the most basic and common is that of the *prison as world*, an image that was particularly relevant in the early modern period when prisons reflected the social stratification of society. In addition to this, the fact that the world was conceived of as a vale of tears from which death absolves us and propels us either into heaven or hell provided a neat parallel to the prison inmate's experience of suffering during their jailing, followed by trial (parallel to the Last Judgement) with subsequent release (~ heaven) or hanging (~ death and hell). Both of these facets are, for instance, foregrounded in the following passage from Sir Thomas More's 'On the Vanity of this Life':

> We are all shut up in the prison of this world under sentence of death. In this prison none escapes death. The land within the prison is divided into many sections, and men build their dwellings in different sections. As if the prison were a kingdom, the inmates struggle for position. The avaricious man hoards up wealth within the dark prison. One man wanders freely in the prison, another lies shackled in his cave; this man serves, that one rules; this one sings, that one groans. And then, while we are still in love with the prison as if it were no prison, we are escorted out of it, one way or another, by death. (More 1984, pp. 167–9)

As one can observe, the radical diversity of human fates is emphasised – today, we would call this inequality. The passage highlights both the end point of life and imprisonment, respectively, through death and the social diversity inside jails and in the world at large. Other Renaissance authors foreground the social parallelism in even greater detail by pointing to the trades practised in prisons just like outside. As William Fennor puts it:

> And, lastly, as in a city there is *all kinds of trades*, so is there here; for here you shall see a *cobbler* sitting, mending old shoes, and singing as merrily as if he were under a stall abroad. Not far from him you shall see a *tailor* sit cross-legged like a witch on his cushion. (Fennor qtd. in Judges 1930, p. 485; my emphasis)[2]

Similar global homologies can be found in the traditional conception of *the body as a prison*, an image that has even given rise to illustrations in the emblem literature. In Francis Quarles's *Emblems*, volume V, Emblem 8, in the 1634 edition illustrated by Charles Bennet and W. Harry Rogers, a homunculus looks out from a skeleton's ribcage (1861, p. 286). Other popular metaphors of global homology are the PRISON AS SHIP, PRISON AS UNIVERSITY, the PRISON AS HOSPITAL. (For a fuller list, see Fludernik 2019, pp. 65–71.) In all of these cases, extended parallels between aspects of the situation in prison and that in the frame of the source domain/vehicle of the image are delineated, thus implementing a *blend* in the sense of Turner and Fauconnier (Fauconnier & Turner 2008).

What I have called a *partial homology metaphor* also compares the prison to an external realm of experience, frequently from a subjective perspective, and

---

[2] For the much longer passage and the PRISON AS WORLD homology, see Fludernik (2019, pp. 69–70).

focuses on a particular aspect of the prison which legitimates the comparison. However, no total structural homology can be posited. Thus, when prison is described as a school ('it is an university of poore Schoolers, in which three Artes are chiefly studyed. To pray, to curse, and to write letters' – Overbury 1936, pp. 83–4), the triad of praying, cursing and writing begging letters touches on only one particular feature of the school curriculum, the triple qualifications of the trivium. Other such comparisons include the prison as dicing house or brothel. (In the latter case, one's bondage to sin is seen as the shared trait between a prisoner and frequenters of bawdy houses.[3]) I have also put Dickens's garden metaphor for Newgate in *Great Expectations* with its ostensibly positive source domain among the partial homologies, since Wemmick's macabre depiction of inmates as flowers to be culled by the gibbet displays an extremely subjective, or peculiar, view on the law in action:

It struck me that Wemmick walked among the prisoners, much as a gardener might walk among his plants. This was first put into my head by his seeing a shoot that had come up in the night, and saying, 'What, Captain Tom? Are *you* there? Ah, indeed!' ... Wemmick with his post-office in an immovable state, looked at them while in conference, as if he were taking particular notice of the advance they had made, since last observed, towards coming out in full blow at their trial. (Dickens 1996, p. 246)

It is noticeable that the PRISON IS X metaphors in the two categories described so far, but also more generally, reflect different perspectives on the prison. There are metaphors that focus on the carceral experience of inmates – it is for them that the analogy of school and prison is relevant; other homologies appear to derive from a more objective viewpoint from outside that truly observes the heterotopic quality of the carceral world; and yet others seem to cast a very one-sided or idiosyncratic glance at the institution (as in our last example). It is for this reason that PRISON IS X metaphors are much more given to negative associations of a condemnatory cast, mirroring worldviews or ideologies, cultural or moral assumptions or religious and political orthodoxies.

Among a second group of ideologically slanted metaphoric descriptions of the prison, external and internal (or subjective) viewpoints should be distinguished. Among the external viewpoints, there are those that are critical of the institution of penal confinement, that is, metaphors like PRISON IS CRIME and PRISON IS INJUSTICE, as well as metaphors which I have labelled 'symptomatic' of particular social or political frameworks. Among the latter group, one finds the prison imaged as symbolic of, for instance, colonialism, patriarchy or the *ancien régime*. Such metaphors highlight the fact that the injustices of (neo)

---

[3] See John Cook's *City Gallant* (1875, p. 244). For the dicing house metaphor, see Fennor (1930, p. 434).

colonialism are reproduced and exacerbated in prison such that the prison becomes an emblem of, say, apartheid. (The metaphor occurs with some frequency in South African prison memoirs – see Fludernik 2019, pp. 385–96). Likewise, when Mary Wollstonecraft's eponymous heroine Maria says that marriage had 'bastilled' her 'for life' (1994, p. 87), the MARRIAGE IS PRISON metaphor – in the context of the book, in which Maria is shut up in a lunatic asylum by her husband – also implies that prison is a symbol of patriarchy. And, of course, the Bastille itself developed into an emblem of the *ancien régime*.

While these two groups of ideological critiques of prison focus on the institution per se as an analogue of a political or social system, another set of metaphors picks out a particular trait of the prison or its inmates, one which elicits negative associations, and equates the prison with that feature. In this way, journalistic and legal discourses in particular describe the prison as representative of, for instance, filth and sewers, of dishonour, guilt, but also of exile, punishment or slavery. All of these metaphors see the prison as a place of *exclusion* for moral or legal reasons, with the filth/sewer association deploying a metonymy of the very real insanitariness of carceral institutions to point to the moral shortcomings of inmates. These discourses therefore imagine the prison as a heterotopia into which society has exiled those who are guilty in order to punish them and mark their dishonourable status. Such metaphors moreover conceive of the prison as a site of just punishment and deserved slavery. Early nineteenth-century reform propaganda against inacceptable conditions of employment in factories – but also against the employment situation of female dressmakers and seamstresses – underline the unjust slavery of these men and women by juxtaposing them with the well-deserved slavery of prisoners, who 'work for crime' (Hood 1980, st. 7).[4]

In Figure 3.1, I have also in this category added PRISON IS SURVEILLANCE/PANOPTICON/DISCIPLINE, on the understanding that these metaphors are employed to endorse policies of discipline or surveillance in relation to prison inmates. However, in more recent times, these analogies play out more frequently in the category of symptomatic prison images since the generalisation of surveillance mechanisms in our societies may result in an analysis of prison as a site of enhanced surveillance, which can be interpreted to be typical or emblematic of the surveillance panopticism affecting society in general (compare Fludernik 2020).

A final big category of metaphoric prison descriptors are what I have called *prisons of subjective experience*. These are metaphors that depict predominantly negative experiential qualities of carcerality. Such analogues can be very

---

[4] See Fludernik (2019, pp. 138–41) for more details.

general (PRISON IS POVERTY/DEPRIVATION or PRISON IS DISHONOUR/GUILT). The majority of these metaphors are more specific and refocus the exclusionary quality of penal confinement from the perspective of inmates' suffering from that exclusion. As a result, such metaphors are predominantly derogatory, though some positive instances can also be noted. In Figure 3.1, I have separated the various manifestations of this category into a number of subgroups, namely those of the PRISON IS HELL, PRISON IS DEATH, PRISON IS ABATTOIR, PRISON IS WILDERNESS, PRISON IS CAGE, and PRISON IS MACHINE. Only in the first of these, where the idea of prison as a counterworld predominates, have I found positive examples of the prison as hermitage, pilgrimage, even paradise – in analogical counterpoint to hell; and the prison as a space of reformation and purification in contrast with purgatory on the negative side. These positive variants are, I believe, different from those in the separate category of positive prison images like the prison in the shape of a garden, a home or a refuge, where the counterworld idea is less prominent.

These negative experiential analogues focus on several key experiences of confinement. Thus, prison is identified as a place of death (closely related to PRISON AS HELL) and therefore of live burial, entombment, iciness and silence. But death (static) can also be conceived of as active, for example, referring to the process of being killed: hence the idea of the prison as abattoir – a key metaphor in Breyten Breytenbach's work (1984, pp. 112–19; see Fludernik 2019, pp. 305–6).[5] This image also implies a categorisation of the prisoner as an animal (see Olson 2013) and invokes the cage metaphor as well as that of the prison as wilderness or jungle. For instance, in reference to Brendan Behan's book about his Borstal experiences, a reviewer writes: 'But the impression is of a jungle that is only temporarily cleared, and at any moment the tigers will take over and the laws of the forest will be supreme' (qtd. in Mikhail 1979, p. 82).

The cage metaphor, in its turn, relates to more recent conceptions of confinement that foreground the image of locking people up and throwing away the key ('The public begins to say, in effect: Build more prisons, lock up more people, AND throw away the keys' – Whitney 2017, p. 149) as well as, particularly, to the WAREHOUSING metaphor (Jarvis 2019).[6] With warehousing, one enters associations of the prison with anonymity and bureaucratic insensitivity, which in turn give rise to metaphors such as the PRISON AS MACHINE, AS

---

[5] See also Parenti (1999), title of chapter 9. The image is also used by Jack Mapanje (1993, p. 68).

[6] See Herivel and Wright (2003). The phrase 'warehousing' was already used in 1985 by Stanley Cohen. According to Beckett and Sasson (2000) congressional candidate Frederick Kenneth Heineman recommended sending prisoners to Mexico 'where they can be warehoused more cheaply' (p. 72), a proposal that acquired unfortunate topicality with Trump's policies of dealing with asylum seekers from south of the Mexican border.

FACTORY or INSANITY. One could add the recurrent image of the iciness of prison to this list.

As I have tried to demonstrate, there exists a wide variety of ascriptors that try to characterise the experience of confinement and the prison as institution. While the external viewpoints on the institution foreground its heterotopic and exclusionary qualities, the more experiential metaphors map out a whole range of associations that are historically and culturally variable as well as dependent on penal policies in specific contexts. For instance, the association of confinement with loneliness and silence is one typically relatable to the penitentiary. For the eighteenth-century prison, by contrast, sociability, drinking and even sexual activity were key features, and PRISON IS PROMISCUITY/PROMISCUOUSNESS would have been a possible metaphoric analogue of the carceral experience.

3.3 Our Imprisoned Lives: What Epistemological Metaphors Tell Us about the Prison

My use of the term *epistemological* alludes to W. B. Carnochan's phrase *epistemological prisons* (1977, p. 7) for X IS A PRISON metaphors:

> Prisons are real, but we characteristically think of them as *standing metaphors of existence*: to talk of the 'basic prison metaphor' is to show how smoothly, here, reality slips over into the service of representation – and how, by the same token, *we think of mental states as real confinements*. The line that separates the real from the metaphorical thing is in this case very thin. (p. 3; my emphasis)

As one can see in almost any context, prison metaphors of this type abound, and they have done so even before coronavirus times. There are huge numbers of these metaphors, characterising almost any human experience as confining. Some of these metaphors can claim continued prominence as, for instance, the LOVE IS A PRISON and the MARRIAGE IS A PRISON tropes. Falling in love is described as a kind of assumption of (in)voluntary imprisonment, just as being bound by marriage ties feels like a disagreeable or even insupportable confinement for people of any gender. For the former trope, William Blake's prince of love can be cited: in the poem 'How sweet I roamed' he shuts up the speaker in his 'golden cage' and 'mocks' her 'loss of liberty'; for the latter, Mary Wollstonecraft's 'bastilling' of Maria in the novel of the same name was referred to above.[7]

Besides institutions (patriarchy, apartheid, education, the army, schools, etc.), many places and houses naturally invoke the possibility of real or metaphoric imprisonment, most prominently in purdah environments, but

---

[7] See Blake (2002, p. 6).

more generally in the recurrent HOME IS PRISON trope. This can be supplemented by the office (MY JOB IS A JAIL) or the common pre-modern conception of the ship as a moving prison (already in Samuel Johnson's apt dictum that 'being in a ship is being in jail, with a chance of being drowned' [Boswell 1953, p. 247]).

Besides institutions and environments that are perceived to be prison-like, this type of metaphor attributes confining quality to a large number of abstracts: concepts, ideas, ideologies and social rules. Thus, among these instances one finds, for example, the following:[8]

A. Abstract Concepts
- religion (Sterne) ('Behold *Religion*, with *Mercy* and *Justice* chained down under her feet')
- religious zeal (de Quincey) ('enthralment with a religious zeal')
- superstition (Godwin) ('I would not shackle you with the fetters of superstition')
- mind (Blake) ('In chains of the mind locked up')
- 'Reason' (Coleridge)
- community (Emerson) ('that jail-yard of individual relations in which he [man] is enclosed')
- relationship (Austen) ('fettered inclination')
- death (Hawthorne) ('connect the idea of death with the dungeon-like imprisonment of the tomb')
- service to the public (Twain) ('writers of all kinds are manacled servants of the public')
- vice (Pope)
- decorum (Godwin) ('fetter her with those numerous petty restrictions')
- convention (Meredith)
- politeness (Coleridge) ('For, not a silken son of dress, / I clink the gilded chains of *politesse*')
- 'restrictions and ceremonious observances' (Twain)
- 'doting scruples' (Scott) ('which fetter our freeborn reason')
- illusion (Bierce)
- ignorance and sloth (O. Henry)

This list is based on the LION (Literature Online) database and a search for a number of key terms such as *prison*, *fetter*, *shackle*, *manacles*, *chains* (see Fludernik 2019, p. 599, for the full list) – terms that directly or metonymically invoke the prison scenario and therefore allow a search for X IS PRISON metaphors.

---

[8] This is a very short extract from a much longer and by far not exhaustive list provided in Fludernik (2019, pp. 613–16).

Besides these abstract correlates of imprisonment, the epistemological prisons in Carnochan's sense are particularly frequent in attributing the impression of confinement to feelings and emotions. Hatred, envy and contempt may be described as captivating a person's heart and mind just as despair, enthusiasm or laziness may be depicted as keeping somebody in their thrall.

B. Feelings, Emotions
- disdain (Chaucer)
- futility, despair (Conrad)
- despair (Matthew Lewis)
- 'desperate and brooding' (Brontë) ('reminded me of some wronged and fettered wild beast or bird')
- ignorance (Douglass) ('Light had penetrated the moral dungeon where I had lain')
- feelings (Conrad) ('fettered by the long chain of disregarded years')
- 'arrogance and frivolity' (Radcliffe)
- jealousy (Blake)
- 'Cruel jealousy! selfish fear!' (Blake)
- 'cunning of weak and tame minds' (Blake)
- frenzy (Wordsworth)
- perversions (Hawthorne) ('cramped and chained by their perversions')
- curiosity (Meredith) ('What could be the riddle of Renée's letter? It chained him completely')

What does the proliferation of these metaphors tell us, and can one argue for it to have an impact on people's conception of penal confinement? There are several possibilities of explaining the prevalence of these metaphors in our utterances and thoughts. One of these explanations recurs on the actual quality of restriction and restraint exercised by various social, political and ideological contexts and frameworks. Apartheid and patriarchy could be argued to be almost literally confining, just as purdah is equivalent to a system which shuts women up inside their homes. Yet this is not an adequate account of the MARRIAGE IS PRISON trope since not *all* marriages need to be experienced as prison-like, certainly not happy ones. There is almost no immediate connection between confinement and decorum, community or ignorance (to take examples from list A above), or between a jail and disdain, curiosity or arrogance (from list B). These attributions of confinement are to some extent very subjective; they resemble similes more than downright metaphoric equations to the extent that they imply a comparison between, say, decorum as a set of rules that one may find restrictive and the prototype of restriction, that is, the prison. Likewise, a person 'imprisoned' by arrogance is somebody whose pretensions are keeping them apart from their fellow men and women, thus erecting a barrier and excluding them – as being in a prison would do. (Another reading is that of arrogance – or jealousy etc. – to operate like a jailer, oppressing the subject.) The rather fanciful attribution of confinement in these examples does not really extend all the way to a single-scope blend in which more than one aspect of the source is projected onto the target domain. However, though many instances of these metaphors are to be taken as comic and playful, some of them do express experiential qualities. Despair does feel imprisoning and may require therapy to unlock the metaphorical door behind which the subject suffering from depression is languishing. Irascible persons in the grip of an attack of fury can likewise feel themselves to be held in captivity by the emotion. There exists thus a scale between more life-like and more extravagant manifestations of the X IS A PRISON metaphor.

A second line of explanations is more emphatically psychological in attributing to humans an inborn fear of restriction and subjection. Our prenatal confinement in the womb and our ambivalence towards mothers, parents and authority figures in general can be cited here (Klein 1975). It would be worth exploring to what extent a fundamental anxiety about enclosure and one's own loss of freedom are modern and accidental facets of our subconscious: Would societies in which community plays a much more important role than in the West have fewer prison metaphors? Are prison metaphors less widespread in medieval texts? (This latter question may be difficult to discern with medieval authors depending so much on antiquity, where the metaphor was popular.) Certainly, the LOVE IS PRISON trope (*la prison amoureuse*) was a standard rhetorical figure in medieval poetry (see C. S. Lewis 1958; Margolis 1978; Göller 1990, pp. 129–33; as well as Fludernik 2019, pp. 478–96, for further references).

What we could note in the examples I have provided is the unexpectedly empathetic nature of almost all of these metaphors. The focus is on what it would feel like to be imprisoned. These texts therefore invoke the sufferings of confinement in inviting the addressees to imaginatively project themselves into the carceral scenario. Epistemological metaphors of confinement on the whole do *not* see the carceral experience as a just punishment for past crimes or as a reformative process; even metaphors that use the source term *purgatory* in fact emphasise the suffering undergone rather than the purification of the metaphorical inmates' souls. (See Mynshul's [1618] 'Purgatory which doth afflict a man with miseries more than euer he reaped pleasures', p. 4.)

It is therefore a somewhat surprising result of the analysis of carceral metaphors that they project an image of incarceration that relates to anxiety, misery and affliction, without considering the subjects' actions and responsibilities which might have resulted in penal confinement. The question then is: does literature, and do these metaphors, produce a carceral imaginary that benignly erases the issue of guilt and accountability and concentrates on the ordeal of enclosure as punishment? Or is the penal context one which supplies the source terms for the misfortunes of confinement, which are conceptualised as extra-penal, as inherently accidental? In other words: do these metaphors suggest that experiences of confinement occur everywhere and that penal confinement – owing to its enhanced modes of constraint – serves as the prototype that therefore provides useful analogues for the quality of the common experience?

In *Metaphors of Confinement* I have argued that literary texts for the most part depict prison as a place of suffering and misery and therefore convey a sympathetic view of prisoners and their situation. Paradoxically, such a reading of the carceral imaginary can also be interpreted as performing the cultural work of legitimating the penal status quo. To the extent that prisons are perceived as abodes of distress, they underline the undesirability of penal confinement and validate the recommendation to desist from actions that might result in such punishment. Though the metaphors emphasise the pains of imprisonment, they therefore tacitly legitimate penal policy by an implicit strategy of deterrence. However, in spite of this argument, one will need to recognise that this unacknowledged participation in the economy of justice and retribution is not patently visible on the surface of the texts, whose authors do not deliberately implement didactic (moral and retributive) aims. In fact, many authors explicitly criticise the penal system of their day when they present carceral scenarios. Metaphors that are deployed in the service of retributional policies do not, as a general rule, choose carceral metaphors but images that underline the threatening or dangerous quality of offenders. Which takes me to my final comments.

3.4 Concluding Remarks

While the tropes that predominate in the x is a prison format elicit sympathy for the carceral experience, some of the representations of the prison is x mode imply a much less understanding view of the individuals confined in penal institutions. Above, I referred to the prison is filth/sewer and the prison as wilderness/jungle tropes. Both ascriptions highlight an exclusionary vision of the prison as a location that is conceived as prototypical of the abject and as the epitome of a lack of culture and civilisation. The jungle metaphor betokens a realm in which the rules of society have been set aside, especially the rule of law. However, this metaphor can be deployed as well to criticise society in general, linking with the world as prison trope, a good instance of which is Upton Sinclair's *The Jungle* (1906) with its depiction of the oppression of workers by an unscrupulous capitalist meat industry. Jungles and the wilderness moreover invoke the image of wild beasts romping these environments, yet in *The Jungle* the comparison of men and animals is one that sympathises both with the factory workers treated like beasts and with the slaughtered hogs that are presented in anthropomorphic fashion as 'trusting[ ]' individuals who have been betrayed into their tragic fate:

> they [the hogs] were so innocent, they came so very trustingly; and they were so very human in their protests – and so perfectly within their rights! They had done nothing to deserve it; and it was adding insult to injury, as the thing was done here, swinging them up in this cold-blooded, impersonal way, without a pretence at apology, without the homage of a tear.... It was like some horrible crime committed in a dungeon. (Sinclair 1986, pp. 44–5)

The image of the prison as jungle or wilderness with its associated equation of the inmate with an animal is ambivalent – the caged animal may be an object of sympathy as well as abhorrence or fear.[9] When we turn to the PRISON AS FILTH OR SEWER, the inherent ambivalence resides entirely in the observer's attitude towards the abject (slime, mud, faeces, etc.). The objects and people thus focused on are conceptualised in exclusively negative terms as that or those which must be washed off, avoided and excluded. At the same time, the abject constitutes a fascination for the observer.

These ambivalences have been discussed very insightfully by Martha Grace Duncan (1996), who has demonstrated the consistent associations of prisoners and criminals with the abject. This association is both metaphoric (a transfer of moral evaluations to waste and detritus) and metonymic (since, traditionally, prisons were places of acknowledged insanitary quality). Filth and sewers exert a fascination on middle-class subjects which can be linked to negative exotic stereotypes (orientalism), for instance in the representation of Arab and South Asian countries (see Said on manifest orientalism [1978, p. 206]). A typical instance of this is the notorious depiction of the inhabitants of Marrakech by George Orwell (1998), in which the omnipresent flies are metonymically equated with the natives. The narrator even wonders whether the mass of poor 'brown faces' (their having nothing but 'rags' as clothes is insisted on repeatedly) are at all human:

> Are they really the same flesh as yourself? Do they even have names? Or are they merely a kind of undifferentiated brown stuff, about as individual as bees or coral insects? They rise out of the earth, they sweat and starve for a few years, and then they sink back into the nameless mounds of the graveyard and nobody notices that they are gone. (p. 417)

As Michelle Brown puts it, prisons attract a 'certain voyeuristic sensationalism' (2009, p. 4) which invokes the aesthetic of the ugly (Rosenkranz 2003; Cohen & Johnson 2005).

---

[9] Compare my discussion of the cage metaphor and the BIRD IN THE CAGE VS. BEAST IN THE CAGE imagery (2019, pp. 295–304).

The association of inmates and criminals with animals, particularly vermin, has a long history not only in English literature (Olson 2013). Thus, in *Little Dorrit*, Dickens's narrator refers to Blandois and Rigaud as the 'seen vermin, the two men' in juxtaposition to 'rats and other unseen vermin' (1978, p. 40). The denigration of the criminal as animalistic links up with the BEAST IN THE CAGE trope and the jungle or wilderness association for the carceral environment. Hence, many Elizabethan texts provide similes and metaphors that characterise inmates as lions and tigers or wolves, as well as bears, bloodhounds and dogs. The same epithets do, however, also apply to warders and creditors from the inmates' perspective. Mynshul, for instance, describes these as 'blood-suckers' (1618, p. 31), 'leaches' (p. 25) and as 'more merciless then [*sic*] Tygers' (p. 14). The jungle of the prison is thus a moral wilderness both for those looking in as well as for those confined in it.

What this use of imagery suggests is that critical attitudes towards crime and prisoners focus on the character of the inmate as the source of their immorality and do not blame the prison – which, from that perspective, is justifiedly an abode of misery and suffering. As I have argued, even the basically sympathetic representation of the ordeal of incarceration has an implicitly didactic, that is, deterrent function and does not necessarily criticise the legal or penal status quo. However, one does need to qualify this account by pointing out that until the late nineteenth century (i.e. the Bankruptcy Act of 1869) large numbers of inmates were debtors and hence not jailed for felonies or misdemeanours. Moreover, before the penitentiary, the jail population included those held on remand or in pre-trial detention before their trial came up and even witnesses; with the result that many who survived jail were proved innocent at the assizes and were set free, hence could not be considered to be 'criminals'. This situation therefore worked to avoid an automatic equation of prisoners with felons. Nevertheless, the association of innocent people with the thieves and highwaymen they were lodged with in prison was prevalent and supported the PRISONER IS ANIMAL metaphors in their use as derogational discourse. At the same time, the more sympathetic accounts of the prison experience focused on the terrible conditions of incarceration and on the resulting suffering in the prison environment.

References

Beckett, K., & Sasson, T. (2000). *The Politics of Injustice: Crime and Punishment in America*. Thousand Oaks, CA: Sage.
Behan, B. (1958). *Borstal Boy*. London: Hutchinson.
Blake, W. (2002). *Collected Poems* [1905]. Ed. W. B. Yeats. New York: Routledge.
Boswell, J. (1953). *The Life of Samuel Johnson* [1791]. Ed. Geoffrey Cumberlege. London: Oxford University Press.

Breytenbach, B. (1984). *Mouroir: Mirrornotes of a Novel* [1983]. New York: Farrar, Straus and Giroux.

Brown, M. (2009). *The Culture of Punishment: Prison, Society, and Spectacle.* New York: New York University Press.

Carnochan, W. B. (1977). *Confinement and Flight: An Essay on English Literature of the Eighteenth Century.* Berkeley: University of California Press.

Charteris-Black, J. (2009). Metaphor and Political Communication. In A. Musolff & J. Zinken, eds., *Metaphor and Discourse.* Basingstoke: Palgrave Macmillan, pp. 97–115.

— (2011). *Politicians and Rhetoric: The Persuasive Power of Metaphor*, 2nd ed. Basingstoke: Palgrave Macmillan.

— (2019). *Metaphors of Brexit: No Cherries on the Cake?* Basingstoke: Palgrave Macmillan.

Cohen, S. (1985). *Visions of Social Control.* London: Polity Press.

Cohen, W. A., & Johnson, R., eds. (2005). *Filth. Dirt, Disgust, and Modern Life.* Minneapolis: University of Minnesota Press.

Cook, J. (1875). Greene's Tu Quoque; or, The City Gallant [1614]. In W. Carew Hazlitt, ed., *A Select Collection of Old English Plays*, 4th ed. London: Reeves and Turner, pp. 173–289.

Daddow, O. (2019). GlobalBritain™: The Discursive Construction of Britain's Post-Brexit World Role. *Global Affairs*, 5(1), 5–22.

Dickens, C. (1978). *Little Dorrit* [1856–7]. Ed. John Holloway. Harmondsworth: Penguin.

— (1996). *Great Expectations* [1860–1]. Case Studies in Contemporary Criticism. Boston: St. Martin's Press.

Duncan, M. G. (1996). *Romantic Outlaws, Beloved Prisons: The Unconscious Meanings of Crime and Punishment.* New York: New York University Press.

Fauconnier, G., & Turner, M. (2008). Rethinking Metaphor. In Ray Gibbs, Jr., ed., *The Cambridge Handbook of Metaphor and Thought.* Cambridge: Cambridge University Press, pp. 53–66.

Fennor, W. (1930). *The Counter's Commonwealth; or, A Voyage Made to an Infernal Island* [1617]. In A. V. Judges, ed., *The Elizabethan Underworld.* New York: Dutton, pp. 423–87.

Fludernik, M. (2003). The Prison as World – The World as Prison: Theoretical and Historical Aspects of Two Recurrent Topoi. *Symbolism*, 3, pp. 147–89.

— (2004). Prison Metaphors: The Carceral Imaginary? In M. Fludernik & G. Olson, eds., *The Grip of the Law: Prisons, Trials and the Space Between.* Frankfurt: Lang, pp. 145–67.

— (2005). Metaphoric (Im)Prison(ment) and the Constitution of a Carceral Imaginary. *Anglia*, 123(1), 1–25.

— (2017). Panopticisms: From Fantasy to Metaphor and Reality. *Textual Practice*, 31(1), 1–26.

— (2019). *Metaphors of Confinement: The Prison in Fact, Fiction, and Fantasy*, Oxford: Oxford University Press.

— (2020). Surveillance in Narrative: Post-Foucauldian Interventions. In B. Wasihun, ed., *Narrating Surveillance – Überwachen erzählen.* Baden-Baden: Ergon, pp. 43–73.

Foucault, M. (1984). Des espaces autres [1967]. In *Architecture, Mouvement, Continuité*, 5, pp. 46–9. Reprinted in D. Defert & F. Ewald, eds., *Dits et Ecrits, 1943–1988, vol. IV: 1980–1988*. Paris: Gallimard, 1994, pp. 752–62.
  (2002). Of Other Spaces. In N. Mirzoeff, ed., *The Visual Culture Reader*. London: Routledge, pp. 229–36. Available at http://web.mit.edu/allanmc/www/foucault1.pdf (accessed 9 March 2016).
Göller, K. H. (1990). The Metaphorical Prison as an Exegetical Image of Man. *Fifteenth-Century Studies*, 17, 121–45.
Herivel, T., & Wright, P., eds. (2003). *Prison Nation: The Warehousing of America's Poor*. London: Routledge.
Hood, T. (1980). The Song of the Shirt [1843]. In W. Jerrold, ed., *The Complete Poetical Works of Thomas Hood*. Westport, CT: Greenwood, pp. 625–6.
Islentyeva, A. (2019). The Europe of Scary Metaphors: The Voices of the British Right-Wing Press. *Zeitschrift für Anglistik und Amerikanistik*, 67(3), 209–29.
Jarvis, J. (2019). *Lock 'em Up and Throw Away the Keys*. San Francisco: Blurb Incorporated.
Judges, A. V., ed. (1930). *The Elizabethan Underworld*. New York: Dutton.
Klein, M. (1975). Love, Guilt and Reparation [1937]. In *Love, Guilt and Reparation and Other Works, 1921–1945*. Introduction by R. E. Money-Kyrle. London: Hogarth Press, pp. 306–43.
Lewis, C. S. (1958). *The Allegory of Love: A Study in Medieval Tradition* [1936]. Oxford: Oxford University Press.
Mapanje, J. (1993). *The Chattering Wagtails of Mikuyu Prison*. Oxford: Heinemann.
Margolis, N. (1978). The Human Prison: The Metamorphoses of Misery in the Poetry of Christine de Pizan, Charles d'Orléans, and François Villon. *Fifteenth-Century Studies*, 1, pp. 185–92.
Marks, M. P. (2003). *The Prison as Metaphor: Re-imagining International Relations*. Frankfurt: Lang.
McGee, L. (2019). Boris Johnson Is Trapped in a Brexit Prison He Helped Build. *CNN*, 14 September. Available at: https://edition.cnn.com/2019/09/14/uk/boris-johnson-is-trapped-in-a-brexit-prison-he-helped-build-intl-gbr/index.html (accessed 6 July 2020).
Mikhail, E. H., ed. (1979). *The Art of Brendan Behan*. New York: Barnes & Noble.
Mio, J. S. (1997). Metaphor and Politics. *Metaphor and Symbol*, 12(2), 113–33.
More, Sir T. (1984). In huius vitae vanitatem [1518]/On the Vanity of This Life. In C. H. Miller, ed., vol. III of *The Complete Works of St. Thomas More*. New Haven, CT: Yale University Press, pp. 166–9.
Musolff, A. (2004). *Metaphor and Political Discourse: Analogical Reasoning in Debates about Europe*. Basingstoke: Palgrave Macmillan.
  (2016). *Political Metaphor Analysis: Discourse and Scenarios*. London: Bloomsbury.
Mynshul, G. (1618). *Certaine Characters and Essayes of Prison and Prisoners*. London: M. Walbancke. Ann Arbor, MI: University Microfilms.
Olson, G. (2013). *Criminals as Animals from Shakespeare to Lombroso*, vol. VIII of *Law & Literature*. Berlin: de Gruyter.
Orwell, G. (1998). Marrakech [1939]. In P. Davison, ed., *Facing Unpleasant Facts: 1937–1939*. Vol. XI of *The Complete Works of George Orwell*. London: Secker & Warburg, pp. 416–21.

Overbury, Sir T. (1936). *The Overburian Characters, to Which Is Added, a Wife* [1614]. Ed. W. J. Paylor. Oxford: Blackwell.

Parenti, C. (1999). *Lockdown America: Police and Prisons in the Age of Crisis*. London: Verso.

Quarles, F. (1861). *Quarles' Emblems* [1634]. Illustrated by Charles Bennett and W. Harry Rogers. London: James Nisbet. https://openlibrary.org/books/OL6611936M/Quarles%27_emblems (accessed 6 November 2015).

Rosenkranz, K. (2003). *Ästhetik des Häßlichen* [1853]. Ed. Dieter Kliche. Stuttgart: Reclam.

Said, E. W. (1978). *Orientalism: Western Conceptions of the Orient*. New York: Pantheon.

Schoor, C. (2015). Political Metaphor, a Matter of Purposeful Style: On the Rational, Emotional and Strategic Purposes of Political Metaphor. *Metaphor and the Social World*, 5(1), 82–101. Available at: https://doi.org/10.1075/msw.5.1.05sch (accessed 6 July 2020).

Sinclair, U. (1986). *The Jungle* [1906]. Penguin Classics. Harmondsworth: Penguin.

Tapper, J. (2019). The Many Metaphors of Brexit: How Do Metaphors Shape Political Perceptions? And What Do They Mean for the Future of Europe? *JSTOR Daily*, 9 January. Available at: https://daily.jstor.org/many-metaphors-brexit/ (accessed 6 July 2020).

Whitney, K. S. (2017). *Sitting Inside: Buddhist Practice in America's Prisons*. Deerfield, MA: Prison Dharma Network.

Withnall, A. (2016). EU Referendum: Boris Johnson Calls the EU 'a Jail with the Door Left Open' and Says It Would Be 'Wonderful' to Leave. *Independent*, 6 March. www.independent.co.uk/news/uk/politics/boris-johnson-says-eu-is-a-jail-with-the-door-left-open-for-uk-to-leave-a6915241.html (accessed 6 July 2020).

Wollstonecraft, M. (1994). *Maria; or, The Wrongs of Woman* [1798]. Introduction by Anne K. Mellor. New York: Norton.

4 Ideology in Mainstream Crime Fiction

John Douthwaite

4.1 Introduction: The Ideology behind a Successful Tradition

The back cover blurb for Caroline Graham's novel *Written in Blood* contains the following publicity quotes:

'Simply the best detective writer since Agatha Christie' (*The Sunday Times*)
'Swift, tense and highly alarming' (*TLS*)
'Guaranteed to keep you guessing until the very end' (*Woman*)
'Enlivened by a very sardonic wit and turn of phrase, the narrative drive never falters ... a most impressive performance' (*Birmingham Post*)
'Her books are not just great whodunnits but great novels in their own right' (Julie Burchill)

Caroline Graham is the author of seven 'Inspector Barnaby' novels which gave rise to the highly successful television series *Midsomer Murders*. The TV programme has now been running since 1997 and has produced over 120 episodes which have been sold all over the world (Turnbull 2014).

Clearly, the television scripts have been written by various authors over the period, the actors have changed, as have the times, but the basic approach and underlying ideology have remained the same.[1] Furthermore, the series'

---

[1] Zahlmann (2019) argues that the series changes at Season 15, when cousin John Barnaby takes over as DCI from Tom Barnaby on the latter's retirement. The change actually came about following producer Brian True-May having publicly declared that the series was 'a bastion of Englishness' and consequently excluded ethnic minorities. This stance was interpreted as racism and True-May later resigned as producer. However, including characters belonging to minority groups does not necessarily involve dealing with the social issues revolving around those groups. I contend that the series continued in its conservative, non-critical trend, as in the analysis I offer. A typical example is 'Habeas Corpus' (S18 ep. 1). This episode introduces a new forensic pathologist (a high-status occupation). In addition to being female, the pathologist is of Asian origin. Of the three people who turn out to be criminals, one is a doctor (another high-status occupation) of Black African origin. Of the other major suspects one is of Arab origin. However, the Black doctor's 'crime' turns out to be the comic one of burying bodies not in a cemetery, but where the deceased had asked to be buried, such as in a lake, and the suspect of Arab origins turns out to be totally innocent, though not a nice person, like many of the characters in *Midsomer Murders*. The real murderer turns out to be a white male. All nicely politically correct. There is no mention of race and ethnicity in the episode, no connection between ethnicity and the crime committed, no social discussion of any type. The *Midsomer* leopard has

57

attraction has not waned. Nor have Graham's novels' sales waned. Such an achievement – stability and success – clamours for an explanation.

The over-arching thesis argued in this chapter is that the most important reason behind this tremendous achievement is the fact that Graham's novels and the television series are an integral part of the British tradition of conservative crime writing, falling into the furrow dug principally, but not only, by Agatha Christie and which the back cover blurbs refer to.[2]

Within this tradition, the prime factor which makes the *Midsomer Murders* novels and television production popular is the underlying worldview or ideological stance which the works efficaciously convey and which they effectively reinforce by adroitly positioning the reader into accepting that underlying stance. The human embodiment of that ideology is the figure of the hero of the series, Chief Inspector Tom Barnaby – a 'nice' husband, father and boss, as well as a first-class but extremely humane detective, with his positive and negative personality features which present him as fully human and not as a symbolic, superior, god-like Sherlock Holmes character, hence a figure the reader can identify with. Viewed in this light, referring to Barnaby as 'Tom' and not as 'Thomas' or as 'Chief Inspector' is instantly an indication that a relationship of 'intimacy' and 'companionship' is being established between reader and character. Tom Barnaby thus wins the hearts of the audience through his humane, middle-of-the-road stance which reflects the unsuspecting audience's own worldview. In this subtle way the reader is unconsciously positioned into accepting the basic ideological standpoint that Barnaby conveys through his being and through his actions.[3]

---

not changed its spots, but merely put on a fresh coat of paint which can be easily washed away. See also note 12.

[2] Christie was dubbed one of the four queens of crime of the so-called Golden Age of crime fiction which purportedly reigned between the two world wars. The other three queens were Dorothy L. Sayers, Margery Allingham and Ngaio Marsh.

[3] The principal feature we are therefore concerned with here is motivation, why people (i.e. the general public, and not the specialist, the critic) read or view crime fiction. Given the objective of this chapter, space allows only the briefest outline of the topic here. The major motive generally adduced in criticism and in folk knowledge for the enormous interest in crime fiction (and most fiction in general) is plot, curiosity about what will happen, the emphasis residing in the denouement and consequently in the narrative structure that leads to the outcome (formalism, classic narratology). Calculating what will happen in life on the basis of our knowledge of the world is an essential cognitive skill for survival, for without prediction we would soon come amiss (Douthwaite 2000). We would be unable to carry out even the simplest of daily acts such as crossing the road safely, if we were incapable of successfully computing whether the approaching car will hit us if we start out immediately.

Solving problems, from the simplest to the most complex, an example of the latter category being the inferring of the internal mental states of others (goals, intentions, motivations, emotions) by observing their behaviour (termed 'Theory of Mind', or ToM), thus gives satisfaction, demonstrated also by the common adage 'I told you so!', as when you confirm to your wife that the headmaster has indeed fallen for the secretary. Zunshine (2006) argues that ToM is the motivating force in reading literature, since the pleasure obtained from reading/viewing novels/

Ideology in Mainstream Crime Fiction   59

We now turn to the specific content of the two analytical sections which follow.

The second part of this chapter will identify the main traits of Christie's writing, all of which are taken up by Graham, to show how *Midsomer Murders* continues the tradition (Bergin 2012, p. 86), a tradition which is very different from other types of detective fiction, such as American hard-boiled, which, on the one hand, is critical of the capitalist society it analyses, but which, on the other hand, and in a somewhat contradictory fashion, epitomises the American frontier spirit of individualism on which capitalism thrives. That same frontier spirit is at least in part responsible for the machoism expressed by that sub-genre, as Reddy (2003, p. 193) points out: 'the intense masculinity of the hardboiled ... its positioning of women as either dangerous, seductive villains or nurturing but essentially insignificant individuals'. The British tradition is important in accounting for *Midsomer Murders*' success since it constitutes the attempt on the part of the genre voicing the interests of a certain sector of society to embody and bolster the conservative ideology it represents through writing about crime in the way it does (i.e. through content and technique).

---

films is 'grounded in the awareness of our successful mind-reading adaptations, in the respite that such a reading offers us from our every-day mind-reading uncertainties, or in some combination of the two' (p. 20). However, Zunshine does not consider other sources of motivation. Her explanation offers no account of why many books that fail to challenge our ToM are more popular than those which do (Roberts 2007).

Two further motives for the popularity of crime (and not just crime) fiction are escapism and wish fulfilment (on a more general level than Zunshine's statement above). These two motives are no less intense today in a world of economic crisis, pandemics, political instability, organized crime, in which the rich get richer and the poor poorer, and where the 'security' of the past seems to have disappeared (as it generally does as we get older). What is crucial to understanding 'pleasure', however, is not the motives in themselves, but what causes wishes to be satisfactorily fulfilled through 'escapist literature'. My contention is the value system, the worldview that underpins all decisions, determining survival as well as secondary drives, or, in simplistic terms, what we 'like' and 'dislike'.

Further important motives that have emerged since at least the 1980s are aesthetics, heritage and tourism (or to put it simply again, beautiful visuals), as well as the sense of nostalgia such motives trigger (Bergin 2012; Turnbull 2014; Trimm 2017; Zahlmann 2019). Nostalgia is closely linked to one's sense of identity (real, or presumed, or desired), and the latter is determined in part by one's worldview. Related to nostalgia is another major theme dealt with by many critics quoted in this chapter and in Chapter 15: that of national identity and the related topic of 'the condition of England' novels and films dealing with Britain under Thatcher and under Blair (e.g. McCaw 2011).

This brings us to the final major theory advanced as motivational I will mention: storyworlds (Gavins 2007; Bell & Ryan 2019). Dechêne (2020), taking up Ryan, argues that what accounts for the great popularity of crime fiction is 'a shift from plot to worldbuilding'. This thesis cannot be engaged with here. However, the central point concerning storyworlds is that once again, the world a person builds depends on how that person views that world.

Ideology is thus fundamental. It is the most important motivating feature and, without wishing to detract from any of the various excellent reasons propounded for indulging in crime fiction may, I contend, be 'subsumed' under the category 'ideology'.

The third, and major part of the chapter, will examine a cross-section of the characters appearing in *Written in Blood*[4] to illustrate both the content and the linguistic and narrative techniques employed by Graham to position the reader into accepting her ideological stance without openly engaging in an ideological debate so that the reader is blithely unaware of Graham's suasive objective.

4.2   Following in Christie's Footsteps

This section has two main concerns. The first is to highlight the nature of Christie's worldview and aspects of her writing technique which are relevant to conveying that worldview. The second is to identify what Graham 'inherits' from Christie in terms of both ideological content and suasive techniques employed. A third concern is, consequently, that of establishing a tradition and its continuity throughout the twentieth century, since successful cultural phenomena, of which ideologies are an embodiment, require reinforcement. Like any social formation, extant cultural formations attempt to breed the conditions for their survival.

Christie is standardly classified as a Golden Age writer (Knight 1980; Mandel 1984; Douthwaite 2013a, 2013b), a supposedly 'idyllic' period (for the detective story) where the whodunit clue puzzle 'invited' readers to pit themselves against the detective and try to solve the crime before the detective manages to do so (see also Chapter 7 by Zupan in this volume). As Van Dine (1928) puts it, 'The detective story is a game. It is more – it is a sporting event. And the author must play fair with the reader. He can no more resort to trickeries and deceptions and still retain his honesty than if he cheated in a bridge game. He must outwit the reader, and hold the reader's interest, through sheer ingenuity.' Hence, writers were supposed to observe regulations in writing, such as the twenty rules stipulated by Van Dine (1928), which would guarantee that the cards were not entirely stacked against the readers. The readers' goal was twofold: obtaining pleasure and relaxing by pitting their wits against the detective in a non-threatening atmosphere, since the venture is entirely private and the readers consequently run no risks, in stark contrast to real life.

Pleasure and relaxation have an ideological counterpart. On the ideological plane, the entire Golden Age school (and mainstream crime fiction in general) was seen as performing a conservative function where the status quo was taken for granted as being just and therefore to be upheld. This did not, however, mean that society was held to be perfect, hence not to be criticised and

---

[4] The choice of this novel was purely fortuitous, since all seven novels proffer basically the same stance and employ the same constructional tools.

improved, a factor which strengthened its ideological hold, since brazen attempts to uphold extremism were rare, but implied a stance of 'enlightened government'.

In addition to bolstering the conservative worldview, the detective always getting his man and justice always being done served to reassure the public that they were safe in their beds, a vital function which lies at the origin of the police as a social body (Mandel 1984; Kayman 1992). As Mandel (1984, p. 48) puts it, 'Crime never pays. Bourgeois legality, bourgeois values, bourgeois society, always triumph in the end. It is soothing, socially integrating literature, despite its concerns with crime, violence and murder.' Viewed in this light, in part the fairness rules of writing derive ideologically from the justness of the extant order. Since society is just, crime fiction of the Golden Age does not, as a rule, debate social issues, another aspect of its conservative nature.

Golden Age products, which are basically British, thus stand in sharp contrast to genres such as the hard-boiled fiction being written during the same period in the United States, which is more explicitly socially and politically oriented, criticising the (corrupt) status quo, and where crime, especially big-time crime, including white-collar crime, pays and where achieving justice is not a frequent result. Golden Age writers like Agatha Christie focus on 'the intricacies and nuances of domestic life as opposed to the workings of public power' (Pepper 2016, p. 133) on which hard-boiled is fixed. Not by chance, Golden Age is centred in the (peaceful, isolated) countryside, while hard-boiled is in the (large, violent) towns and cities. Thus, the 'traditional British detective (Sherlock Holmes, for example, or Hercule Poirot) is a detached figure, immune from danger; the hard-boiled investigator, on the other hand, is a man who is very directly involved in [the] violent, dishonest, unfragrant world of urban corruption and criminality' (Horsley 2009, p. 136).

The atmosphere in the American genre is much more disturbing in contrast to the tranquilising, if not narcotising, effect Golden Age writing aimed at or produced. Thus Grossvogel (1979, p. 43) accuses Christie of nostalgia for a bucolic England and of conservative formulaic certainty, a criticism echoed by Stowe (1983, pp. 374–382), who also contrasts Christie with the open and undecidable works of the hard-boiled genre which question the structure of society but fail to find a reassuring solution to the problems dealt with. In examining the underlying ideological thrust of the two schools, Hilfer (1990, p. 31) points out that 'the American detective novel is escapist and wish-fulfilling but in an American as opposed to English mode. If the English escape is into a dream of a (re)ordered society, the American escape is into the dream of the last just man whose integrity *is* his alienation' (original emphasis).

Reduced to bare essentials, hard-boiled fiction is viewed as the consequence of the failure of the American Dream, while Golden Age as the response of a placid, sleepy country (the UK) steeped in a tradition which the writers of that school upheld and wished to preserve. Literature, like all social phenomena, is the product of its socioeconomic and historical context.

The newspaper comments on Graham's novels quoted initially clearly situate Graham's crime novels in the Golden Age tradition, implying that she is the heir of Christie (e.g. *The Times*). The pleasure is all and Graham is a master craftswoman ('best', 'swift', 'tense', 'guaranteed to keep you guessing to the very end', 'the narrative drive never fails'), keeping the 'game afoot', to put it with Conan Doyle, who in turn had borrowed it from Shakespeare (*Henry V*, Act 3, Scene 1).

However, there are two far more important traits shared by the two female writers, Christie and Graham. The first is related to the politically important fact that consumption of crime in the media has increased significantly. Already over two decades ago crime fiction was pervasive on Western television (McCaw 2009; Douthwaite 2013a; Turnbull 2014). The vast amount of critical attention devoted to crime writing, which has increased exponentially in recent years, is yet another clear indicator of the cultural importance this sub-sector of literature (in whatever medium) has gained.

The main reasons I hypothesise explaining this phenomenon are the two functions of the sub-genre identified in the first paragraph of this chapter: its entertainment value and its being essentially a site of ideological or discursive struggle, to put it with Bakhtin (1981), championing comforting conservatism. These two reasons apply to both Christie and Graham.

The second trait shared by the two female writers concerns the economic and historical context. Christie has generally been claimed as having written in defence of the country middle class, protecting their economic position, based on stocks and shares, and in some cases on land, which the economy of the period was threatening. Were Christie alive today, she would doubtlessly discover that the economic trend has not changed significantly, with the middle class finding their economic situation progressively weakening. Nor has the political and cultural response to that situation changed profoundly either. It should also be borne in mind that the radicalisation of that economic crisis – which was one step away – is one of the fundamental factors, if not *the* fundamental factor, that ushered in Nazism and fascism. Today witnesses comparable strong nationalist feelings and consequently anti–European Union discontent. This conservative tradition is still represented in crime literature by novelists such as Alison Golden and her Inspector Graham mysteries.[5]

---

[5] Golden calls her various detective series 'Cozy Mysteries', with the letter 'z' replacing standard letter 's' to draw attention to the fictive nature of her work. The term 'cozy' is quite appropriate to the content and tone of her work, which she describes to her (would-be) fans in a series of

Furthermore, Christie's novels, too, are replete with seemingly racist comments, many of which would appear to confirm a right-wing stance (though appearances can be deceptive, as argued in Douthwaite 2013a, 2013b). Graham, too, deals with racism, as we shall see.

This classic interpretation of Christie has been partially challenged (Birns & Birns 1990; Rowland 2001; Makinen 2006; Douthwaite 2017a). Douthwaite (2013b) has contended that Christie criticises all sectors of the population on a variety of counts – money, age, gender, status – and that her criticism is across the board and not simply directed at protecting the interests of one specific social class. Criticism of all social groups is directly linked to Christie's central belief that evil is almost a hard-wired human trait (a widely held position at the time).

In this Christie pertains to that strong conservative current which believes in innatism and which has its roots in biology, medicine, psychiatry and psychology, and is linked to anthropology and sociology. Nisbet (1966/1970) typifies the conservative interpretation of sociology as a domain of knowledge and investigation. In criminology the influence of this brand of thought is to be found in thinkers such as Cesare Lombroso and positivist criminology (Horn 2003).

Caroline Graham, I contend, is aligned with Christie's stance, as is the television series. Her novels, like Christie's, are set in the countryside, where tradition and staticity are somewhat stronger than in the large town, and the main characters tend again to belong to the petit bourgeoisie. Graham's stance is equally conservative, and here, too, scathing criticism is directed at a myriad of characters representing a gamut of social positions. Indeed, the impression the reader/viewer takes away from these works (especially the TV series) is that Britain is a country of criminals, lunatics and inept, sad individuals.

Text 1
[1] 'That mad woman's here again,' said Sergeant Troy.
[2] 'What mad woman's that?' asked Barnaby. [3] He never seemed to meet any other sort these days. [4] Recently he had successfully concluded a case featuring a poet who wore only latex, lived on liquorice allsorts and worshipped a horse she believed to be a reincarnation of Radclyffe Hall. [5] And she was the straight man. (*A Ghost in the Machine*, p. 253)

---

emails. Here is a snippet from her account of the Roxy Reinhardt Mysteries: 'The stories in this series are whimsical, fun, and light. They are fast, easy reads and, of course, as with all my books, there is nothing to worry about in them. You, and your grandchildren if you have them, are in safe hands (apart from the odd murder or two)' (email communication, 24 September 2019). Of her Reverend Annabelle Dixon series, she writes, 'The series is a fun, literary romp featuring Annabelle and her cast of colorful characters from the village of Upton St. Mary' (1 August 2019). Her website (www.alisongolden.com) states that 'Her aim is to write stories that are designed to entertain, amuse, and calm.' The England she describes seems to go back to Christie's epoch. None of the economic and social upheavals characterising recent decades appears in her novels. (See also Turnbull 2014.)

Abnormality (Otherness) as the norm is, of course, one of the major weapons Graham deploys to position her readers, for 'normality' is represented by 'the good detective', professionally and, above all, morally 'good'.

That this point is central is confirmed by technique. 'What mad woman is that?', Sentence 2 (S2), is presented as direct speech and thus constitutes Barnaby's response to Troy's attention-getter 'That mad woman's here again' (S1), also in direct speech. While the following sentence (S3) continues the theme of English madness, contrary to linguistic usage which thematic continuity would lead the reader to expect (thus respecting the Gricean manner maxim, sub-maxim: be orderly) (Grice 1989), namely, the continued deployment of direct speech, S3 is presented as Free Indirect Thought (FIT), as can be demonstrated by forward shifting: 'I never seem to meet any other sort these days.' Had Graham continued deploying direct speech, then the sentence would have realised the illocutionary forces of Barnaby criticising Troy for lack of clarity and demanding clarity. Instead, by couching the sentence in FIT, it cannot count as a response to Troy's attention-getter but becomes an 'aside' – Barnaby thinking to himself – hence an independent, evaluative comment launched by Barnaby and connected to the preceding two sentences only by having been triggered by an association of ideas. Its (subtly) hidden independence underscores its importance as a global, and not a local, theme.

Two important differences must be noted between Christie and Graham. First, while Christie makes extremely frequent explicit statements regarding human nature as being evil, this feature is generally implicit in Graham's work. This, I suggest, may be attributed not to a different ideology but in part to a changed cultural climate,[6] producing perhaps less ingenuousness on the part of the reader and viewer as well as responding to the presence of greater 'equal rights' feelings in part of the population, and in part to the second difference (discussed in the following paragraph). The effect of this first difference is that the ideological, discursive work done by Graham and the TV series is less obvious. Reading and viewing thus require more attentive critical appraisal, or resistance (Fetterley 1978), on the part of the readers if they are to disentangle the skein and identify the ideological elements lying below the surface meaning of linguistic and behavioural acts.

Second, Graham's novels are generally much longer than Christie's. This is because a significant proportion of each novel provides a (relatively) detailed portrait of the characters. Thus, where Conan Doyle's Sherlock Holmes short

---

[6] The changed cultural climate is also reflected by, if not influenced by, a change in scientific approaches. In criminology, Lombrosian Positivism is superseded by sociological studies investigating how the socioeconomic structure of society influences behaviour in general and crime in particular. From the plethora of important works, I quote only Cloward and Ohlin (1960), Becker (1963), Matza (1964) and Mannheim (1965).

stories offer a summary description of the characters, functionally related to their role in the crime story, Christie furnishes more information, but often stereotypical and externalising the prejudices of the time. Instead, Graham gives a much more detailed account of her characters. For instance, *Death in Disguise* is 434 pages long. Barnaby and the crime are introduced only in the second section of the novel, at page 153! Hence Burchill's critical appraisal quoted above that Graham's 'books are not just great whodunnits but great novels in their own right', a generous evaluation given that there is, I would contend, little character development, the portraits remaining more still shots than moving pictures.

However, such portraits are, in the final analysis, functional to the stance Graham conveys, since, given Graham's often excellent linguistic technique, she manages not only to get the reader to suspend disbelief but also to empathise, sympathising with those that are to be sympathised with, to the point of identifying with some of those characters, and criticising those that are to be taken to task, when not abhorred. Stated differently, Graham is excellent at mimesis and at positioning her audience so as to covertly induce them to share her ideological stance. Her novels epitomise perfectly the crime novel as a site of struggle. The remaining part of the chapter is devoted to examining Graham's sophisticated technique, the main contributor to the success of the ideological operation just described.

4.3   Positioning the Reader

As stated above, one of the major differences between Christie and Graham is that Graham provides a portrait of her characters, whereas Christie's characters are totally flat (Forster 1927; Culpeper 2001). This does not mean to say that Graham's characters are totally round. They correspond more to stereotypical categories which are symbolic, in the sense that they serve Graham's purpose of conveying her ideology in a persuasive fashion, as I will immediately explain.

I suggest that Graham's characters fall into three broad categories, which for convenience's sake I will dub the 'bad', the 'non-entities' and the 'good'. The latter constitute a stark minority, the non-entities the majority (illustrating a whole range of human weaknesses), and the 'bad' a minority far larger than the 'good' (though in the television series the percentage of wicked characters increases noticeably). This sub-division is in itself an indication of Graham's goal and means: she presents characters whom she criticises (the nonentities and the bad), 'leaving' the reader to identify with the (very few) positive characters and their values (as well as unconsciously praising himself for being one of the few good people in the world). The positive characters, of which the principal is Tom Barnaby, project a worldview which, I will argue, is akin to that conveyed in Christie's novels.

I will examine the two major bad characters in the novel *Written in Blood*, two non-entities, each related to one of the bad characters, two policemen (who fall into the inadequate group but help demonstrate Graham does not absolve a 'wrongdoer' simply because they are a member of the Establishment) and one good character. Since the texts selected will inevitably refer to more than one character, then presentation is cumulative. Thus, the two bad characters are scrutinised together with the two non-entities they ferociously maltreat psychologically. Such juxtaposition in the novel constitutes another narrative device whereby Graham makes the reader 'automatically' (viz. unconsciously) judge the characters negatively since the technique implicitly 'invites' the comparison to be made. Hence, having eliminated the bad, the reader then pities the non-entities ('there but for the grace of God go I') to finally side with the good characters. Space allows for little illustration in such a wide panorama of characters, but the examples selected are representative for the points made.

4.3.1   The Bad

The two most 'evil' characters, Honoria Lyddiard (a sociopath) and Brian Clapton (an egocentric with no reality principle), just happen to be right- and left-wing extremists, respectively, another stark indication of Graham's worldview. Despite occupying opposite stances on the political spectrum, they are similar personality-wise: dishonest, conceited, racist, haughty, thick-skinned, blind to reality and totally self-centred. Both subjugate their 'living companion', Honoria her sister-in-law, Amy, and Brian his wife, Sue. Both are willing to employ any means to realise their objectives, murder included, in Honoria's case. They are so harshly presented that readers cannot but criticise them most severely. Since personality is closely linked to worldview, in the real world as well as in literature, readers consequently reject Honoria's and Brian's political stances as a result of criticising their characters, again unconsciously. Thus, the 'middle way' is the only value system with any social and moral credibility left standing in the novel.

4.3.1.1   Honoria Lyddiard – And Amy As name and surname suggest, Honoria is an aristocrat. 'Honoria' is viciously ironic, since her actions and values do anything but honour the aristocratic code, in stark contrast to Chaucer's 'parfit gentil knight'. The situation is exacerbated by the fact that although Honoria's aristocracy is of the type that has become penniless, she nevertheless upholds the feudal system with all her might and, to her diseased mind, her right.

Text 2
[1] Honoria despised people. [2] Especially the lower orders. [3] 'Unwholesome barbarians breeding like bacteria in their squalid little hutches' was one of her less extreme descriptions. [4] How her aristocratic spirit looked down on them! [5] Barely civilised rabble.

[6] Ralph had always laughed at this nonsense and could not understand why Amy didn't do the same, but she found Honoria's insistence on a 'natural aristocracy of the blood' far from funny. [7] To Amy it seemed dehumanising, smacking of eugenics, born leaders and chilling attempts at social engineering. (pp. 18–19)

At a preliminary (decontextualised) first reading, Text 2 (T2) may be stated to constitute Narration (N) focalised through Amy, Honoria's mild and dominated sister-in-law by marriage to Lydia's now defunct brother Ralph. Ironically, we later learn that Ralph, a naval officer, enjoyed the company of males as well as that of females, and died of AIDS, and not in battle, a secret Honoria desperately attempts to hide to avoid ensuant devastating social disgrace. This 'peccadillo' actually provides the vital clue that allows Barnaby to track down Honoria as the murderess in what approaches a biblical parable or a medieval morality play in which sin leads to death.

In reading the novel, it should be borne in mind that Amy, in contrast to Honoria, is a totally reliable character. She is a cross between a non-entity (for she is annihilated by Honoria) and a good character (i.e. one embodying sound human values which are presumably shared by the average reader). Consequently, her assertions and views may confidently be taken at their face value. Indeed, Graham makes the reader feel very sorry for her and overjoyed when she finally rebels (by deciding to leave Honoria's house despite the fact that she is penniless).

Speech and thought presentation (STP[7]), which is one of the principal linguistic tools Graham deploys to achieve the effects of intensity of perception and of positioning the reader throughout the novel, plays a crucial role in this extract. I first prepare the deeper analysis of T2 by providing a summary overview of STP in Text 2.

---

[7] Given its great analytical power, speech and thought presentation has been subjected to intense theoretical scrutiny and has been applied extensively in text analysis. A highly selective overview of the field may be provided by referring to Pascal (1977), Fludernik (1993), Palmer (2004), Fludernik (2011), Herman (2011), Thomas (2012) and Rundquist (2017). This brief list shows that many workable schemes have been developed. As a stylistician, I personally employ the Leech–Short–Semino analytical framework to speech, thought and writing presentation (Leech & Short 1981; Semino & Short 2004).

Two major points are relevant to the selection of the STP methodology adopted. First, no analytical scheme or theory is perfect and comprehensive. As Semino and Short (2004) point out, texts (and language, we might add) are far more complex than a single theory can embrace. Consequently, frameworks must be adapted to accommodate the reality of the object under scrutiny. The hybrid forms identified in this chapter bear ample witness to this fact, S6 of T2 which is examined below constituting a cogent and timely exemplification. The second point follows from the first: the framework employed must give valid results. Thus, while Rundquist's (2017) recent volume, for instance, offers an undoubtedly fruitful approach, many stylisticians continue to employ the Leech–Short–Semino framework to great effect. For a brief overview of my methodological position, see Douthwaite (2017b). For illustrative concrete applications from my own work, see Douthwaite (2007b, 2017b). References to other stylisticians may be found in Douthwaite (2017b).

Sentence 1 (S1) is seemingly written in narrative mode but is actually focalised through Amy. Evidence for this comes from preceding co-text (not included) and succeeding co-text, which we now examine. For instance, S2 is realised by a single, verbless clause, hence by definition a subordinate clause. It is consequently ungrammatical. It thus indicates a highly informal style typical of conversation rather than of formal, objective, heterodiegetic narration. S3 constitutes direct speech. What is especially significant about this sentence is that the reporting clause displays a modalising expression (Douthwaite 2007a) – 'one of her *less extreme* descriptions' (my emphasis) – an expression which conveys a value judgement. Consequently, the question requiring an answer is: Whose opinion is being expressed in that noun phrase – the narrator's or that of one of the characters? Significantly, as we shall see shortly, the reporting clause fails to display a reporting verb, hence hiding its function. In addition, the style and tone of the expression are mild, mirroring Amy's character and standing[8] in harsh contrast to the starkly explicit and heavy-handed linguistic variety employed by Honoria. S4 again constitutes N mode focalised through Amy, again realising the function of evaluation. The deployment of the evaluative noun 'spirit' with its connotation of religion may be read as Amy 'innocently' (i.e. verbatim) reporting Honoria's own elevated evaluation of herself. It may concurrently be interpreted as the omniscient narrator's dual voice expressing ironic criticism of Honoria, a recurrent trait of the novel, and another ploy used to align readers with the narrator's worldview. S6 might also give the impression of being in N mode because it begins as Narrative Report of Speech Act (NRSA) ('Ralph ... laughed at this nonsense'), a form which is very near N mode in the Leech–Short–Semino model since it is under the narrator's control, given that the narrator is making a stark summary of the character's words and because the general reader is unaware of the existence of such sophisticated linguistic categories. However, an extremely significant feature which is easily missed in a non-analytical reading is that S6 is a subtle hybrid form, thanks to the deployment of proximal deictic 'this' pre-modifying the evaluative noun 'nonsense'. This marker indicates that we are actually being concurrently presented with Amy's thought in that first clause, in lieu of distal deictic 'that', which would have signalled the narrator's voice in a pure form. In other terms, the deployment of deictic 'this' brings the 'action' close to the speaker instead of distancing it as it would in N or NRSA modes. Hence, the deictic expression also paves the way for the transition into FIT ('Ralph ...

---

[8] Mildness may be seen in S6–S7 where Amy expresses her own view of Honoria's position. Thus, 'far from funny' (S6) and all of S7 reveals a restrained, controlled, unaggressive tone, and not the anger and directness that a stronger personality wishing to challenge Honoria might display.

could not understand ...' may be transformed into: 'I can't understand this nonsense ...'). This analysis coupled with the various linguistic signals identified above enable our initial impressions to be modified and the claim made that T2 is essentially Amy's FIT in which she has 'reported' to herself some of Honoria's many assertions.

This preliminary analysis of S1–S6 enables us to return to S1 and hypothesise that that sentence too is not the omniscient narrator but Amy's Free Direct Thought (FDT) and that the entire paragraph is actually tracking Amy's mental activity, with only a minimal contribution by the narrator. Appearances can be deceptive, as they should be in a detective novel.

Further evidence may also be mustered in support of the argument that the first paragraph is solidly Amy's voice (bar the undercurrent of the narrator's dual voice). I will furnish only one example of a linguistic device which is employed throughout that paragraph, a factor indicating that T2 is a unit of discourse. Alliteration is pervasive, both intra-sententially and extra-sententially. S2 plays on the letter 'b' when quoting Honoria's words: 'barbarians', 'breeding', 'bacteria', key words indicating Honoria's extremist stance and concurrently criticising it. Extending the analysis, all sentences abound with 'b', 'd', 'l', 'r' and 's', generally linking ideologically redolent content words conveying value judgements, such as 'despised', 'especially', 'lower', 'orders', 'unwholesome', 'squalid', 'little', 'hutches', 'less', 'extreme', 'descriptions', 'aristocratic', 'spirit', 'down', 'barely', 'civilised', 'rabble'. That this is deliberate is demonstrated not only by a quantitative fact but also by qualitative examples. Thus 'descriptions' could have been substituted by 'definitions' which does not contain the letter 'r', the latter letter 'harmonising' the noun 'descriptions' with the adjective 'extreme' which pre-modifies that noun.

Given the preceding discussion, if S6 at first appears to be presented in N mode or a mode related to N, since it appears to constitute external description reported in the past tense, diverse linguistic features are present which suggest this is actually FIT. First S6 is parallel in form and function to S1: past simple, assertion of values and opinions. Second, S6 is parallel to S3 in exhibiting embedded direct speech: 'natural aristocracy of the blood' in S6 graphologically paralleling 'Unwholesome barbarians breeding like bacteria in their squalid little hutches' in S3. Third, informal linguistic selections characterise these sentences (e.g. 'far from funny'). The expression just quoted, together with the lexeme 'insistence', also illustrates the fourth parallel feature, Amy's standard toning-down of some of Honoria's value judgements, again typifying Amy's remissive character, for what she is talking about here is her sister-in-law's total domination of herself. Parallelism (Douthwaite 2000) is thus employed to counterpose Honoria's worldview to her brother's and Amy's own contrasting worldview. Thus, if S1 is Amy's FIT, then S6 must be in the same mode.[9] The simple demonstration of the plausibility of this hypothesis is obtained by forward shifting to obtain the 'original' version, that is, Amy's possible thoughts/words:

Ralph always laughed at this nonsense and could not understand why I didn't do the same, but I find Honoria's insistence on a 'natural aristocracy of the blood' far from funny.

S7 also parallels S1 and S6, since it continues recounting Amy's own position. Hence, while 'To Amy' in sentence-initial position might first appear to indicate N mode, remove that prepositional phrase and the sentence takes on the features of the preceding discourse, enabling it to be classified as Amy's FIT yet again. The list of features, for instance, with its ungrammatical final noun phrase ('and chilling attempts at social engineering') again seems to indicate that the sentence reflects Amy's flow of thoughts. The adjective 'chilling' is a strong negative evaluator, again begging the question whose point of view is being expressed. Since there is no indication of the dual voice being operative here, then the opinion cannot but be Amy's.

What has just emerged, therefore, is a 'chilling' indictment of Honoria, especially effective because it is revealed through the flow of consciousness of Honoria's major victim, who reports Honoria's words verbatim and in so doing expresses her victimhood without violence of expression or intention and without extremism, thus furnishing the distinct impression that she is 'of sound mind', hence reliable, hence 'persuasive'.

Two major linguistic features heighten the effects of intensity and identification described above. First, conceptual simplicity. Not only are the concepts crystal clear, but they are also readily identifiable as pertaining to extreme right-wing ideology, with its emphasis on racism and (total) social control in order to maintain a given social group in power ('social engineering').

Second, this ideology is evoked by classic biological and medical metaphors, metonyms and symbols closely and intensely associated with the linguistic realisation of that ideology. Thus 'breeding' and 'hutches' equates the lower orders with ANIMALS, hence with Otherness (see Chapter 2), and with reproductive functions beyond human control, consequently implying a fixed, 'natural' (S6) order of things, hence inviolable, unchangeable and consequently unchallengeable, politically and socially – feudal, if you will. 'Bacteria' belongs to the biological and medical lexical fields, as does 'breeding', in one sense (S1). Both terms are employed metaphorically. The former term again evokes the concept of (Darwinian) struggle (to keep the 'lower

---

[9] Note, however, that S6 also contains embedded FIT, since Amy's FIT is 'reporting' her husband's words: 'he couldn't understand why I didn't do the same'. This feature strengthens the argument in favour of FIT as basic presentational mode.

orders' from infecting the upper echelons) and the latter metaphor reiterates the idea of hard-wiring, another concept championed by ultra-conservatives. '*Natural* aristocracy of the *blood*' (my emphasis) (S6) and 'eugenics' and 'born leaders' (S7) confirm the biological imprint view which typifies that worldview.

The effects are enriched by the deployment of various linguistic devices in each sentence. Space allows only two exemplifications. Being in paragraph-initial position, S1 is a thematic sentence. The devastating nature of the value judgement expressed by the lexical verb 'despised' together with the object of Honoria's contempt, 'people' (which, phrased as it is, allows for no exception as well as implying Honoria is something different, something higher – only God remains above her), is reinforced by the brevity of the sentence.

The exploitation of the Gricean quantity maxim continues in S2, which counts one word more. That this is deliberate may be readily demonstrated: replace the full stop at the end of S1 with a comma and you obtain one sentence, and not two, as well as removing the ungrammatical construction of S2. Such brevity highlights the ideas expressed: 'despised', 'people', 'lower orders', as well as achieving a crescendo emphasising class relations. Further confirmation comes from the contrasting lengthiness of S3: seventeen words compared with the previous three and four in the first two sentences.

In conclusion, eighty-two words of the novel suffice to advance the claim that Graham's technique in positioning the reader, characterising Honoria and, to a lesser extent, also Amy, is highly effective.

4.3.1.2 Brian Clapton – And Sue As stated earlier, Brian is the radical equivalent of conservative Honoria. First and foremost, he too believes he is well above other humans and consequently despises them – alterity again. Coming from someone who claims to be a socialist, this is in itself a sufficiently damning contradiction. In exactly the same political vein, the way this paragon of advanced views treats his wife may be likened to a medieval lord having his way with women, yet another contradiction between proclaimed beliefs and actual behaviour. This, too, constitutes a perfect parallel with the way Honoria treats her 'inferiors', with Amy in the vanguard. (Below we will see Honoria deal 'suitably' with the police -Text 6.)

Brian's wife Sue, like Amy, is one of the many inadequates in Graham's novels (and in the TV series). However, unlike the vast majority of this large category of characters, these two ineffectual women win out in the end. This statistically rare phenomenon is also unusual behaviour-wise since there is generally very little character change in the novels, and even less so in the TV episodes, for obvious reasons. In addition, in the real world weak people do not tend to obtain the 'best' results (as measured by the realisation of socially prized goals such as high economic status).

The reason motivating Graham's narrative strategy is that by highlighting the interaction between couples with diametrically opposed personality features, in which the dominant partner is the 'bad character' but also the one who in the long run ironically loses out to the weak character, Graham is suggesting that, as in Shakespearean tragedy, good will eventually discomfit evil or, in King John's words, 'So foul a sky clears not without a storm' (*King John*, Act 4, Scene 2). The conclusion to be drawn therefrom is that society as it is structured works essentially for the general good, despite all the evil that besets it (the ideology of the Protestant Ethic which also lies behind this ideological stance is dealt with in Section 4.3.1.3). In other terms, narrative strategy mimics and bolsters the author's ideology.

Text 3
[1] Slu**gg**ar**d**ised **b**y wakefulness an**d** **b**a**d** **d**reams, **B**rian sa**t** on the fa**k**e **p**ine **b**rea**k**fast **b**ench attache**d** to the **t**a**b**le. [2] Actually, he did not so much sit as lurch, semi-upright. [3] A posture that, should anyone else in the family have adopted it, would have brought about an immediate lecture on slovenly behaviour. (p. 283, my emphasis)

T3 appears to deal with body posture, that is to say, seemingly simple, intellectually low-level motor acts and behavioural acts. However, such acts are highly significant, since they are indicative of etiquette, hence of the culture that lies behind the movement, and specifically of the meanings and values that that culture attaches to given acts. Consequently, they instantly reveal Brian's double standard, his insincerity, his inability to see reality.

The extract is presented in N mode. The critical voice of the narrator is heavily to the fore.

In S1, 'Sluggardised' constitutes external description. It employs a creative lexical verb ('sluggardise') to produce a creative ANIMAL metaphor debasing Brian ('slug'). Note that this is deliberate, since Graham could have opted for a construction employing the codified adjective 'sluggish'. There would consequently have been no foregrounding, hence the reader would not have made the link with the animal which Graham's novel verb draws attention to.

'Wakefulness' is ironic because of the following:

(1) In terms of the code, it is either a value-free term or positively value-loaded. Here, instead, it indicate negativity.
(2) 'Sluggardised by wakefulness' is an oxymoron, since 'wakefulness' generally leads to full activity and not to 'sluggish' movement.
(3) It is also indirect, since what it refers to is Brian having been unable to sleep due to 'bad dreams', an indirect reference to a bad conscience, since Brian has just had sexual intercourse with Edie, a fifteen-year-old student of his.

Infidelity and statutory rape place Brian well beyond the pale for 'normal' human beings. Brian abusing his position as a teacher intensifies the reader's condemnation. Ironically, Brian having a bad conscience also means that he is, at least dimly or occasionally, aware that his supposedly libertarian, 'revolutionary' ideas are not justifications, not 'advanced' moral values championed to bring progress to society, but sham excuses, hiding his own 'base' desires and frustrations. This aspect too intensifies the reader's critical stance: If Brian knew he was doing wrong, why did he not stop?

Brian lays claims to cultural superiority: a teacher, a writer, one who in his spare time devotes himself to attempting to instil in his backward, working-class pupils[10] the joys and intellectual and emotional stimuli of creating their own 'theatre'.

Such cultural superiority is instantly debunked by the metonym '*fake* pine' (S1, my emphasis): striving to achieve superiority but dismally and patently failing, even in the choice of furniture, even if the choice was financially constrained. Again, the detail has been selected by the narrator, for Brian is not one to admit his own faults. Were this not so, then the description of the furniture would be redundant, violating Gricean relevance. Indeed, Brian has no faults, he thinks. The point is reinforced by the expression 'attached to the table', which violates the Gricean maxims of relevance and manner since there is no immediately apparent reason why such a specification should be provided (i.e. of what possible interest could it be to the reader?)

Phonology also plays an important role in S1 in critically mimicking Brian's character. The heavy play on alliteration, especially the plosives 'p', 't', 'k', 'b', 'd', 'g', brings the reader's attention to those words: the sound is harsh, reflecting Brian's character – he never has a good word for anyone – bar young Edie whom he wants to take to bed. Hardly the greatest aspiration for a would-be artist.

Further evidence corroborates the hypothesis that this paragraph represents N with the narrator venting his opinions. 'Actually' in sentence-initial position in S2 is a strong indicator of conversational style, of dialogism, again suggesting narratorial intervention. The syntactic construction 'so much … as'

---

[10] While outwardly treating his students as human beings with a brain of their own and a right to equal opportunity and to the possibility of the full development of their potential, in actual fact Brian sees them as 'backward'. This emerges starkly in the final school scene in the gym where the pupils practise 'theatre' (pp. 389–398), with Brian openly and cruelly insulting his pupils in the final paragraph: 'I must have been mad to have ever wasted five minutes let alone five months of my life on any of you. Or to have thought that the stinking squalid sewers that pass for minds in your tiny pointed heads could ever begin to understand the first thing about literature or music or drama' (p. 398). Although the trick the pupils played on him caused the vicious outburst, Brian reveals his limited intellectual capacity and his inability to control himself in this scene, since he should have realised the students were only making fun of him while concurrently trying to impress him as having succeeded as a teacher.

intensifies the negativity exuded by the lexical verb 'lurch' and constitutes an external description. S3 is colloquial, since it is ungrammatical. However, it also bears markers of a relatively formal conversational style: the deployment of the inverted syntactic structure 'should anyone else have adopted' and the formality of the lexical verb (in lieu, for instance, of colloquial 'use'). The sentence thus mimics 'professorial style' and the superiority this radiates. Such a stance can only represent the critical voice of the narrator. To complete the picture of narratorial censure, 'lecture' is sarcastic, again making fun of Brian's role as a teacher. Again, external criticism.

Text 4
[1] But he tried not to dwell on those. [2] And it wasn't as if matters could not be put right. [3] It had, after all, been the first time. [4] A certain amount of awkwardness was only to be expected. [5] But now that he knew what Edie wanted, what turned her on, things would be very different. (p. 283)

T4 reports Brian's debacle with Edie, his premature ejaculation and trying to justify it.

S1 is in N mode. The remaining sentences are in FIT, as may be demonstrated by applying the forward-shift test, for example, (a) 'And it isn't as if matters can't be put right', (b) deictic 'now' employed instead of 'then', had the sentence been grammatically correct.

The picture that emerges is a sarcastic one of an unknowledgeable schoolboy ('first time', 'a certain amount of awkwardness was only to be expected'). Unbelievably, Brian 'believes' that rape and adultery can be 'put right', as if nothing really serious had happened. Of course, in T4, Brian is referring only to his sexually disastrous encounter with Edie. It is the very fact of his failing to consider he has a wife and daughter when thinking he can put 'matters ... right' that shows Brian is a total egoist, insanely so, since he wishes to persist. Equally insane is the fact that Brian has to 'learn' what 'turns Edie on' (S5). It is hard to believe that Brian is a grown man with a teenage daughter, and a teacher to boot. His self-centredness and stupidity have no bounds. In this extract, it is Brian himself who alienates the reader, highly effectively so by having his flow of thoughts revealed in the direct fashion of FIT.

Presentation in FIT (bar S1) and the connector 'after all' introducing a justification also heighten the sensation of whingeing, denoting emotional and cognitive immaturity. The fifty-year-old male presents himself as blameless compared with the fifteen-year-old girl.

Text 5
[1] Keenly fraught with lust, he shifted uneasily back and forth staring sourly across the room at his earnest shambles of his wife. [2] He wished her moon face far away. [3] And her saggy, russet-aureoled boobs and big feet. [4] Christ, how was it possible for a woman with legs like Olive Oyl to take size eights? [5] He'd thrown himself away

there, all right, by God he had. [6] Casting the pearls of his intellect and talent before such an unpractised simpleton.

[7] There was little doubt in Brian's mind where the main responsibility for last night's shortcomings lay. [8] Why, when finally holding the girl who had fired his red-hot imaginings for so long in his arms, he had reacted like a puritanical schoolboy.

[9] A more sensitive partner, a more perceptive, caring partner, would have found ways to develop her husband's sensuality. [10] Made him wise in the paths of carnal knowledge, for were not the skills of the harem in every woman's blood?

[11] OH! [12] Why had he ever let his parents persuade him into 'doing the right thing'? [13] Why hadn't he had the courage to just clear off and leave Sue and her infant to fend for themselves? [14] Other men did. (p. 284, my emphasis in S1)

T5 is a powerful portrait of a frustrated, incapable, ignorant, totally self-centred husband, hating his wife and viciously blaming her for what are actually his own imperfections. In T4 Brian had been aroused by thinking about Edie. As a result, in T5 he is 'keenly fraught with lust'. Frustration causes him to move uncomfortably in his seat ('shifted uneasily back and forth', S1, the verb and adverb conveying the same type of cultural negative value judgement as those in T1). Opposite him he sees his wife. He 'instinctively' pours his frustration and anger onto her ('staring sourly') as the cause of his ills ('the earnest shambles of his wife').

While S1 is basically in N mode, the final noun phrase ('earnest shambles of his wife'), with its ravaging criticism, presents Brian's own words and constitutes the transition into Brian's mind for the rest of the paragraph. This brings us to the next point.

Alliteration pervades T5 as it does T2 and T3, performing the same function of drawing attention to the brutal criticisms the evil characters pronounce. This is borne out by the deployment of the letter 's' in S1 of T5, where almost half of the words display the letter and, significantly, seven of the eleven open-class items bear that consonant. This rhetorical device also helps account for the unusual collocation 'earnest shambles' (the noun both beginning and ending with 's'), an oxymoron expressing incredulity together with criticism. One can imagine Brian thinking something along the lines of 'that shambles of a wife of mine really [viz. 'earnestly'] believes she is God's gift to her husband'. In S2 Graham employs deletion to juxtapose 'face far' to highlight the play on the letter 'f', thereby intensifying Brian's criticism of his wife's face with the creative expression 'moon face', implying not only a fat face, but also a medical disorder as its cause (Cushing's syndrome), demeaning his wife even further (cf. the form without the deleted lexical verb: 'He wished her moon face was far away'). Graham's creative use of language is at a premium here.

S2 is presented as NRTA ('wished'). It therefore represents the second step into penetrating Brian's consciousness. S3 begins colloquially with 'And' in sentence-initial position, is realised by a verbless clause realised in its turn by a single noun phrase, and is consequently ungrammatical, thus constituting FDT and bringing the reader into direct contact with Brian's mind. S4–S6 are in FIT, since the verb is back-shifted as are other deictic markers ('his' in S6 in place of 'my' in DS). Again FIT (together with FDT, in this extract), is one of the major factors accounting for the emotional intensity of the passage.

S2–S4 convey the physical abhorrence Brian feels for his wife. Note just how important the physical aspect is for Brian. S2–S3 again display verbosity since they could have been collapsed into one sentence, as in 'He wished her moon face and her saggy, russet-aureoled boobs and big feet far away.' By presenting the same information in two sentences, each is stressed as important independent information, thereby hiding the fact that the underlying concept is only one – physical beauty. The intensity with which the concepts in S1–S4 are expressed demonstrate that the fact that the passing of time generally diminishes a person's sexual attractiveness is unacceptable for Brian. This aspect concurrently confirms his disinterest in the psychological and emotional aspects of marriage. Furthermore, this emphasis on physicality is yet another manifestation that the 'blame' for Brian's incapacity lies with the 'ugly wife', as the subsequent two paragraphs will underline.

S5 again underscores Brian's self-reputed superiority. The metaphor 'thrown himself away' (making himself an inanimate object), implies (a) that he is now almost worthless (ironically true and another of his many own goals) and (b) that the fault is his wife's, since the presupposition is that before marriage he was worth something or, more precisely, a lot! This interpretation is bolstered by the use of the biblical reference in the following sentence to 'casting one's pearls before swine', which recalls the expletive 'by God he had' in S5, with its touch of righteousness.

Physical criticism turns to mental by classifying his wife as an '*unpractised*' 'simpleton' (S6) while concurrently reiterating self-praise ('the pearls of his intellect and talent'). S6 is the occasion for yet another of Brian's many own goals, since if his wife really is 'unpractised', then one may rightfully ask whose fault that is.

The ultimate irony will be that, after having criticised Sue's drawings for children in his usual 'gentlemanly' fashion, Sue ends up winning a contract from a big publisher for those very drawings while Brian will never complete a single work. Thus, when Sue discovers her husband's infidelity she rebels and locks him out of the house. Hurrah, the reader will be induced to think.

S6, with its direct onslaught at his wife's mental prowess, constitutes the climax of that paragraph.

S7, the opening sentence of the subsequent paragraph, moves back into the hybrid form of N, akin to S1, with an intermingling of Brian's words ('the main responsibility for last night's shortcomings lay') and deictic reference to the present ('last night's') rather than to the past ('the previous night's'). Like S3 and S6, S8 is ungrammatical. Lack of grammaticality is due to ellipsis, since what has been omitted from this sentence is the main part of the preceding sentence: 'There was little doubt in Brian's mind ... [W]hy, when finally holding the girl who had fired his red-hot imaginings for so long in his arms, he had reacted like a puritanical schoolboy'. Hence, S7–S8 could have been formulated as one. By presenting them as two sentences, the value of the information conveyed by each is increased. This contrasts with the standard communicative effect of violating the Gricean quantity maxim, for in one sense, S8 is simply a recouching of the concept conveyed by S7. Hence, S8 should not, in theory, exist because it is redundant. Its presence, like that of most of the sentences in Text 5, is accounted for by the fact that they represent Brian venting his spleen. Strong emotion on an important topic is not brought under control in two seconds.

One does not need to be a rabid feminist to realise the raving, racist lunacy, harking back to the biological imprint stance upheld by Honoria, betokened by 'were not the skills of the harem in every woman's blood?'

S11–S14 demonstrate Brian's total lack of emotional and moral concern for his family.

The central point here, with regard to positioning the reader, is that in the main, Brian condemns himself with his own hands (and mouth), as does Honoria – the most effective way of convincing onlookers that a person is wrong!

It is extreme portraits of this kind that inform the TV series, with its gallery of mentally unsound and otherwise inadequate people populating most episodes.

4.3.1.3 The Police: Inspector Meredith and Sergeant Troy Graham's position is not simply 'conservative' *tout court*. Rather, it is that of the good bourgeois who is a true inheritor of the Protestant Ethic (Weber 1905/2002). Thus being a policeman is not automatically synonymous with being good. Quite the contrary. To get to heaven one must work hard for the individual good in order to achieve the social good. Consequently, those (not infrequent) policemen not conforming to the work ethic, and other 'traditional' Western values, also come in for heavy flack.

Inspector Ian Meredith is the 'apex' of the group: 'One of the shortcutters. A Bramshill flyer. Out of Oxbridge with his degree round his neck like an Olympic gold ... plus, most galling of the lot, connections in high places. And without the grace to wear this largesse lightly' (p. 148). Although these are the envious thoughts of Sergeant Troy, Barnaby's bagman, presented in FDT mode, the values are concurrently those of Barnaby and of the author. For Meredith is not prone to hard work, exploits his social status to gain

78   John Douthwaite

promotion, is constantly trying to appear the top brain (failing badly almost every time), tells lies to further his personal ends (pp. 280–282) and refuses flatly to cooperate with the group (e.g. pp. 289–294), a point Barnaby continually indicates is the essence of police work, publicly commending his subordinates whenever they make a significant contribution to the investigation in order to reinforce the team spirit and get the best out of his group. Barnaby's persistently and relentlessly bettering Meredith each time, to the joy of the other police officers, is another strategy Graham employs to underscore the Protestant Ethic and turn her readers against those violating that code.

Prototypically, detectives have a foil, whose functions may be myriad, such as highlighting the genius of the super-detective and passing on information to the reader under the guise of informing the partner. Barnaby's foil is Sergeant Troy, a young policemen with some merits but also with several faults. This central feature makes Troy perfect for Graham's task of outlining Barnaby's own merits through comparison with Troy's numerous defects, some of which are exemplified in the next extract.

Text 6 illustrates Sergeant Troy's character, comparing and contrasting it with Honoria Lyddiard's and Tom Barnaby's. The two policemen are leaving Honoria's residence after having interviewed her.

Text 6
[1] [BARNABY] 'What sort of man was Hadleigh?'
[2] [HONORIA] 'He was a gentleman.'
[3] ... As Amy was showing them out she [Honoria] could be heard declaiming loudly, 'Jumped up clowns!'
[4] *A Gentleman.* [5] Troy kicked savagely at the gravel as they made their way back to the rusty gate. [6] Of course we all know what that means. [7] The upper crust on life's farmhouse. [8] He lit a cigarette. [9] A member of the club. [10] Right tie. [11] Right accent. [12] Right attitude. [13] Right sort of monkey. [14] Right wing. [15] (Troy himself was extremely right wing, but from quite a different jumping off point. [16] And for quite different reasons.) [17] And, of course, blue balls.
[18] 'You can't believe folk like that, can you?' [19] He opened the gate and stood aside to let Barnaby pass through. [20] 'In this D and A. [21] I bet she's never done a stroke of work in her life. [22] Bloody parasite.'
[23] 'Now look.' [24] Barnaby, his voice sharp and irritable, stopped in mid-stride. [25] His back ached from standing and he liked being patronised no more than the next man. [26] 'Your prejudices are your own affair, Gavin, unless they interfere with your work. [27] In which case they also become mine. [28] Our job is to extract information and to persuade people to reveal themselves. [29] Anything that hinders this procedure is a time-wasting bloody nuisance. [30] And I don't expect to find it coming from my own side of the fence.' (88–89, original emphasis)

By classifying Hadleigh, the murdered man, as a 'gentleman' (S2) Honoria Lyddiard immediately flaunts her social standing and her ideology. She continues doing so by insulting the policemen as they leave without any restraint or compunction, deliberately putting into ironic practice through her racist manner the edict *noblesse oblige* (S3). That she is indeed flaunting, and not simply displaying, her self-assigned social status is confirmed both by her denigratory comment 'jumped up clowns' (S3) and by the fact that it is an 'aside' that is intended to be heard by the insulted parties ('declaiming loudly').

Given that Troy wishes to 'escape' from his lowly origins (contextual information), he immediately takes umbrage at having his lower status exposed and berated in public (S4). The intensity of his emotional reaction is conveyed in S4 by the brevity of the sentence, by its ungrammaticality, by its occupying paragraph-initial position, by being written in italics (hence conveying emphasis) and by being presented in FDT. What Troy's reaction also demonstrates is the deep-rootedness of the English class system.

Sentence 5 immediately moves out of Troy's head and is presented in N mode. It confirms Troy's anger through external description of action expressed by two highly negative modalisers, 'kicked' and 'savagely', which also call into question Troy's human status, not for the first, nor last, time in the novel. Troy is more animal than gentleman. Furthermore, S5 also depicts Troy as powerless and frustrated, since kicking 'at the gravel' (viz. complementing the aggressive lexical verb with an adverbial and not with a direct object, as in 'kicked Mrs Lyddiard') indicates an action whose negative consequences are severely limited, since Troy does not act directly on the world affecting that world, as is standard when deploying a transitive syntactic construction, as the example of kicking Mrs Lyddiard shows. Hence the way Troy has selected to vent his feelings is limited by significant contextual, social factors, factors which impede his will and his capacity to act on the world. Seeing himself as a victim of his 'birthright',[11] he regularly takes this out on the world. Indeed, at one point the narrator says that Troy 'had, by nature, an unkind heart' (p. 111). The classification 'by nature' tallies perfectly with Christie's view of human character as inborn (Douthwaite 2013b).

S6 returns immediately to FDT, as is indicated by, *inter alia*, the deployment of the present tense, of inclusive 'we' and of conversational and evaluative 'of course' in perceptually prominent (hence important) sentence-initial position. The return to FDT is one of the linguistic devices employed to convey great intensity of emotion, namely, Troy's anger and frustration at the (or rather his) situation.

This presentational mode dominates the fourth paragraph. Indeed, S4–S17 (bar S5, S8 and S15–S16) exhibit strong parallelism:

---

[11] This concept actually places Troy in the same ideological category as Honoria and Brian, with their views on biological and social imprinting.

(1) short sentences (often realised by a single noun phrase, hence short because, *inter alia*, ungrammatical)
(2) identical conceptual content (pinpointing the social identity of the referent)
(3) identical illocutionary forces: criticism, venting frustration and anger
(4) lexical repetition of 'Right', in strong graphological and pragmatic sentence-initial position (parallelism), with its implied attack on aristocratic 'hereditary' power (as exemplified in the novel by Honoria and by her symbolic name), concurrently revealing, through induction, Troy's belonging to the have-nots
(5) the use of prototypical cultural symbols – 'club', 'tie', 'accent', evoking the high status and ideology of the referent
(6) creativity in the exploitation of prototypical cultural symbols and conventional metaphors: 'blue balls' in lieu of the traditional symbol 'blue blood', the conventional metaphor 'upper crust' innovatively blended with the creative metaphor 'life's farmhouse', both expressions conveying criticism, anger, frustration and envy.

For ultimately, Troy is not a social rebel, but simply envious that he is not at the top and, above all, that he was not born at the top.[12] Ideologically, this puts him on the same plane as Meredith.

Before proceeding with the linguistic analysis, it should be noted, however, that Troy also has several positive qualities which will save him as he 'grows' (thanks also to Barnaby's expert tutelage).

Highly significant are the three interruptions to the pattern of parallelism: they break the paragraph into four major sections which convey Troy's thoughts and feelings, while the three interruptions represent the narrator's stance. S4 is graphologically isolated, foregrounded by paragraph-initial position, brevity (two words) and italics. These linguistic devices work together with presentation in FDT to convey the great intensity of Troy's emotional reaction. The functions of S5 as confirmation and addition through the use of N mode have already been pointed out. S6–S7 (section two) return to FDT. Their function is to explain critically the meaning of 'gentleman'. S8 parallels S5. Both construe material processes betraying emotional states (anger and the attempt to alleviate frustration). S9–S14 are redundant on a conceptual level,

---

[12] To underscore the entrenchedness of the class system, one might note that the novel *Room at the Top* by 'angry young man' John Braine was first published in 1957, thirty-five years before *Written in Blood*. Nothing seems to have changed greatly despite much social protest. For a more radical interpretation of *The Killings at Badger's Drift* as a novel depicting policing Englishness to retain ethnic purity and Troy as a right-wing extremist, see McCaw (2005). McCaw's 'Oriental' interpretation refers to Graham's first novel and the pilot film of the TV series and sheds more light on Graham's conservative position. This point is developed further in Chapter 15, note 16.

since they constitute further exemplifications of the concept expressed in S7. S14 also functions as new information, in the limited sense of adding an explicit political identification. Such prolixity mimics typical human behaviour when anger is the dominant sentiment.

Significantly, the third interruption carries the additional linguistic signal of being in brackets. Here the author, rather than the narrator, is talking directly to the reader. S14 was explicit because it was political. In S15–S16 the author is making her presence felt in order to criticise right-wing extremism, as exemplified both by Honoria Lyddiard and by Sergeant Troy.

S17 constitutes the fourth and final section. This section is one sentence long, the sentence is very short (hence perceptually salient), and it contains the deliberate 'mistake' made by Troy of mixing his metaphors ('blue balls'). It thus constitutes the climax of the paragraph and Troy's attempt at one-upmanshipping Honoria to show his greater intellectual prowess, or so he thinks.

Not by chance, in other parts of the novel, Troy is depicted almost as a Nazi (movement and dress mode included: 'Troy ... made his leather coat crack fiercely round his boots as he strode along', p. 79), with violence and a sense of superiority coming to the fore. Clearly, Graham positions the reader against what Troy stands for in no uncertain terms.

4.3.2   *The Good: Inspector Tom Barnaby*

We end this analysis with the central character, the unvanquishable detective. In contrast to the flat, stereotypical figure of Sherlock Holmes (a thinking machine pre-dating computers, rarely manifesting human emotions bar those connected to his detective work; see Chapter 8 by Anne Furlong in this volume), Barnaby is portrayed as a human being, with his strong and weak points, but always honest, extremely hard-working, devoted to catching the criminals, as well as a good husband and father. He also acts as a model for Troy, his 'bag-carrier', or Watson-like figure. Although Barnaby is frequently hard on his subordinate, this is how the boss trains the novice to bring the latter up to scratch. In stark contrast to Honoria and Brian, Barnaby is far from the heavy-handed boss wielding power to satisfy his sadistic instincts. Instead, he is the superior officer genuinely seeking to offer his subordinate the best experience possible to improve, a fact which Troy is fully aware of: 'Trouble was, he knew Barnaby was right' (p. 89). Finally, Barnaby is always understanding and sympathetic as well as scandalised and outraged precisely where the 'normal' human being would be. The moral aspect is so central to the character that Barnaby may be said to embody the Protestant work ethic. Indeed, strong evidence of this is offered by the final paragraph of T6. S26 indicates Barnaby's humanity. S29 underscores the importance of work. S30 emphasises the need for team work ('my own side of the fence') to obtain a positive social outcome in the domain of work.

One short extract towards the close of the novel is exemplary in bringing to light Barnaby's character and demonstrating Graham's skill at covertly aligning her readers.

Text 7
[1] But it said here she had a headache. [2] Barnaby cursed himself for not being more specific. [3] If only he had phrased his question more precisely. [4] Did you go to bed straight away? [5] Or even, did you go upstairs? [6] Then, providing of course Amy was telling the truth, he would have caught Honoria out in a deliberate lie. [7] Barnaby was mildly disconcerted to realise how pleased he was at the thought and how much he would have enjoyed confronting her with it. (p. 413)

At this point, Barnaby becomes highly suspicious that Honoria might have told a lie of such consequence that it would instantly render her a prime suspect.

The paragraph begins in Barnaby's head, for S1 is a hybrid construction where FIT dominates but is 'contaminated' by FDT, as indicated by the abnormal use of 'here', which shifts the time forward and nears the reader (perceptually, psychologically, emotionally) to the deictic centre, namely, to Barnaby.

This subtle form of foregrounding (namely, hybridising the STP construction), together with the use of the inner voice, produces the illocutionary force of Barnaby identifying the locus of an error he has committed. There is also an undertone of (self)disdain ('it said here' – what the document says differing from what Barnaby now believes, thus implying self-criticism). The critical effect is achieved by Barnaby quoting from the transcription of his own interview. Stated differently, through the anonymity of the document referred to (exploiting Gricean manner through vagueness), Barnaby is distancing himself from the contents of the document, hence criticising his own work.

In conclusion, the linguistic form makes the reader experience the thought and emotion in a relatively direct, or mimetic, fashion. This is the first step (in this particular extract, since I must perforce ignore co-text and context for lack of space) in making the reader identify with the character.

S2 moves almost out of Barnaby's head into NRTA ('cursed' constituting a reporting verb, the original being hypothesisable as: 'Damn it, why on earth wasn't I more specific!'). This is yet another subtle move akin to that performed in S1, for it distances Barnaby from the conceptual content of the sentence and, consequently, from empathetic readers, who have already identified with Barnaby thanks to S1. In other terms, the self-reproach Barnaby expresses in S1 at having made a mistake is signalled in S2 by the narrator as not to be taken that seriously but as having to be evaluated more as Barnaby venting his frustration and anger at not yet having solved the case and at having missed an opportunity to do so earlier. In this way readers are further encouraged to sympathise and identify with Barnaby since they understand Barnaby is human, admitting his mistake, while the other major police characters fail to do so – quite the opposite, as we have seen with Meredith.

S3 returns inside Barnaby's head with FIT (change 'he' and 'his' to 'I' and 'my' and FDT is obtained), hence the strong emotions of frustration, anger and regret, with Barnaby mentally kicking himself over his error, are also powerfully experienced by the reader, who again empathises with Barnaby.

S4 moves into FDT, generally the STP mode creating the most intense form of readerly participation. Here Barnaby (mentally) pronounces the question he should have asked the witness when he first interrogated her and which would have avoided committing the error, thereby confirming that the illocutionary forces conveyed by the previous sentence are those of self-criticism and anger/frustration at his blunder. Barnaby is also underlining the simplicity of the question (hence of the point he missed), reiterating his concomitant frustration and anger. Simplicity is conveyed both by the nature of the conceptual content (concrete, mundane) and by the brevity of the sentence (exploiting Gricean quantity).

S5 employs another extremely subtle device. Starting with 'Or even' followed by a comma (hence a verbless clause), and then following with a finite clause, hides the formal structure:

Or he might even have asked 'Did you go to bed straight away?'

This variant would have clearly constituted FIT with embedded FDT. Instead, through ellipsis, the sentence continues to *appear* to be in 'pure' FDT, again contributing to making the sentence more direct and highly emotively involving for the reader. Of course, the author's objective is also to foreground 'Or even' through its lack of grammaticality and its graphological brevity in order to convey Barnaby developing his thought (in contrast to external narration) and being even more critical of his error, thus providing the climax to this rhetorical move and paving the way for the next sentence.

While, in formal terms, S6 could embody both N and FIT, given that the preceding sentences are all in Barnaby's consciousness (bar S2, which constitutes an exception for the functional reason hypothesised above), then this is how S6 is to be interpreted too (Gricean manner maxim, sub-maxim: be orderly – the reader [correctly] presumes that the status quo has not changed until the author provides a signal indicating that something has indeed changed). Sentence-initial 'Then' indicates the introduction of a cause–effect chain, hence Barnaby (and not the narrator) reasoning. The illocutionary force of the subordinate clause 'providing of course Amy was telling the truth' is that of enunciating a condition on which the conclusion is dependent – a clear signal of logical activity, hence of mental activity, Barnaby's mental activity. The adverb 'of course' is an expression typically employed in informal conversation rather than in formal written language. The forward test lends further weight to the argument: 'providing of course Amy is telling the truth, then I will have caught her out in a deliberate lie'.

In contrast to T. S. Eliot's renowned finale, S7 concludes the paragraph with a bang and not a whimper. Barnaby's logical analysis has come to an end with S6. S7 constitutes his realisation (a mental process) of his own emotional reaction to his conclusion – the recognition that his line of reasoning is not just functional to solving the case and consequently upholding decent 'human' values (a social act), but that he is also overjoyed at being able to put a highly malevolent human being behind bars, and the further realisation that this emotional reaction does not represent the flowing of the milk and honey of human kindness (i.e. social values), to mould Exodus with Deuteronomy and Shakespeare. That is to say, Barnaby is moderately ('mildly') surprised and ashamed ('disconcerted') at what he sees as his own sadistic vindictiveness. He is human, and his values and emotions are those of 'the man in the street', that is to say, our (we readers') values and emotions, including those which are commonly deemed less praiseworthy.

In a nutshell this climactic sentence epitomises 'the good policeman', a person who does his job well, who is morally sound, for he wishes to catch the culprit to defend society, as shown by his emotional reaction, and who realises that he must not be judge, jury and hangman. To conclude, Barnaby embodies goodness and the ideal policeman that no one can take exception to, bar the criminals. Hence the reader, who also embodies goodness (at least while reading the novel!), identifies with and finds comfort in Barnaby. With consummate writing skill Graham has positioned her reader to perfection.

The TV series underscores, and even intensifies, the themes and communicative strategies (duly modified and augmented to take advantage of the medium) adroitly deployed by Graham. A cogent example is episode 1 of series 11, entitled 'Blood Wedding'. It contains several murders, wickedness (e.g. the illegitimate offspring of a noble family is 'passed on' to a woman of the lower orders to act as mother) and consequent social criticism. Barnaby appears as the great detective and excellent husband and father (saving the day by finding caterers for his daughter's wedding at the last minute when all the other professionals contacted have fallen through, resolving the hysteric crisis his family is going through with great aplomb), thereby providing the perfect model, served up with liberal doses of emotion and beautiful English scenery. Evil is again discomfited and the natural order restored. How can the traditional viewer resist?!

References

Bakhtin, M. (1981). *The Dialogic Imagination*. Ed. M. Holquist, trans. C. Emerson & M. Holquist. Austin: University of Texas Press.

Becker, H. (1963). *Outsiders. Studies in the Sociology of Deviance*. New York: Free Press.

Bell, A., & Ryan, M. (2019). *Possible Worlds Theory and Contemporary Narratology*. Lincoln: University of Nebraska Press.

Bergin, T. (2012). Identity and Nostalgia in a globalized World: Investigating the International Popularity of *Midsomer Murders*. *Crime Media Culture*, 11(3–4), 466–484.

Birns, N.. & Birns, M. B. (1990). Agatha Christie: Modern and Modernist. In R. G. Walker & J. M. Frazer, eds., *The Cunning Craft*. Macomb: Western Illinois University Press, pp. 120–134.

Cloward, R. A., & Ohlin, L. E. (1960). *Delinquency and Opportunity: A Theory of Delinquent Gangs*. New York: Free Press.

Cohen, A. K. (1955). *Delinquent Boys: The Culture of the Gang*. New York: Free Press.

Culpeper, J. (2001). *Language and Characterisation: People in Plays and Other Texts*. Harlow: Longman.

Dechêne, A. (2020). Detective Storyworlds: Longmire, True Detective, and La trêve. *Crime Fiction Studies*, 1(1), 41–58.

Douthwaite, J. (2000). *Towards a Linguistic Theory of Foregrounding*. Alessandria: Edizioni dell'Orso.

(2007a). A Stylistic View of Modality. In G. Garzone & R. Salvi, eds., *Lingue e Linguaggi Specialistici*. Roma: CISU editore, pp. 107–156.

(2007b). Using Speech and Thought Presentation to Validate Hypotheses Regarding the Nature of the Crime Novels of Andrea Camilleri. In D. Hoover & S. Lettig, eds., *Stylistics: Prospect and Retrospect*. Amsterdam: Rodopi, pp. 143–167.

(2013a). The Social Function of the Detective Fiction of the Golden Age. In *Lingua e Diritto. La Lingua della Legge, la Legge nella Lingua*. Publifarum, no. 18, ISSN 1824-7482; http://publifarum.farum.it/show_issue.php?iss_id=19.

(2013b). Agatha Christie and the Social Function of the Detective Fiction of the Golden Age – A Linguistic Analysis. In *Lingua e Diritto. La Lingua della Legge, la Legge nella Lingua*. Publifarum, no. 18, ISSN 1824-7482; http://publifarum.farum.it/show_issue.php?iss_id=19.

(2017a). Natural Complexity. From Language to Text to Tradition. *AION: Pragmatics and the Aesthetics*, 21(1), 111–140.

(2017b). Tracking the Mind in Edith Wharton's Writing. *Status Quaestionis*, no. 13 (July). https://doi.org/10.13133/2239-1983/14387.

Fetterley, J. (1978). *The Resisting Reader: A Feminist Approach to American Fiction*. Bloomington: Indiana University Press.

Fludernik, M. (1993). *The Fictions of Language and the Languages of Fiction*. London: Routledge.

(2011). 1050–1500: Through a Glass Darkly; or, The Emergence of Mind in Medieval Narrative. In D. Herman, ed., *The Emergence of Mind*. Lincoln: University of Nebraska Press, pp. 69–102.

Forster, E. M. (1927). *Aspects of the Novel*. London: Edward Arnold.
Gavins, J. (2007). *Text World Theory: An Introduction*. Edinburgh: Edinburgh University Press.
Graham, C. (1992/2007). *Death in Disguise*. London: Headline.
  (1994/2007). *Written in Blood*. London: Headline.
  (2005/2016). *A Ghost in the Machine*. London: Headline.
Grice, P. (1989). *Studies In the Way of Words*. Cambridge, MA: Harvard University Press.
Grossvogel, D. J. (1979). *Mystery and Its Fictions: From Oedipus to Agatha Christie*. Baltimore: Johns Hopkins University Press.
Herman, D., ed. (2011). *The Emergence of Mind*. Lincoln: University of Nebraska Press.
Hilfer, T. (1990). *The Crime Novel: A Deviant Genre*. Austin: University of Texas Press.
Horn, D. (2003). *The Criminal Body: Lombroso and the Anatomy of Deviance*. New York: Routledge.
Horsley, L. (2009). Hard-Boiled and Noir in Twentieth-Century American Crime Fiction. In A. Seed, ed., *A Companion to Twentieth-Century United States Fiction*. Oxford: Wiley-Blackwell, pp. 135–146.
Kayman, M. A. (1992). *From Bow Street to Baker Street: Mystery, Detection and Narrative*. Basingstoke: Macmillan.
Knight, S. (1980). *Form and Ideology in Crime Fiction*. London: Macmillan.
Leech, G., & Short, M. (1981). *Style in Fiction*. Harlow: Longman.
Makinen, M. (2006). *Agatha Christie: Investigating Femininity*. Basingstoke: Palgrave Macmillan.
Mandel, E. (1984). *Delightful Murder: A Social History of the Crime Novel*. London: Pluto.
Mannheim, H. (1965). *Comparative Criminology: A Textbook*, 2 vols. London: Routledge & Kegan Paul.
Matza, D. (1964). *Delinquency and Drift*. New York: John Wiley & Sons.
McCaw, N. (2005). Those Other Villagers: Policing Englishness in Caroline Graham's The Killings at Badgers's Drift. In J. H. Kim, ed., *Race and Religion in the Postcolonial British Detective Story*. Jefferson: McFarland & Company, pp. 13–28.
  (2009). The Ambiguity of Evil in TV Detective Fiction. In S. Dam & J. Hall, eds., *Inside & Outside of the Law*. Oxford: Inter-Disciplinary Press, pp. 21–29.
  (2011). *Adapting Detective Fiction: Crime, Englishness and the TV Detectives*. London: Continuum.
Nisbet, R. A. (1966/1970). *The Sociological Tradition*. London: Heinemann.
Palmer, A. (2004). *Fictional Minds*. Lincoln: University of Nebraska Press.
Pascal, R. (1977). *The Dual Voice*. Manchester: Manchester University Press.
Pepper, A. (2016). *Unwilling Executioner. Crime Fiction and the State*. Oxford: Oxford University Press.
Reddy, Maureen T. (2003). Women Detectives. In M. Priestman, ed., *The Cambridge Companion to Crime Fiction*. Cambridge: Cambridge University Press, pp. 191–208.

Roberts, T. (2007). Why We Read Fiction: Theory of Mind and the Novel (review). *College Literature*, 34(4), 210–212.

Rowland, S. (2001). *From Agatha Christie to Ruth Rendell: British Women Writers in Detective and Crime Fiction*. Basingstoke: Palgrave Macmillan.

Rundquist, E. (2017). *Free Indirect Style in Modernism: Representations of Consciousness*. Amsterdam: John Benjamins.

Semino, E., & Short, M. (2004). *Corpus Stylistics: Speech, Writing and Thought Presentation in a Corpus of English Writing*. London: Routledge.

Simpson, Paul (1993). *Language, Ideology and Point of View*. London: Routledge.

Stowe, W. (1983). *The Poetics of Murder: Detective Fiction and Literary Theory*. San Diego, CA: Harcourt Brace Jovanovich.

Thomas, B. (2012). *Fictional Dialogue: Speech and Conversation in the Modern and Postmodern Novel*. Lincoln: University of Nebraska Press.

Trimm, R. (2017). *Heritage and the Legacy of the Past in Contemporary Britain*. New York: Routledge.

Turnbull, S. (2014). *The TV Crime Drama*. Edinburgh: Edinburgh University Press.

Van Dine, S. S. (1928). Twenty Rules for Writing Detective Stories. Reprinted in H. Haycraft, ed., *The Art of the Mystery Story: A Collection of Critical Essays*. New York: Bilbo and Tannen, 1975, pp. 189–193.

Weber, M. (1905/2002). *The Protestant Ethic and the Spirit of Capitalism*. Trans. P. Baehr & G. C. Wells. London: Penguin

Zahlmann, S. (2019). Landscapes of Thrift and Dwelling: Dwelling and Sociality in Midsomer Murders. *Culture Unbound Journal of Current Cultural Research*, 11(3–4), 466–484.

Zunshine, L. (2006). *Why We Read Fiction: Theory of Mind and the Novel*. Columbus: Ohio State University Press.

5 A Critical and Stylistic Analysis of the Depiction of the Transnational Human Trafficking Victim in Minette Walters' *The Cellar*

Christiana Gregoriou

5.1 Introduction

Transnational human trafficking crime fiction can potentially have a significant impact on public awareness of this crime and its victims, and partly so because of the wide readership the broader crime genre enjoys (Beyer 2018). As such books therefore deserve serious attention, this chapter offers a critical and stylistic analysis of the literary depiction of one transnational human trafficking crime fiction victim while elucidating aspects of this crime's popular perception. Specifically, I explore Edgar winner Minette Walters' 2015 novel *The Cellar*, a third-person novel focalised through fourteen-year-old trafficking victim Muna. Following a brief plot summary, I outline some of the benefits and limitations of the book's human trafficking–related representations. It is in the chapter's main part, Section 5.2, that I undertake detailed analysis of the book's literary language so as to investigate the ways in which the text creates certain impressions of what one such victim's experience may be like. Analysing the language of this domestic slavery narrative also sheds light on the effect this crime may well have on actual victims.

5.1.1 Plot Outline

'Stolen' (p. 123) from an African orphanage by the Songoli family when she was eight, Muna is trafficked to, and enslaved in, Britain, under the pretence of Muna supposedly being immigrant Yetunde and Ebuka Songolis' mentally disabled daughter. However, Muna is neither the couple's daughter nor disabled, and, despite appearances, the girl has even taught herself to understand English, something that her captors are unaware of at the book's start. In addition to being kept captive and being forced to sleep in the cellar after spending her days serving the Songoli family's various domestic needs, the girl is regularly sexually assaulted by her pretend-father Ebuka, and is sexually attacked and threatened by his two sons, and her pretend-brothers, Abiola and Olubayo. Ultimately, Muna frees herself from slavery by causing the death of

Yetunde and her two sons. Though Ebuka survives an altercation with Muna, he is reduced to a rather powerless wheelchair-user and instead becomes Muna's 'prisoner', in effect (p. 211).

All the while, the house that Muna lives in seems to be inhabited by an evil spirit of sorts, a 'darkness' or 'devil' which readers may find ambiguous to interpret. As crime novels tend to abide by the notion of realism, as in purport to 'the illusion of life' (Gregoriou 2007, p. 52), experienced crime fiction readers are likely to interpret this dark power as one generated by Muna's imagination. After all, the text's style suggests not only a troubled mind but also a girl whose narration is not wholly reliable. In this sense, the 'darkness' can be readable as a metaphor for the domestic slavery crime itself, which, like 'darkness', is hidden, unknown and incites fear. Having said that, the end of the book coincides with the cellar's 'darkness' seemingly taking literal dimensions, and appearing as a supernatural force dragging Muna back down to the cellar (p. 245), which leaves the readers unsure about her fate, or the meaning this 'darkness' ultimately comes to have. In a metaphorical reading of the ending, Muna is not pulled back to the cellar in fact, but merely finds herself unable to leave the house's 'darkness', as her (understandably, perhaps) vengeful behaviour toward her captors has now led her to a life of criminality she can never escape from. Having destroyed evidence of her real identity, she remains trapped in the house and its cellar's 'darkness', regardless of her new-found so-called freedom. Not unlike Abigail in Abani's (2006) *Becoming Abigail*, Walters' novel also ends with Muna being ultimately traceless in the system, and this perhaps offers 'a much needed neocolonial critique of structural problems that create conditions that oppress and exploit people in [trafficking] situations' (Hall 2015, pp. 57, 59). Before engaging with the novel stylistically, the next section approaches the novel with such critiques in mind.

5.1.2 Critical Reading

Whether fictional or otherwise, transnational human trafficking narratives enable readers' engagement with an otherwise hidden crime. As Hartlaub (2016) notes when reviewing Walters' book,

> '[t]he things that give rise to the events described here occur. We know they do, though, more often than not, we turn away from them when confronted by them in a newspaper article that one quits reading after the third paragraph, or in an investigative report televised on the nether regions of a cable channel. There is no turning away from THE CELLAR once you start it, and that is chief among its many strengths.'

In other words, further to enabling reader engagement, literary texts of this sort arguably encourage readers to socially and morally confront this crime, and particularly so because trafficking is here portrayed through a victim whose experience we, uniquely, get direct access to.

However, modern slavery depictions too come with risks, one such risk being that of failing to capture the structural global causes leaving people vulnerable to trafficking (Gregoriou & Ras 2018a, p. 8). Another is the risk of depicting this crime's victims as one-dimensional (Gregoriou & Ras 2018b), or what Forster [1927] (1987) would describe as 'flat', as in constructed round a single idea or quality (a tendency not limited to trafficking victims alone, but true of all victim portrayals in fact). Further to such texts failing to focus on what precisely drives, and enables, trafficking, then, they also over-focus on 'ideal victims' (Christie 1986) who are young, female, non-white, naïve, helpless, coerced, and sexually abused (see Gregoriou & Ras 2018b), like Walters' Muna (see also Kinney 2015, p. 104). Reinforcing the trafficking victim stereotype as such runs the risk of failing to recognise non-ideal victims, such as men facing labour exploitation, and establishing 'a victim hierarchy, resulting in many non-ideal, but real, victims being denied services and rights, to the extent where they are prosecuted' (see Gregoriou & Ras 2018a, pp. 9–10), and hence treated as criminals rather than victims. In short, such narratives' stereotyping of trafficking victims potentially damages real non-fictional victims who come to be, at best, denied the help they deserve and, at worst, conversely face unfair punishment. To put this in real terms, Kelly (2005, p. 243, cited in Gregoriou & Ras 2018a, p. 10) estimates that only half of trafficking victims in need of assistance actually receive it.

Even more importantly, Walters' novel portrays Muna's trafficking into the United Kingdom as a problem that is not domestic, but imported, as it is generated by foreigners/the Songolis, to whom similarly foreign Muna 'belonged' (p. 16). For Muna is an 'unpaid servant' (p. 205) and a paperless 'illegal immigrant in a foreign land' (p. 236), helplessly brought into slavery in London. Her traffickers and captors are also non-British citizens; the novel shows them to be unentitled to the normal sorts of privileges UK's British enjoy, like employment and education benefits (see p. 201). In portraying all these characters as foreign, not to mention manipulative, the novel implicitly perpetuates the portrayal of trafficking as a problem generated by foreigners/'others' alone (see, for instance, Szörényi 2016, p. 79). Media discourse also favours the portrayal of trafficking as an imported crime, which problematically criminalises transnational movement, legitimises strict border control and migration policies, and 'distracts from the fact that many local causes of trafficking (e.g. poverty, conflict) are the result of the foreign policies of countries such as the US and the UK' (Gregoriou & Ras 2018a, p. 15). In reality, this crime is not one only 'others' inflict and suffer from; though the victims of transnational human trafficking may well be foreign in the country in which they are exploited, what often causes trafficking ultimately comes down to matters, and structural causes, which are domestic.

The remaining part of this essay will stylistically examine Walters' crime novel which, however problematic in its representation of modern slavery, is nevertheless still highly effective in shedding light on a human trafficking victim's experience, albeit fictional. A stylistic analysis of this text which deals with the human trafficking victim also enables an enhanced critical understanding of the irreparable damage that this crime can generate.

5.2   The Language of *The Cellar*

This section analyses Walters' novel through Fowler's (1977) notion of 'mind style', a term used to refer to the use of linguistic unusualness employed to project Muna's unusual view of the world. As I next illustrate, the unusualness of her world view relates directly to her imprisonment from a young age, and the extreme and vicious verbal and physical abuse she finds herself enduring while being forced to work without pay in the Songoli household. The linguistic mind style features contributing to Muna's trafficking victim mind impression are the Muna-focalised narration's speech presentation, naming strategies, metaphor, transitivity,[1] and (deontic) modality,[2] features which are next analysed in turn.

5.2.1   Reporting Speech

The Cellar is in the third-person narrative mode, and is internally focalised through Muna, while its (English) language reflects the girl's understanding of the world in a number of ways. First, the book is printed in English, but the Songoli family members' communication with one another and also with Muna is said to be in the African Chadic language Hausa. Nevertheless, Muna unobtrusively learns how to speak in English too, through access to media such as television, and also one of the boys' English lessons, privately delivered by a tutor at home. Being able to understand and, eventually, speak English, and this being unknown to her captors for the duration of most of the book's plot, empowers Muna. The language allows her to eavesdrop on important conversations amongst her captors, and also provides opportunities

---

[1] Transitivity is the grammatical system through which the reader is presented with 'clear notions of who is in control, who is a victim and so on' (Jeffries 2010, p. 47). As exemplified in Gregoriou (2011, p. 52), 'active material processes (of the 'X stabbed Y' kind) can be reformulated into passive voice structures (of the 'Y was stabbed (by X)' kind), the suppletion of agentless passives by intransitive clauses (of the 'Y died' kind), and nominalisations – the turning of verb processes into noun phrases which background the process to its product (of the 'The stabbing proved fatal' kind)'.

[2] Modality, in the form of modal verbs (like 'may') and adverbs (like 'probably'); evaluative nouns ('victim'), adjectives ('innocent'), and adverbs ('perhaps'); lexical verbs ('have to'), verbs of knowledge, prediction, and evaluation; and generic sentences, is concerned with the attitude and stance toward the propositions people express. Among other attitudes, modality can express hope, commitment, and possibility/likelihood.

such as calling for help, something she imagines doing, but finds herself unable to do. Importantly, all character speech is reported mostly in the Free Direct Speech[3] mode such as in the following extract, where a female police officer is called upon to investigate Abiola's disappearance:

'She was too small and thin to resist the woman's pull. Don't show fear, Yetunde warned in Hausa. Smile when this policewoman smiles at you, and speak in answer to the questions I ask you. It won't matter what you say. She's white English and doesn't understand Hausa.' (p. 7)

Speech segments (see all but the first sentence in the extract above) are placed alongside the novel's Muna-focalised narration (see first sentence above), and lack a reporting clause, quotation marks, or both. Seeing that the novel is focalised through Muna, and the freeness of the speech reporting is quite marked through a noticeable lack of quotation marks, the choice of speech presentation mode proves significant in generating the impression of the focaliser distancing themselves from those speaking. In other words, speech being reported in the Free Direct mode suggests that Muna is lacking control over, and is unable to respond to, those whose words she reports; she is exposed to speech but merely registers what she hears, unquestionably, and is powerless over who it is that is actually doing the speaking.

Elsewhere, snippets of Free Indirect Speech[4] blend other characters' voice with the Muna-focalised narration within the same sentence and instead suggest a disputable tone over what it is that these characters say. Such speech reporting mode is employed, for instance, where, as a result of Abiola's disappearance, Ebuka 'strode angrily about the carpet, cursing the day he'd brought his family to this godforsaken country' (pp. 11–12). The narrative reference to Ebuka striding is followed by a Free Indirect Speech report of his cursing. This speech report can be described as Free Indirect as it mixes the voices of the reporter and reported; whereas the wording ('godforsaken') is character-appropriate and hence character-coloured, the tense ('had brought' as opposed to 'brought') and pronouns ('he' and 'his' as opposed to 'I' and 'my') are narrator- rather than character-specific. Similarly, the Muna-focalised narration reports Abiola's searchers asking the parents a series of questions, one of which is 'How much did his parents know about his

---

[3] According to Leech and Short (2007, p. 275), 'Direct speech has two features which show evidence of the narrator's presence, namely the quotation marks and the introductory reporting clause. Accordingly, it is possible to remove either or both of these features, and produce a freer form, which has been called Free Direct Speech: one where the characters apparently speak to us more immediately without the narrator as an intermediary.'

[4] In Free Indirect Speech (FIS) linguistic features associated with characterological directness are found alongside some associated with narratological indirectness. According to Leech and Short (2007, p. 261), 'FIS is a sort of halfway house position, not claiming to be a reproduction of the original speech, but at the same time being more than a mere indirect rendering of that original.'

friends?' (p. 12). This speech report is again Free Indirect; the structure being grammatically in the form of a question suggests a character voice, but, again, the tense ('did' as opposed to 'do') and pronouns (notice the reference to 'his parents' as opposed to 'you') suggest that of the narrator. The opting for Free Indirect Speech, and hence the blending of character and narrator voice, generates irony[5] over the speech Muna reports; the reporting mode is effective in suggesting that Muna mocks those talking, and even anticipates her ultimately taking power over them in the end.

A similar effect is achieved through the novel's speech summaries, which Short (1988) describes as abbreviated forms of longer pieces of discourse; much like Free Indirect Speech reports, summaries too suggest the narrator's distance over those reported speaking. Where the police interrogate Ebuka over Abiola's disappearance, the Muna-focalised narration reports Ebuka having 'accused the police of being racists for putting him and his wife through the indignity of an interrogation, and raged at Scotland Yard for appointing a woman to run the investigation' (p. 30). The speech summary mode of speech presentation suggests a contemptuous tone over what Ebuka is saying. So does the content of what he actually says; after all, Ebuka, a man proven capable of horrible indignities (i.e. his consistent raping of Muna), accuses the police of indignity and racism, and all the while expressing a sexist view of his own (i.e. that of a woman running the investigation being infuriating to him). Similarly, when trying to explain why he was not at home when he ought have been so on the day, Muna is said to have 'listened to Ebuka huff and puff about being caught in traffic' (p. 34). Further to the mode itself suggesting her reporting him ironically, the reference to him 'huffing' and 'puffing' also clearly mocks him, and suggests that he is lying about the traffic, and is not to be trusted. The opting for speech summaries, and hence a mode of speech presentation that allows the narrator to interfere with the speech reported, indirectly encourages the reader to critically engage with what is being said.

In short, the modes of speech representation employed (and specifically the opting for Free Direct Speech, Free Indirect Speech, and speech summaries) suggest a focaliser who lacks power in relation to those talking, all the while casting irony over what it is that these others say.

5.2.2 Naming Strategies

With regard to Muna's narrative voice, its unusualness is manifested partly through the referring strategies this 'frail little slave' (p. 206) opts for in

---

[5] 'This ability to give the flavour of the character's words but also to keep the narrator in an intervening position between character and reader makes FIS an extremely useful vehicle for casting an ironic light on what the character says' (Leech & Short 2007, p. 262).

relation to all others, which reflect the type of social relationships Muna believes she has with them, not to mention her evaluation of these relationships.

The Muna-focalised narration's naming choices are not constant where her captors are concerned, partly because of the need for the novelist to employ stylistic variation perhaps. Nevertheless, these naming strategies are telling. Despite their appalling behaviour toward her, Muna initially refers to the Songolis by title and surname ('Mr and Mrs Songoli', p. 5), which suggests distance, subservience, and – initially, at least – fear, particularly since Muna (p. 5) is herself contrastingly first-named throughout the book. The Muna-focalised narration thereafter referring to the Songolis by first names ('Yetunde' on p. 5, 'Abiola' on p. 6), full names ('Yetunde Songoli', p. 5), or through kinship terms ('Aunt Yetunde' on p. 19 or 'Mamma' on p. 27) contrastingly suggests an inevitable affinity or familiarity between Muna and her captors. The latter set of kinship terms also clearly suggests dishonesty. Though referring to a family friend as one's 'Aunt' is common in a number of cultures, the friendship this alludes to is far from genuine. As for 'Mamma', the term ironically reflects the supposed mother–daughter relationship the two females are presented as having to others, but clearly do not share. When directly addressing, or orally referring to, her captors, Muna is only 'permitted' (p. 9) to refer to Yetunde as 'Princess' (p. 9), and her own rapist as 'Master' (p. 46), which solidifies her complete subordination to them both. What is more, Muna persists in using this set of subservient terms even when she kills Yetunde, and finds herself in complete control of wheelchair-bound Ebuka, this suggesting an ironic tone once more, but also an inescapability from her domestic slavery, even with her no longer being their actual slave at the novel's end.

White race characters, all of whom are placed outside the Songoli household she is imprisoned in, are unnamed, and referred to merely as 'whites' (p. 10), with one singled out particularly negatively through the term 'witchy-white' (p. 135) even. This consequently 'others' these non-blacks, and suggests that, for her own community, and in the black 'piccaninny' (p. 238) girl's mind, they cannot be trusted because of their race. As a result, these 'whites' remain unaware of the realities of Muna's predicament and prove powerless to assist her in her plight, despite Muna's hopes that they might help her somehow. Hence, for her to gain her freedom, she has no choice but to become the agent of her own release from slavery instead. She comes to take revenge over her captors, all without anyone else's help.

Last, Ebuka referring to Muna as a 'Temptress' and 'Polluter of men' (p. 57) also reverses the question of guilt, as is often the case with victims of rape. What Ebuka insinuates here is that Muna is somehow responsible for the violence inflicted upon her (in that she 'tempts' the men who abuse her), not to mention that she is 'polluting' the men who act violently on her; in addition to denying Muna's victimhood status, Ebuka's descriptions of Muna suggest that she is a victimiser of her abusers instead. Expressions such as 'witchy' in 'witchy-white' and 'polluter' in 'polluter of men' can also be read metaphorically, an area I turn to next.

5.2.3 Metaphors

Throughout the book, the Muna-focalised narration portrays the Songolis' behaviour along animalistic metaphorical lines. Following the cognitive view of metaphor[6], this suggests the SONGOLIS ARE ANIMALS underlying conceptual metaphor. Though animals are not associated exclusively with bestiality, linguistic realisations of this metaphor suggest that, for Muna, they are certainly a negative domain through which to describe her captors. See, for instance, references to Yetunde and Ebuka's snake-like 'hiss[ing]' (pp. 5, 57) at Muna when verbally abusing her, Ebuka's 'pig-like grunts' (p. 18) when 'maul[ing]' (p. 83) her in rape, her captors 'growl'ing (p. 181) at one another in anger, and Olubayo's 'animal grunts as he worked on himself' (p. 38) when masturbating, all of which suggest violence and aggressiveness. In Muna's mind, her captors are inhuman, and the metaphors employed reflect this.

Male ejaculation is metaphorically referred to as 'filth' that 'leak[s]' (p. 38), or 'slime' that is 'emptied' (p. 89), out of male bodies and 'into her' (p. 38), which cements her disgust at male body functions, particularly as these are the result of sexual violence directed at her. The Muna-focalised narration referring to Muna's body as a vessel for these filthy male liquids through the ontological[7] MUNA IS A CONTAINER metaphor suggests that she is treated as a mere agentless object for them to manipulate as they see fit.

Conceptualising her own body as a container for them to exploit is linked to her captors employing the MUNA IS NON-HUMAN metaphor, too. See, for instance, references to Olubayo dismissively referring to her as a 'filthy bitch in a filthy kennel' (p. 42) while, when angered by all misfortune brought to the family, she is called 'a monster' (p. 60) by Ebuka, and a 'witch and a demon' (p. 6) or someone who 'had demons' (p. 7) 'inside her' (p. 20) by Yetunde. Whereas Muna's animalistic metaphors for her captors suggest their lack of

---

[6] Lakoff and Johnson (1980) argue that metaphors reflect underlying thought processes and are central in the way we conceptualise our experiences and the society we live in. Following the cognitive metaphor tradition, one would employ the A is B structure through which to indicate how the metaphor's mapping is constructed, with A referring to the metaphor's target domain (the item described) and B referring to its source domain (what it is described through).

[7] According to Lakoff and Johnson (1980), ontological metaphors concern ways of viewing events, activities, emotions, ideas, etc. as entities and substances. The abstract is here made concrete.

humanity which is no doubt related to their appalling behaviour toward her, the dehumanising metaphors her captors use when verbally abusing her suggest that, for them, her human identity is actually entirely erased. She is either objectified for them to utilise, an animal for them to dismiss, or a supernatural species they can blame for all family hardship.

The novel reader also encounters many metaphorical mappings relating to the target domains of verbal and physical abuse. The ontological metaphor VERBAL ABUSE IS LIQUID conceptualises the verbal attacks the girl suffers, that is, something abstract, as concrete, and liquid-like. In '[a] torrent of pent-up abuse poured from her mouth' (p. 75), verbal abuse, which had so far been held back ('pent-up'), becomes physical, and strong and fast-moving 'torrent' as it pours out of her captor's mouth, for instance. Such constructions vividly create an aggressive and physical image of verbal abuse, not to mention an unfavourable image of the abuser, as one who physically generates an unwelcome substance for others to deal with. PHYSICAL ABUSE IS also conceptualized as YETUNDE'S SPORT:

'It was Yetunde's favourite sport to beat the Devil out of the girl, and Muna had come to welcome the punishment. If the Devil was so hard to expel, it meant He must be real.' (p. 54)

Here, the physical abuse Muna endures is all but an enjoyable and harmless hobby ('favourite sport') for the abusers and, rather than referring to the girl as a Devil, her captors refer to 'the Devil' as something within her, for which reason they abuse her, in order to expel it out of her. In other words, the captors conceptualise their vicious acts as ones supposedly designed to help free her from 'the Devil' inside her, for which reason Muna welcomes their 'punishment' in return. This can be described as an attempt to dominate Muna through brainwashing; control over her is effectively maintained not only through violence but also through the medium of ideology, which is consistent with Gramscian notions of hegemony.[8] In short, the abuser's language here manipulates and indoctrinates Muna into accepting her violence as natural and common-sense. Last, the novel featuring various metaphors for abuse also suggests that abuse is a kind of experience that Muna is all too familiar with, and cannot escape from; since the novel is focalised through Muna, these metaphors suggest that verbal and physical attacks are but a daily, and ineluctable, occurrence for her.

As noted, the girl too appears to believe in the existence of evil spirits; she understands 'the Devil' (p. 56) or 'demons' (p. 76) as literally inhabiting the

---

[8] The term 'hegemony' is used by Neo-Marxist Gramsci to refer to 'the maintenance of one social group's dominance over subordinate groups through relations of consent and coercion' (Gramsci, 1971, cited in Ekers and Loftus 2008, p. 702).

cellar she lives in, and uses references to such supernatural existence so as to explain all misbehaviour therein, including Olubayo's seizures ('Muna didn't doubt it was the Devil who jumped into Olubayo's body and cause him to behave as he did', p. 55). The novel's prologue and epilogue even refer to a personified cellar 'Darkness' that, in a series of grammatically paralleled structures, 'speaks', 'breathes', 'feels', and 'hears' (p. 1), and is elsewhere said to be 'alive' (p. 17), 'whisper[ing] rebellion in Muna's ear' (p. 43), and in one instance 'encourag[es]' her, asking her to 'bide' her time so as to ultimately 'inflict a more lingering pain' (p. 54) upon her captors. The reader could read such expressions along the lines of the ontological DARKNESS IS ALIVE metaphor or, alternatively, read the existence of a 'dark' supernatural being literally, much as it is for Muna.

Even when freed from 'her prison' (p. 11) toward the novel's end, Muna chooses to remain hidden in the Songoli house, and readers begin to wonder as to the extent to which the references to the darkness all need (re)reading, not metaphorically, but literally. Even though Muna intends that the Devil really exists, readers are invited to do the same. When Ebuka attacks her, Muna refers to 'a few clear memories of what happened next' (p. 57), and recalls

'a series of half-formed images. She saw the black bowels of the earth open before her, felt Ebuka being lifted over her by a giant fist, watched his body tumbling down the stairs. More clearly than anything, she heard the Devil laugh.' (pp. 57–8)

The extract is ambiguous. Though Ebuka here gets actually physically harmed, which later results in him being confined to a wheelchair, the reader is left wondering as to what exactly happened, and whether a supernatural force was actually at play. The use of metaphor (notice the reference to memories as 'half-formed images', the personified earth's 'bowels', and the personified Devil's 'laughter') and that of the passive voice with an unclear agent (with Ebuka 'being lifted' by an unnamed source's 'giant fist') do not allow the reader to uncover who is the agent of the lifting and the violence inflicted upon Ebuka, this time. If the reader resists a supernatural reading of the scene, they are left wondering whether Muna proved capable of overpowering Ebuka somehow.

Similarly, when attacking Yetunde, Muna hears '[a] deep guttural rumble that drew a hollow echo from the walls' (p. 108), and 'the Devil's laugh rise from the caverns of the earth and see[s] his hand reach out of the darkness to drag Yetunde down' (p. 108), suggesting that she is not the agent of dragging Yetunde down, but that this 'Devil' actually is. The text's metaphors (the rumble 'drawing' an echo from the walls, the personified Devil's laugh 'rising', his hand 'reaching out' of concretised darkness) disguise the agent of what/who it is that dragged Yetunde down, and leave it up to the reader to interpret this force as either Muna or an actual evil spirit of sorts.

When vengeful, the Muna-focalised narration even portrays the girl in animalistic terms also; the MUNA IS AN ANIMAL metaphor is found in references to her having 'vibrated her tongue against her palate to produce a snakelike hiss' (p. 74), 'dropped into a cat-like crouch and jumped at Olubayo, her lips drawn back in a snarl' (p. 178). She here conceptualises herself as a snake or cat when liberating herself from slavery while also inflicting violence, and murder, on others. Even if justified, her own behaviour is shown to be not dissimilar to that of her own tormentors; she loses her own humanity by treating them not unlike the way they treated her. By the end of the book, Muna's thus far perhaps metaphorical allusions to demons take on literal dimensions. The book ends as follows:

'She reached out to pull the cellar door to, but her fingers were numb and unfeeling. Hard as she tried, she could not make her hand close round the knob. She stared into the darkness below. Something moved. Something stirred. And the air that came from it smelt of death and corruption.

A weight descended on her neck, forcing her to her knees. She bowed her head in terror when a voice, absent of pity or love, spoke.

Do you think to cheat Me out of what is Mine? I am Vengeance. I am Retribution. I am Wrath. I take lives in payment for those that have been taken. There is no escape.

Sinewy coils bound around Muna's chest, squeezing the breath from her lungs. In her mind, she saw an image of Yetunde, eyes pleading for mercy as her life ebbed away. Muna tried to cry out that she was sorry but her mouth wouldn't open, and in despair, she turned towards Ebuka. But his wheelchair was empty and he was gone.

She felt the Darkness pull her down. She heard the cellar door close.

And she knew the Devil was laughing.' (pp. 244–5)

Here, the personified 'Darkness'/'Devil' actually talks in the Free Direct Speech mode, identifying itself as 'Vengeance', 'Retribution', and 'Wrath' (p. 245), the darkness itself drawing on further metaphors, which again construct abstract concepts (such as 'vengeance') in ontological terms of a physical 'being'. The darkness then pulls Muna back down to the cellar, possibly metaphorically suggesting that the girl will be forever trapped by the consequences of her own vengeance. In the epilogue, the personified and here vengeful Darkness 'hides', 'deceives', and 'wait[s]' 'within' (p. 246). Clearly, the conceptual metaphors DARKNESS IS BAD and DOWN IS BAD are persistent throughout, though it is perhaps left up to the reader to decide to what extent these are to be interpreted literally with the darkness now having possibly become, if not having always been, an actual living entity of its own.

The novel also draws on certain links between size and physical domination, which also can be read along the lines of conceptual metaphor. Throughout the story, the Muna-focalised narration draws attention to her captors' large size ('Yetunde Songoli's heavy tread', p. 6; 'mother and son were as fat and bloated as each other', p. 13) in contrast to Muna's 'small and thin' (p. 7) frame. The character size alludes to the captors' lack of grace ('heavy tread'), and their greed/excess ('fat and bloated'), compared with Muna's lack of nourishment. Having said that, size also functions as a visual metaphor of the large power they physically hold over her, hence alluding to the conceptual metaphors BIG IS POWERFUL and SMALL IS POWERLESS. Size is interpretable as relevant to her captors' domination and here suggests the impossibility of rebellion on her part, even though Muna nevertheless manages to overpower them regardless (if through the physical darkness that appears to help her). Last, the negatively connoted largeness of the captors' size is linked to the ugliness/unsightliness of the violence they enforce upon Muna, but is also related to the ugliness that Muna herself, too, portrays when proving violent herself shortly after. Slavery proves negative all round.

Ontological conceptual metaphor is also employed to personify Muna's lack of mobility and quietness as a friend or servant. The STILLNESS IS A PERSON metaphor is found in reference to 'Immobility [having] become a friend over the years' (p. 6) and 'Stillness and silence [having] served her well over the years' (p. 72). Similarly, HER DREAMS ARE TEACHERS ('Her beautiful, vibrant dreams of hurting Yetunde hadn't taught her to deal with the consequences of inflicting pain', p. 126). Since Muna clearly lacks allies of her own, and feels the need to personify abstract concepts, these conceptual metaphors signal her need of socialisation, and particularly in the form of friendship, assistance, and education. It is for this reason that pleasant human interaction in the form of laughter is all but 'alien' to her ('But humour and laughter were as alien to her as smiling and speaking', p. 10); her present circumstances are so dire that they have sadly come to allow no social pleasantries in the form of friendly speaking to, smiling, and laughing with others. Domestic slavery is here portrayed as clearly stripping victims of humanity and disallowing them access to interaction that is in any way pleasurable.

5.2.4 *Transitivity and (Deontic) Modality*

'The idea behind analysing Transitivity is to explore what social, cultural, ideological and political factors determine what Process type (verb) is chosen in a particular type of discourse', for '[r]elations of power may be implicitly inscribed by the relationship between Actor and Goal' (Mayr 2008, p. 18). Of particular interest here is the agency behind material processes, defined in the context of traditional transitivity research as 'doing' (here, violent) actions, and matters of control and responsibility surrounding those involved in these actions. It is in the discussion of responsibility that deontic modality[9] also plays a role.

When others look at, or do things to, Muna, their body parts often take on agency. When a white policewoman interrogates the family members in relation to Abiola's disappearance, Muna found 'the [woman's] blue eyes staring at her' (p. 11) or 'boring into her head' (p. 21). When the 'witchy-white' (p. 129) neighbour Mrs Hughes tries to help Muna, the narration refers to the woman's 'hand [having] caressed her cheek' (p. 129) and '[a]n arm [having] slipped beneath Muna's neck' (p. 130). Even if one reads such excerpts metonymically, with the body part being used in place of the agent's body, the pattern is, nevertheless, hinting at Muna's extreme sensitivity to others' gaze and touch, most probably as a result of her suffering. The girl appears to have endured physical and verbal abuse to such an extent that she is prone to reading innocent physical interaction (see the reference to eyes staring and a hand caressing) as negative (see the reference to eyes aggressively 'boring', and the arm uninvitingly 'slipping' behind her). Her own body parts also take on similar agency at times. In 'she struggled to make her mouth say [English words]' (p. 24) and 'Muna's agile finger took her unerringly through the steps' of typing in Yetunde's password on the latter's smartphone (p. 160), the grammar is instead suggestive of a detachment from her body parts, which, like all else, she sometimes feels herself unable to control (see 'struggle'). Similarly, weapons that harm her also take on agency ('the knife sliced through those parts that were private to little Muna', p. 17) or often disguise such violent agency through passive voice structures ('she'd learned those skills through being beaten with a rod when she made a mistake', p. 18). What such constructions do is obscure individual agency, and suggest a collective kind of responsibility for Muna's predicament which, after all, is caused by combined actions from not just one, but all members of the household.

Fear characterises Muna's action and behaviour throughout the first half of the book. See the use of 'afraid' (pp. 7, 21, 56), 'fear' (pp. 10, 20), 'tremble' (p. 11), 'terror' (pp. 17, 57, 102), 'dread' (pp. 20, 26), and 'frightening' (p. 24), among others. This semantic field of fear being no longer evident in the later parts of the book shows Muna to have surpassed this fear she had of her captors, which consequently allows her to fearlessly take revenge over their abusive actions. When vengeful, she acts upon her captors ('Muna pursued her', p. 106) or, with somewhat diminished responsibility, directs weapons in the direction of them ('Muna swung the hammer at Yetunde's kneecap', p. 107).

---

[9] Simpson (1993) outlines four main modal systems (deontic, epistemic, boulomaic, and perception modality) into which modality features can be grouped. Deontic is the modal system of duty and commitment, and is concerned with one's 'attitude to the degree of obligation attaching to the performance of certain actions' (Simpson 1993, p. 47).

Agentless passives feature in Muna's attacks too ('something sharp was thrust into the muscle of his right arm', p. 177), taking focus away from her as the doer of the violent attack. Similarly, weapons also feature as taking over her own violence; in 'the solid head of the hammer smashed into [Yetunde's] bulging midriff' and her 'blow[s] landed' upon Yetunde (p. 106), the readers encounter a metonymic reference to the hammer's head and Muna's blows, respectively, which emphasises the violence of the act performed while also distancing the doer from it. Last, when the text addresses Muna's attack on Olubayo, there is reference to the boy not seeing 'the open cellar door or the hammer that smashed against the side of his head' (p. 212), as if the door and hammer somehow came to willingly smash the victim's body, without a human agent driving or guiding them. Even though, much like her captors, Muna is implied to be a violent predator here, which is consistent with the novel's portrayal of trafficking as a problem perpetuated by foreigners alone, this distancing nevertheless absolves Muna of some responsibility for what she does. What contributes to an impression of Muna having limited responsibility over her violent actions is the text's deontic modality, which I briefly touch on next.

Muna being imprisoned and living in conditions of slavery mean that she is portrayed as limited to only doing whatever others 'allow' her to do. These limitations are shown by the Muna-focalised text's deontic modality. See, for instance, references to 'words she was permitted to use' (p. 9), to her not being 'allowed to raise her eyes to anyone' (p. 20), and to her being 'forbidden to watch television or listen to a radio' (pp. 23–4).

But even when acting within these limitations, Muna is still able to somewhat break free and retaliate. Later on, though still, willingly this time, confined in the house, she finds herself freed from fear and others' dictating of her own doings. She acquires confidence and, 'moulded' by her violent attackers into 'mirrors of themselves' (p. 108), becomes agent of her own, if violent, vengeful, and maybe even (morally/legally) justified actions. What comes to be implied is that Muna's vindictive violence is the result of others' violence; what she ended up doing to them was somehow inevitable.[10]

---

[10] Muna's lack of emotion (p. 236) and also her violence, and references to a personified Darkness, are reminiscent of Jeff Lindsay's Dexter novel series, in which a vengeful Dexter conceptualises his murdering urges into a force referred to as a 'Dark Passenger' (see Gregoriou 2011, chapter 4). Also reminiscent of this series are references to Muna's mother having died when the girl was as young as four, and Muna having cradled her head in her lap for days before neighbours came to check on her (p. 214), which somewhat explains references to her experiencing 'pleasure' when 'lov[ing] and caress[ing]' (p. 234) her own victims' corpses at the end of the book, corpses she refers to as 'trophies' she later plans to 'dismember' (p. 238). Dexter's very similar childhood trauma is a means through which his, again similar, subsequent killing actions are also explainable and justified in the Lindsay series.

Ultimately, Muna's vindictive action and Ebuka's apologetic attitude toward the end of the book problematise both Muna's classification into the category of 'victim' and Ebuka's into that of 'unapologetic abuser'. Besides, by the end of the book, Muna is no longer the 'ideal victim' she initially was, and the only surviving Songoli family member, Ebuka, is no longer an 'ideal offender'[11] either. Where he was once unrepentant and physically powerful, he is now remorseful and weak, solely depended on his former victim for survival. Unlike other crimes, perhaps, trafficking's perpetrators and victims are never 'ideal', after all, and though focusing on individual behaviour is typical of crime narratives, trafficking is a crime the structural causes of which instead demand attention.

5.3   Conclusion

As Beyer argues (2018, p. 110), 'crime fiction has the capacity to put a human face to TCT [transnational child trafficking] through nuanced portrayals created through political use of literary language and form'. And yet, I have tried to show that such representations need to be approached with caution, for human trafficking fiction tends to reproduce hegemonic discourses about such aspects as gender, sex, and race, and fails to focus on the global causes of trafficking (see also Szörényi & Eate 2014). This is true of Walters' novel, for the novel problematically portrays trafficking as a crime merely imported, and caused exclusively by foreign others. Having said that, though Muna initially seems to fit the 'ideal' human trafficking victim category (as female, non-white, young, sexualised, and so on), her vengeful behaviour means that she too is a victim that problematises this stereotype too.

It is the linguistic analysis of this Muna-focalised novel that illuminates the domestic slavery victim. The Muna-focalised narration's reporting of speech is telling; the chosen modes of presentation suggest lack of control over those talking, but also cast distance over the abusive way in which others speak to/about her, an ironic light over what it is that those talking actually say, and even show her building up courage for her revenge to come. The naming strategies reveal Muna's uncomfortable closeness to, but also fear of, her captors, and an inescapable distance from others who might actually be able to give her help; besides, the tragedy of the novel is that Muna is unable to seek help, and cannot articulate the sentences she has taught herself, telling someone her name and what has happened to her. Her not trusting others not only left her isolated, but also contributed to turning her into a predator herself.

---

[11] In line with Christie's (1986) criminological theory, the ideal victim is a weak, blameless, and respectable individual, who falls victim to an ideal offender who is large, evil, and completely unknown to them.

The metaphors employed suggest that trafficking isolates, dehumanises, and objectifies victims, and the transitivity that the responsibility for the crimes Muna endures is down to the collective rather than an individual. Last, when vengeful, the language distances Muna from her violent actions, and suggests not only a coping mechanism and diminished responsibility, but also inevitability for what she eventually has come to do, even if she loses some reader sympathy as a result. Ultimately, Muna proves to be a complex trafficking victim, something that may well be true of all trafficking victims, in fact. She is what Forster [1927] (1987) would describe as a 'round' character, as in constructed by a range of qualities and not just one. Abusive experiences of the kind the novel portrays create not only non-ideal victims, but also uncertainty over the extent to which they need to be liable for what they come to do, an uncertainty that perhaps bears links to the novel's own ambiguous, and somewhat mysterious, cellar 'darkness'.

References

Beyer, C. (2018). 'In the suitcase was a boy': Representing Transnational Child Trafficking in Contemporary Crime Fiction. In C. Gregoriou, ed., *Representations of Transnational Human Trafficking: Present-Day News Media, True Crime, and Fiction*. Houndmills: Palgrave, pp. 89–115.

Christie, N. (1986). The Ideal Victim. In E. A. Fattah, ed., *From Crime Policy to Victim Policy*. London: Palgrave Macmillan, pp. 17–30.

Ekers, M., & Loftus, A. (2008). The Power of Water: Developing Dialogues between Foucault and Gramsci. *Environment and Planning D: Society and Space*, 26(4), 698.

Forster, E. M. [1927] (1987). *Aspects of the Novel*. Harmondsworth: Penguin.

Fowler, R. (1977). *Linguistics and the Novel*. London: Methuen.

Gramsci, A. (1971). *Selections from the Prison Notebooks*. Trans. Quintin Hoare and Geoffrey Nowell-Smith. New York: International Publishers.

Gregoriou, C. (2007). *Deviance in Contemporary Crime Fiction*. Basingstoke: Palgrave.

(2011). *Language, Ideology and Identity in Serial Killer Narratives*. London: Routledge.

Gregoriou, C., & Ras, I. (2018a). Representations of Transnational Human Trafficking: A Critical Review. In C. Gregoriou, ed., *Representations of Transnational Human Trafficking: Present-Day News Media, True Crime, and Fiction*. Houndmills: Palgrave, pp. 1–24.

(2018b). 'Call for purge on the people traffickers': An Investigation into British Newspapers' Representation of Transnational Human Trafficking, 2000–2016. In C. Gregoriou, ed., *Representations of Transnational Human Trafficking: Present-Day News Media, True Crime, and Fiction*. Houndmills: Palgrave, pp. 25–59.

Hall, S. L. (2015). The Uncanny Sacrifice: Sex Trafficking in Chris Abani's Becoming Abigail. *Critique – Bolingbroke Society*, 56(1), 42–60.

Hartlaub, J. (2016). Review: *The Cellar*, by Minette Walters. Book Reporter. www.bookreporter.com/reviews/the-cellar-0 (accessed April 2022).

Jeffries, L. (2010). *Critical Stylistics: The Power of English*. Basingstoke: Palgrave.

Kelly, L. (2005). 'You can find anything you want': A Critical Reflection on Research on Trafficking in Persons within and into Europe. *International Migration*, 43 (1–2), 235–65.

Kinney, E. (2015). Victims, Villains and Valiant Rescuers: Unpacking Sociolegal Constructions of Human Trafficking and Crimmigration in Popular Culture. In M. J. Guia, ed., *The Illegal Business of Human Trafficking*. Cham: Springer, pp. 87–108.

Lakoff, G., & Johnson, M. (1980). *Metaphors We Live By*. Chicago: University of Chicago Press.

Leech, G., & Short, M. (2007). *Style in Fiction*, 2nd ed. London: Longman.

Mayr, A. (2008). *Language and Power: An Introduction to Institutional Discourse*. London: Continuum.

Short, M. (1988). Speech Presentation, the Novel and the Press. In W. van Peer, ed., *The Taming of the Text*. New York: Routledge, pp. 61–81.

Simpson, P. (1993). *Language, Ideology and Point of View*. London: Routledge.

Szörényi, A. (2016). Expelling Slavery from the Nation: Representations of Labour Exploitation in Australia's Supply Chain. *Anti-Trafficking Review*, 7, 79–96. www.antitraffickingreview.org (accessed April 2022).

Szörényi, A., & Eate, P. (2014). Saving Virgins, Saving the USA: Heteronormative Masculinities and the Securitisation of Trafficking Discourse in Mainstream Narrative Film. *Social Semiotics*, 24(5), 608–22.

Walters, M. (2015). *The Cellar*. London: Penguin.

6 The Linguistic Construction of Political Crimes in Kurdish-Iraqi Sherko Bekas' Poem *The Small Mirrors*

Mahmood Kadir Ibrahim and Ulrike Tabbert

6.1 Introduction

Sherko Bekas was born on May 2, 1940. He is a contemporary Kurdish poet and the son of Faiq Bekas (1905–1948), a well-known poet within traditional Kurdish poetry. Sherko was born in the Kurdistan Region of Iraq and published his first book when he was seventeen years old. Bekas lived in an era (from the inception of modern Iraq up until 1991) when the Kurds had been viewed as being second-class citizens. The discrimination increased during Saddam Hussein's regime and was practiced in the educational and cultural sectors as well as in the job market. In the 1970s, Kurds were displaced, their areas Arabised and destroyed in an attempt to demolish the Kurdish dream of having their own autonomous state. The situation further escalated in 1988 with the destruction of over 3,000 Kurdish villages and more than forty chemical attacks – one even killed over 5,000 Kurds in Halabja (an event discussed later in this chapter) – and 100,000 civilians buried after mass killings.

Bekas started his political activities and his fight against the regime in 1964. He joined the Kurdish Liberation Movement in 1965 and worked for their radio station (The Voice of Kurdistan). He published eighteen collections of poetry in 1968 and two dramas. In seeking 'new aspects and dimensions' for the thus far heavily Arabised Kurdish poetry, Bekas turned to international texts and, for example, translated Hemingway's *The Old Man and the Sea* into Kurdish. He joined the second Kurdish Liberation movement in 1974. After the failure of that movement, the Baath regime exiled him to the middle of Iraq where he stayed for three years.

At a very young age Bekas enlisted in the Peshmerga and worked as a 'party poet' for the Political Union of Kurdistan, a major political party in the Kurdish Regional Government (KRG), a semi-autonomous region in Iraq (Levinson-LaBrosse 2018). He continued writing poetry about his experience as a soldier. On 8 August 1987 in a speech at Folkore Hois ('The Whole Sky of My Borders')[1] he stated that he considered himself the poet 'of all Kurdish nation, the poet of revolution and Peshmergas' and continued by saying, 'I consider myself the mother poet of Kurdistan'. His poetry depicts his political, literary beliefs and cultural community wishes, aims, and preferences (Bekas 2006, p. 16). Thus, his poetry represents ideal, personal, and cultural ideologies.

In 1986, he was exiled by the Iraqi regime to Sweden where he published *The Small Mirrors* in 1987 and *Butterfly Valley* in 1991. In both collections, he mourns the victims of Kurdistan. Following the uprisings in Kurdistan in March 1991, Bekas returned to Iraqi Kurdistan. After the 1991 Gulf War, the already mentioned semi-autonomous Kurdish region KRG was created in northern Iraq and the Iraqi government withdrew its troops. The allied Western troops declared a no-fly zone which was patrolled regularly by aircrafts from the United States, Great Britain, France, and Turkey. In the first regional election, Bekas was elected a member of the Kurdish parliament and became Minister of Culture in the first Kurdish government. In 1993, he resigned from his position because of what he regarded as violations of democracy. All of his work is compiled in one anthology of eight thousand pages.

In 1970, together with other poets and writers of his generation, Bekas founded the Rwanga movement (Fahmi & Dizayi 2018). Rwanga[2] poetry was a reaction to the social and political situation and is considered to be 'one of the fruitful consequences of the socio-political developments' (Fahmi & Dizayi 2018, p. 72). Poets from the Rwanga movement tried to adjust poetry to real life (Naderi 2011, p. 32); thus, it breaks from the traditional rules of rhyme and rhythm to express many beautiful fantasies. Rwanga allows poets to express their vision accurately and overcome the boundaries of language. This was a radical change in Kurdish poetry (Riengard & Mirza 1998, p. 8) because Bekas identified 'new elements in the world literature' and utilised them in his own poetry (Fahmi & Dizayi 2018, p. 73). Bekas stated in an interview that this movement aims to explain that their desires are 'free to discover what has not yet been discovered, to mix local and global languages in new and creative writings, and to support freedom all over the world' (Dhiab 2007, p. 132).

Bekas' poetry expresses sympathy towards the oppressed (Tabari et al. 2015, p. 1299). According to Naderi (2011, p. 12), the movement aims to gain justice

---

[1] The Whole Sky of My Borders, Speech at Folkore Hois, 8 August 1987, www.rudaw.net/english/opinion/12092013.
[2] Rawanga means 'immediate observation' in Kurdish.

and to fight suffering. It deals with realism, which stimulated the founders of the movement because of their interest in the Liberation Movement.

The poets of Rwanga proclaimed in 1970 (Naderi 2011, p. 12):

- Our writing is full of suffering ... Thus we are fighting against suffering.
- Beauty is the center of our writing ... Therefore, it is against ugliness.
- It is free and independent ... Hence it breaks boundaries.
- It is revolutionist ...

Bekas' poetry exemplifies his preoccupation with a range of political problems in his homeland, particularly the rise of the mentioned Kurdish Liberation Movement and his work for their radio station. These aspects are reflected in his poetry, particularly in *The Small Mirrors,* to be examined in this chapter.

Bekas died in exile in Sweden on 4 August 2013.

Many of his poems emphasise the importance of poetry as a powerful weapon to pursue global recognition of Kurdish culture and rights. Political attempts to oppress Bekas, as mentioned by Bachtyar Ali (Bekas 2019), failed. On the contrary, his tireless work for the Kurdish people and against oppression was recognised by him being honoured with the Swedish Tucholsky Award in 1988.

6.2 Bekas' Poetry and *The Small Mirrors*

Beka's work is widespread and well-known beyond the borders of his homeland, which allows for studying his oeuvre in several languages because some of his works have been translated into Arabic, Italian, Swedish, French, German, and English. He has read his poetry in Sweden, Denmark, Norway, Germany, Switzerland, Austria, the United Kingdom, Russia, and Italy, where he was named an honorary citizen of Milan. He paid a visit to the United States in 1990 and has a proven international reputation for his literary works.

His poetry is mainly studied from the perspective of literary criticism (Abdulqadir 2019; Ali 2009; Darwish & Salih 2019; Fahmi & Dizayi 2018; Mala 2012; Mohammad & Mira 2018; Muhammed 2001; Omer 2011; Tabari et al. 2015). These studies reveal the different techniques Bekas uses in his writings to depict his political and social situation. The present author (Ibrahim 2018), however, attempted a Critical Stylistics perspective to primarily reveal ideological meaning in Bekas' texts and is thus the first to apply Critical Stylistics (Jeffries 2010) to Kurdish poetry.

The Small Mirrors/Awena buchkalakan is a collection of Bekas' poems published over a period of two years (1987–1988) in Kurdish and European magazines. Most of the poems now belonging to the collection of *The Small Mirrors* were published for the first time only in 2006, namely, in the second volume of Bekas' *Diwan* (2006). This collection is characterised by 'exceptional aesthetic value, unparalleled facility with words, a poetry that is emotionally, historically, cognitively, and existentially accessible to the public through its rich yet simple everyday language' (Sharifi & Ashouri 2013). In *The Small Mirrors*, Bekas depicts the war in Kurdistan and its victims. Victims of war (as individuals and as a group, even if they are not regarded as victims of genocide) can rightfully claim victimhood status (Van Wijk 2013). How Bekas depicts them and the respective offenders sheds light on his (if not the Kurds') ideological perspective on these atrocities, which are most effectively revealed by using the framework of Critical Stylistics (Jeffries 2010).

In order to present a Critical Stylistics analysis with the aim of detecting ideological meaning in Bekas' texts, we focus on the following extract from *The Small Mirrors*. The text was translated by one of the present authors who is a native speaker of Kurdish. For a more comprehensive analysis of Bekas' *The Small Mirrors* we refer the reader to Ibrahim (2018); for an analysis of Bekas' poem *Snow* the reader is invited to follow up with Ibrahim (2016).

Example 1: Extract from The Small Mirrors (Bekas 2006, pp. 651–652)

xanûyek juriyêkî liyê mird	A room of a house died
le prseda çawî giyêrrra	in the consolation it looked
bo jûrekanî drawsiyê	for the neighbouring rooms
eweyi neydî	those whom it did not see
eweyi nehat	those who did not come
lenaw dlêyi pencereyda bû bergriyê!	became, in the heart of window, a knot!
gerrrekî malêyêk kujra	A house of a neighbourhood is killed
le prseda çawî giyêrrra	in the consolation
bo rriyê û ban û ,	It looked for the roads
bo gerrrekî em law ula	for this and that neighbourhood
eweyi neydî	those whom it did not see
eweyi nehat	those who did not come
le naw dlêyi ber heywan û serkolaên û gorrrepaniya bû be griyê!	in the heart of the courtyard and district! became a nob
axir xo min kurdistanm	At the end I am Kurdistan
leyek tirûkeyi çawa bû	It was in a blink of an eye
<u>piyênc hezar kanîyi liyê kujra</u>	<u>Five thousand springs of it are killed</u>
<u>piyênc hezar rezî liyê xinika</u>	<u>Five thousand fruits of it are suffocated</u>
<u>piyênc hezar şî'rî liyê kujra</u>	<u>Five thousand poems of it are killed</u>
piyênc, piyênc, piyênc, piyênc,...	Five five five five,...
wa şeş mange le prsedaye mewlewîm	It has been six months since my Malawe is in consolation
<u>dar be darm guyê heléexa</u>	<u>Tree eavesdrop for tree*</u>
<u>berd be berdm sorax ekaw</u>	

şax be şaxm çaw egiyêrrriyê	Stone search for stone*
eweyi dûkelêyi cergmî nasî û nehat	Mountain look for mountain*
eweyi nemdî	Those who recognise the smoke of my
çon leber çawî em miyêjuwe sk	offspring and did not come, those I did not see
sutawem	How for the sake of my abdomen-burnt
rreş, rreş, rreş, rreş	history do not turn
danagerrriyê !	black, black, black, black!
kotelê	Sculpture

In this chapter, we particularly focus on the linguistic construction of victims in *The Small Mirrors*, given that perpetrators are mentioned only implicitly. We argue that offenders are nevertheless present due to a binary opposition between victims and perpetrators. We use the tools of Critical Stylistics (Jeffries 2010) combined with Kövecses' (2018) developed and expanded version of Lakoff and Johnson's (2003) Conceptual Metaphor Theory (see Chapters 2 and 3 in this volume) to explore the construction of victims and its impact on the construction of the unmentioned offenders.

Critical Stylistics is a means to identify ideological meaning in texts by offering a framework of ten textual conceptual functions performed by texts (see Table 6.1). Under each of these functions Jeffries (2010) groups 'formal realisations' which can be looked for in texts in order to systematically analyse a text. This allows for rigour and replicability of the analysis, which is not only a principle of any stylistic analysis but particularly important when it comes to ideological meaning as it allows for the analyst to avoid bias and to prevent criticism that the analysis proves only pre-fabricated results.

Jeffries takes Halliday's (1971) three metafunctions of language (textual, ideational, interpersonal) as a starting point and argues that ideology 'enters the picture ... where these ideational processes in texts produce worlds which have values attached to them' (Jeffries 2015b, p. 384)**.** These values need to be explored and extracted in order to detect ideological meaning. Table 6.1 lists and explains the ten textual-conceptual functions from Critical Stylistics.[3]

In the following sections we analyse the extract from *The Small Mirrors* (Example 1) using all ten textual-conceptual functions and explain how victims are constructed and how their construction impacts on the construction of the not explicitly mentioned offenders. As the ten textual-conceptual functions often interlock, it is sometimes necessary for the sake of argument to briefly mention findings from other textual-conceptual functions. Given the short extract from the poem as well as space constraints, we occasionally pair two of the ten textual-conceptual functions and discuss them together. To make it easier for

---

[3] For a more in-depth introduction to Critical Stylistics, refer to Jeffries (2010).

Table 6.1. *The tools of Critical Stylistics and their conceptual categories*

Conceptual category/textual function	Analytical tool/formal realisations
Naming and Describing	The choice of nouns to signify a referent; nominalisation; the construction of noun phrases with pre-/post-modification to identify a referent
Equating and Contrasting	Equivalence (parallel structure), antonymy, and opposition (Jeffries 2015b)
Representing Actions/States and Events	Transitivity and verb voice
Enumerating and Exemplifying	Three-part lists to imply completeness, without being comprehensive (Jeffries 2010, p. 73) and four-part lists (indicating hyponymous and meronymous sense relation), apposition
Prioritising	Transforming grammatical constructions: clefting, passive and active voice, subordination, and syntactic structure
Negation	The construction of negated meaning (Nahajec 2009)
Assuming and Implying	Presupposition and implicature
Hypothesising	Modality
Presenting Other's Speech and Thought	Speech and thought presentation
Constructing Time and Space	Choice of tense, adverb of time, deixis

Adapted from Tabbert 2015, pp. 45f.

the reader to follow, we adapted the order of the ten textual-conceptual functions in Table 6.1 to the order they will be examined in this chapter.

6.2.1 Naming, Describing, and Equating Victims

In this section, we present the findings related to the textual-conceptual functions of Naming and Describing as well as Equating and Contrasting. Due to the complexity of even such a short passage like Example 1, we would like to zoom in on three lines from Example 1 to start with:

Example 2 (extract from Example 1)
Five thousand springs of it are killed
Five thousand fruits of it are suffocated
Five thousand poems of it are killed

Example 2 provides evidence for Bekas' preference for parallelism as not only do all three lines share the same syntactic structure (subject–predicator) but also, within the subject slot, the three noun phrases consist of almost exactly the same words (same pre- and postmodifier, only the three head nouns differ ['springs', 'fruits', and 'poems']). However, although the semantics of the three head nouns differ, their plural form is similar. Further, verb tense (present) and verb voice (passive) are identical in all three lines with 'killed' being repeated as if to girdle 'suffocated', both participles belonging to the semantic field of 'dying', although 'to kill' portrays the act from an offender's perspective, whereas 'to suffocate' brings in a victim's perspective.

Parallelism is additionally present in the fact that in all three lines the actors of these three material action intention processes (Simpson 1993) are absent. The people responsible for the killing and suffocating remain unmentioned. This, however, does not mean that these three lines provide no information about them. On the contrary, the construction of victims of crime always simultaneously presents the respective offenders based on a binary opposition between victim and offender (the effect of which has been discussed by Jančaříková [2013] and Tabbert [2015, 2016])

Answering the question of how the victims (and thus the respective offenders) are constructed brings back the aforementioned parallelism. As noted, only the semantics of the three head nouns differ, which leads to a heavy foregrounding of the meanings of these three nouns (all having positive connotations). 'Springs', however, can have two different meanings: as sources of water or as one of the four seasons. One of the two present authors, who is a native speaker, argues that the preferred meaning in this context is spring in the sense of one of the four seasons. Therefore, 'springs' as one of nature's seasons and 'fruits' as one of nature's products associate 'poems' with nature in a prosodic sense relation. Although poems are man-made and thus only indirectly created by nature, the parallelism the noun 'poems' occurs in aligns it with the semantic category of nature and its products. Additionally, the noun 'poems' brings with it connotations of art and expression which extend onto 'springs' and 'fruits' and thus describes the killing as an act of destroying nature, beauty, and art. It constructs the killings also as affecting (artistic) expression and as such touches upon the freedom of expression and the topic of censorship.

Killing people has become a destruction of nature itself by means of the strategies employed to name the victims and thus enlarges the dimension of the atrocities as they concern mankind in its entirety. What underlines this is the postmodifying prepositional phrase 'of it', meaning there are many more people affected through bereavement, mourning the death of their loved ones. This links with the notion of 'indirect victimisation' (Shapland & Hall 2007, p. 179) and means that if a person falls victim to a crime, family and friends are affected as well, arguably even more so in case the victim suffers fatal injuries.

To fully grasp the meaning of the three foregrounded head nouns, their metaphorical use needs to be examined given the fact that in their literal meaning they denote inanimate ('fruits', 'poems') or even abstract ('springs') objects. What links them to humans is, in the case of 'springs', that the four seasons are in fact a man-made concept to understand changes in nature over the course of a year with time also being a human concept. 'Fruits' with a primarily reproductive purpose for nature itself are used by humans as food for their bodies, whereas 'poems' are an artistic product and as such regarded as nourishment for the human soul. It is through these multi-layered relationships between the three head nouns as well as their individual meanings that all three are metaphorically used to name the victims of these atrocities. The metaphor does not stop here, however, but extends onto the offenders and, in terms of transitivity choices, the actors of the three material action processes. The absent actors in their anonymity have not merely killed human beings and thus a part of nature but with it also killed nature itself, which, in conclusion, ostracises them from nature by making them in fact enemies of the living.

Another example further illustrates the importance of Bekas' naming strategies for the presentation of ideological meaning:

Example 3 (extract from Example 1)
A room of a house died
...
A house of a neighbourhood is killed

These two clauses consist exclusively of subject and predicator and show a parallel syntactic structure which we will be dealing with in the following section. As only little information as to the number of constituents is provided, this brings about the cooperation principle, in this case the maxim of quantity (Grice 1975), meaning how much information is needed to make these lines informative. This leads to graphological foregrounding of these two lines. In this section we focus on the two noun phrases exclusively because we are still examining naming choices. Note that these two lines do not appear next to each other in the poem but are separated by six lines.

By naming the victims in relation to urban structure, these two lines add a different notion in comparison to the nature theme mentioned in regard to Example 2. A house and a neighbourhood are man-made and serve not only to accommodate people but to create a living space and structure. Here, families raise their children, friendships are built and nourished, acquaintances are maintained. Illness and other negative experiences are combatted, creating love and solidarity. Both noun phrases in their consecutive order zoom out from the smallest unit (a room in a house) to the larger unit (a neighbourhood). Bekas uses a metonymic relationship between the three nouns (room, house, neighbourhood) to broaden the dimension of destruction. By not mentioning any specifics about the neighbourhood, the reader is able to associate with it by drawing on schematic knowledge and thus bringing in the reader's own neighbourhood, which increases immediacy and proximity of the killings as well as their devastating nature as it is not only a killing of individuals.

6.2.2 Presenting Actions, States, and Events

This section starts with a further exploration of Example 3, this time with a focus on verb choice. 'Died' and 'is killed' are two material actions (arguably so in the case of 'died'), both factive verbs with the emphasis on the result. However, 'died' might be arguably regarded as a supervention process in this context, which means that an actor and thus a culprit is not necessarily needed. If this argument is followed through, it underlines that 'room' is regarded an animate entity as the verb choices that follow in these six lines demonstrate:

> **Example 4 (extract from Example 1)**
> A room of a house died
> in the consolation it looked
> for the neighbouring rooms
> those whom it did not see
> those who did not come
> became, in the heart of window, a knot!

The verbs 'looked for', 'did not see', and 'did not come', alongside 'died', all lead the reader to expect animate entities when instead we find 'a room' and 'the neighbouring rooms' in the noun slots. The verbs 'to look for' and 'see' are mental processes of perception, usually carried out by people. The verb 'to come' is material action intention, an act of movement and changing position which a room is usually incapable to do. In Example 4, however, 'a room' is carrying out these perception and action processes which deviate from the norm.

Further, this room is being described as in need of consolation, which entails that 'a room' has human emotions. Such deviations are highly foregrounding and allow us to understand that 'a room' and 'neighbouring rooms' are naming choices for people, in fact, victims of the killings. By naming them in relation to urban structure, Bekas achieves proximity in the perception of these atrocities, and, furthermore, he is able to construct those affected as innocent victims, which aligns with Christie's (1986) notion of ideal victims. Ideal victims are weak, sick, either very young or very old, are carrying out a respectable project at the time of crime, have no personal relationship with the offender, and cannot be blamed for being attacked. Such an ideal victim, for example, is the character 'Little Red Riding Hood' from the same-named fairy tale (Walklate 2007, p. 28). Victims of international crimes, however, 'face much more difficulty in publicizing their fate and consequently "benefiting" from their status as victim' (Van Wijk 2013, p. 159). This is particularly relevant here as the Iraq-Kurdish conflict is a very complex one with no clearly carved good/bad dichotomy and thus goes against Van Wijk's (2013) criteria, according to which 'potential [victim]-status givers' prefer 'comprehensible' conflicts that have a unique selling point, 'have a limited time span', and are 'well-timed'. Further, 'domestic policies, geopolitical interests, accessibility to the region and the possibility of donors identifying with the victims' (2013) are prerequisites for a conflict to attract public attention and for those victims to be perceived as 'ideal'. All this is absent from the Iraq-Kurdish conflict because at that time media coverage and human rights groups were not allowed to watch and report the conflict and its results. Therefore, the conflict continued and left thousands of civilian victims, which Bekas writes about.

6.2.3 *Enumerating and Prioritising*

In this section we return to Example 2 from above and examine it from a different perspective, namely, how information in these three lines is prioritised and how these three lines further provide an example of enumeration, namely, a three-part list that suggests completeness.

Prioritising can happen by means of syntactic structure or by means of transformation as, for example, by changing verb voice (from active to passive or vice versa). Imagine the first phrase would read, ' [He/she/they] killed five thousand of its springs.' In such a phrase, the main focus would be on the actors 'He/she/they', whereas the victims because of their object position would remain in the background. By transforming the phrase into passive verb voice, the victims become a priority because they are now to be found in a subject position. The cognitive effect of this is of particular interest for cognitive grammarians (Giovanelli & Harrison 2018, pp. 44ff.; Langacker 1991). They would describe the cognitive effect of such transformation in relation to the principle of figure–ground, namely, that a figure in the foreground is set against a less important background. In other words, passive can be used to foreground the recipient of an action, in our case the victims. Following from their subject position, the victims are being regarded as a 'figure' against the ground of the (absent) offenders who would if mentioned be found in an object position. Cognitive grammar in contrast to systemic-functional grammar (Halliday 1971) focuses on cognition and thus text perception, whereas Halliday's grammar explores meaning in context as well as interpretative effects of texts (Giovanelli & Harrison 2018, pp. 5f.). One could also regard both as two different ways of expressing the same experiential concept. As Critical Stylistics, the framework applied in this chapter, is based on Hallidayan systemic-functional grammar, this discussion of prioritised meaning allows for a short detour to explain the different approaches the two grammars take and how close they actually are when it comes to the textual-conceptual function of prioritising. Some would even argue they are, in fact, the same.

As transformation into passive voice allows for the actors to be omitted, Bekas provides the reader with an opportunity to fill in the picture of the seemingly missing offenders by drawing on image schemas readers have about atrocities committed by a government and carried out by anonymous offenders. A Western reading of this poem immediately brings to mind the Third Reich and its countless offenders carrying out orders given by a Nazi government or, not too long ago, the Balkan war. Such image schemas readers possess allow for the poem to be understood in various cultures as individual cultural backgrounds bring about individual schemas of politically motivated atrocities. This transformation simultaneously allows for the numeral 'five thousand' to stand at the beginning of the phrase, which evokes negative connotations because of its link with the five thousand murdered in Halabja by the chemical gas bombardments in March 1988.

Further, the repetition of 'five thousand' and even more often of 'five' (see Example 1 for context) enhances these negative connotations. The numeral 'five' is mentioned seven times in just four lines. Hence this repetition is highly foregrounding. However, it can be understood only against the cultural context of the poem.

The already mentioned parallel structure of the three lines in Example 2 further allows for the three differing head nouns 'springs', 'fruits', and 'poems' to appear as an enumeration, in fact, a three-part list suggesting completeness. It is this rhetorical completeness that leads to the interpretation that these three nouns name the victims comprehensively and ties in with what was discussed in Section 6.2.1 of this chapter and the interpretation outlined there.

6.2.4 *Negating, Implying, and Assuming*

Negation raises the possibility of presence (Nahajec 2012, p. 39; 2014) and produces a 'hypothetical version of reality' (Jeffries 2010, p. 107). This is particularly powerful as it allows for the construction of two alternative scenarios, one that is actually happening and another that could be happening. What could happen but does not is presented in the following two instances of negation, realised by means of a negative particle ('not'):

> those whom it did <u>not</u> see
> those who did <u>not</u> come
> Extract from Example 4

Note that these two lines are repeated in the context of 'neighbouring rooms' looking for 'roads' who did not come.

We have already established in Section 6.2.2 that the two negated verbs 'see' and 'come' are processes of perception and action, usually assigned to animate entities. In Example 1 these processes are carried out by 'a room' and we have discussed how this deviation from expectation not only foregrounds the verbs but allows for the interpretation that 'a room' and 'neighbouring rooms' are in fact naming choices for victims.

This extends to the second instance where the focus zooms out from 'a house of a neighbourhood' to 'neighbourhood' and 'roads', adding these nouns/noun phrases to the group of naming choices for victims.

In this section, we take the argument further by examining the role of negation in this context. Negation, as Nahajec (2012, p. 35) argues, is presuppositional and produces implied meaning. We therefore discuss the two textual-conceptual functions of 'negating' as well as 'implying and assuming' here together. Whereas implicature arises from flouting cooperation maxims (Grice 1975), 'pragmatic presuppositions reside in the shared conventions of language use' (Simpson 1993, p. 128).

Negation in Example 4 pragmatically presupposes that the reader as discourse participant expects the house/neighbourhood/roads to be there, to be visible and be able to 'come' when in fact they cannot anymore because they died/were killed. Negation then has a further, implied level of meaning that arises from deliberately not observing the cooperative principles (Grice 1975). To fully grasp the implied meaning here means to take the metaphorical naming choices for victims into account, based on the conceptual metaphor PEOPLE ARE URBAN STRUCTURE. By using a man-made structure of a 'neighbourhood', the victims are no longer regarded as individual, separate casualties but are instead tied together structurally, through their relations with one another. They build a complex system of interrelations because of family relations, friendships, and acquaintances like roads running through a neighbourhood, connecting one house and its rooms with another. The killing thus not only becomes meaningful in terms of the already mentioned indirect victimisation (where family and friends are affected when somebody falls victim to a crime) but gives rise to the notion of a systematic killing, a deliberate attempt to erase an ethnic group and thus constructs the crime close to the notion of genocide.

6.2.5. *Hypothesising and Presenting Others' Speech and Thoughts*

It can be argued whether modality is able to produce 'a hypothetical alternative reality' (Jeffries 2015a, p. 165) comparable to negation as outlined in the previous section, or is rather related to point of view in that it expresses a speaker's/writer's opinion about or attitude towards a proposition (Simpson 1993, p. 47). Whichever argument is followed, a closer examination of Example 1 from *The Small Mirrors* reveals no instance of modality. All sentences are categorical as the following example illustrates:

Example 5 (extract from Example 1)
At the end I am Kurdistan

This example not only is of relevance to illustrate Bekas' preference for categorical and unmodalised assertions in Example 1 but also provides the only evidence in this extract for the presence of a first-person narrator and thus speech presentation. It is arguably a presentation of speech rather than thought as the poet foremost speaks these words and intends them to be published rather than merely thinking them.

This sentence further illustrates that the entire passage is actually Direct Speech, which enhances the immediacy of what is being said, and the passage, if not the entire poem, becomes Bekas' personalised and individual speech. As such, Bekas acts as a contemporary witness to the crimes that happened in Kurdistan. In relation to crimes of the state (as well as corporate crimes; see Chapter 14 in this book), Cohen (2003, pp. 546f.) acknowledges the problem 'that the state is not an actor and that individual criminal responsibility cannot be identified', leading to a common perception that the resultant action is not '"really" crime'. Cohen goes as far as to state that 'the political discourse of the atrocity is ... designed to hide its presence from awareness'. Bekas' poem in its political background is written to resist hegemonic discourse, and it apparently takes the weight of the author's own prominence to raise awareness of a counter-hegemonic narration of events. One means to achieve this is Direct Speech. In a culture of denial (Cohen 2003, p. 548) with regard to institutionalised crime, Bekas acknowledges the anonymity of the offenders by not mentioning them explicitly. However, the offenders are nevertheless present and are constructed by means of their binary opposition to the respective victims.

6.2.6   Representing Time, Space, and Society

We wish to dwell on Example 5 and talk about identification by means of deixis. Deixis is regarded as a linguistic pointer (Semino 1997, p. 32) to time, space, or social relations, among others. In Example 5, Bekas achieves immediacy not only by means of Direct Speech (see the previous section) but also by means of temporal deixis (present tense) as well as personal deixis (personal pronoun 'I') and a relational process intensive. A closer examination of Example 1 for such linguistic pointers reveals a repeated use of 'it' as a third-person pronoun. This appears to be of relevance as we have established earlier that 'room' and 'house of a neighbourhood' are in fact naming choices for people, namely, the victims.

As for pointers of temporal reference, it appears that Example 5 marks a shift from past to present tense, which carries on throughout the subsequent Example 2. These time pointers by means of verb tense separate the killings in the past from the present impact they have on Kurdistan and thus the Kurds, as a people spread across several countries (Turkey, Iran, Iraq, and Syria) and without a yet internationally recognised state of their own. By means of spatial deixis ('Kurdistan') Bekas refers to a foremost geographical and cultural area but also brings in the notion of ongoing efforts for independence. This again underlines the importance of detecting values attached to ideational or world-building processes, which are the carriers of ideological meaning.

6.3   Conclusion

The study has found out that all the textual conceptual functions are consistent in confirming the overall argument that the construction of the victims is due to a binary opposition between the victims and the perpetrators, and the offenders are only implicitly represented.

Bekas avoids mentioning the offenders and does not state specific victims. By doing so, Bekas leaves the slot empty for the reader to fill in by drawing an image of the victims and the atrocities carried out by anonymous offenders under government order. The perpetrators are constructed as cruel and the victims as ideal, both inextricably bound together in an unavoidable relationship. However, the victims face much more difficulty in receiving a global recognition of their fate, and consequently the Iraq-Kurdish conflict is a very complex one with no clear good/bad dichotomy.

Similarly, the ten textual conceptual functions are compatible in the construction of a systematic and wide victimisation in an attempt to erase an ethnic group. The victimisation involves not only killing people but also destroying nature. This constructs crime as close to the notion of genocide.

The complexity of state crime is clear in the data where the offenders are not mentioned, and Bekas resists hegemonic discourse by manipulating his wide reputation to raise awareness of a counter-hegemonic narration of events. In addition, *The Small Mirrors* shows that Bekas longs for an independent state for the Kurds.

References

Abdulqadir, B. (2019). Alienation in Sherko Bekas' Poetry, *Chair Human* as a Model. Arabic Language Department, College of Education/Shaqlawa, Salahaddin University.

Ali, A. (2009). *The Structure of Artistic Imagery in Sherko Bekas' Poems*. Sulaymanya: Koya University.

Bekas, S. (2006). *Awena buchkalakan (The Small Mirrors)*. In Dewane Sherko Bekas, *Barge Dwam (The Diwan of Sherko Bekas)*, vol. 2. Iraq: Kurdistan.

(2019). *Geheimnisse der Nacht pflücken: Mit einem Vorwort von Bachtyar Ali. Gedichte*. Berlin: Unionsverlag.

Christie, N. (1986). The Ideal Victim. In E. A. Fattah, ed., *From Crime Policy to Victim Policy*. Basingstoke: Macmillan Press, pp. 17–30.

Cohen, S. (2003). Human Rights and Crimes of the State: The Culture of Denial. In E. McLaughlin, J. Muncie, & G. Hughes, eds., *Criminological Perspectives: Essential Readings*. London: Sage Publications, pp. 542–560.

Darwish, N., & Salih, S. (2019). A Comparative Study of Soul's Alienation in Poe's *The Raven* and Bekas's *The Cemetery of Lanterns*. *Journal of University of Garmian*, 6(1), 510–516.

Dhiab, S. (2007). Reality Precedes Poetic Vision (trans. Chenwa Hayek). *Masarat Magazine*.

Fahmi, I. M., & Dizayi, S. (2018). The Thematic Presence of *The Waste Land* in Sherko Bekas' *Jingl*. *University-Erbil Scientific Journal*, 1, 71–90.

Giovanelli, M., & Harrison, C. (2018). *Cognitive Grammar in Stylistics*. London: Bloomsbury.

Grice, H. P. (1975). Logic and Conversation. In P. Cole & J. Morgan, eds., *Syntax and Semantics, vol. 3: Speech Acts*. New York: Academic Press, pp. 41–58.

Halliday, M. A. K. (1971). Linguistic Function and Literary Style: An Inquiry into the Language of William Golding's *The Inheritors*. In S. Chatman, ed., *Literary Style: A Symposium*. London: Oxford University Press, pp. 330–368.

Ibrahim, M. (2016). A Critical Stylistic Analysis of Sherko Bekas' Snow. Paper presented at the Annual Conference of the Poetics and Linguistics Association (PALA). www.pala.ac.uk/uploads/2/5/1/0/25105678/ibrahim_mahmood.pdf.

(2018). The Construction of the Speaker and Fictional World in The Small Mirrors: Critical Stylistic Analysis. Doctoral thesis, University of Huddersfield. http://eprints.hud.ac.uk/id/eprint/34586/.

Jančaříková, R. (2013). Simplification in the British Press: Binary Oppositions in Crime Reports. *Discourse and Interaction*, 6(2), 15–28.

Jeffries, L. (2010). *Critical Stylistics: The Power of English*. Basingstoke: Palgrave Macmillan.

(2015a). Critical Stylistics. In V. Sotirova, ed., *A Companion to Stylistics*. London: Bloomsbury, pp. 157–176.

(2015b). Language and Ideology. In L. Cummings & N. Braber, eds., *Introducing Language and Linguistics*. Cambridge: Cambridge University Press, pp. 379–405.

Kövecses, Z. (2018). Metaphor in Media Language and Cognition: A Perspective from Conceptual Metaphor Theory. *Lege Artis*, 3(1), 124–141.

Lakoff, G., & Johnson, M. (2003). *Metaphors We Live By*. Chicago: University of Chicago Press.

Langacker, R. W. (1991). *Foundations of Cognitive Grammar: Descriptive Application*, vol. 2. Stanford, CA: Stanford University Press.

Levinson-LaBrosse, A. M. (2018). A Portfolio of Kurdish Poetry. *World Literature Today*, 92(4), 42.

Mala, A. (2012). *Binbest le şî'rî şêrku bêkesda û çend babetêkî tir (Bases in Bekas' Poetry and Some Other Subjects)*. Avda: Université de Castilla la Mancha-Espagne.

Mohammad, M. D. A., & Mira, A. M. R. (2018). Sherko Bekas's Rebellion Poetic Language in the Volume of: *Now a Girl Is My Country*. *International Journal of Kurdish Studies*, 4(2), 534–561.

Muhammed, S. H. (2001). Alienation in Sherko Bekas' Poetry. MA thesis, University of Sulaimani.
Naderi, L. (2011). *An Anthology of Modern Kurdish Literature: A Short Study of Modern Kurdish Poetry in Southern Kurdistan*. Sanandaj: University of Kurdistan.
Nahajec, L. (2009). Negation and the creation of implicit meaning in poetry. *Language and Literature*, 18(2), 109–129.
   (2012). Evoking the Possibility of Presence: Textual and Ideological Effects of Linguistic Negation in Written Discourse. PhD thesis, University of Huddersfield.
   (2014). Negation, Expectation and Characterisation: Analysing the Role of Negation in Character Construction in *To Kill a Mockingbird* (Lee 1960) and *Stark* (Elton 1989). In S. Chapman & B. Clark, eds., *Pragmatic Literary Stylistics*. London: Palgrave, pp. 111–131.
Omer, S. (2011). Realism in Bekas' Poetry. MA thesis, University of Sulaimani.
Riengard, & Mirza, S. (1998). *A Journey through Poetic Kurdistan, The Secret Diary of a Rose*, 2nd ed., by Sherko Bekas, trans. Riengard and Shirwan Mirza. Suleimani: Khak Press.
Semino, E. (1997). *Language and World Creation in Poems and Other Texts*. Harlow: Longman.
Shapland, J., & Hall, M. (2007). What Do We Know about the Effects of Crime on Victims? *International Review of Victimology*, 14, 175–217.
Sharifi, A., & Ashouri, A. (2013). A Tribute to Sherko Bekas, the Kurdish Poet of the Century. www.rudaw.net/english/opinion/12092013.
Simpson, P. (1993). *Language, Ideology and Point of View*. London: Routledge.
Tabari, P., Parsa, S., & Gozashti, M. (2015). Humanism in Intellectual Style of Sherko Bekas, the Contemporary Poet from Iraqi Kurdistan. *International Journal of Review in Life Sciences*, 5, 1299–1303.
Tabbert, U. (2015). *Crime and Corpus: The Linguistic Representation of Crime in the Press*. Amsterdam: John Benjamins.
   (2016). *Language and Crime: Constructing Offenders and Victims in Newspaper Reports*. London: Palgrave Macmillan.
Van Wijk, J. (2013). Who Is the 'Little Old Lady' of International Crimes? Nils Christie's Concept of the Ideal Victim Reinterpreted. *International Review of Victimology*, 19(2), 159–179.
Walklate, S. (2007). *Imagining the Victim of Crime*. Maidenhead: Open University Press.

7   Stylistic Aspects of Detective Fiction in Translation
The Case of 'The Murders in the Rue Morgue' in Slovenian

Simon Zupan

7.1   Introduction

Translation has played a crucial role in the development of detective fiction. Edgar Allan Poe (1809–1848), often cited as the inventor of the detective story, serves as a good example. In the early 1840s, his detective fiction was virtually unknown outside the United States. Then, in 1846, two plagiarised versions of his detective story 'The Murders in the Rue Morgue' almost simultaneously appeared in two French newspapers, causing a major scandal after it was revealed that their real author was actually Poe himself (Ascari 2007, p. 100). Paradoxically, the bogus authorship contributed to Poe's fame in France, leading to his work being translated into French over the course of the following years. However, this process was important for two other reasons. On the one hand, Poe's stories inspired the development of native French detective fiction, as exemplified by Emile Gaboriau, '[t]he other "founding father" of detective fiction' (Priestman 1990, p. 56), as well as the Série Noire, the most famous and prestigious French detective fiction series, whose advent was at least indirectly connected to Poe (see Rolls 2016). At the same time, Poe's stories increased the popularity of detective fiction in many other countries, such as Russia, Germany, Austria, Norway, Belgium and Japan (see Vines 1999 and further Chapter 8 on adaptations of Sherlock Holmes in Russia and Japan).

The development of crime fiction across cultures raises various questions about the effects of translation on its style, such as the following: How does style travel between languages, cultures and literary systems? What does detective fiction stylistically lose (or gain) in the process of translation? How do the stylistic conventions and constraints of the target language affect the style of the source text? How do stylistic translation shifts influence the reading of detective fiction in the target language? What is the effect of stylistic translation shifts on the reception of detective fiction? Some of these aspects have already been addressed; however, linguistic studies of the style of detective fiction in translation remain relatively scarce given the popularity of the genre. This chapter aims to contribute to filling that void. The study focuses on Edgar Allan Poe's short story 'The Murders in the Rue Morgue' (TMRM hereafter) and its translations in Slovenian. The following two sections, respectively, provide an overview of stylistic studies on translation of detective fiction and present Poe's short story along with its Slovenian translations. The fourth and central part of the chapter comprises a stylistic analysis of an excerpt from the original and two of its translations in Slovenian, followed by concluding remarks.

7.2   Detective Fiction, Stylistics and Translation

Detective fiction has been the subject of scholarly interest for decades. A good illustration is a comprehensive collection of fifty essays on detective fiction from 1946, which, according to its editor, were selected from 'several hundred possible candidates to illustrate the nature and evolution of detective story criticism through the years' (Haycraft 1946, p. 2). Understandably, the volume of research has grown in the meantime, as, for example, is indicated by the *Reference Guide to Mystery and Detective Fiction*, which in 1999 listed almost 800 resources on detective fiction (Bleiler 1999). On the other hand, research on detective fiction in translation has been more limited. The relatively few monographs in this field include three collections of essays (Cadera & Pavić Pintarić 2014; Seago et al. 2014; Rolls et al. 2016) and a volume on the migration of crime fiction between languages, cultures and media by Gregoriou (2017). However, the majority of these publications address translation of crime fiction in general, not specifically the translation of detective fiction. The few exceptions addressing style, detective fiction and translation include Espunya's (2014) examination of the narrative point of view in Spanish translations of Agatha Christie's novel *Third Girl*; Brumme's (2014) chapter about the translation of Austrian conversational style in Wolf Haas's detective novels; Linder's (2000) article on slang in three translations of Raymond Chandler's detective novel *The Big Sleep*; and Bassnett's (2017) study on reception of translated detective fiction. In Slovenia, the situation is not much different. Although crime fiction has been the subject of a few studies (e.g. Zupan & Sosič 2001; Gadpaille 2014), none primarily deals with translation-related aspects of detective fiction, especially not with a stylistic approach.

In spite of the limited amount of research on stylistic aspects of detective fiction in translation, stylistics and translation studies have recently engaged in a rewarding relationship. One of the key authors in the field in the recent two decades has been Boase-Beier, whose monograph *Stylistic Approaches to Translation* (2006) is a standard reference work. Boase-Beier takes stylistics beyond the traditional framework of structuralist stylistics to include the socio-historical and other contexts and cognitive processes involved in literary translation. In addition to the formal properties of texts that had been central to the study of style for a long time, Boase-Beier considers the author and the translator as individuals whose reading and (re)writing depend on a variety of factors (Boase-Beier 2014). An equally intriguing venue has been translational stylistics, a concept introduced by Malmkjær (2004). She claims stylistics has the capacity to analyse any text and explain how readers respond to it, but those analyses fail to delve into the relationship between translations and their source texts because translators shape translations the way they do (Malmkjær 2004, p. 16). By comparing passages from H. C. Andersen's 'The Little Match Girl' in Dutch and its English translation, Malmkjær demonstrates how even modifications of less prominent stylistic features such as grammatical tense or repetitions can significantly alter the effect of the same text in the target language. In translational stylistics, the emphasis lies not so much on a given translator's personal style and their preferences but rather on those elements in the source text that make translators employ particular stylistic elements in the target text (Malmkjær 2006).

Malmkjær's approach to the study of style in translation has since been successfully applied in translational analyses of poetry (Giugliano 2017) and prose (Morini 2014; Douthwaite 2018) and will also be employed in the present chapter.

7.3 Introduction to the Story

'The Murders in the Rue Morgue' (TMRM) is one of Edgar Allan Poe's stories of *ratiocination* (reasoning), first published in 1841. It is often considered the first ever detective story (Fisher 2002; Frank 2003; Cook 2014). The story develops around the double murder of Madame L'Espanaye and her daughter in Rue Morgue in Paris. Its main protagonist is the friend of an unnamed first-person narrator, C. Auguste Dupin, destined to become the prototype of a modern detective, who solves the mystery by using his superior acumen and discovers that the two women were murdered by an orangutan that had escaped its owner, a sailor.

Over the course of a century, the story has appeared in four different Slovenian translations, some of which were reprinted multiple times. Of these four translations, two were published in Slovenian daily newspapers as adaptations (in 1907 and 1963) and two as integral translations in book editions. The first book edition appeared in 1952 and was translated by Zoran Jerin and Igor Šentjurc (Poe 1952; TMRM1 hereafter). The second was included in a collection of Poe's short stories entitled *Zlati hrošč* (The Gold Bug), published in 1960 (Poe, 1960; TMRM2 hereafter); it was translated by Jože Udovič.

Given that the newspaper translations were ephemeral in character, while the translations in book form have been available for decades and have reached considerably more readers, the analysis will primarily focus on TMRM1 and TMRM2. The original English text (TMRM) used in the analysis is the hypertext Raven Edition of *The Works of Edgar Allan Poe* in Project Gutenberg (Poe 2008; hereafter referred to as the Original); hence, page numbers are not provided.

7.4 Comparison of TMRM1 and TMRM2 to the Original

The passage analysed is from the opening part of the story and introduces the reader to the central crime in TRMR, the killing of two women. In addition to being the first mention of the crime, the excerpt represents several stylistic characteristics of the text as a whole. After engaging in a philosophical debate during one of their regular nocturnal strolls, Dupin and the narrator stop to read a newspaper report on a mysterious murder that had taken place in Paris on the same day (Original):

[1] Not long after this, we were looking over an evening edition of the 'Gazette des Tribunaux', when the following paragraphs arrested our attention. [2] 'Extraordinary Murders. [3] – This morning, about three o'clock, the inhabitants of the Quartier St. Roch were aroused from sleep by a succession of terrific shrieks, issuing, apparently, from the fourth story of a house in the Rue Morgue, known to be in the sole occupancy of one Madame L'Espanaye, and her daughter, Mademoiselle Camille L'Espanaye. [4] After some delay, occasioned by a fruitless attempt to procure admission in the usual manner, the gateway was broken in with a crowbar, and eight or ten of the neighbors entered, accompanied by two gendarmes. [5] By this time the cries had ceased; but, as the party rushed up the first flight of stairs, two or more rough voices, in angry contention, were distinguished, and seemed to proceed from the upper part of the house. [6] As the second landing was reached, these sounds, also, had ceased, and everything remained perfectly quiet. [7] The party spread themselves, and hurried from room to room. [8] Upon arriving at a large back chamber in the fourth story, (the door of which, being found locked, with the key inside, was forced open,) a spectacle presented itself which struck every one present not less with horror than with astonishment.'

Let us now compare sentence 1 in the Original with TMRM1 and TMRM2, each followed by my own back-translation into English:

[Original] Not long after this, we were looking over an evening edition of the 'Gazette des Tribunaux', when the following paragraphs arrested our attention.

[TMRM1, 16] Ne dolgo po tem dogodku sva prelistovala večerno izdajo »Gazette des Tribunaux«, kar vzbudi najino pozornost sledeči odstavek:

   Not long after this event we were leafing through an evening edition of the 'Gazette des Tribunaux', when the following paragraph draws our attention:

[TMRM2, 57] Kmalu nato sva pregledala večerno izdajo lista Gazette des Tribunaux, kjer je pritegnil najino zanimanje naslednji članek:
    Soon after this we looked over an evening edition of the paper 'Gazette des Tribunaux', where the following article attracted our interest:

Sentence 1 is Narration, describing the narrator and Dupin's physical action (looking over a newspaper) (Semino & Short 2004, the framework for speech, thought and writing presentation used in this chapter). At first glance, the two translations do not deviate much from the Original. Syntactically, both TMRM1 and TMRM2 comprise a phrase functioning as a time adverbial (not long after this/soon after this), followed by a main clause and a subordinate clause conveying time. Both translations also include the same two propositions as in the Original: the protagonists are reading a newspaper and one article in it attracts their attention (notice the difference between 'when' – temporal – and 'where' – locative); both target texts also retain the original transitive patterns with an anaphoric animate subject (we) in the first clause and an inanimate subject (paragraphs) in the second clause.

However, a detailed examination reveals several stylistic differences between the target texts and the Original. The first appears in the adverbial 'not long after this' (note the comma after this which is omitted in both translations). While this adverbial has an identical structure in both TMRM1 and the Original, its internal logic reverses in TMRM2, where the negated adverb 'not long' is replaced by the affirmative adverb 'soon'. In contrast to the Original, where the negative form requires the reader to take an additional step to establish the time deixis (long and not long), TMRM2 partly interprets and simplifies the Original, sparing the reader that extra mile with an affirmative form of the adverbial. A stylistic shift in the same temporal adverbial can be observed in TMRM1. Unlike the Original, where the point in time is referred to anaphorically with the pronoun in the prepositional phrase 'after *this*', the temporal reference becomes explicit in TMRM1: 'after this *event*'. Specified time deixis means that the reader of TMRM1 is not required to fill in the missing pronominal information; at the same time, however, if admittedly to a limited extend, the reader is deprived of the challenge of thinking like a detective. The reason for explicitation, which by definition refers to the technique of 'making explicit in the target text information that is implicit in the source text' (Klaudy 2011, p. 104), in TMRM1 is not entirely clear, especially since the original leaves the reference deliberately opaque. As TMRM2 shows, the shift is not mandated by the target language. Possibly, the translator feared that the reader would be unable to follow the story and deliberately made the reading easier for them.

It turns out that this is not the only explicitation in sentence 1. Another one appears in the nominal phrase 'an evening edition of the "Gazette des Tribunaux"' in TMRM2. As can be seen from the Original, the narrator refers to the newspaper by its name in French, leaving it to the reader to infer from co-text (the preceding sentence) and the phrasal verb 'look over' that reference is being made to a newspaper. The translator, however, inserts the generic noun 'list' (newspaper) before the French name thus making the reference more explicit. Again, while the reader of the source text has to infer what the title refers to, the reader of TMRM2 is spared that inference. Possibly, this happened for the same reason stated above; it is, however, even more likely that the shift is an example of a common problem in translation: that the act of translation is not based on an accurate reading of the source text but rather on the translator's representation of the source text in their mind (De Beaugrande 1978, p. 25). The problem is that the addition is redundant because – as indicated by the Original and TMRM1 – the narrator need not tell the reader the obvious, possibly underestimating them.

A similar shift appears in relation to the phrase 'the following paragraphs'. In TMRM2, the phrase is translated as 'naslednji članek' ('the following article'), with the singular noun 'article' replacing the Original plural noun 'paragraphs'. This shift does not affect the source text syntactically but has elocutionary repercussions. In the Original, 'paragraphs' functions as a metonymy for the printed words/sentences that drew the narrator and Dupin's attention to the newspaper article as a whole. Evidently, this inference has to be made by the reader, with the figure of speech adding sophistication to the narrator's discourse. In TMRM2, on the other hand, where 'article' replaces 'paragraphs', the metonymy and that extra inferential step are missing. As a result, the reader of TMRM2 is spared one more, admittedly minor, intellectual challenge. In addition, the same shift has another significant stylistic repercussion for TMRM2: it affects the metaphorical meaning of the clause. In the Original, the syntactic pattern of the second clause displays an inanimate grammatical subject ('paragraphs') performing an action ('arrested') on an animate object ('our attention'), creating a metaphorical meaning of the predicator. Poe uses a metaphor to highlight the event that marks the beginning of a criminal investigation for Dupin and the narrator. The plural form of 'paragraphs', emphasising the multitude of individual parts, creates a dramatic effect, strengthened by the verb 'arrest' that fits the context because of its relation to crime and policing. In TMRM2, the metaphor is retained; however, by using a subject in its singular form ('article') and, more importantly, a lexically weaker verb 'pritegniti' (to attract'), which can suggest abrupt physical action but lacks the social connotations of the verb 'arrest', the dramatic effect appears less striking than in the Original. The problem with grammatical number of the subject also affects TMRM1. Although the subject noun from the Original ('paragraph') is retained, it is used in its singular form, causing a similar loss of dramatic effect as in TMRM2. It can further be observed that in contrast to the Original, the translators of TMRM1 used the verb 'vzbudi' (draw) in the present tense. This shift makes the text appear more informal in my English back-translation; however, in Slovenian, the switch in tense in fact has the opposite effect as it is an example of 'narrative' or 'dramatic' present tense, used to add vividness to narrated past events (Toporišič 2000, p. 292–293). The same shift thus also partly compensates for the use of the verb 'vzbudi' (draw) in TMRM1, which lexically and particularly in terms of its connotation is weaker than 'arrest'.

Finally, minor stylistic shifts can also be observed in the translation of the verbal phrase 'were looking over' in sentence 1. In the Original, the progressive aspect is used to emphasise that one action, the casual reading of the newspaper, is suddenly interrupted by another, more important event: learning about the crime. In TMRM1, the same aspect is retained and with it the relationship between the two actions described. The only difference is that the verb 'prelistovati' (to leaf through) replaces the verb phrase 'were looking over', suggesting less engagement in the reading by the two protagonists than in the Original. In TMRM2, on the other hand, present-simple 'sva pregledala' (we looked over) is used. Given that in Slovenian the simple aspect in such context is used to describe completed actions (Toporišič 2000, p. 353), the wording suggests that the narrator and Dupin first read the newspaper in its entirety, and only then focused on the crime, seemingly less surprised and consequently attracted by the news item than in the source text.

As is indicated by the inverted commas, sentence 2 marks the beginning of a verbatim rendition of the text from the 'Gazette des Tribunaux', including its headline, indicating that sentences 2–8 represent Direct Writing[1] (Semino & Short 2004). The quotation is indicated by inverted commas. Although comprising only two words, the translations of the headline in TMRM1 and TMRM2 show that it poses an intriguing translation challenge:

> [Original]: 'Extraordinary Murders.
>
> [TMRM1, 17]: Nenavaden dvojni umor.
> Extraordinary double murder.
>
> [TMRM2, 57]: 'Dva čudna umora.
> Two strange murders.

In English, the headline comprises a simple noun phrase, informing the reader that a violent crime (murder) has taken place. The premodifying adjective 'extraordinary' suggests that the crime deviates from the murder template, constructing it as newsworthy by combining elements of unexpectedness and

---

[1] Admittedly, Direct Writing based on the accounts of multiple witnesses in sentences 2–8 comprises several layers of embedded discourse. However, a preliminary analysis showed that the embedding is not affected by the translations. The adverb 'apparently' from sentence 3 undergoes partial modification in this respect and is discussed below.

superlativity (Bednarek & Caple 2017). It also arouses curiosity on the part of the readers, who probably ask themselves why the murders are classified as 'extraordinary'. Another notable characteristic of the vague phrase[2] is that Poe does not disclose the number of victims or murders in the headline, although he could have used a phrase such as 'double murder'. Instead, the head word 'murders' is in its plural form, allowing two interpretations: one is that the crime left behind two or more victims; the second is double the number of criminal acts. The reader learns the precise facts a few paragraphs later when the two victims are explicitly identified.

In Slovenian, however, the translator cannot follow the Original. In contrast to English, which distinguishes between a singular and plural form, Slovenian also uses the dual as a grammatical number, indicated by the use of pronouns and suffixation, which refer specifically to 'the value of two (or a couple of something)' (Toporišič 2000, p. 271). Given the two murder victims, the translators thus have relatively few options available in Slovenian from a grammatical point of view, and both translations reveal the precise number in the headline already although in different ways: TMRM1 premodifies the noun 'umor' (murder, singular form) with the multiplicative adjective 'dvojni' (double), while TMRM2 premodifies the head noun 'umora' ([two] murders) with the cardinal adjective 'dva' (two). The noun form indicating the dual number in TMRM2 makes the premodifying adjective tautological. As a result of this shift, the Slovenian reader is given the relevant information earlier and thus has an advantage over the reader of the Original.

The meaning of this headline is of further relevance in relation to the title of the story, 'The Murders in the Rue Morgue'. Here, Poe uses the same head noun, again deliberately not disclosing the number of victims nor criminal acts. In contrast to the translation of the headline in sentence 2, the translators use two different approaches to translating the title of the story in Slovenian. In TMRM1, the title is translated analogously to the headline as 'Dvojni umor v ulici Morgue' (Double Murder in the Rue Morgue), revealing the number of victims and criminal acts right at the outset. TMRM2, on the other hand, translates the title as 'Umor v ulici Morgue' (Murder in the Rue Morgue), using the singular form which does not necessarily mean one act only but, in an abstract sense, can also refer to several victims (such as in a mass murder). The effect of TMRM2, in that it does not reveal too much too early, bears a greater similarity to Poe's original title. The reason this element of secrecy

---

[2] For sake of comparison: on 22 December 2019, the Corpus of Contemporary American English (Davies 2008) included no occurrences of the phrase 'extraordinary murders'. The singular form 'extraordinary murder', however, appeared three times. In none of the three instances the adjective 'extraordinary' premodified 'murder' as a head noun; instead, 'murder' premodified another head noun (e.g., 'extraordinary murder trial').

should be maintained is that the reader of the Original learns most details about the crime much later in the story.

Another interesting minor shift in TMRM1 is that the headline is missing the introductory angle quotes, which by rule are used in Slovenian as the standard quotation marks (»like this«). As it turns out at the end of the quoted passage, however, this is just a typographical error, given that angle quotes appear at the end of it. Nevertheless, the missing quotation mark technically changes Direct Writing to Free Direct Writing for the duration of the entire quoted stretch. At the same time, given that 'the effect of dramatization and immediacy associated with (F)DS [(Free) Direct Speech] are considerably diluted with (F)DW' (Semino & Short 2004, p. 109) and that the preceding introductory clause ends with a colon, signalling that what follows is a quote, the shift does not significantly alter the readers' comprehension of the text.

In sentence 3, following the newspaper headline, the opening sentence of the report provides rudimentary facts about the crime as reported by witnesses. In compliance with the genre, the time and location of the incident are described as well as the protagonists. Overall, the sentence is characterised by an objective style with multiple nominal structures and passive voice in the verbal structures. Comprising the main and two subordinate clauses, sentence 3 was translated as follows:

[Original]: – This morning, about three o'clock, the inhabitants of the Quartier St. Roch were aroused from sleep by a succession of terrific shrieks, issuing, apparently, from the fourth story of a house in the Rue Morgue, known to be in the sole occupancy of one Madame L'Espanaye, and her daughter, Mademoiselle Camille L'Espanaye.

[TMRM1, 17]: – Davi okrog treh je prebivalce četrti St. Roch vrgla iz spanja vrsta strašnih krikov, ki so očivdno prihajali iz četrtega nadstropja hiše v ulici Morgue, za katero vedo, da v njej prebivata le gospa L'Espanaye in njena hči gospodična Camille L'Espanaye.
 – This morning at about three a series of terrific shrieks threw out of sleep the inhabitants of the Quartier St. Roch, which [the shrieks] were evidently coming from the fourth story of a house in the Rue Morgue, for which they know that reside in it solely Madame L'Espanaye and her daughter, Mademoiselle Camille L'Espanaye.

[TMRM2, 57]: – Danes navsezgodaj okoli tretje ure je prebivalce četrti St. Roch prebudilo iz spanja več zaporednih strašnih krikov, ki jih je bilo slišati, kakor se je zdelo, iz četrtega nadstropja hiše v ulici Morgue, o kateri je znano, da v nji stanuje samo neka gospa L'Espanayeva in njena hči gospodična Camille L'Espanayeva.
 – Today very early at about three o'clock did the inhabitants of the Quartier St. Roch arouse from sleep several successive terrific shrieks, which could be heard, so it seemed, from the fourth story of a house in the Rue Morgue, of which it is known that live in it solely some Madame L'Espanaye and her daughter, Mademoiselle Camille L'Espanaye.

Both translations include multiple shifts. In TMRM1, the first appears in the prepositional phrase 'okrog treh' (at about three), where a less formal elliptical structure is used to emphasise the full hour instead of the more formal 'okrog tretje ure' (at about three o'clock), which, in comparison, is used in TMRM2.

The next notable shift, apart from a syntactical one (the apposition is gone), appears in relation to the collocation 'were aroused from sleep'. In contrast to the Original, in TMRM1 the active voice is used instead of the passive ('vrgla iz spanja' – threw out of sleep), placing 'shrieks' in a subject position.[3] This shift, which will be discussed further in the next paragraph, is not surprising because the active voice is the preferred option in Slovenian in such instances. However, the translators also replace the lexical verb: unlike in the Original ('to arouse from sleep'), the metaphorical meaning of the verb phrase 'vrgla iz spanja' (threw out of sleep) in TMRM1 underlines the force of the disturbance. The verb in the Original has connotations of unexpectedness, abruptness and shock, whereas 'successive shouts' together with 'aroused' in TMRM2 indicate a more gradual awakening. In TMRM1, however, the action appears to be even more dramatic.

Another notable shift lies in the translation of the disjunction 'apparently'. This type of disjunction is used to express 'some degree of doubt' (Quirk et al. 1992, p. 620) about the truth of the proposition and thus constitutes epistemic modality, signalling the witnesses' uncertainty about the exact location from where the shrieks were coming. In the original, the concept is expressed by one word, which is graphologically highlighted by being between two commas, which also means that the phrase functions as a clause – hence the word conveys highly important information. In TMRM1, on the other hand, the lexeme is replaced by 'očividno' (evidently), a disjunction expressing a higher degree of certainty about where to locate the disturbance. The reporter in TMRM1 thus appears more certain about the spatial coordinates of the shrieks than his counterpart in the Original. In TMRM2, 'so it seemed' additionally includes a syntactic shift (subordinate clause), which de-emphasises doubts. Additionally, by being expressed by several words, words constituting a standard clause, the crucial conceptual component 'seemed' is 'hidden' among other words, thereby decreasing its value as information compared with the original.

Several other stylistic shifts can be observed in TMRM1, some of which are mandated by the language-systemic differences between English and Slovenian. The first is a voice shift in the verb phrase 'were aroused', where passive voice from the Original becomes active voice in TMRM1: 'a series of terrific shrieks threw out of sleep the inhabitants'. This shift would suggest that TMRM1 places greater emphasis on the cause of action than on its target. However, as was pointed out above, active voice is the preferred form in

---

[3] In Slovenian, an inflected language, the case is indicated by the suffix; in turn, the syntax is also less rigid.

Slovenian and the pragmatic choice. In addition, the loss of passive voice is partly compensated by the word order. Instead of placing the grammatical subject ('the shrieks') first, the translators turn the syntactic flexibility of Slovenian to their advantage and present the object ('the inhabitants') first, followed by the grammatical subject. The verb phrase in TMRM1 and the Original thus have a comparable effect.

The gerund 'issuing' in the Original is a different case: it makes the information dense and increases the level of implicitness because the reader has to disentangle the elliptic structure. Grammatically, a non-finite form ('prihajajoč') is also available in Slovenian; however, it has become notably rare in Slovenian language use in the last hundred years (Ahačič et al. 2017, p. 66). Instead, the translators in TMRM1 chose a finite verb form, accentuating the subject 'shrieks' through the relative pronoun 'ki' (which). At the same time, the low-register verb 'prihajati' (to come from) replaces the high-register verb 'to issue' from the Original. Thus, the TMRM1 reader is yet again spared another minor intellectual challenge, but, on the other hand, the register is now less consistent with the rest of the report.

Unsurprisingly, the list of shifts in TMRM1 does not end here. Another one appears in the translation of the prepositional phrase 'in the sole occupancy'. In the Original, the noun phrase 'the sole occupancy' increases information density and places emphasis on the occupants, presented in a formal register. In TMRM1, on the other hand, the verb 'prebivata' ([the two of them] reside) is used. Given that the verb ending in Slovenian indicates two implied subjects, TMRM1 also places emphasis on the two women. The change from noun (occupancy) to verb (reside) makes TMRM1 a degree more personal than the Original. It should also be mentioned that the degree of subjectivity also increases by changing the passive voice of the preceding verb (known to be) to the active voice (for which they know) and by consequently introducing a grammatical subject.

Due to space constraints, merely one other shift should be mentioned, namely, the omission of the determiner 'one' (one Madame L'Espanaye). While the determiner in the Original implies that the woman is unknown among the general public and thus constructed as distal in terms of social deixis, the omission of the determiner in TMRM1 suggests that Madame L'Espanaye is known in her neighbourhood, changing her social status from distant and unknown to even prominent.

Stylistic shifts also appear in sentence 3 of TMRM2. The first happens in the sentence-initial time adverbial '[t]his morning, about three o'clock': instead of the equivalent phrase 'to jutro' (this morning), the descriptive phrase 'danes navsezgodaj' (today very early) is used, with the modifying adverbial 'very early' specifying the part of the day. Given that the ensuing prepositional phrase 'okoli tretje ure' (at about three o'clock) further details the exact hour, the modifying phrase is tautological and hyperbolic. Interestingly, another redundancy appears in the translation of the prepositional phrase 'by a succession of terrific shrieks': in the Original, the head noun is 'succession', indicating that witnesses had reported a series of subsequent shrieks. In TMRM2, on the other hand, 'več zaporednih strašnih trikov' (several successive terrific shrieks) are reported. The two premodifying adjectives in Slovenian emphasise individually both the number and timeline of the shrieks, although it is already indicated by the plural noun form that there was more than one shriek. It follows that this segment in TMRM2 appears over-dramatic compared with the Original. The reason for such intervention might be that the translator wants to make sure that the reader does not overlook any of the facts.

The next shift appears in the translation of the verb phrase 'were aroused', where the passive voice is replaced by the active voice in TMRM2 (did the inhabitants arouse). This shift is the result of the same grammatico-pragmatic reasons as outlined in relation to TMRM1 and has a similar stylistic effect. One difference between the two translations, however, is that TMRM2 and the Original both use the same lexical verb (arouse) to reduce the stylistic gap, which TMRM2 does not. A similarity between TMRM2 and TMRM1 is the translation of the participle 'issuing'. Neither of the two uses a participle. In contrast to TMRM1, which focuses on the spatial origin of the shrieks ([the shrieks] *were coming* from the fourth story), TMRM2 by means of a mental perception process (Simpson 1993, p. 91) focuses on the witnesses' experience of the shrieks: '[the shrieks] *could be heard* from the fourth story'. In contrast to a focus on the sender/origin of the shrieks in the Original and TMRM1, TMRM2 emphasises perception and thus the receiver, making the description more subjective by involving the reader as participant more. In analogy to TMRM1, the noun 'occupancy' undergoes transformation in TMRM2 and also appears as a verb ([the two of them] live), with a similar effect as above although even less formal.

However, it can be noted that the preceding verb 'know', which in TMRM1 is in the active voice, remains in the passive voice in TMRM2; hence, who knows does not have to be mentioned explicitly. With regard to TMRM2, a minor shift affects the disjunction 'apparently'. In the Original, this disjunction is a single adverb. In TMRM2, its meaning is expressed with the clause 'so it seemed', whose key element is the verb 'seem' carrying modal meaning. Toolan (1998) calls this '"metaphorised"' or "advanced" modality'. Although a different syntactic structure is used in TMRM2 compared with the Original, its effect is similar: the proviso makes it clear that the report is based on second-hand evidence.

In sentence 4, the text describes the response of the witnesses to the reported shrieks and the manner in which they entered the house. In contrast to sentence

3, which focuses on the auditory aspect of the crime, sentence 4 focuses on physical action, breaking in the gateway and entering the house:

[Original]: After some delay, occasioned by a fruitless attempt to procure admission in the usual manner, the gateway was broken in with a crowbar, and eight or ten of the neighbors entered, accompanied by two gendarmes.

[TMRM1, 17]: Po kratkem zadržku, ki ga je povzročil brezuspešen poskus, da bi prišli v hišo na običajen način, so vlomili vrata s pomočjo železne palice; v vežo je vdrlo osem ali deset sosedov in dva orožnika.

After some delay, occasioned by a fruitless attempt that they would enter the house in the usual manner, they broke in the door using an iron rod; into the entrance hall broke eight or ten neighbours and two gendarmes.

[TMRM2, 57]: Po kratki zamudi, ki jo je zakrivil brezuspešen poskus, priti v hišo po navadni poti, so z železnim drogom vlomili vežna vrata, in v hišo je vdrlo kakih osem ali deset sosedov, spremljal pa jih je orožnik.

After some delay, occasioned by a fruitless attempt to enter the house in the ordinary way, they broke in the gate with an iron rod, and into the house broke some eight or ten neighbours, accompanied by a gendarme.

Again, both TMRM1 and TMRM2 show numerous translation stylistic shifts. In TMRM1, the first involves the collocation 'to procure admission'. In the Original, this combination of an infinitive verb and an abstract noun, which also constrains the suppression of the agent, helps create a formal, matter-of-fact and static description of the witnesses' attempt to get past the gateway and enter the house. However, it is notable that only the gateway is mentioned in the Original and that the 'fruitless attempt' implies that the gate was locked. Since no textual signal is provided to indicate a change of context or a different referent, the reader logically infers that the house entered is the one introduced in sentence 3. TMRM1, however, makes use of a relative clause 'da bi prišli v hišo' (that they would enter the house), thereby personalising the construction. In addition to a lower level of formality, 'the house' is explicitly mentioned, depriving the reader of inferencing as in the Original. The verbal structure increases the dynamics in TMRM1 and adds subjectivity by means of the added pronoun: 'they'. A similar shift appears with regard to the subject–verb combination 'eight or ten of the neighbours entered'. In the Original, the verb is used intransitively so that the part of the house that the group enters is to be inferred by the reader. In TMRM1, however, the area is specified: 'v vežo' (into the entrance hall). Given that two explicitations appear in the same sentence in TMRM1, neither of which is required by target language nor context, this suggests that explicitation is a conscious or controlled part of the translation process (Gil Bardaji 2009). Yet another stylistic fingerprint corroborates the latter hypothesis: the verb co-occurring with 'entrance hall' in TMRM1. While the Original uses the verb 'entered' (eight or ten of the neighbors entered), the same action is referred to as 'into the entrance hall broke eight or ten neighbours and two gendarmes' in TMRM1, modifying the character of the action from neutral to violent. The effect is enhanced by the parallel between the physical act of opening the gate by force (broke in the door) and the metaphorical act of breaking into the hall (into the entrance hall broke). Given that the verb 'to enter' from the Original has a one-to-one equivalent in Slovenian (vstopiti), it seems that a different verb is used to make the situation appear more dramatic to the reader.

In addition to these two shifts, another grammatical shift appears in the phrasal verb 'was broken in'. While passive voice is used in the Original, active voice is used in both instances of 'broke' in TMRM1. In turn, the agent in the position of subject is identified (they/eight or ten neighbours and two gendarmes), unlike the Original where passive voice allows Poe to leave the agent (agents?) of the breaking act unidentified. It might be inferred in the Original that some of the neighbours/gendarmes broke the gateway, whereas TMRM1 explicitly refers to neighbours and gendarmes by means of a cataphoric personal pronoun 'they'.

In the Original, the report mentions that the neighbours were 'accompanied by two gendarmes', indicating that the police control the group of individuals as they enter the house and puts authority in a superior position. In TMRM1, however, the verb 'accompanied' disappears. Instead, 'eight or ten neighbors and two gendarmes' are connected with the conjunction 'and', placing both groups on the same level and removing any hierarchical relationship between them. As a result, the police seemingly adopt a less authoritative role than in the Original. In addition, the wording 'osem ali deset sosedov' (eight or ten neighbours) instead of 'eight or ten of the neighbors' in the Original suggests that the size of the crowd in TMRM1 is limited to twelve (including gendarmes) and that all of them enter the house. A smaller crowd makes the situation appear less dramatic. The same shift appears in TMRM2 with 'kakih osem ali deset sosedov' (some eight or ten neighbours), likewise suggesting that no neighbours remain in front of the house, as is the case in TMRM1.

Several other notable translation shifts can be observed in sentence 4 in TMRM2. The first concerns the verb 'was broken' from the Original, which again appears twice and undergoes the same shift from passive to active voice as in TMRM1. Here again the pronominal subject 'they' is added. Both TMRM1 and TMRM2 change 'to procure admission' to 'to enter the house', the verb 'enter' being stylistically closest to the Original in Slovenian, given that a mechanical or literal translation of the Original phrase ('to procure admission') is not an option. The finite verb form does not mention the doers of action, making the report less subjective. The stylistic effect is thus similar to the Original, although less formal. Further similarities between the two translations appear with regard to the predicate '[the neighbors] entered'. As pointed out above, TMRM1 changes the character of the action from neutral to violent by using the phrasal verb 'je vdrlo' (into the entrance hall *broke* eight or ten neighbours and ...). Interestingly, in TMRM2, the predicate is translated in the same way as 'je vdrlo' (into the house broke ...). One possible explanation of a matching shift in the two translations is that the translators either misunderstood the source text or – more likely – that they each wanted to make the situation appear more dramatic. It is notable that both translations include syntactic inversion, with their grammatical subjects (the neighbours) in Slovenian following the verb. Subjects' case endings, which allow Slovenian syntax to be much less rigid than that of English, reveal their semantic roles in translation; however, such inversion is still stylistically marked in Slovenian and emphasises the inverted parts (Toporišič 2000, pp. 677–678), although considerably less than inversion would foreground the subject in English (see Quirk et al. 1992, pp. 1379–1381). Consequently, the Given-New information link with sentence 5, which relates back to the preceding sentence, is not heavily affected. One phrase that distinguishes both translations is the handling of the adverbial 'in the usual manner', describing how the group attempted to enter the property. In contrast to the Original and TMRM1, in TMRM2 the adverbial 'po navadni poti' (in the ordinary way) entails ambiguity: it can be understood that they tried the door handle but found it locked, but it can also be interpreted that the group first tried one entrance into the house and then the gateway, making the report less succinct than the Original.

It should also be noted that both TMRM1 and TMRM2 share one minor lexical shift in the noun phrase 'a crowbar', referring to the tool that is used to break in the gateway. In the Original, a technical term is used, whereas in both translations a generic term 'železna palica' (iron rod) is used. Although a synonym for 'crowbar' is available in Slovenian (lomilka), the 'iron rod' allows the crowd to achieve the same result; yet stylistically, the reporters of TMRM1 and TMRM2 appear lexically inferior and, again, less formal compared with the Original. Additionally, given that the group includes police officers, it is possible that the tool has been provided by the police, who – and in turn the reporter – would know its name.

Some of the types of shifts identified above also appear in sentence 5. Here the report focuses on the experiences of the group after they enter the house, comprising four clauses and one apposition ('in angry contention') in the form of a reduced relative clause:

[Original]: By this time the cries had ceased; but, as the party rushed up the first flight of stairs, two or more rough voices, in angry contention, were distinguished, and seemed to proceed from the upper part of the house.

[TMRM1, 17]: Takrat so kriki prenehali, toda ko je skupina hitela po spodnjem stopnišču, so slišali še dva ali več razburjenih glasov v hudem prepiru – zdelo se je, da prihajajo iz zgornjih prostorov.

At that time the cries had ceased, but as the party rushed on the lower flight of stairs, [they] heard two or more agitated voices in bitter contention – it seemed that they were coming from the upstairs rooms.

[TMRM2, 57]: Tedaj so kriki prenehali, toda ko so ljudje planili na prvo stopnišče, je bilo mogoče razločiti dva ali več glasov v jeznem prepiru, in zdelo se je, da prihajajo iz zadnjega nadstropja.

At that time the cries had ceased, but as the people rushed up the first flight of stairs, it was possible to distinguish two or more voices in angry contention, and it seemed that they were coming from the top floor.

This syntactically complex sentence undergoes multiple shifts in TMRM1 and TMRM2. In TMRM1, the first difference lies in the choice of preposition in the second clause in relation to the verb 'rushed'. In the original the preposition 'up' in the prepositional phrase 'up the first flight of stairs' indicates the direction in which the group moved; in TMRM1, on the other hand, only the location of the group is indicated – 'je skupina hitela po spodnjem stopnišču' (the party rushed on the lower flight of stairs) – and not their direction of movement. In addition, the adjective 'first', premodifying 'flight of stairs' in the Original, is replaced by 'spodnjem' (lower) in TMRM1, which might suggest fewer flights of stairs (the upper and the lower?) than in the Original.

Both texts, however, make it clear that the search party is still a long way from the fourth floor and thus less likely to reveal the key information: the identity of the perpetrator although the distance to go is less evident in TMRM1. These two shifts in TMRM1 require more inference from the reader than in the Original, which could also be considered a compensation (Harvey 1995) for explicitations in the preceding sentences as discussed above.

Another grammatical shift appears in the verb phrase 'were distinguished'. In the Original, the passive voice helps the reporter to avoid naming the person(s) who distinguish the voices. Conversely, using the active voice in the phrase 'so slišali' ([they] heard) in TMRM1 means that the grammatical subject (they) reveals the senser (Simpson 1993, p. 91). Consequently, the focus to some extent shifts from the phenomenon to the senser. At the same time, the verb 'distinguished' is replaced by 'heard' in TMRM1, reducing perception plus identification of the voices from the Original to perception only. The senser whose prominence increases in TMRM1 thus at the same time has a more reduced capacity for identification than their unmentioned counterpart in the Original.

However, this is not the only lexical shift in the third clause. At the same time, 'rough voices' become 'razburjenih glasov' (agitated voices) in TMRM1. While the adjective in the source text describes merely the acoustic properties of the voice, the target text emphasises their emotional character, possibly triggering the schema of human voices and thus unnecessarily affecting Poe's extremely subtle hint that one of the voices might not be human, which the finale will show to be the truth.

Another minor lexical shift appears in the phrase 'from the upper part of the house'. In the Original, this adjunct describes the location from which the witnesses thought the voices were coming. The location is referred to in general terms, which is understandable from a narratological perspective, given that the focalisers (Genette 1983) at this point have just entered a building (presumably) for the first time and are unfamiliar with its layout. In TMRM1, conversely, the phrase 'upstairs rooms' is used. Although 'prostorov' could also be translated back as 'spaces/areas', it does suggest that the focalisers in TMRM1 seem to know that the floor they have in mind is compartmentalised (and not, for example, one large area such as the attic), which is information that the reader does not obtain from the report in the Original.

Sentence 5 in TMRM1 also sees a notable punctuation shift in clauses three and four. In the Original, the clauses are conjoined by 'and' (were distinguished, and seemed to proceed . . .). In TMRM1, conversely, a dash is used to separate the two actions. Initially, this shift does not seem prominent. However, Poe had a very distinct and clear idea about the use of the dash, which he explained in one of his poetological columns. He believes that the dash should be used exclusively to denote apposition, or, in his words, '*a second thought – an emendation* . . . that gives the reader a choice between two, or among three or more expressions, one of which may be more forcible than another, but all of which help out the idea' (Poe 1902, p. 131). In TMRM1, however, the dash is used as a break suggesting and emphasising that the clause following it is a conclusion based on deliberation, which conflicts with the Original style, where no causal relationship exists. On the other hand, a semicolon after the first clause in the Original represents a caesura, marking the silence that ensues the commotion in the house described in the preceding clause; the semicolon thus performs an iconic function (Henry 2001).

As is the case in TMRM1, TMRM2 also partly deviates from the Original in punctuation. As can be seen, the semicolon after the opening clause is replaced by a comma, with the same effect as described above; the rest of the sentence follows the original punctuation.

Another shift can be observed in the subject of the second (subordinate) clause, where a collective noun 'party' from the Original is replaced by the plural noun 'people'. The difference between the two is that 'party' refers to 'a particular group of people who are involved in an activity' (Cambridge Dictionary 2020), that is, as one unit, while 'people' as the plural form of 'person' emphasises the individuals in a group. Whereas the Original constructs a herd instinct that drives crowds in dramatic moments and making them lose individual human traits, in TMRM2, this characteristic is less distinct.

With regard to 'were distinguished', TMRM2 avoids a change of verb voice: in contrast to TMRM1 but in accordance with the Original, TMRM2 uses the passive voice while making use of a structure equivalent to the pleonastic 'it' structure[4] ('it was possible'), followed by an infinitive. This allows the translator to avoid naming the experiencer explicitly. This way, the stylistic effect of this segment is comparable to the Original, although again sounding less formal.

However, in the same sentence, an omission can also be observed. While in the Original the noun 'voices' is premodified by 'rough', this premodifier is omitted in TMRM2. Initially, this shift appears minute, particularly because some characteristics of the 'voices' are included in the attribute 'angry' describing a conflict (in angry contention). Nevertheless, 'rough' is foregrounded in the Original because it typically does not co-occur with 'voice', which Poe uses as a subtle clue to suggest that at least one voice belongs to the orangutan. By omitting the premodifier in TMRM2, the hint is gone.

As was the case in TMRM1, there is also a shift in the prepositional phrase 'from the upper part of the house', which becomes 'from the top floor' in TMRM2 and is more specific compared with the Original, presuming that the crowd – the focalisers – know for certain which floor the cries came from, which suggests that they are more knowledgeable than their counterparts in the Original. In addition, by denying the possibility of another floor being above the fourth one, TMRM2 rules out the possibility that the perpetrator escaped over the roof, even further up than the fourth floor. Consequently, TMRM2 restricts the readers' options of inference compared with the Original. Finally, the introductory phrase 'by this time' also changes in both translations. In the Original, this adverbial indicates that the shrieks ceased at the latest (but possibly earlier) when the search party broke into the house, suggesting that the preceding commotion might already have led to their discontinuation. In TMRM1 and TMRM2, on the other hand, the synonymous adverbs 'takrat' and 'tedaj' (at that time) indicate that the shrieks ceased at one particular moment: given the cohesive links with the preceding sentence, either at the first unsuccessful attempt, the moment the door gave in or the moment the party entered the house. Although this represents a minor shift for the newspaper readers in Poe's original text world, it is nevertheless interesting because it could have had repercussions for a meticulous criminal investigation. It is equally interesting that the same shift appears in both translations, which shows how deeply immersed in the Original were the translators.

---

[4] Slovenian being a pro-drop language, the pronoun is not explicit.

After the report describes the witnesses' account of the rough voices that they heard, sentence 6 focuses on the moment when those voices cease to be heard:

[Original]: As the second landing was reached, these sounds, also, had ceased, and everything remained perfectly quiet.

[TMRM1, 17]: Ko so dospeli do druge ploščadi med stopnicami, so umolknili tudi ti glasovi, in slišati ni bilo ničesar več.
As they reached the second landing between the stairs, these sounds also had ceased, and nothing else could be heard.

[TMRM2, 57]: Ko so prišli na drugo ploščad, so utihnili tudi ti glasovi in vse je zajela popolna tišina.
As they reached the second landing, these sounds also had ceased, and perfect silence enwrapped all things.

Syntactically, both translations follow the Original and comprise a subordinate and two coordinate main clauses. A cohesive link with the preceding situation is established through double anaphoric reference ('they' – although not in the Original; 'these sounds').

In the Original, none of the clauses includes an explicit human actor or senser. One human subject is implied in the introductory subordinate clause but is not made explicit because of passive voice. The other two subjects are inanimate ('these sounds') and pronominal ('everything'). As a result, the description appears impersonal and objective.

In the course of translation, some of these stylistic characteristics undergo modification. In TMRM1, two shifts appear in the subordinate clause. The first regards the voice of the verb. While the passive voice is used in the Original ('was reached'), the active voice is used in TMRM1: 'so dospeli' ([they] reached). In analogy with previously identified shifts in voice, the TMRM1 makes the protagonists more prominent than the action itself and has the effect of making the text more personal and less formal compared with the Original.

The second shift concerns an expansion of the noun phrase 'the second landing', describing the platform between two flights of stairs. In the Original, the stairs are not explicitly mentioned but require logical inference. In TMRM1, the micro location is more specific: 'druge ploščadi med stopnicami' (the second landing between the stairs). It is unclear why the translators add such detail, possibly emphasising that the search party still cannot see anything because they are still at least two floors away from the crime scene. By mentioning this detail, the translators divert the reader's attention from solving the mystery too early and thus maintain suspense.

Additional shifts appear in the second coordinate clause of TMRM1, which describes the silence that the search party experience on the second landing. In the Original, silence is referred to positively, indicated both by the choice of adverb ('perfectly quiet') and by the use of the universal indefinite pronoun 'everything' in the sense of 'all things/all matter' (Quirk et al. 1992, p. 378). In TMRM1, on the other hand, the formulation 'slišati ni bilo ničesar več' (nothing else could be heard) suggests that silence is inferred from the absence of 'else' noises, as if the reader expects them, possibly those made by the perpetrator. The silence in TMRM1 is thus more complex because negated noises can be understood only after they have been imagined first. In addition, the verb 'remained' is replaced by a verb of perception 'slišati' (could be heard), which indicates that the perspective shifts from an external to an internal one, increasing the subjectivity of the report.

TMRM2 undergoes fewer stylistic shifts in sentence 6. The first two clauses are almost identical to the Original; the only difference beside word order is a shift in verb voice in the subordinate clause, which turns from passive to active, with identical stylistic repercussions the same shift has in TMRM1. A more prominent shift in TMRM2 appears in the third clause: in analogy with the Original, the silence is still referred to positively. However, in contrast to the Original, where silence is implied by the subject complement '(perfectly) quiet', silence is nominalised in TMRM2 (perfect silence) and made the subject of the clause. This shift is not coincidental given the idiomaticity of the collocation 'tišina zajame' (silence enwraps) in Slovenian. In addition to turning silence into an entity, the collocation carries a metaphorical meaning in combination with the dynamic verb 'enwrap' (SILENCE IS A BLANKET) (Lakoff & Johnson 2003), making silence even more prominent (for the importance of metaphor in the construction of Otherness, I refer to Chapter 2). TMRM2 is closer to the Original than TMRM1 because of a focus on the phenomena instead of their perception, retaining the objectivity of the Original.

Sentence 7 describes the reaction of the search party after the voices are no longer heard. Following a static closure of sentence 6, sentence 7 again builds on dynamism and physical action:

[Original] The party spread themselves, and hurried from room to room.

[TMRM1, 17]: Skupina se je razkropila, da bi posamezniki preiskali prostor za prostorom.
The party spread themselves in order for the individuals to examine one room after the other.

[TMRM2, 58]: Ljudje so se razdelili in hiteli od sobe do sobe.
The people divided themselves and hurried from room to room.

Excluding the headline, sentence 7 is the shortest in the passage and the only one without a subordinate clause. The subject of both the main and the coordinate clauses (the latter being elliptical) is the noun 'party', referring to the same noun as in sentence 5 and thus establishing a cohesive link between the two sentences. The verbs in both clauses are intransitive and relate to the manner in which the group moved around the house after reaching the second landing. Intransitivity also suggests that the group does not (yet) know what to expect. Although the sentence is brief, stylistic shifts appear both in TMRM1 and TMRM2.

In TMRM1, one shift affects the coordinate clause. In the Original, the clause is introduced by the conjunction 'and', syntactically placing both clauses on the same level. In TMRM1, the coordinate clause becomes an adjunct of purpose, introduced by the conjunction 'da' (in order to), changing the generic properties of the report. While the Original lists only two subsequent actions in chronological order, complying with the fundamentals of newswriting, according to which reporters are expected to 'present factual information succinctly and in an impartial or objective manner ... [and] [r]eporters and editors strive to keep opinions out of news stories' (Fedler et al. 2005, p. 59), TMRM1 breaches those principles by explaining the purpose of the first action. An objective report thus becomes subjective speculation. The translators' intervention is particularly out of place because it appears as part of the newspaper article which serves as the starting point of Dupin and narrator's investigation.

This is not the only shift in the second clause. The translators also change the elliptically omitted subject from 'the party' to 'posamezniki' (the individuals). This shift not only makes explicit an implicit actor but also affects the collective nature of the search party's actions in the Original. The significance of the collective effort reflects itself in the fact that the group is consistently referred to as 'the party',[5] seemingly acting as one. The translation chosen in TMRM1 underscores its individual members. Further, the translators change the verb 'hurried' to 'examine' in its finite form in the second clause of TMRM1. While this verb in the Original suggests that the movement was quick, the use of the verb 'preiskali' (to examine) in TMRM1 suggests that the individuals' focus was on discovering something. In turn, a neutral description of rapid movement turns into a more systematic search for the perpetrators/ victims.

In contrast to TMRM1, two notable shifts appear in TMRM2. The first is a change of the subject noun from 'party' to 'ljudje' (people). This shift has an effect similar to that in the second clause of TMRM1: while the group acts as a single entity in the Original, the plural form 'people' underscores the individuals in it, shifting focus from the events to the protagonists.

The second shift affects the verb 'spread'. In the Original, the verb is employed in line with its basic meaning: 'to move from one place to another' (Cambridge Dictionary 2020). The formulation does not suggest that the

---

[5] The noun 'party' appears nineteen times in the text as a whole; in thirteen of those appearances, its reference is identical to that in sentences 5 and 7 discussed here.

movement was organised, at least not in an explicit manner. In TMRM2, on the other hand, the formulation 'so se razdelili' ([they] divided themselves) implies that the search party first agreed on how to carry out the search and then proceeded with it. As a result, a haphazard search turns into a systematic one, changing the character of the search party from spontaneous to an organised one. In this regard, the shift is similar to the one described in the corresponding part of TMRM1.

The passage closes with the description of the scene that the witnesses find after they have reached the crime scene on the fourth floor:

[Original]: Upon arriving at a large back chamber in the fourth story, (the door of which, being found locked, with the key inside, was forced open,) a spectacle presented itself which struck every one present not less with horror than with astonishment.

[TMRM1, 17]: Ko so prišli do velike sobe v zadnjem delu četrtega nadstropja (vrata, ki so bila zaklenjena z notranje strani, so s silo odprli), se jim je ponudil prizor, ki je navdal prisotne bolj z osuplostjo kot pa z grozo.

When [they] arrived at a large chamber at the back side of the fourth story (the door, which was locked from the inside, [they] opened by force), a spectacle presented itself to them which struck those present more with astonishment than with horror.

[TMRM2, 58]: Ko so prišli v veliko sobo na dvoriščni strani v četrtem nadstropju (vrata, ki so bila zaklenjena in je v njih znotraj tičal ključ, so s silo odprli), so zagledali prizor, ki so se ob njem vsi navzoči prav tako zgrozili, kakor začudili.

When [they] arrived inside a large chamber on the backyard side in the fourth story (the door, which was locked and had in it on the inside a key, [they] opened by force), they saw a spectacle at which everyone present equally horrified and astonished themselves.

Sentence 8 is the second longest in the passage with forty-one words. Compared with sentence 7, it is syntactically more complex, comprising the main clause 'a spectacle presented itself ...' and an adjunct of time ('upon arriving ...') preceding it. In parentheses, sentence 8 also includes an embedded relative clause on what might be called a subordinate level 2, postmodifying the noun 'chamber'; and the same embedded clause, in turn, has embedded in it an additional non-finite clause ('being found locked, with the key inside') on subordinate level 3, postmodifying the noun 'door'. Yet another relative clause ('which struck ...') postmodifies the noun 'spectacle' in the main clause on subordinate level 2.

The syntactic complexity is important for at least two reasons: first, in spite of the complexity, the central proposition is straightforward, 'a spectacle presented itself', meaning that the rest of the sentence comprises additional circumstantial and peripheral information. Second, complex syntax means that the reading process necessarily slows down. This manifests itself, for example, in the Original head noun 'spectacle', postmodified by the relative clause 'which struck ...'. Typically, the postmodifier completing the noun phrase is found immediately after the head noun, followed by the next sentence element, in this case the predicator. Here, however, the head noun and its postmodifier are split by the predicate that would normally follow the extended noun phrase and makes the processing of the information difficult. Such untypical syntactic pattern also appears in parentheses. The genitive relationship between the noun 'chamber' and its postmodifier 'door', for example, is not expressed by means of a possessive pronoun (e.g. 'whose door'); instead, the of-phrase ('the door of which') is used, moving the anaphoric pronoun 'which' even further from its referent and thus further impeding comprehension. In addition, the of-phrase could be regarded as redundant as the referent is clear from context.

Another similar syntactic pattern involves the subject 'door', which is also separated from the predicate 'was forced' by an embedded non-finite clause ('being found locked') and a prepositional phrase ('with the key inside'). The result is an information-dense, processing-intensive staccato clause. As it turns out, such wording is not coincidental. Instead, the syntax here is an iconic representation of the search party's frustration because new obstacles continuously slow down their effort to find the origin of the shrieks.

Another characteristic of the sentence is the reduction of human presence to the minimum. Although the sentence describes human experience, none of the five verbs in it couples with a human grammatical subject: three are in non-finite form and/or passive voice ('arriving', 'being found locked', 'was forced'), whereas two dynamic verbs ('presented', 'struck') are in conjunction with inanimate subjects, creating metaphorical meaning. Therefore, the sentence has matter-of-fact characteristics, complying with the genre of an objective newspaper report.

Given the complexity of the Original sentence 8, several shifts appear in both translations with noticeable stylistic repercussions. Syntactically, both translations initially seem to follow the structure of the Original. However, a more detailed analysis indicates that that is not entirely the case.

In TMRM1, one syntactic shift appears in relation to the postmodifier 'being found locked, with the key inside': the prepositional phrase 'with the key' is left out and a change in syntax appears: 'ki so bila zaklenjena z notranje strani' (which was locked from the inside). As a result, the distance between the subject 'vrata' (door) and the predicator is shorter, seemingly simplifying the search efforts.

The phrase 'with the key inside' undergoes a syntactic shift in TMRM2 as well. In contrast to the Original, the phrase turns into a complete clause 'je v njih znotraj tičal ključ' (had in it on the inside a key). Given that a relational process (have a key on the inside) is implicit in the Original, the explicitation is stylistically redundant; on the other hand, the long clause retains the iconic effect described above and could thus be an example of compensation for the shifts encountered elsewhere.

Both translations undergo several other grammatico-lexical shifts. Among the more salient ones is the shift in verb voice as a result of language-systemic differences described above which affect both TMRM1 and TMRM2. In sentence 8 in the Original, passive voice allows the reporter to leave out the identity of the human agents and experiencers behind the action ('forced open') or perception ('found locked'), describing and emphasising the events and phenomena instead of the protagonists. The non-finite clause 'being found locked' presents a perception process and is turned into a relational process (which was locked) in TMRM2 (Simpson 1993, pp. 91, 92). Given that perception implies the presence of a human senser, the omission of the verb 'found' in both TMRM1 and TMRM2 makes the clause appear more factual than in the Original, possibly partly compensating for the shift in voice. The finite verb phrase 'was forced open', on the other hand, is transformed into active verb voice 'so s silo odprli' ([they] opened by force) in both TMRM1 and TMRM2. As is the case with other shifts from passive to active voice, both TMRM1 and TMRM2 emphasise the protagonists instead of the action itself.

In TMRM2, another prominent shift affects the transitivity of its main clause. As mentioned above, the subject of the main clause is the noun 'a spectacle' (in the Original as well as in TMRM1). Given that the subject is abstract, metaphorical meaning is created in combination with the predicate 'presented itself', with the subject adopting a semantically active role. The same metaphor continues in the relative clause 'which struck everyone ...', postmodifying the head noun 'spectacle' by means of a relative clause. Such formulation helps the reporter to avoid using a mental perception process (for example, 'the search party saw'), which would require mentioning the senser. It turns out that this is precisely what happens in TMRM2: the pronoun 'they' becomes the subject of the clause, followed by a verb of perception and the 'spectacle' as the phenomenon in an object position: 'so zagledali prizor' ([they] saw a spectacle). Human protagonists thus again become more prominent in TMRM2. Moreover, TMRM2 also changes the transitive pattern in the postmodifying relative clause. While '[a spectacle] ... struck every one not less with horror than with astonishment' in the Original, in the translated passage 'at which everyone present equally horrified and astonished themselves' the role of 'everyone' changes from object to subject. In addition, instead of objectifying the emotions through nominalisation in the Original ('horror', 'astonishment'), the same emotions are presented as verbs in TMRM2 ('horrified and astonished), emphasising subjective perception.

Both translations include additions in sentence 8. The first appears in the main clause. In the Original, the central part of the main clause (a spectacle presented itself ...) is formulated without explicitly identifying anyone witnessing the 'spectacle'. In TMRM1, however, the translators add the pronoun 'jim' (to them), which indicates that the scene is witnessed by the search party: 'se jim je ponudil prizor ...' (a spectacle presented itself to them ...). In contrast to the Original, where the reporter avoids mentioning the experiencers, the latter become more noticeable in TMRM1. Similarly, an addition appears in TMRM2 in the sentence's initial subordinate clause. In the Original, the report says that the 'spectacle" presented itself '[u]pon arriving at a large back chamber in the fourth story', without specifying the micro location (inside or outside the chamber) from where the scene is witnessed. In TMRM2, in comparison, this micro location is given more precisely in the sentence initial temporal clause '[w]hen [they] arrived inside a large chamber'. As is evident, the adverb 'inside' explicitly positions the witnesses inside the chamber. Although the Original permits such interpretation, it is not limited to it. On the contrary, the Original makes it highly likely that the search party see the crime scene the moment the door opens, underscoring the magnitude of the crime, while TMRM2 reduces this effect.

7.5   Conclusion

A comparison of a passage from Poe's 'The Murders in the Rue Morgue' and two of its Slovenian translations has revealed several stylistic discrepancies between the source and target texts. Some of them appear in both TMRM1 and TMRM2, while others are restricted to either of the two. Notable examples of stylistic translation shifts that appear in both translations are explicitations, which manifest themselves in the form of translators' interventions through which implicit parts of the Original text become explicit in the target text, or omissions, where parts of the Original text are left out.

On the other hand, a comparison with the Original showed that the translators of TMRM1 change the modality of the Original text, while the translator of TMRM2 modifies transitivity pattern. The same applies to the translators' interventions that affect the iconicity of the text, change of register and others. As was also argued, some shifts appear because of the language-systemic differences between English and Slovenian. What is particularly notable is that certain translation shifts alter the generic properties of TMRM as a detective story. It was thus found that the translators, in an apparent urge to clarify or interpret the Original text, unnecessarily deprive the target readers of inferring, often an integral element of reading crime fiction (Cohen 2000, pp. 27–28).

However, the implications of the present chapter go beyond the particular two translations for at least three reasons. First, the study shows that the stylistic analytical toolkit can be applied to any crime fiction text in translation in order to establish its relationship with the source text, confirming

Gregoriou's observation that '[s]tylistics is ideally placed when offering a set of tools with which to unpick ... linguistic devices ... in relation to translation' (2019, p. 230). This is particularly important for critical examinations of crime fiction in translation that aim to be intersubjectively verifiable. Second, stylistics has an applicative value for practicing literary translators. Although the present study is based on a relatively short passage, the results show how to avoid stylistic pitfalls in translating crime fiction. Finally, the study also reiterates the need for the further development of translational stylistics, a relatively new subdiscipline of translation studies. Again, Slovenian serves as a good example. Although the style of translated prose has been addressed by several authors over the last three decades (e.g. Mozetič 1997; Onič 2005, 2013; Trupej 2017), it turns out that their approaches vary and above all place insufficient emphasis on the source text in the sense proposed by Malmkjær (2006), particularly when it comes genre-specific stylistic features, such as those of crime fiction.

References

Ahačič, K., Vukotič, J., Smolej, M., Šekli, M., & Žele, A. (2017). *Slovnica na kvadrat: slovenska slovnica za srednjo šolo*. Ljubljana: Rokus Klett.

Ascari, M. (2007). *A Counter-History of Crime Fiction: Supernatural, Gothic, Sensational*. Basingstoke: Palgrave Macmillan.

Bassnett, S. (2017). Detective Fiction in Translation: Shifting Patterns of Reception. In L. Nillson, D. Damrosch & T. D'haen, eds., *Crime Fiction as World Literature*. New York: Bloomsbury, pp. 143–155.

Bednarek, M., & Caple, H. (2017). *The Discourse of News Values: How News Organizations Create Newsworthiness*. New York: Oxford University Press.

Bleiler, R. (1999). *Reference Guide to Mystery and Detective Fiction*. Englewood, CO: Libraries Unlimited.

Boase-Beier, J. (2006). *Stylistic Approaches to Translation*. Manchester: St. Jerome Publishing.

  (2014). Stylistics and Translation. In M. Burke, ed., *The Routledge Handbook of Stylistics*. New York: Routledge, pp. 393–407.

Brumme, J. (2014). The Narrator's Voice in Translation: What Remains from a Linguistic Experiment in Wolf Haas's Brenner Detective Novels. In S. M. Cadera & A. Pavić Pintarić, eds., *The Voices of Suspense and Their Translation in Thrillers*. Amsterdam: Rodopi, pp. 161–176.

Cadera, S. M., & Pavić Pintarić, A. (2014). *The Voices of Suspense and Their Translation in Thrillers*. Amsterdam: Rodopi.

Cambridge Dictionary. (2020). [online]. https://dictionary.cambridge.org/ (accessed 21 February 2020).

Cohen, M. (2000). *Murder Most Fair: The Appeal of Mystery Fiction*. Madison, NJ: Fairleigh Dickinson University Press.

Cook, M. (2014). *Detective Fiction and the Ghost Story: The Haunted Text, Crime Files*. Basingstoke: Palgrave Macmillan.

Davies, M. (2008). *The Corpus of Contemporary American English (COCA): 560 Million Words, 1990–Present.* www.english-corpora.org/coca/.
De Beaugrande, R. A. (1978). *Factors in a Theory of Poetic Translating.* Assen: Van Gorcum.
Douthwaite, J. (2018). The Method and Practice of Translational Stylistics. *Token: A Journal of English Linguistics,* 7, 159–191.
Espunya, A. (2014). Shifting Points of View: The Translation of Suspense-Building Narrative Style. In S. M. Cadera & A. Pavić Pintarić, eds., *The Voices of Suspense and Their Translation in Thrillers.* Amsterdam: Rodopi, pp. 193–206.
Fedler, F., Bender, J. R., Davenport, L., & Drager, M. W. (2005). *Reporting for the Media,* 8th ed. New York: Oxford University Press.
Fisher, B. F. (2002). Poe and the Gothic tradition. In K. J. Hayes, ed., *The Cambridge Companion to Edgar Allan Poe.* Cambridge: Cambridge University Press, pp. 72–91.
Frank, L. (2003). *Victorian Detective Fiction and the Nature of Evidence: The Scientific Investigations of Poe, Dickens, and Doyle.* Basingstoke: Palgrave Macmillan.
Gadpaille, M. (2014). Elementary Ratiocination: Anticipating Sherlock Holmes in a Slovene Setting. *Elope,* 11 (Spring), 67–82.
Genette, G. (1983). *Narrative Discourse.* Trans. J. E. Lewin. Ithaca, NY: Cornell University Press.
Gil Bardaji, A. (2009). Procedures, Techniques, Strategies: Translation Process Operators. *Perspectives: Studies in Translatology,* 17(3), 161–173.
Giugliano, M. (2017). What the Analysis of Style in Translation Can Say: Disentangling Styles in Giovanni Giudici's Translations of Poetry. *Lingue e Linguaggi,* 21, 107–127.
Gregoriou, C. (2017). *Crime Fiction Migration: Crossing Languages, Cultures and Media.* London: Bloomsbury Academic.
  (2019). Untranslatable Clues: Reader Manipulation and the Challenge of Crime Fiction Translation. In S. Sorlin, ed., *Stylistic Manipulation of the Reader in Contemporary Fiction.* London: Bloomsbury Academic, pp. 215–233.
Halliday, M. A. K. (1996). Linguistic Function and Literary Style: An Inquiry into the Language of William Golding's *The Inheritors.* In J. J. Weber, ed., *The Stylistics Reader: From Roman Jakobson to the Present.* London: Arnold, pp. 56–86.
Halliday, M. A. K., & Matthiessen, C. M. I. M. (2004). *An Introduction to Functional Grammar.* London: Arnold.
Harvey, K. (1995). A Descriptive Framework for Compensation. *The Translator,* 1(1), 65–86.
Haycraft, H., ed. (1946). *The Art of the Mystery Story: A Collection of Critical Essays.* New York: Grosset & Dunlap.
Henry, A. C. (2001). Iconic Punctuation: Ellipsis Marks in Historical Perspective. In O. Fischer & M. Nänny, eds., *The Motivated Sign: Iconicity in Language and Literature 2.* Amsterdam: John Benjamins, pp. 135–156.
Klaudy, K. (2011). Explicitation. In M. Baker & G. Saldanha, eds., *Routledge Encyclopedia of Translation Studies.* London: Routledge, pp. 104–108.
Lakoff, G., & Johnson, M. (2003). *Metaphors We Live By.* Chicago: University of Chicago Press.

Linder, D. (2000). Translating Slang in Detective Fiction. *Perspectives: Studies in Translatology*, 8(4), 275–287.

Malmkjær, K. (1994). Stylistics in Translation Teaching. *Perspectives: Studies in Translatology*, 2(1), 61–68.

(2004). Translational Stylistics: Dulcken's Translations of Hans Christian Andersen. *Language and Literature*, 13(1), 13–24.

(2006). Translational Stylistics. In E. K. Brown & A. Anderson, eds., *Encyclopaedia of Language & Linguistics*. Amsterdam: Elsevier Pergamon, pp. 104–108.

Morini, M. (2014). Translation, Stylistics and *To the Lighthouse*: A Deictic Shift Theory Analysis. *Target*, 26(1), 128–145.

Mozetič, U. (1997). Splošni in posebni problemi prevajanja angleških in ameriških leposlovnih besedil v slovenščino. In M. Grosman, ed., *Književni prevod*. Ljubljana: Znanstveni inštitut Filozofske fakultete, pp. 57–73.

Onič, T. (2005). Translating Recurrences in Pinter's Plays. *ELOPE*, 2(1–2), 293–299.

(2013). Vikanje in tikanje v slovenskih prevodih Albeejeve drame Kdo se boji Virginije Woolf? *Primerjalna književnost*, 36(1), 233–251.

Poe, E. A. (1902). Marginalia – Part X. In J. A. Harrison, ed., *The Complete Works of E. A. Poe*. New York: Thomas Y. Crowell & Company, pp. 130–131. www.eapoe.org/works/harrison/jah16m00.htm.

(1952). *Propad hiše Usher in druge zgodbe*. Trans. Z. Jerin and I. Šentjurc. Ljubljana: Polet.

(1960). *Zlati hrošč*. Trans. J. Udovič. Ljubljana: Cankarjeva založba.

(2008). *The Murders in the Rue Morgue*. In *Project Gutenberg's The Works of Edgar Allan Poe, The Raven Edition*. Urbana, IL: Project Gutenberg, www.gutenberg.org/files/2147/2147-h/2147-h.htm.

Priestman, M. (1990). *Detective Fiction and Literature: The Figure on the Carpet*. Basingstoke: Macmillan.

Quirk, R., Greenbaum, S., Leech, G. N., & Svartvik, J. (1992). *A Comprehensive Grammar of the English Language*. London: Longman.

Rolls, A. (2016). Whose National Allegory Is It Anyway? or What Happens When Crime Fiction Is Translated?. *Forum for Modern Language Studies*, 52(4), 1–16. DOI: 10.1093/fmls/cqw054.

Rolls, A., Vuaille-Barcan, M.-L., & West-Sooby, J., eds. (2016). Translating National Allegories: The Case of Crime Fiction. Special Issue. *The Target*, 22(2).

Seago, K., Evans, J., & De Céspedes, B. R., eds. (2014). Special issue on Crime in Translation. *The Journal of Specialized Translation*, 22 (July). www.jostrans.org/issue22/issue22_toc.php.

Semino, E., & Short, M. (2004). *Corpus Stylistics*. London: Routledge.

Simpson, Paul (1993). *Language, Ideology and Point of View*. London: Routledge.

Toolan, M. J. (1998). *Language in Literature: An Introduction to Stylistics*. London: Arnold.

Toporišič, J. (2000). *Slovenska slovnica*. Maribor: Obzorja.

Trupej, J. (2017). Strategies for Translating Racist Discourse about African-Americans into Slovenian. *Babel*, 63(3), 322–342.

Vines, L. D., ed. (1999). *Poe Abroad: Influence, Reputation, Affinities*. Iowa City: University of Iowa Press.

Zupan, S., & Sosič, A. (2001). Kriminalna uganka [Crime puzzle]. *Slavistična revija*, 49 (1–2), 41–53.

Zurru, E. (2008). Translating Postcolonial English: The Italian Translation of D. Walcott's The Odyssey: A Stage Version. *ELOPE. As You Write it: Issues in Literature, Language, and Translation in the Context of Europe in the 21st Century*, 5(1–2), 229–241.

8 Transnational Adaptations of Sherlock Holmes
A Relevance-Theoretic Discussion

Anne Furlong

8.1 Introduction

My objective in this chapter is to explore the ways in which transnational versions of the Holmes stories of Arthur Conan Doyle shed light on the process of adaptation. This chapter thus goes beyond Zupan's Chapter 7 on translation, acknowledging that a translated text can also be considered an adaptation of the original. Critics have long been impressed by the longevity, proliferation, creativity, innovativeness, and richness of adaptations of the Holmes narratives. From their first appearance in *Beeton's Christmas Annual* in 1887, these stories have been adapted at home and abroad; indeed, translations and locally inflected versions of the stories appeared literally around the world within a year or less of publication. Adaptors encourage, invite, require, or impose the non-spontaneous interpretation of adapted texts. The additional or augmented contextual effects (propositional and non-propositional) more than offset the increased cognitive effort expended by the audience. Indeed, adaptors and audiences implicitly recognise that without augmentation – through transmediation, to be sure, but also through alteration, revision, extension, or correction – an adaptation cannot succeed at the most fundamental level. In the case of the Sherlock Holmes tales, the proliferation of adaptations raises the issue of how many times the well can be revisited; on the evidence thus far, it seems indefinitely often.

The distinctive stylistic and narrative elements of these texts (as pointed out by Zupan's fine-grained analysis of a text by Edgar Allan Poe), emerging in the context of the development of modern crime and detective fiction, are readily imitable, occurring in recognisable form in virtually every adaptation, no matter how many alterations have been made or equivalents have been found. They include the intense but unequal friendship; the domestic arrangements of Holmes and Watson; the ascetic, acerbic nature of the detective; the complicated evidence chain that is laid bare through a combination of fieldwork and ratiocination; the integration of salient cultural concerns; and the narrative structure which typically begins with a summons and often ends with a sententious philosophical bromide. The most successful and complex adaptations build on Conan Doyle's tales, repaying non-spontaneous interpretation with a wider range of poetic and contextual effects than the source works; they also demonstrate the enduring appeal of the source texts in part by virtue of their extraordinary capacity to generate new works.

I approach adaptation studies from a relevance theoretic perspective. I propose that adaptors encourage their audience to develop non-spontaneous interpretations that may be more rewarding than the source works might warrant or support. Adaptors achieve this effect by encouraging audiences to invest considerable cognitive effort in constructing complex contexts and in developing intricately detailed readings which go well beyond either implicatures or even implications of the source works.[1] In the discussions that follow, I consider the relationship not only between a *source work* and its adaptations, or the *adaptation* and its audience, but also between the *adaptor* and the audience. In doing so, I distinguish adaptation from translation (see Chapter 7), touch on the status of parody (see Chapter 9), and argue that adaptations must produce new or augmented effects which may represent significant 'improvements' over the source works if they are to achieve relevance. My focus represents a significant shift from much of the work in adaptation studies, where questions of fidelity, value (including literary value), and mediation still tend to dominate.[2] It is my view that an adaptor has no duty to 'respect' the source, except as this serves their communicative purpose.

Relevance theory does not produce 'new' readings of texts.[3] Relevance theorists explore how readers arrive at the interpretations they do. They investigate the relationship between these interpretations and those manifestly intended by the author ('manifest' in relevance theory literature means capable of being mentally represented and accepted as true or probably true). Further, they examine the relationship between the text and the specifics of any given reader interpretation. Relevance theory can 'help produce richer and stronger analyses of the kinds of interpretations which it is the business of literary studies' to deliver, providing 'a vehicle for meta-critique, a systematic account

---

[1] Relevance theory follows Grice in distinguishing implications and implicatures. An implication is a proposition which follows logically from processing an utterance in a context; an implicature is an intended implication. The narrator of Seamus Heaney's poem 'Mid-Term Break' describes his brother's coffin as 'A four-foot box, a foot for every year'. A mischievous reader might argue that the line suggests that a five-year-old child should have a five-foot box (and so on), though it is extremely unlikely that Heaney intended this implication.

[2] See Albrecht-Crane and Cutchins (2013) for a relatively recent survey of the field; Bluestone (1957) for an introduction to some of the earliest principled treatments of adaptation in the twentieth century; Blankier (2014) for an demonstration of the application of adaptation taxonomies to fairy tales; and Leitch (2003) for a trenchant critique of the dominance of questions of fidelity.

[3] I suggest why this is not the case in 'A Modest Proposal: Linguistics and Literary Studies.' As I wrote: 'Literary and critical theorists ... [ask] How can linguistics produce fresh new readings of literary texts? ... but this criterion – the production of fresh readings – will not work for ... pragmatics any more than it will for phonology' (Furlong 2007, pp. 324–325).

of how a reader decides "what is meant" by a text' (Furlong 2007, p. 326). In contrast to literary and critical theories, which act as interpretive frameworks rendering certain aspects of the text or context more salient, relevance theory can offer 'an insight into the process of interpretation', thus allowing audiences and scholars the basis on which to evaluate interpretations and 'understand the bases of their conclusions' (Furlong 2007, p. 326). Below I provide a very brief introduction to some fundamental concepts of relevance theory, and develop my notion of non-spontaneous interpretation, making the case for its application to the study of adaptation.

8.2 Relevance Theory, Non-Spontaneous Interpretation, and Adaptation

Relevance theory, developed by Dan Sperber and Deirdre Wilson, based on the conversational maxim of relation as introduced by Grice, claims that readers are equipped with a single, universal, exceptionless criterion for evaluating interpretations as they occur to the audience. Something 'is relevant to an individual when its processing in a context of available assumptions yields a positive cognitive effect … [i.e.], a worthwhile difference to the individual's representation of the world' (Wilson & Sperber 2004, p. 622) – that is, achieves relevance. Relevance is a property (Sperber & Wilson 1995, p. 261), subject to extent conditions of effect and effort. Successful communication takes place if the addressee recognises (an adequate subset of) the set of assumptions the communicator intended their utterance to convey. The central claim of relevance theory is that audiences are guided to this intended interpretation by the principle of relevance – that every utterance communicates the presumption of its own optimal relevance. This presumption drives the generation, evaluation, and acceptance of a given interpretation at a given time by a given reader or audience.[4]

The relevance theory comprehension heuristic runs as follows:

(1) Follow a path of least effort in deriving cognitive effects: test interpretive hypotheses (disambiguations, reference resolutions, implicatures, etc.) in order of accessibility
(2) Stop when your expectations of relevance are satisfied (or abandoned).

While this protocol may seem to suggest the audience should never go beyond *initial* readings, Sperber and Wilson never intended this. An audience carrying

---

[4] Clearly, this rudimentary introduction grossly oversimplifies relevance theory's central claims and mechanisms. Readers wishing to know more about relevance theory can find the theory laid out in detail in Sperber and Wilson (1995); for a more succinct and accessible description, they may consult Allott (2013) or Wilson and Sperber (2004).

out a relatively spontaneous interpretation arrives at key conclusions and then moves on to think about something else. An audience carrying out a *less* spontaneous interpretation might dwell on further aspects of what the communicator might have intended. The *more* evidence the interpretation takes into account, and the *more broadly* the audience extends the context in looking for evidence to support particular conclusions, the *less* spontaneous it is. Thus, non-spontaneous interpretation involves extended cognitive effort as the audience aims for *maximal* relevance – accounting for as much of the evidence of the text as they can discern, and generating a core set of global inferences which are highly manifest in the context in which any part of the text is interpreted. Wilson (2011) describes an analogous process in her discussion of the open-endedness of interpretation, arguing that 'communication is not simply a yes-no matter, but a matter of degree' (p. 5), adding that 'in recognising the author's informative and communicative intentions, readers must necessarily go beyond them and derive some contextual implications (or other cognitive effects) of their own' (p. 6).

Audiences routinely carry out 'non-spontaneous interpretation'. The interpretation protocol described in standard relevance theory literature obtains, over a longer period, on the audience's responsibility. A text may impose an increased cognitive demand (as with legal texts [see Chapter 13] or puzzles) or raise expectations in the audience that investing more effort will result in increased cognitive effects (as with poetic texts). Alternatively, a hearer or reader may continue the interpretive process beyond the immediate communicative situation of their own volition without any prompting or guidance from the communicator. While it may appear that non-spontaneous interpretation is simply literary interpretation in a new coat, this is not the case. All literary interpretations are the outcome of non-spontaneous interpretation (whether pursued purposely or generated as the result of prolonged reflection sparked by individual tastes and preferences). From the author's point of view, a text may require non-spontaneous interpretation if the author has literary pretensions; from the audience's perspective, non-spontaneous interpretation will be undertaken only if relevance is achieved – if the effort of developing new contextual premises is more than adequately compensated by new (additional or augmented) contextual effects. Seen in this light, non-spontaneous interpretation is integral to the recognition and interpretation of adaptations, providing a way of understanding adaptations as communicative acts in their own right.[5] Adaptations *which are recognised as such*[6] ostensively invite some degree of non-spontaneous interpretation. The audience is encouraged to construct a context that includes not

---

[5] I have developed this argument at more length elsewhere: Furlong (2007, 2008, 2012, 2019).
[6] When an audience does not recognise a text as an adaptation, they treat the work as they would any new text, and the standard relevance theoretic heuristic applies.

only the evidence presented by the adaptation, but also assumptions derived from the source work itself, from any pre-existing adaptations, and from the audience's interpretations of these multiple texts.

While this discussion suggests that, from a relevance theoretic perspective, there are clear overlaps between translation and adaptation, I argue that these can be distinguished in principled terms by appeal to the objective of their creator. Ethical translators aim to produce the same (or similar) effects through the translation that the author created in the source work (see Chapter 7).[7] They know, of course, that it is impossible to create identical effects in the target language that the author has done in the source (sometimes due to the differences between languages as Zupan has demonstrated), and they know also that all translations present interpretations of the source work. Finally, when they are translating complex works, translators understand that their version of the source may be treated as a literary text in its own right, subject to non-spontaneous interpretation and critical reading.[8] Consequently, they will take care to make use of literary devices in the translation that will function as equivalents to techniques employed by the author of the source. However, no matter how many 'liberties' they may take, ethical translators aim to satisfy or meet their audience's expectation: that in reading the translation, the target audience can be assured that the interpretation they arrive at will be reasonably similar to the interpretation they could achieve were they able to read the work in the original language.

Adaptors, on the other hand, may well aim at replicating a work created in one medium in another (story to stage, for instance); on the other hand, they may present a different version in the same medium (abridged or condensed novels, for instance). In the case of parody (see Chapter 9), an adaptor will create a version which is superficially 'faithful' (i.e., one which preserves many of the narrative or textual features) but which ostensively communicates a humorous or mocking attitude toward the source.[9] Ultimately, it is the adaptor's interpretation of the source work, and not the interpretation manifestly intended by the author, which shapes the adaptation.[10] In contrast to translators, who 'speak for' the author (to put it metaphorically), making the source work available in a new language, adaptors speak for themselves.

---

[7] See Gutt 2000.

[8] So, for example, Heaney's translation of *Beowulf* is studied as a work of poetic art as well as a translation of the Old English text.

[9] Parody is readily accommodated within translation studies (Edwards 2007) and accounted for in relevance theory's treatment of irony and echoic speech more broadly considered.

[10] The value and creativity of an adaptation is not dependent on its difference from the source: there is no inherent advantage in either punctilious imitation or radical transformation. The audience's evaluation may be influenced by their expectations of replication, but adaptations are independent communicative acts and so are not bound by the intentions of the author of the pre-existing work. Here, too, they differ in principle from translation.

Though this discussion grossly oversimplifies the complexities of translation, the broad distinction between translation and adaptation is robust, granting that every translation requires some adaptation to the target audience, and that every adaptation effectively translates the source by placing it in a new context or medium.

Typically for many transmediated adaptations, as when the source moves from text to cinema, for example, much of the value is added through non-linguistic evidence for the adaptor's intended interpretation of the adaptation. The new contextual premises that support non-spontaneous interpretation repay the effort required by the repetition of familiar textual elements. The new material is not normally available through reading alone: even experienced, widely read, imaginative audiences will have difficulty conjuring up and retaining specific details of appearance, dress, and setting. Few readers will be able to continuously represent aural information, such as ambient sound, traffic, household noises, and all those results of physical movement which are created by Foley technicians in film.[11] And virtually none will devise an accompanying score specific to the story, the sequence, or the scene.

At the very least, then, a cinematic or television adaptation is expected to provide richer and more varied and detailed information than the textual source.[12] Moreover, some textual elements, such as scene-setting narrative, are redundant in visual media such as film, television, and graphic novels: there is no point telling audiences what they can see and hear for themselves. In relevance theoretic terms, such redundancy fails to achieve relevance, since it imposes gratuitous processing effort without achieving adequate contextual effects. Finally, the actors' contributions are critical: their expressiveness, their line readings, their interpretation of the character, their physical and emotional relationship to other actors, to the scene, and to the narrative present an almost overwhelming wealth of information for the audience; and while some members of the audience may recognise the actors' choices and evaluate them, most viewers will subject the acting to the relevance theoretic comprehension protocol and derive contextual effects spontaneously and automatically.

Adaptations thus provide evidence for the intended interpretation of the *new* work that exploits its resemblance to the earlier text; typically, readers rate

---

[11] Foley sound artists provide the incidental effects which help with cinematic world-building. Footsteps, the rustling of clothing, bird songs, wind and water noises, the crumpling of paper, the sound of tires, even the metallic slide of a sword from its sheath are all created by Foley artists in the sound studio during post-production. Scoring, which I also mention, is a separate process, and far more complex; musical scores in contemporary film and television are created by composers in collaboration with directors, producers, editors, and showrunners.

[12] Indeed, this expectation drives the conversion of novels into film. When the Twitter account Waterstones Swansea (@swanseastones) asked their followers, 'Which book, or series of books, would you most like to see adapted for the screen (film or tv)?', there were fifty-seven replies within hours.

most highly adaptations that more or less replicate the effects of the original. But to achieve relevance, adaptations must yield at least some effects that could not be produced by the source. Some of these may be created by the medium into which a work is transmediated, as I have indicated. Stage versions, movies, and television or streaming series provide rich visual and aural evidence. Graphic novels are not temporally constrained, and fan fiction typically addresses what the adaptor regards as deficiencies in the source.

One question raised by the practice of adaptation is whether these alterations add value or detract from the effects of the source work, and the answer depends on how we conceive of 'value'. I do not hold that literariness is inherent or immutable; nor do I accept that it is nothing more than a cultural construct, an expression of constantly shifting norms. Instead, I propose that audiences (in the case of the Holmes narratives, readers) produce 'literary' interpretations, carrying out non-spontaneous interpretation and deriving a wide range of positive cognitive effects. Some texts support such treatment (non-spontaneous interpretation aiming for exhaustiveness and the generation of global inferences) across a broad spectrum of readers, over a considerable period of time, and – in certain cases – in translation in other cultures and historical periods. Most texts treated in this fashion, however, would require so much cognitive effort that they would fail to achieve relevance, and fail to support this level of non-spontaneous interpretation.[13] Texts such as Conan Doyle's Sherlock Holmes narratives, through their influence and their capacity to attract new audiences, are treated as literary, and more than repay the effort required to produce non-spontaneous interpretations that achieve relevance. The wealth and variety of adaptations of the novel suggest that the typological and structural qualities of the text – as well as Conan Doyle's undoubted skills as a writer of fiction – underpin the enduring popularity of his Holmes narratives.

Irrespective of its final form, each adaptation constitutes an independent and original communicative act, neither restricted to nor constrained by the intended interpretation of the earlier text. As Hogan (2005), discussing Austen's influence on the twentieth-century Japanese writer Nogami Yaeko, notes, 'it is the second author or artist who has agency, not the first' (p. 79), in contrast to those who assume that an adaptation succeeds in part to the extent to which it retains crucial elements or retells the 'original', that is, by its fidelity, however this is construed. To support this view I will discuss in some

---

[13] The result of subjecting texts which are unlikely to support it to non-spontaneous interpretation can be disorienting. A nineteenth-century critic, John Bellenden Ker, read deep political and religious meanings into nursery rhymes. He claimed that 'There was an old woman lived under a hill' was a seditious poem that described the Roman Catholic Mass in cryptic and symbolic terms (see Baring-Gould & Baring-Gould 1962).

detail Maslennikov's 1981 Russian language made-for-television film of *The Hound of the Baskervilles*. I will also briefly consider the BBC-TV series *Sherlock*, the CBS series *Elementary*, and the HBO-Asia series *Miss Sherlock*, noting the ways in which these recent adaptations exploit elements of previous television and stage productions as well as the central narrative component of Doyle's stories.

8.3 Transnational Adaptations: *The Hound of the Baskervilles*

In the last quarter of the nineteenth century, the empires of England, Russia, and Japan were undergoing profound social, economic, and political change. In Japan and Russia, these shifts were often framed as 'modernisation', and raised questions of national identity. In England, transformations in work and leisure, though not calling into question the notion of 'Englishness', began to chip away at long-established norms and practices. Not surprisingly, such far-reaching transformations made citizens and authorities acutely conscious of threats to personal security and the critical need to maintain law and order, concerns which found expression in popular literature in the rise of detective and crime fiction. In England, tales from the Newgate calendar had long circulated in the press; along with these salacious accounts of doings of the poor and vicious, audiences could find the stories of James McLevy, the mid-century Edinburgh detective. In late imperial Russia, Ivan Dmitrievich Putilin, the head of the criminal investigative division in St Petersburg, published an autobiography (*Forty Years among Robbers and Murderers*) in 1889 that capitalised on the growing appetite in that country for such stories. In Meiji-era Japan, *Tantei Jitsuroku* (*Real Tales of Detection*) aimed at 'both instructing the public officials and enlightening the general public on how investigation and judiciary matters ought to be handled' (Tsutsumibayashi 2015). The ground was thus prepared for the appearance of Sherlock Holmes in all three cultures (the source work in Great Britain, and the translations in Russia and Japan).[14]

Almost immediately after the stories were first published in *The Strand*, Russian and Japanese translators produced precise, accurate target-language versions. The earliest adaptations in both Russia and Japan domesticated the Holmes narratives, lifting them from their historical and cultural origins and retelling them as if the tales had been written for the translator's or adaptor's non-English audience. The characters' names were replaced entirely with Russian or Japanese names (sometimes through phonetic matching), or native forms were exploited (e.g., the approach taken by the contemporary Japanese

---

[14] I am indebted to McReynolds (2013), Nepomnyashchy (2005), Okabe (2019), and Tsutsumibayashi (2015) for much of the historical and literary background information in this section.

HBO series *Miss Sherlock*: John Watson is now Wato Tachibana, or Wato-San). The stories were situated locally ('The Secret of the Nizhni Novgorod Storehouse'), and the crimes were aligned with local and contemporary genre preferences: Japanese popular crime fiction preferred female poisoners, Russian pulp fiction drew on accounts of spectacular thief-catchers. In Japan, the translations that were best received by the influential educated classes – the intelligentsia – were accompanied by detailed, painstaking footnotes or explanatory notes which explicated the context of the source texts. In some quarters, these translations were regarded as scholarly works in their own right, whose purpose was to educate the police and judiciary as well as to entertain lay readers; the translators hoped to provide models of rational, orderly, logical police and detective work for the emulation of the authorities. Russian adaptations also emphasised Holmes' methods, implicitly comparing them with those employed by famous, real-life detectives such as Putilin of St Petersburg. Unlike those produced in Japan, Russian translations for mass consumption lacked explanatory supplementary texts; moreover, the translators did not aim for precision and accuracy but played up the sensational aspects of crime and punishment. This difference is culturally significant: whereas the Japanese adaptors and audiences hoped to learn something for real-life policing, the Russian adaptors and readers treated the tales as pure entertainment. The distinction suggests contrasting perceptions of Western approaches to the detection and prevention of crime; the Russian versions merely added Holmes to a flourishing indigenous detective tradition, while the Japanese translations indicate a degree of anxiety about the need for reform and the adoption of modern methods of policing.

In Russia, apart from competent translations for cultured audiences (Charskii's had gone into its third edition by 1908 [McReynolds 2013, p. 217]), the *Adventures* were almost immediately domesticated and adapted in tales such as 'The Secret of the Nizhni Novgorod Storehouse'. Adaptations from this pre-revolutionary period, whether praising or mocking the authorities and the police, demonstrate Russians' 'cultural preference for the "whydunnit"', with a partiality for developing motive rather than emphasising process (McReynolds 2013, p. 222). Russian versions of Holmes were marked by a fatalism that rejected 'the closure found in Sherlockology' (p. 223), suggesting the degree to which the quintessentially English character was reconceptualised for this new audience.[15] What mattered from the first,

---

[15] McReynolds (2013) explains that Russian audiences appeared to prefer tragic conclusions that confirmed their conviction that no effort on an individual's part can influence the future; she argues that this attitude is diametrically opposed to the Western insistence on 'closure', a conclusion that makes sense of the crime and re-establishes the possibility of control and order.

however, was whether the adaptors expected their audiences to recognise their new works as adaptations at all. The answer is that for all their nativisation, the new versions featured original personae explicitly based on foreign (literary) texts; the appetite for these new genre-specific characters and plots, once created, could not be sated.

The multiplicity of these nineteenth-, twentieth-, and twenty-first-century Russian and Japanese adaptations of the Holmes narratives demonstrates the transnational appeal of such specifically situated tales. They also raise the question of how adaptors over the past century or so deal with the significant cultural differences, particularly during periods (such as Meiji-era Japan, late imperial Russia, and late Soviet Russia) when the cultural bias would presumably be against typical British imperial attitudes as expressed by the characters and implied by the narratives. Several adaptation strategies emerge, all dealt with in the standard adaptation studies literature: domestication, replication, re-invention, and modernisation, to name a few of the many possibilities.[16]

I have selected *The Hound of the Baskervilles* not only for the range and variety of its adaptations, but because the 1981 Russian television film represents an acme of both domestication and exoticism, against which other versions (and the source itself) can be profitably discussed, and because comments by the adaptors (directors, producers, writers) explicate their goals, their views on the value of the film and on the cultural and historical context in which the film was made and broadcast. Where an element is eliminated, the adaptor's communicative act will differ markedly from Conan Doyle's, or from the authors of crime and detective fiction generally. When virtually all the elements are retained, we may initially expect the adaptation will convey more or less the same set of effects as the source; but such is not always the case. Here, for instance, we will find that though the 'signature' features are preserved, the adaptation conveys implicatures not consistent with Conan Doyle's text, and in some ways antithetical to it. At this point, a quick review of the text is in order.

The Hound of the Baskervilles is Conan Doyle's third novel featuring Sherlock Holmes, appearing originally in volumes 22–23 (August 1901–April 1902) of 'The Strand', and set before Holmes' ostensibly fatal encounter with his arch enemy, Professor Moriarty, at the Reichenbach Falls. The text consists of fifteen chapters (2,250 to a little under 5,000 words each), structured to suit the demands of serial publication: chapters that end with a startling revelation ('they were the footprints of a gigantic hound!') tend to be followed by chapters that begin *in media res* ('I confess at these words a

---

[16] Blankier (2014) and Leitch (2003) rehearse a number of possible 'types' of adaptation. Taxonomies swell and diminish, depending on the writer, but all express some attitude toward the source work, and some intention regarding the intended audience.

shudder passed through me'), while chapters that conclude less sensationally ('we will postpone all further thought upon this business') are followed by chapters with scene-setting openings ('Our breakfast table was cleared early'). Important details provided in earlier chapters are alluded to explicitly in later ones, and repeated descriptions are truncated. These devices help guide readers by increasing the saliency of old information without putting the reader to unnecessary effort, in effect reducing processing effort by stimulating retrieval from memory. However, other pieces of information – concerning Holmes and Watson's domestic arrangements and personal relationship, for example – are repeated, not only within individual stories, but across the entire canon. So we learn, in each entry in Watson's casebooks, about the pair's domestic habits (including Holmes' dressing gown, his smoking, his violin-playing or his philistinism) and personalities (Watson's hero-worship, his weakness for pretty women, his sensitivity to weather and landscape); the specifics may vary, but the narratives unvaryingly tread the same round.

The Hound trades on some of the staple motifs and tropes of sensation fiction in English. It incorporates elements from Gothic fiction (wild, remote settings; inchoate evil; crumbling ancestral manors or estates), ghost stories (generational curses, ghost dogs, night-time terrors, frightened women), and crime fiction (murder, assault, imprisonment). All are subordinated to the framing narrative of a dominant strand of detective fiction, the resolution of a (criminal) puzzle by a brilliant, super-rational, eccentric genius.[17] Many of these elements appear in the majority of the Holmes tales, in assorted combinations. So, for example, *A Study in Scarlet*, though set in London, originates in the wilds of Mormon-controlled Utah; *The Adventure of the Copper Beeches* draws Holmes and Watson from the crowded streets of London to an isolated manor where a young woman is being held captive; and the racist *The Adventure of the Yellow Face* involves the generational 'curse' of 'miscegenation'.

Adaptations of *The Hound* thus have a wealth of material to draw from: the adaptors' choices suggest their communicative intentions, and their methods reveal a formidable range and flexibility. The novel has been adapted for stage, screen, television, graphic novels and comic books, and board and video games (and this list is incomplete). Since the late 1970s, several television

---

[17] More than one critic has pointed out that Holmes does not employ deduction at all. Keller and Klein (1990) take up this thread, arguing that 'the hypotheses of fictional detectives are not always arrived at through induction, neither are they always at first formed abductively' (p. 46). They assert that 'tacit knowledge' – 'principles and internalised scripts of which we are not always consciously aware' (p. 46) – plays a crucial role in detective fiction. In relevance theoretic terms, tacit knowledge is captured in part in the notion of 'cognitive environment', that is, the set of assumptions manifest to an individual at a given time (Sperber & Wilson 1995, p. 39), though Keller and Klein explicitly incorporate work on knowledge schemas.

films of *The Hound* have appeared. Among the earliest is a 1981 made-for-television film (147 minutes) on Soviet television, directed by Igor Maslennikov, with the actors Vasilij Livanov as Holmes and Vitali Solomin as Watson, remarkable for its blend of domestication and exoticism.

8.3.1   The Russian 'Hound'

In the Soviet Union in the 1980s, Russian-language television produced a truly outstanding series of film adaptations which some Holmes fans consider to be among the most 'faithful' ever produced. Nepomnyashchy (2005) notes that 'the Soviet Holmes is very much the iconic Holmes of the ongoing visual and cinematic tradition and, second, in cinematic quotations' (p. 132). She argues that this adaptation reflects 'the urge to evade the rigours and political disenchantments and pitfalls of the age'. In its director's words, Nepomnyashchy notes, the series was '"playing at being British (*igra v anglichanstvo*). It's boyishness for adults" (quoted in Rtishcheva 2000)', p. 131).

A direct comparison of the Soviet film with the source text only is insufficient; the visual allusions strongly suggest that the filmmakers were aware of the many previous film treatments as well as the iconography that has grown up around the figures of Holmes, Watson, and the hound. The discussion that follows, then, will include cinematographic and visual elements that appear in earlier adaptations, but which are missing from the source. As well, I will identify and comment on those features which, though intended to represent the England of the late nineteenth century, are indisputably Russian. Casting choices, interiors, locations, dress, and domestic details which are intended to stand in for those of the source (or of previous adaptations) blend the exotic (life among the British bourgeoisie) with the domestic (tea and coffee services, complete with samovars; standards of male and female beauty; stereotypes of household staff). Some of these were doubtless Hobson's choices, as it was well beyond the capabilities of the producers to replicate late nineteenth-century England. In such cases, the *mise-en-scène* aims for an acceptable representation rather than a historically faithful reproduction. Other decisions, however, seem intended to bring Holmes and Watson into line with the cultural expectations of the audience. Still other choices, as Nepomnyashchy (2005, p. 134) suggests, were deliberately taken to position *The Hound* as manifestly non-political.

Textually, the film follows the source work very closely. I am relying on the subtitled version of the film, but even without translation, the departures from Conan Doyle's story are relatively minor so far as the plot is concerned. Much of the dialogue is reproduced, with such alterations as translation and acting choices may require. Most of the characters in the source narrative are preserved, along with their relationships to one another, their roles in the plot, and their moral values.

From the outset, then, Maslennikov's direction emphasises the close resemblance of his version to the source, drawing attention to the film's status as both adaptation and translation. During the opening credits, a hand unrolls the scroll describing the Baskerville curse (a scroll that will reappear in the first scene); a second sheet is laid over it, with strategically placed openings that transform the English letters into Cyrillic. As a result, the title, the actors' names, and so forth seem to arise 'naturally' out of Conan Doyle's narrative, suggesting the adaptor intends to provide a Russian-language version of the story with few if any variations from the source. Yet the *mise-en-scène* at once complicates the implicated relationship: the costumes, the set design, and the props are plainly Russian, from about the last decade of the nineteenth century. Here, we will encounter a Holmes who is not just Russian-inflected, but re-created in Russian (though emphatically not Soviet) form. Maslennikov's *Hound* opens with a promise of fidelity – that is, identity of text *and* of interpretation – which is immediately both fulfilled and undermined. I will focus on three aspects – characterisation, *mise-en-scène*, and cultural relevance – in my analysis of the effects and limitations of this adaptation.

Characterisation We all know what Sherlock Holmes looks like: tall, thin, with nervous fingers and a vigorous tread. But the details of that knowledge are not in fact derived from Conan Doyle's text. There, Watson focuses on Holmes' behaviour (tossing a cigarette into the fireplace, leaning back on a settee, looking keenly at Dr Mortimer, laughing heartily when one of his plans is foiled), and characterises the man as 'keen', 'intent', 'impatient', and 'mischievous' but says almost nothing about his friend's appearance, dress, or expression. For the fullest physical description of Holmes we must turn to 'The Science of Deduction', the second chapter of the first Holmes adventure, *A Study in Scarlet*:

In height he was rather over six feet, and so excessively lean that he seemed to be considerably taller. His eyes were sharp and piercing, save during those intervals of torpor to which I have alluded; and his thin, hawk-like nose gave his whole expression an air of alertness and decision. His chin, too, had the prominence and squareness which mark the man of determination. (Doyle 1930, p. 20)

Virtually the only addition to this description in *The Sign of the Four*, the next Holmes narrative, comes from Watson's remark that the detective has 'long, white, nervous fingers'. Otherwise, either Holmes' appearance is merely alluded to (on the assumption that the reader is familiar with previous narratives), or the original traits appear in compressed form.

Compare Watson's account of his intimate friend with his description of Mary Morstan in that novel:

> Miss Morstan entered the room with a firm step and an outward composure of manner. She was a blonde young lady, small, dainty, well gloved, and dressed in the most perfect taste. There was, however, a plainness and simplicity about her costume which bore with it a suggestion of limited means. The dress was a sombre greyish beige, untrimmed and unbraided, and she wore a small turban of the same dull hue, relieved only by a suspicion of white feather in the side. Her face had neither regularity of feature nor beauty of complexion, but her expression was sweet and amiable, and her large blue eyes were singularly spiritual and sympathetic. (Doyle 1930, p. 94)

And compare both with his account of Dr Mortimer, the friend and mentor of Henry Baskerville, in *The Hound*:

> The appearance of our visitor was a surprise to me, since I had expected a typical country practitioner. He was a very tall, thin man, with a long nose like a beak, which jutted out between two keen, grey eyes, set closely together and sparkling brightly from behind a pair of gold-rimmed glasses. He was clad in a professional but rather slovenly fashion, for his frock-coat was dingy and his trousers frayed. Though young, his long back was already bowed, and he walked with a forward thrust of his head and a general air of peering benevolence. (Doyle 1930, p. 671)

In both cases, we are given not only some physical attributes ('grey eyes, set closely together', 'large blue eyes', 'blonde young lady') but characterisation as well ('spiritual and sympathetic', 'peering benevolence'). Further portrayals reinforce the initial impressions, but of course as neither Morstan nor Mortimer appear in other tales, these are the only accounts provided. Holmes' physical appearance is not described again in either *Study* or *Hound*.[18]

As it turns out, the 'classic' appearance of Holmes in filmic adaptations owes little to Conan Doyle's text. It originates in the drawings of Sidney Paget, who illustrated the Holmes stories for *The Strand*.[19] William Gillette, the actor who made the role his own on stage and screen from 1899 until the 1940s, perpetuated this image and added innumerable details of wardrobe, including

---

[18] It is often unclear whether Watson is speaking for himself or focalising Holmes. If the latter, it might account for the differences here. However, Watson is capable of close observation, though as Holmes puts it, 'You see, but you do not observe' ('A Scandal in Bohemia', chapter 1). Moreover, he has a keen eye for feminine beauty (which Holmes lacks), a predilection for sentiment, and a marked tendency to equate moral and aesthetic qualities, all of which appear in his descriptions of people, including Holmes.

[19] Moffatt and Gatiss allude to the influence of Paget and others in the script of 'The Abominable Bride', an original episode of *Sherlock*. When the housekeeper, Mrs Hudson, complains that Watson's narratives 'make the rooms so drab and dingy', he replies, 'Oh, blame it on the illustrator. He's out of control. I've had to grow this moustache just so that people would recognize me.'

the deerstalker hat and the meerschaum pipe.[20] Basil Rathbone, perhaps the most famous film Holmes, layered on yet more incidental elements. Vasilij Livanov's Russian Holmes is fairer than Rathbone or Gillette, more slender than Gillette but less wiry than Rathbone, and apparently slightly shorter than either.[21] In all other ways, however, his fundamental characterisation is in line with the iconic version first created by Paget, though inflected for a Russian audience.

However, Livanov, presumably under the guidance of the director Maslennikov, makes little attempt to create a 'realistic' portrayal of an English gentleman of the period; instead, his performance is 'playing at being British' (Nepomnyashchy 2005, p. 131) as a Russian audience in the Soviet Union might conceive of this in 1981. Solomin, as Watson, creates a less obsequious and block-headed Watson; though hardly Holmes' intellectual equal, he is brave, susceptible, fond of good living, and willing to show his annoyance with Holmes' mockery. Even Dr Mortimer, though his gestures are too delicate, even effeminate, for the taste of a British or American audience of the time, nevertheless seems constructed to convey the stereotyped notion of an English man of science: an amateur, despite his dedication, and more than faintly ridiculous in his preoccupation with phrenology and Celtic mythology.[22] So far as these characters are concerned, they may reflect an outsider's understanding of British society, but they do not challenge it.

On the other hand, Baskerville and his household are notably un-English. Nikita Mikhalkov portrays Henry Baskerville as a giant of a man with an impressive handlebar moustache, far from the 'small, alert, dark-eyed man about thirty years of age, very sturdily built, with thick black eyebrows and a strong, pugnacious face' of the novel (Doyle 1930, p. 685). He props his dirty booted feet on the dining table in the great hall, drinks excessively, behaves with almost childish resentment when he is crossed, and rides horses like a Cossack. Indeed, Mikhalkov plays Baskerville very much along the lines of the King of Bohemia in the story that introduced Irene Adler: blustering, full-blooded, given to excess in drink and amorous passion. Similarly, the short, swarthy, shifty Barrymore of the movie, with his chinstrap beard (not the 'full black beard' of the novel) is equally out of place, as is his wife; neither would pass muster as household staff in an ancestral hall in the remotest part of England. Most remarkable, however, is the film's treatment of Laura Lyons. Her situation – deserted by her husband, rejected by her father – follows the

---

[20] The pipe specified in the text, a black clay pipe, would have had a straight stem, and obscured Gillette's lower face on stage. The meerschaum, with its curved stem, posed no such difficulty.

[21] Rathbone established the cinematic Holmes as Gillette established the stage version on which it was based.

[22] The adaptation completes the burlesque by giving Mortimer's 'curly-haired spaniel' the name 'Snoopy'.

novel, but the film makes clear that she has left any pretence of conventional respectability behind. In the aesthetically ornamented rooms she occupies, she casually smokes a long black clay pipe like any fin-de-siècle New Woman.

These performances and interpretations effectively domesticate the film, presenting the viewers with the Russian notion of an English household, an ancient manor, and a properly dominating hereditary lord. Maslennikov's direction thus ensures that both audiences and political censors will recognise that no undue praise of Western methods is intended; at the same time, he brings the exotic world of the late Victorian bourgeoisie into the homes of viewers for their amusement. None of the effects arising from these portrayals and directorial decisions are available through reading: all require the amplification of cinema. To this end, the adaptation relies heavily on *mise-en-scène*.

Mise-en-scène The filmmakers have taken great care in bringing Baker Street and Baskerville Hall to the screen. However, few if any of the details of setting, set dressing, lighting, sound design, and composition are drawn from Conan Doyle's text. Instead, the *mise-en-scène* reflects the contributions of the director, screenwriter, producer, cinematographer, and crew of this production – and, indeed, of innumerable previous adaptations for stage and screen. While the Baker Street set conforms broadly to pre-existing visualisations (again going back to Paget's illuminations), Baskerville Hall and the moors are presented more freely; they will strike Western viewers familiar with the conventions guiding the depiction of the English landscape and country manors as inexplicably 'foreign'. The landscape in which Baskerville Hall sits is appropriately desolate, but low, marshy, and flat: the hills and hollows of the Devonshire moors are nowhere in evidence.

The interiors of the Hall are great cavernous spaces devoid of comfort and ornament. The furniture, great knobbed nineteenth-century pieces, imply grandeur but also scarcity. For instance, Barrymore locks up the bottles of spirits and wine, so that we know there are ample supplies available. At the same time, the bare walls, the plain staircases, and the lack of ornamentation convey not just gloom but a poverty of invention. The architectural spaces suggested by the studio set do not represent but stand in for the proportions of a stately home. For an audience whose knowledge of comparable spaces relies on films instead of historic sources, or pre-revolutionary *dachas*, Maslennikov's version is more than adequate. But the underdeveloped *mise-en-scène* beyond the confines of Baker Street – including the crooked cobbled lanes that are intended to represent London – means that the adaptation relies for its effect on the pre-existing assumptions of the audience and on the familiarity of the countryside and the built environment. Other peculiarities may owe as much to the financial and production constraints as to the demands of a Russian-language audience. The costumes imitate late Victorian styles: Watson sports tweed hunting jackets and cloth caps in a subdued small check, even at Baker Street, while Holmes' Bohemian leanings[23] are revealed by his velvet smoking-jacket and ostentatiously patterned tie.

Cultural Relevance As McReynolds (2013) and Nepomnyashchy (2005, p. 134) suggest, the Russian-language adaptations of Sherlock Holmes align themselves culturally with the audience's preferences and presumptions. While the pre-revolutionary translations were deliberately domesticated for local consumption, the film treatments of the late 1970s and 1980s provided 'a multiplicity of potential relationships ... between the antiquated, bourgeois values of the text and the realities of the Soviet present'. The adaptation initially achieves relevance not by reproducing the text in transmediated form but by amplifying it, supplying visual and aural information absent from the stories at a level of detail which no reader would think to imagine for themselves. For audiences who carry out a non-spontaneous interpretation of the film, the contrast between this safely encapsulated imperial past and the fraught Soviet present (*The Hound* screened in the last years of the Brezhnev era) could well provoke a wide-ranging, sophisticated, and highly satisfying range of effects.

The vicarious enjoyment of relatively well-to-do Victorians is tempered, and made palatable, by their transformation. A slavish reproduction of fin-de-siècle London would emphasise both the foreignness and the inaccessibility of that society. Displays of excess would not be tolerated or appreciated by the public or by political overseers; nor would the peculiar conventions that governed interpersonal relationships be comprehensible to most audiences without tedious explicatory dialogue. Finally, Livanov's performance pulls Holmes out of the ranks of English gentlemen and remakes him as a quintessentially Russian character. All these effects are readily produced because of the familiarity of so many cultural markers: Baskerville's heroic proportions, the sturdy peasants, the sly serving class, even the decaying grandeur of the Hall, evoke a romantic past without endorsing it. Maslennikov's film adaptation manifestly addresses the cultural and ideological expectations of the Soviet audience. Consequently, its success was produced not by its relation to the source but by the degree to which it conformed to the complexities of Soviet political and aesthetic realities.

Nepomnyashchy (2005, p. 132) notes 'the generally acknowledged priority of literature over film in Soviet culture'; the tension was not between high and low culture but 'between unacceptable, excluded cultural products' and 'those

---

[23] Cottom (2012) argues that if 'Dracula represents the fantasized origin of the bohemian, Holmes is this figure's fantastic end' (p. 537).

works given the official imprimatur of publication or production'. Consequently, those aspects of the Holmes narratives in conflict with approved views were more likely to be lampooned, derided, or treated with light contempt. She further argues that the Soviet adaptations combine 'easy familiarity with the foreign cinematic tradition' with a 'fondly ironic stance towards their predecessor texts' (p. 132). The result is a version that produces a range of aesthetic effects, depending on the characteristics of the audience. For viewers well versed in cinema, particularly foreign film, 'cinematic quotations' (p. 132) may function as confirmations of their privileged, elite status, and as occasions for humour.[24] Less sophisticated audience members may derive pleasure from the domestication of the archetypal British imperialist, remade in the shape of an intellectual from the late Tsarist period. Any hint of (hazardous) nostalgia for that past is negated by the relentless ridiculing of non-sanctioned Western values and mores as expressed by Holmes, Watson, and the rest. At the same time, however, viewers could take unalloyed pleasure in the well-known landscape, the nativist-inflected costumes, and the recasting of characters in the terms of traditional storytelling.

The reception of the adaptation thus rests on a set of complex, often incompatible contextual assumptions. National identity is simultaneously reinforced and destabilised by the domestication of the Holmes narrative. The ironic treatment of English and American characters implies the hollowness of the West and its vanities, while the meticulous recreation of the imperial past seals it off hermetically from the imperial present and renders it harmless. But the indulgence of the tastes of the Victorian empire – for ornament, for the conspicuous display of wealth, for the satiation of appetites and desires – contrasts sharply with the constraints of the Soviet one, subverting the latter's claims to inherent superiority.

8.4 The Russian *Hound* and Contemporary Adaptations in English and Japanese

More current iterations – the BBC limited series, the CBS network series, and the Japanese HBO series – are more ambitious but less culturally or politically fraught than Maslennikov's film. Each engages with the Holmes of the texts but equally with the myriad adaptations of the preceding century. The producers have little interest in hewing closely to the letter of the novels and stories,

---

[24] In one case of cinematic intertextual allusion, 'Holmes beckons the new lodger into his room, shows him an array of photographs and asks if he is acquainted with any of the people in them. Watson somewhat squeamishly responds in the negative, while Holmes maintains that he knows them well. The particularly shady characters exhibited, however, appear all to be shots from vintage films, including Lon Cheney Sr in his famous make-up for his role in the silent film of Phantom of the Opera' (Nepomnyashchy 2005, p. 132).

though in many cases they have incorporated dialogue and important plot points from most of the adventures. Instead, these adaptors aim at engaging both aficionados and neophytes, extending the long reach of Holmesian influence to new generations of readers and viewers.

Two English-language adaptations appeared almost simultaneously in the United Kingdom and the United States, each reflecting not only the cultural preferences of the producers and writers but also the different modes of production and broadcast. In the United Kingdom, BBC produced four seasons of three ninety-minute episodes of *Sherlock*; in the United States, CBS aired seven seasons of *Elementary*, totalling 153 episodes. The constraints of weekly network television led the writers and producers of *Elementary* to reduce or compress screenplays adapted from Conan Doyle (including *Hound*), and to create new narratives for the central characters. By contrast, the BBC series more closely resembles the Soviet version; though produced for television, each episode was consciously written and shot as if it were for cinematic release. So, while the Russian series reveals the blurred lines between film and television in the late Soviet era, the British series deliberately aims at cinematic standards of quality, complexity, and detail. The American series cannot match these features at the level of the individual episode. However, the carefully curated developments in character and the internal and intertextual consistency yield powerful cumulative effects.

The adaptations embark on a form of domestication; one is set in contemporary New York (*Elementary*), the other in contemporary London (*Sherlock*). While *Elementary* necessarily generates a significant number of new plots to fit the demands of American serial television, like *Sherlock*, it retains the central characters and relationships in all relevant respects; the writers of both series typically insert references that encourage an audience familiar with the source to recognise the allusions and develop contextual effects. The political, cultural, and genre preferences of the audience are consciously reflected in their differing treatments of *The Hound*.

In *Sherlock*, the episode is set in what was then present-day England (2012), retaining the Devonshire location, the gigantic spectral hound, and the plot against Sir Henry Baskerville's life. However, the villain is Bob Frankland (not Stapleton), and the hound in question is both a stray dog gone feral on the moors and the acronym for a government research group working on biological weapons some thirty years earlier in the United States. The writers of the *Elementary* episode also preserve the names of the central characters and alter the identity of the murderer (Laura Lyons); but they make a number of other significant changes. The setting shifts to New York, where equivalents for the characters' social status ('venture capitalist') in the US context make more sense than hereditary peer, while suggesting similar levels of wealth, privilege, and predatory behaviour. Both adaptations are intended to appeal to a wide audience: fans of the source works may bring a critical appreciation to inventive parallels, while viewers unfamiliar with Conan Doyle's text may appreciate the episodes as crime and detective fiction.

In both series, the characterisation of Holmes follows the source text, but is deeply informed by a century of cinematic forbears. The actors are lean, dark, and intense, though neither is as tall as specified in the novels, and their facial features are not as sharp as Conan Doyle indicates. The BBC series introduces new characters (police officers, coroners) but otherwise makes no innovations; the CBS series, by contrast, engages in what could have been disastrous recasting. John Watson, veteran of the Afghan wars, becomes Joan Watson, a disgraced surgeon. However, the dynamic at the heart of the Holmes stories, the friendship between the central characters, far from being abandoned, is pleasantly energised by the change. Finally, while the Russian *Hound* entailed a complex *mise-en-scène* that attempted to reconcile the Soviet present with the imperial past, no such difficulties face the makers of the UK and US versions. Both series are mainstream productions that straightforwardly enact the political and cultural sensibilities of the audience.

The recent Japanese television series *Miss Sherlock* is both inventive and slyly derivative. The innovations – casting women as the lead characters, setting the stories in contemporary Japan, finding local equivalents for the crimes and criminals – are less interesting than the deliberate echoes and integration of the visual and cinematic details of other series. The floor plan of Holmes' apartment is laid out along very similar lines to that of the BBC series, down to the colour scheme, set decoration, and placement of the kitchen. The promotional material for the series places Holmes and Wato-san against an ornate wallpaper pattern, which closely resembles the paper in Sherlock's sitting room. The sequences that indicate movement from one location to another incorporate comparable images – successive shots of the city from the air, from street level, following Holmes as she strides up a staircase – to the BBC series. Like Benedict Cumberbatch as *Sherlock*, who wears a distinctive Belstaff coat, *Miss Sherlock*'s Yūko Takeuchi wears a light trench coat with the collar turned up; her stiletto heels allow her to tower over her co-stars, giving the impression of height and leanness. With respect to the *mise-en-scène*, the producers have taken many of the technical devices of the UK series, such as 'floating images' that illustrate Sherlock's thought processes, or close-ups of some detail which has caught the detective's attention. The adaptors have thus resolved the difficulty of domesticating Holmes through the overt appropriation of signature visual and cinematic elements while altering the plots to reflect current cultural concerns, such as the status of women in Japanese culture, the state of the family, and social mobility.

While it is true that there seems never to have been a year without a fresh adaptation or interpretation of the Holmes narratives, reissues of older television and film versions on cable, DVD, and streaming services have allowed earlier variations to persist in cultural memory. The efflorescence of variants on the Great Detective have helped unmoor Holmes from the source texts so that his character has achieved an existence partly independent of Conan Doyle's work. Given Holmes' seminal status in crime and as a detective – not as the first, but as the most heavily and frequently adapted of all crime fiction – it could be said that all crime fiction comes out of Baker Street,[25] allowing Holmes and Watson to settle as far afield as New York, Japan, and the Soviet Union.

8.5 Conclusion

Translators speak, or purport to speak (though this may be merely a pose) for the author. Adaptors, even those who aim at replicating or recreating the range of effects produced by the source works in a new medium, or in reduced or expanded form in the original medium, are speaking for themselves. Adaptations may well support better, richer, more detailed, and more satisfying non-spontaneous interpretation than do the source works. This is, I would argue, particularly the case with the Holmes narratives, which are all too often repetitive, jingoistic, racist, misogynist, and fraudulent.[26] They are also seminal works in the development of crime and detective fiction, and lend themselves to apparently infinite variation and reinvention. Along with Paget, Rathbone, and the hundreds of other stage, film, and television versions over the last century, it is the vast array of adaptations – amplifications, revisions, parodies, celebrations, and recreations – which have lifted the Great Detective out of Doyle's casebooks.

As Cavallaro (2017) writes, 'I have more than 243 adaptations to choose from, not counting the version in my own head.' There are, in fact, many more.

---

[25] As de Jonge (1974) puts it: 'We all came out of Gogol's "Overcoat", the most famous apocryphal saying of Russian literature, ... attributed to Dostoevsky ... suggests not only that Gogol was the great source of the Russian novel but that his works lent themselves to a wide enough range of interpretations for his overcoat to shelter, comfortably, future Turgenevs, Chekhovs, Dostoevskys, and Tolstoys.' Similarly, Holmes has been the inspiration for generations of super-sleuths, reinterpreted and revised with every change in the social and cultural winds.

[26] With regard to fraudulence, Keller and Klein (1990) point out that Holmes' solutions rely on 'tacit' knowledge rather than on deduction or other forms of reasoning. Holmes is described as 'the most perfect reasoning and observing machine that the world has ever seen' (*A Scandal in Bohemia*, Doyle 1930, p. 161) but as Keller and Klein point out, this description is not at all accurate. The Japanese and Russian translations and adaptations were intended 'to educate the police and judiciary as well as to entertain lay readers'; 'the translators hoped to provide models of rational, orderly, logical police and detective work for the emulation of the authorities'. The model they sought to copy, however, was fundamentally flawed and misleading.

Impressive successes or dire failures, they are indisputable evidence of the enduring appeal of the framework on which generations of readers, writers, filmmakers, and artists have raised a remarkably productive, bewildering array of variations, from the canonically precise to the absurd. As long as we gauge the success of adaptations by fidelity to the text, by conformity with our private interpretations, or by reaching some standard of literariness set by the source, we will miss the point. The process and the effects of adaptation, the complex cross-pollination and repurposing of technical, literary, and medium-specific devices, strongly suggest that adaptations work, when they work, because adaptors modify and revise source texts for their own communicative purposes, taking their own audiences into consideration.

References

Abominable Bride, The (2016). *Sherlock*. BBC One, 1 January 2016.
Albrecht-Crane, C., & Cutchins, D. (2013). Introduction: New Beginnings for Adaptation Studies. In C. Albrecht-Crane & D. Cutchins, eds., *Adaptation Studies: New Approaches*. Madison, NJ: Fairleigh Dickinson University Press, pp. 11–22.
Allott N. (2013). Relevance Theory. In A. Capone, F. Lo Piparo, & M. Carapezza, eds., *Perspectives in Pragmatics, Philosophy & Psychology, vol. 2: Perspectives on Linguistic Pragmatics*. Cham: Springer, pp. 57–98.
Baring-Gould, C., & Baring-Gould, W. (1962). *The Annotated Mother Goose*. New York: Bramhall House.
Barquin, A. (2016). *The Arthur Conan Doyle Encyclopedia*. Personal web page. www.arthur-conan-doyle.com.
Blankier, M. (2014). Adapting and Transforming 'Cinderella': Fairy-Tale Adaptations and the Limits of Existing Adaptation Theory. *Interdisciplinary Humanities*, 31(3), 108–123.
Bluestone, G. (1957). *Novels into Film: A Critical Study*. Baltimore: Johns Hopkins University Press.
Brombley, K. (2018). Escaping the *Strand*: The Paratextual Sherlock Holmes. *Critical Quarterly*, 60(3), 49–65.
Cavallaro, B. (2017). Not My Sherlock: A Sherlock Holmes Expert on 'The Six Thatchers' and the Perils of Reinvention. *Literary Hub*, 4 January. https://lithub.com/not-my-sherlock/ (accessed 27 June 2019).
Cottom, D. (2012). Sherlock Holmes Meets Dracula. *ELH*, 79(3), 537–567.
de Jonge, A. (1974). Under the Overcoat. *The New York Review of Books*, 18 April. www.nybooks.com/articles/1974/04/18/under-the-overcoat/ (accessed 10 January 2020).
Doyle, A. C. (1930). *The Complete Sherlock Holmes*. 2 vols. Garden City, NY: Doubleday & Company.
Edwards, P. (2007). Adaptation: Two Theories. *Text and Performance Quarterly*, 27(4), 369–377.
Furlong, A. (2007). A Modest Proposal: Linguistics and Literary Studies. *Canadian Journal of Applied Linguistics*, 10(3), 324–345.

(2008). You can't put your foot in the same river once: Relevance Stylistics and Repetition. *Proceedings of The State of Stylistics, 26th Annual Meeting of the Poetics and Linguistics Association*. Amsterdam: Rodopi, pp. 283–302.

(2012). 'It's not quite what I had in mind': Adaptation, Faithfulness, and Interpretation. *Journal of Literary Semantics*, 41(2), 175–191.

(2019). Adaptations as Communicative Acts. In K. Scott, B. Clark, & R. Carston, eds., *Relevance, Pragmatics, and Interpretation*. Cambridge: Cambridge University Press, pp. 267–278.

Gatiss, M. (2012). The Hounds of Baskerville. *Sherlock*, BBC-TV. Dir. P. MacGuigan.

Gatiss, M., & Moffatt, S. (2016). The Abominable Bride. *Sherlock*, BBC-TV. Dir. D. Mackinnon.

Grice, H. P. (1975). Logic and Conversation. In P. Cole & J. L. Morgan, eds., *Syntax and Semantics, vol. 3: Speech Acts*. New York: Academic, pp. 41–58.

Gutt, E.-A. (2000). *Translation and Relevance: Cognition and Context*. Manchester: St Jerome Publishing.

Hogan, E. J. (2005). Beyond Influence: The Literary Sisterhood of Nogami Yaeko and Jane Austen. *U.S.-Japan Women's Studies*, 29, 77–98.

Hound of the Baskervilles, The. (Приключения Шерлока Холмса и доктора Ватсона: Собака Баскервилей). (1981). Directed by Igor Maslennikov [film]. Moscow: Lenfilm Studio.

Hounds of Baskerville, The (2012). *Sherlock*, Series Two, Episode Two. BBC One, 8 January 2012.

Hounded (2016). *Elementary*, Series 4, Episode 16. *CBS*, 10 March 2016.

Hutcheon, L. (2006). *A Theory of Adaptation*. New York: Routledge.

Kotani, N., Masaike, Y., & Mori, J. (2018). The Wakasugi Family Curse. *Miss Sherlock*, HBO Asia/Hulu Japan. Dir. Y. Taki.

Keller, J., & Klein, K. G. (1990). Detective Fiction and the Function of Tacit Knowledge. *Mosaic*, 23(2), 45–60.

Leitch, T. (2003). Twelve Fallacies in Contemporary Adaptation Theory. *Criticism* 45(2), 149–171.

Maslennikov, I., & Veksler, Y. (1981). *The Hound of the Baskervilles*. Lenfilm. Dir. I. Maslennikov.

McReynolds, L. (2013). *Murder Most Russian: True Crime and Punishment in Late Imperial Russia*. Ithaca, NY: Cornell University Press.

Miss Sherlock (ミス・シャーロック). (2018). HBO-Asia.

Nepomnyashchy, C. T. (2005). 'Imperially, my dear Watson': Sherlock Holmes and the Decline of the Soviet Empire. In S. Hutchings & A. Vernitski, eds., *Russian and Soviet Film Adaptations of Literature, 1900–2001: Screening the Word*. London: Routledge, pp. 128–141.

Okabe, T. (2019). Global Partners against Crime: Rewriting Sherlock Holmes and Watson in Japanese Video Games. *Replaying Japan Journal*, 1(1), 40–51.

Sperber, D., & Wilson, D. (1995). *Relevance Theory: Communication and Cognition*, 2nd ed. Oxford: Blackwell.

Tsutsumibayashi, M. (2015). 'There's a west wind coming': Sherlock Holmes in Meiji Japan. *Keio Communication Review*, 37, 83–109.

Wilson, D. (2011). Relevance and the Interpretation of Literary Works. London: UCL Department of Linguistics. *UCL Working Papers in Linguistics*, 1, 1–11.

Wilson, D., & Sperber, D. (2004). Relevance Theory. In L. R. Horn & G. Ward, eds., *The Handbook of Pragmatics*. Oxford: Blackwell, pp. 249–287.

Wolfe, R. H. (2016). Hounded. *Elementary*, CBS-TV. Dir. R. Fortunato.

9 The Ethical Effects of Voice-Over Narration on a Victim Testimonial
A Text-World Analysis of 'The Bed Intruder' Meme

M'Balia Thomas

9.1 Introduction

To be recognised as a victim is a socially negotiated process in which the label 'victim' entitles an individual to public compassion, respect, and social concern (Van Dijk 2009). Therefore, how a claim to victimhood is framed, narrated, and told is crucial to shaping its public reception. The mediation of a victim testimonial through an advocate or the media can result in perceptual or rhetorical shifts in the telling that endorse or depart from the narrative told. While endorsements may reinforce the credibility of a narrative, departures can adversely affect empathy and ethical response to victims and their claims.

Drawing upon a US broadcast television interview popularly known as 'The Bed Intruder' (Crazy Laugh Action 2012), I demonstrate the impact a mediated telling has had on the public response to a claim to victimisation. This interview-turned–internet meme features victim testimonial by siblings Antoine and Kelly Dodson. The Dodsons adopt a rhetorical style marked by repetition, hyperbole, irony, and strategies of impoliteness (Culpeper 2011) to communicate their claim of home invasion and attempted rape. Since airing in July 2010, the interview has inspired the creation, upload, sharing, and viewing of thousands of video parodies across social media. Through echoic irony (Gavins & Simpson 2015) and ironic inversion (Hutcheon 2000), the parodies endorse and distort the Dodsons' rhetorical style, but often while failing to reference its most serious allegation – the attempted rape of Kelly Dodson.

This chapter addresses the failure of the parodies to take up the Dodsons' claims with compassion, respect, or social concern. I investigate the role the broadcast's content and narrative structure have on public response (e.g. Gibbons 2019; Nuttall 2017; Whiteley 2011). To carry out this work, I adopt Text World Theory (Gavins 2007; Werth 1999), an 'analytical framework through which the textual and conceptual structures of discourse can be examined within the context of their production and reception' (Gavins & Simpson 2015, p. 721). I analyse the textual cues supplied by the broadcast's live reporting and voice-over narration for the ways in which they endorse and then depart from the victims' narrative. I posit the ethical impact of these departures on viewer identification with the Dodsons and their claims as reflected in exemplar postings of bed intruder-themed video parodies uploaded to YouTube during the two years following the broadcast.

The chapter proceeds as follows: I present a broad transcription of 'The Bed Intruder' broadcast in its entirety. I provide an overview of Text World Theory and then I model the discourse architecture of the broadcast. This model highlights the ways in which the broadcast's discourse invites or closes off narrative roles for viewers. Next, I analyse the broadcast's narrative structure for the manner in which the narratorial telling – in particular, the voice-over narration – endorses and ultimately departs from the Dodsons' testimonial claim. I close with a discussion of the ethical implications of these departures on the public's response and their broader significance for the representation of victim testimonials in the news generally.

9.2 'The Bed Intruder'

Produced by Huntsville (Alabama) television affiliate, WAFF-48, 'The Bed Intruder' is a two-minute broadcast news story containing excerpts from WAFF-48 reporter Elizabeth Gentle's interview with Antoine and Kelly Dodson (Gentle 2010). Recorded outside their home earlier that day, the broadcast includes direct speech excerpts from the interview. It also includes inside footage of the home with items overturned due to the break-in, and outside footage of the home with the distinct red brick walls associated with US government-sponsored housing projects, commonly known as the Projects. A transcription of the broadcast follows in paragraph form. Although I exclude visual cues from the transcription, I incorporate these cues into the forthcoming analysis.

9.2.1 The Transcribed Interview

(1) **Mark Thornhill (MT) – In Studio.** Terrifying moments for a woman who woke up to a strange man in bed with her. The woman screamed, her brother rushed in to help and tried to fight the offender off. That break-in happened early this morning in the 500 block of Webster Drive in Huntsville [AL]. WAFF-48's Elizabeth Gentle caught up with the victims. Elizabeth – emotions were running high.
(2) **Elizabeth Gentle (EG) – Reporting Live, Empty Parking Lot.** Hi Mark. The woman, a victim, told us that a man broke into her house and tried to rape her. Her brother br- ... went in and he tried to help her out but the man got away, leaving behind, though, evidence of his visit.
(3) **EG (voiceover):** Kelly Dodson was asleep with her little girl inside their apartment on Webster Drive when ...

(4) **Kelly Dodson (KD)**: I was attacked by some idiot ... from out here in the Projects.
(5) **EG (voice-over)**: Dodson says her attacker used a garbage can to climb onto the unit's ledge, open the upstairs window, and then, he got in bed with her.
(6) **KD**: He ... he tried to rape me, he tried to pull my clothes off.
(7) **EG (voice-over)**: Dodson struggled with her attacker, knocking over items in her bedroom. Antoine Dodson heard his sister scream and ran to help.
(8) **Antoine Dodson (AD)**: Well, obviously, we have a rapist in Lincoln Park. He's climbin' in your windows; he's snatchin' your people up. Tryin' to rape 'em, so y'all need to hide your kids, hide your wife, and hide your husband because they're raping everybody out here.
(9) **EG (voice-over)**: The attacker got loose and went out the upstairs window, but he did leave something behind.
(10) **AD**: We got your T-shirt, you done left fingerprints and all. You are so dumb, you are really dumb, for real.
(11) **EG (voice-over)**: A crime scene investigator photographed and dusted for prints on the lid of the garbage can and the windowpane and ledge. Dodson says he's never seen the perp before, but sends this warning to whoever is responsible.
(12) **AD**: You don't have to come and confess that you did it. We're looking for you. We ... we gon' find you. I'm letting you know now. So, you can run and tell that ... homeboy.
(13) **EG (parking lot)**: Now, if you have any information on this crime you are urged to call the Huntsville Police Department. We'll have much more from the victims of that attack coming up tonight at six. Reporting live from Huntsville, Elizabeth Gentle, WAFF-48 news.

Three levels of narrative telling are evident in the transcription: (1) the live reporting that introduces the news story, (2) the pre-recorded voice-over narration that reports, interprets, and evaluates the news story events (Phelan 2007), and (3) the (Free) Direct Speech excerpts of the Dodsons' pre-recorded victim testimonial. To demonstrate the conceptual and rhetorical manner in which these three narrative levels come together to create an ethical positioning for the broadcast, I turn to Text World Theory (Gavins 2007; Werth 1999), which I describe in the next section.

9.3 Text World Theory

Based on a 'text-as-world' metaphor (Whiteley 2011, p. 24), Text World Theory provides (1) a conceptual framework to map and (2) a methodological approach to analyse reader (or viewer) production, understanding, and emotional and ethical response to discourse. The theory posits the cognitive representation of discourse on three ontological levels. The first level, the discourse-world, represents the perceived and inferred context surrounding a discourse event (Werth 1999). It also incorporates textual projections of actual (or implied) discourse participants – the implied author, story recipients(s), or other participants – and the knowledge, beliefs, and experiences these participants bring to the discourse situation (Gavins 2007; Lahey 2005; Werth 1999).

The second level, the text-world, is constituted by the dynamic and evolving conceptual spaces generated by the referential and deictic elements (of person, space, place, and time) provided by text or talk. These spaces are made up of objects and enactors – text-world versions of actual discourse participants or story narrators, narratees, or characters – as well as plot, scene, person, and argument propositions that advance the actions, states, circumstances, and metonymic relationships depicted by the discourse (Werth 1999).

Represented by deictic and modal world-switches, the third level reflects conceptual departures from the initiating text-world. These departures are triggered by details in the discourse that portray unfolding references to (or inferences about) space, time, and person or that provide accounts of attitudinal or epistemic stances towards unrealised, unverifiable, hypothetical, and remote wish, belief, or negated propositions (Gavins 2007; Werth 1999). A discourse participant's ability to shift into a given text-world is dependent on whether that text- world is participant-accessible (discourse is presented by an enactor emanating from the discourse-world level and thus is verifiable) or character-accessible (discourse is presented by an enactor emanating from within the text-world level and thus is not verifiable). A text-world's accessibility holds implications for a discourse recipient's ability to 'psychologically project' – through 'transportation', 'perspective-taking', or 'identification' – into the narrative roles and textual experiences represented and inferenced by that discourse (Whiteley 2011, p. 27; see also Gavins 2007; Lahey 2005; Stockwell 2009). The type of projection, and the strength of the metaphorical mapping between the discourse participant and textual role/experience, can inform viewers' real-world emotional response (Whiteley 2011).

A text-world analysis also can demonstrate how narrative structure influences viewer accessibility and their ethical response to discourse (Phelan 2007). When the language, voice, and recipient roles of a text's narration endorse the narrative told about an event, viewers are more likely to identify with and express empathy toward that text and its characters (Stockwell 2009). Yet a narration that departs from its told narrative signals unreliability (Phelan 2007), producing a more resistant response by viewers to the narrative told and making it more likely that viewers will disassociate from the text and its characters (Whiteley 2011). Notably, disassociation can result even when viewers are transported by or adopt some degree of perspective-taking with respect to the discourse (Whiteley 2011).

Finally, while text-world analyses have been conducted on a variety of discourse events – face-to-face interviews (Van der Bom 2016), immersive theatre (Gibbons 2016), telecinematic discourse (Gibbons & Whiteley 2021), classroom pedagogical interventions (Giovanelli 2010), and Spanish and English spoken narratives (Lugea 2016) – they have yet to be conducted on a broadcast media event. The present work extends the scope of text-world analyses to such a discourse event. In the next section, I map out the text-world architecture of 'The Bed Intruder' broadcast with its multi-layered act of telling, highlighting the textual features of discourse that influence viewers' ability to psychologically project into or 'map' onto the 'worldview, attitude, emotions, [and] goals' (Whiteley 2011, p. 27) of the Dodsons and their claims.

9.4 The Text-World of 'The Bed Intruder'

The text-world architecture of the broadcast initiates with a split discourse-world consisting of television affiliate WAFF-48 (and by association its reporters) and the broadcast's actual viewers. This latter category is comprised of individuals who watched the broadcast live or watched the recorded broadcast after the fact. The telecast opens with an anchor, Mark Thornhill, seated at a news desk. Drawing upon their background knowledge (schema) of interacting with news story discourse, viewers mentally conceptualise a matrix broadcast text-world, 'The WAFF-48 Broadcast'. Into this text-world, viewers project enactor versions of themselves and the anchor (Gavins 2007; Lahey 2005), taking up the narrative position of 'authorial or ideal' viewer and attributing to the seated reporter the role of 'authorial or ideal' anchor (Gibbons 2019, p. 12).

(1)   Mark Thornhill (In Studio): Terrifying moments for a woman who woke up to a strange man in bed with her. The woman screamed, her brother rushed in to help and tried to fight the offender off. That break-in happened early this morning in the 500 block of Webster Drive in Huntsville [AL]. WAFF-48's Elizabeth Gentle caught up with the victims. Elizabeth, emotions were running high.

Thornhill's opening words ('Terrifying moments') provide the initial world-switch from the matrix text-world to a participant-accessible epistemic text-world, 'In-Studio Reporting'. This text-world is accessible through Thornhill as discourse-world participant. This world-switch is followed by a temporal (deictic) world-switch to a character-accessible 'Event Time' text-world consisting of several enactors ('a woman', 'a strange man', 'her brother') and plot-advancing actions (woman – woke up, screamed; brother – rushed in to help, tried to fight off). Thornhill's next statement – 'That break-in' – indicates a world-switch back ('happened') to the 'Event Time' text-world where the discourse provides additional temporal ('early this morning'), locative ('in the 500 Block of Webster Drive'), and spatial details (an onscreen map labelled 'Home Break-In. Madison County').

Thornhill's relational reference ('WAFF-48's') assigns Elizabeth Gentle a broadcast role, requiring a world-repair (Gavins 2007) in which Gentle is added to the matrix text-world as a discourse participant. Thornhill's temporal reference ('caught up') marks a deictic world-switch to a prior discourse event – an 'Interview' text-world in which Gentle and 'the victims' are present. Onscreen, a split visual image of the two reporters signals a split text-world consisting of Thornhill's 'In-Studio Reporting' and Gentle's 'Off-Site Reporting'. Thornhill's vocative address briefly 'toggles' (Cruickshank & Lahey 2010, p. 76) him into Gentle's 'Off-Site Reporting' text-world. This toggle is followed by a deictic world-switch from 'In-Studio' back to the aforementioned discourse event – the 'Interview' text-world – where 'emotions were running high'.

(2)   Elizabeth Gentle (Reporting Live, Empty Parking Lot): Hi Mark. The woman, a victim, told us that a man broke into her house and tried to rape her. Her brother br- ... went in and he tried to help her out but the man got away, leaving behind, though, evidence of his visit.

Reciprocating the first-name address produces an additional toggle between the split reporting text-worlds. It also reinforces Gentle's link to the broadcast station and nominates Thornhill as an enactor within her text-world. Referencing a previous, and thus spatiotemporally remote, speech event ('a victim, told us'), an epistemic world-switch is generated. This world-switch is followed by a deictic world-switch ('broke into') to a 'Flashback' text-world in which multiple enactors engage in several actions: 'a victim' (telling), 'a man' ('broke', tried to rape', 'got away', 'left evidence') and 'her brother' ('went in', 'tried to help').

(3)   Elizabeth Gentle (voice-over): Kelly Dodson was asleep with her little girl inside their apartment on Webster Drive when ...

Gentle's pre-recorded and dis-embodied reporting voice generates a world-switch from the matrix text-world to an epistemic modal world. This 'Voice-Over' text-world is externally focalised through the metaphorical lens of 'us' (para. 2) – WAFF-48 and the implied reporting crew – and voiced by discourse participant, Elizabeth Gentle. Although a remote world, this epistemic text-world is participant-accessible through discourse-world participant Elizabeth Gentle. The voice-over nominates several entities and world-building locatives, while the onscreen visuals and labels increment into the text-world details that can be inferred about the space – the race, gender, ages, and socioeconomic status of the named and unnamed enactors.

(4)   Kelly Dodson: I was attacked by some idiot ... from out here in the Projects.

Kelly Dodson's pre-recorded Free Direct Speech produces a deictic world-switch to a participant-accessible direct-speech text-world, 'Kelly Dodson Direct Speech'. This direct-speech text-world is an empty text-world in which Gentle ('us') is the implied narratee, the viewing public are 'narrative observers' (Gibbons 2019, p. 12), and from which stem Kelly Dodson's spoken narratives. Lahey (2016) provides a case for this 'empty' text-world, 'where speech and thought presentation indicate a level of reliability greater than that afforded to the matrix focalization-world, the deictic and epistemic modal-worlds prompted by speech and thought will be anchored in the backgrounded "empty text-world"' (p. 34).

From this empty direct speech text-world, a deictic world-switch ('was attacked') shifts 'the narrated action out of the existing temporal parameters of the text world and into a previous time frame' (Gavins 2005, p. 81), resulting in an enactor-accessible 'Flashback' text-world in which the victimisation occurred. The grammatical stance of the flashback discourse is highly evaluative. Kelly Dodson's use of the subject pronoun, 'I', marks an enactor version of herself as the grammatical subject of the attack, while the passive syntactic structure foregrounds this self as the grammatical object (Goal) of the attack. She additionally characterises the perpetrator (Actor) as 'some idiot' whom she metonymically and proximally situates 'from' within a shared space 'out here in the Projects'.

(5)   Elizabeth Gentle (voice-over): 'Dodson says her attacker used a garbage can to climb onto the unit's ledge, open the upstairs window, and then, he got in bed with her.

This second voice-over prompts a deictic world-switch away from the 'Flashback' text-world and back to the 'Voice-Over' text-world. A subsequent epistemic modal world-switch is generated by the historic present tense and the indirect reported speech ('Dodson says her attacker') used to report Kelly Dodson's victim testimonial. Several entities and objects are nominated into this epistemic text-world: 'her attacker ... a garbage can ... climb ... open ... upstairs window ... got in bed with her'.

(6)   Kelly Dodson: He ... he tried to rape me, he tried to pull my clothes off.

The presence of Kelly Dodson's Free Direct Speech initiates a world-switch back to the empty direct-speech text-world. This world-switch gives way to a deictic world-switch back to the 'Flashback' text-world ('he tried') where

Kelly Dodson positions herself as the grammatical object (me, my) of an attempted rape ('tried to rape', 'tried to pull'). She draws upon repetition and parallelism to foreground the attacker's gender and actions. Moreover, her use of the simple past tense ('tried') reinforces the completeness of the action, while the semantic forcefulness of the repeated verb 'try' foregrounds the failed attempt.

(7) Elizabeth Gentle (voice-over): Dodson struggled with her attacker, knocking over items in her bedroom. Antoine Dodson heard his sister scream and ran to help.

Gentle's third voice-over initiates a world-switch back to the 'Voice-Over' textworld with its narrative-advancing details: 'struggle', 'knock over', 'scream', 'ran to help'. Onscreen visuals increment the text-world as the scene shifts to a young man shown earlier wearing a black undershirt and a red bandana that holds back his afro-textured hair. An onscreen headline identifies the young man as 'Antoine Dodson'.

(8) Antoine Dodson: Well, obviously, we have a rapist in Lincoln Park. He's climbin' in your windows; he's snatchin' your people up. Tryin' to rape 'em. So y'all need to hide your kids, hide your wife, and hide your husband because they're raping everybody out here.

Antoine Dodson's Free Direct Speech prompts a deictic world-switch to a new participant-accessible, direct-speech text-world – 'Antoine Dodson Direct Speech'. A subsequent world-switch produces an epistemic modal text-world ('obviously ... have') where the stance towards 'a rapist in Lincoln Park' is expressed through a collective ('we') rather than individual voice. This ambiguous pronominal reference – whether inclusive to the Dodsons, exclusive to the Dodsons and the community of Lincoln Park, or metaphorically to all within earshot of the address (see Sorlin 2015) – implicates an 'ideal' narratee role (Gibbons 2019, p. 12) within the empty direct-speech text-world. Antoine Dodson's use of the historic present to describe the 'rapist's' actions ('climbin' ... snatchin' ... tryin') signals a deictic world-shift. The argument-advancing strategies provide a sense of immediacy and evidential support to his claims. The parallelism of the contracted pronominal ('he's') and progressive verbs ('climbing' and 'snatching') foreground material process verbs of movement, while the pronominal ellipsis before the verb 'try' foregrounds intent, but ultimate failure ('tryin' to rape'). Despite the intruder's failed attempt, obligation undergirds a deontic modal world-switch ('need to'). This text-world is comprised of a hyperbolic and ironic argument-advancing strategy where verbal ('hide') and pronominal ('your') repetition are contrasted with nominative deviation ('kids', 'wife', 'husband') – where 'husband' is not a category typically associated with vulnerability to rape.

The strategy provides rhetorical support to Antoine Dodson's claim that the intruder is a threat to 'everybody out here'.

(9)   Elizabeth Gentle (voice-over): The attacker got loose and went out the upstairs window, but he did leave something behind.

Supported by onscreen visuals, Gentle's discourse signals a return to the 'Voice-Over' text-world and the following world-building elements and narrative-advancing propositions are incremented into the text-world: enactors ('the attacker'), actions ('got loose', 'went out', 'leave behind'), path of actions ('out the upstairs window'), and objects ('something').

(10)   Antoine Dodson: We got your T-shirt, you done left fingerprints and all. You are so dumb, you are really dumb, for real.

Antoine Dodson's Free Direct Speech signals a deictic world-switch back to his direct speech text-world. This world-switch introduces an epistemic modal text-world prompted by Antoine Dodson's apostrophic address ('you') of an unspecified – though inferred to be the intruder – text-world enactor on behalf of unspecified text-world enactors ('we'). This text-world enactor is grammatically linked to a series of person-advancing propositions consisting of relational process verbs ('got/have', 'are') and personal objects ('your T-shirt', 'fingerprints'). Through irony – specifically, the adoption of hyperbole ('so', 'really', 'for real'), impoliteness ('you are dumb), and vague language ('and all') – Antoine Dodson forwards an evaluative stance towards the intruder that is simultaneously personal and distancing.

(11)   Elizabeth Gentle (voice-over): A crime scene investigator photographed and dusted for prints on the lid of the garbage can and the windowpane and ledge. Dodson says he's never seen the perp before, but sends this warning to whoever is responsible.

Gentle's fifth voice-over generates a world-switch back to the 'Voice-Over' text-world. Her initial statement and the on-screen visuals nominate enactors (a crime scene investigator and by metonymic implication – 'prints' – the intruder), material process actions (photographed, dusted), and objects (prints, garbage can, windowpane, ledge) related to the crime scene. The indirect reported speech ('Dodson says he's') prompts an epistemic world-switch followed by a negative world-switch ('never seen'). This negative text-world is a space of negative accommodation where the possibility of Antoine Dodson having 'seen the perp before' is accommodated and then negated. Together with the indirect reported speech, the negated text-world suggests an unverified conceptual space.

The camera flashes to Antoine Dodson, who is facing the camera. He holds a rolled-up sheet of paper in his hand, which he uses to point to and gesticulate toward the camera as he speaks. This shift back to Antoine Dodson generates a deictic world-switch back to the 'Antoine Dodson Direct Speech' text-world.

(12)   Antoine Dodson: You don't have to come and confess that you did it. We're looking for you. We ... we gon' find you. I'm letting you know now. So, you can run and tell that ... homeboy.

The return of the apostrophic address signals an epistemic world-switch from the direct speech text-world. This world-switch is followed by a negative deontic world-switch ('don't have to') into a text-world of negative accommodation and oppositional irony (Sorlin 2014, p. 14) where the obligation ('have to') runs into an epistemic text-world of 'unrealised' and 'intending-future-action' (Gavins 2005, pp. 85–86) in which the intruder is to 'come and confess'. This unrealised obligation is expressed and then negated before switching into a 'Flashback' text-world where the intruder 'did it'. The acts of 'looking' and 'gon' (going to) find' signal a shift back to the epistemic or 'intend-world' of 'future action'. The pronominal shift from 'we' to 'I' ('I'm letting you know') – accompanied by the spatiotemporal adverb ('now') – suggests a shift in evaluative stance (see Chapter 11 by Mayr on Appraisal Framework) rather than deictic movement within the current epistemic text-world of ongoing actions. Finally, an epistemic modal world-switch ('you can') introduces a cline of ironic discourse processing possibilities for viewers – 'can' as in present ability, opportunity, or even permission. Together with the negated clause – 'you don't have to come and confess' – the phrase 'you can run and tell' forms a kind of 'preterition' (Sorlin 2014, p. 14). In denying the desired course of action, the discourse emphasises a real-world distinction between what should be and what is. The argument-advancing propositions of these text-worlds present a conceptual space of oppositional irony that culminates with Antoine Dodson's use of the outdated fraternal term 'homeboy' to refer to the intruder.

(13)   Elizabeth Gentle (Reporting Live, Empty Parking Lot): Now, if you have any information on this crime you are urged to call the Huntsville Police Department. We'll have much more from the victims of that attack coming up tonight at six. Reporting live from Huntsville, Elizabeth Gentle, WAFF-48 News.

The temporal adverb 'now', accompanied by an onscreen shift back to Elizabeth Gentle reporting live, generates a deictic world-switch back to the 'Off-Site Reporting' text-world. There is a world-switch into an epistemic ('if') text-world comprised of a broad ('any') appeal for information. This appeal is followed by a subsequent world-switch (deontic modal) prompted by the call to action ('you are urged'). The discourse closes with a world-switch indicating a future reporting time in which viewers can expect 'much more' of the Dodsons' victim testimonial. The report closes with a final world-switch back to the 'Off-Site Reporting' text-world and a final station identification.

Figure 9.1 presents the broadcast's text-world architecture, specifically the world-building and function-advancing textual cues that signal participant accessibility and narrative roles to be taken up. Of special note is Antoine Dodson's use of the pronominal reference 'we' in his discourse. Despite the 'ontological distance' (Whiteley 2011, p. 29) between his direct speech text-worlds and participants in the discourse-world, the metaphorical ambiguity of 'we' allows viewers to potentially take up the narrative role of 'ideal narratee' (Gibbons 2019, p. 12) and access these more remote and less verifiable text-worlds. This access may explain the public focus on Antoine Dodson's discourse over his sister's, whose use of language is highly restricted to her personal ('I') reflection on events.

While textual cues and inferences are important to the text-world modelling of the broadcast, it is to its narrative structure I turn to next. In the forthcoming section, I describe the ethical dimensions of this structure – with a particular focus on the voice-over narration – and its impact on public response to the Dodsons' victim testimonial. In addition, I incorporate a reader response analysis (Gibbons 2019; Nuttall 2017; Whiteley 2011) where I examine the ethical implications of the broadcast's structure through the echoic and dissociative processes of revoicing, reimagining, retelling, and rekeying of the broadcast evident in the bed intruder–themed parodies.

9.5 The (In)Accessibility of the Dodson's Testimonial Claim

While all three levels of the broadcast's structure – the live reporting, the voice-overs, and the direct speech – contribute to its ethical impact, I focus on the disembodied voice-overs and the ways they endorse and depart from the Dodsons' testimonial narrative. Although the voice-overs appear to mostly echo the testimonial discourse, two types of departures surface in the broadcast: (1) perceptual departures, which impact who sees (the mood of the text) and whose voice (style, grammar, stance) is foregrounded, and (2) rhetorical departures, which alter the textuality (Stockwell 2009) of the discourse (and thus text-worlds) conceptualised by viewers. Both departures undermine the accessibility and reliability of the Dodsons' claims, disrupt the relationship between the Dodsons and viewers, and impact viewers' ethical judgement about and empathetic response to the siblings and their victimisation.

9.5.1 Perceptual Departures

Several perceptual departures figure into the broadcast's structure. First, the broadcast's structure appears to endorse the Dodsons' testimonial in allowing the siblings to report in their own words the events of their victimisation. The

Effects of Voice-Over Narration on a Victim Testimonial

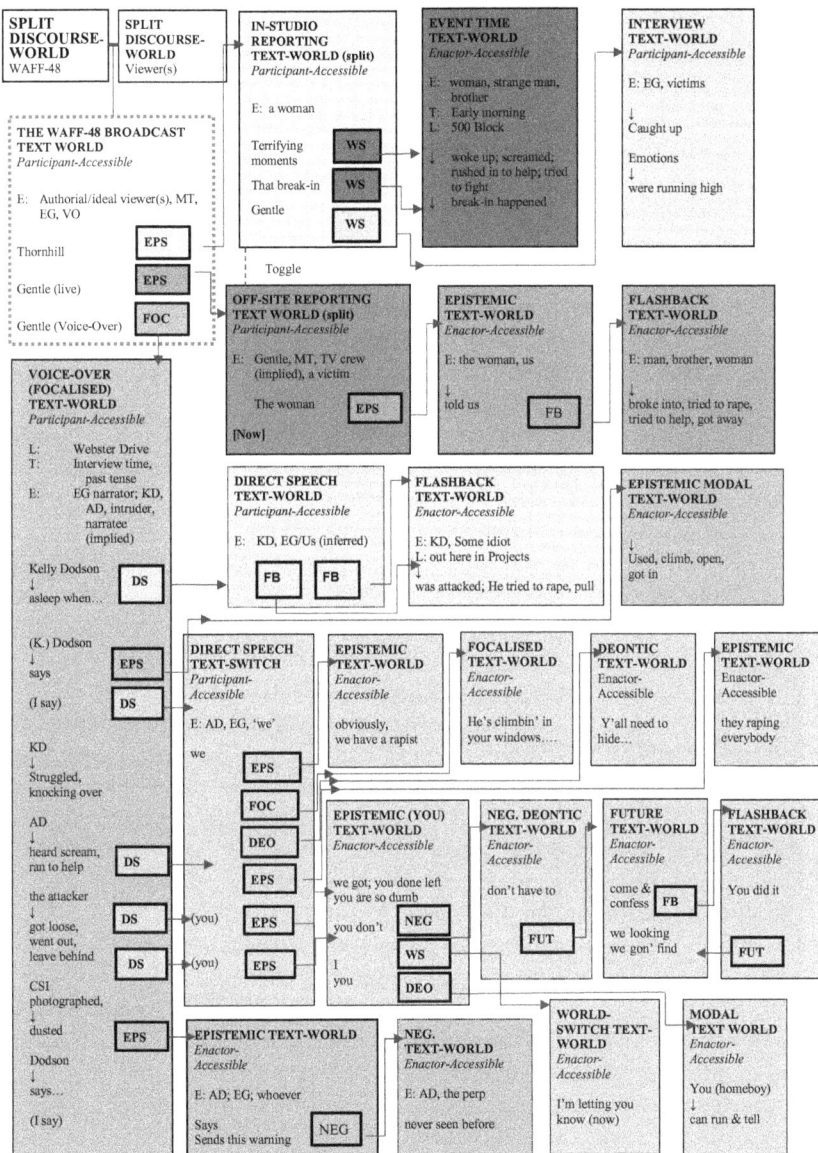

Figure 9.1 Text-world architecture of 'The Bed Intruder'

presentation of these words, which has been edited and structurally embedded at an ontological distance from the discourse-world participants, is mediated by Gentle's voice-overs. Moreover, the disembodied voice-overs permeate the broadcast space from a perceptual distance from the entities, actions, and objects depicted on screen. This is in contrast to the Dodsons' narrative, which is spatially restricted to Lincoln Park. The narrative is also positioned conceptually at a temporal, locative, and epistemic remove from the discourse-world participants. Ultimately, these departures in voice and mood foreground the broadcast telling over the victim testimonial. This foregrounding creates distance between viewers and the Dodsons and it restricts mind-modelling – viewer identification with the explicit or inferred 'knowledge, beliefs and feelings of ... entities' (Stockwell 2009, p. 140). As a result, viewers' empathetic and ethical response to the testimonial narrative is undermined.

Echoes of departures in voice and mood surface in YouTube parodies that revoice the WAFF-48 broadcast. These revoicings appropriate the 'syntactic structure, words, intonation' of the broadcast, but in ways refracted to serve the ideological intentions of the speaker (Bakhtin 1981, p. 293).

A notable revoicing features US actor-comedian John Leguizamo (UrbanoTV 2011, 21,000 views). Dressed in Antoine Dodson's signature red bandana and sleeveless black undershirt (to which he adds a gold chain), Leguizamo delivers a mock interview to an off-screen reporter about 'paparazzi [who] tried to break into my house and snap some shots' (UrbanoTV 2011). Drawing from his personal experience with celebrity, the actor-comedian appropriates discourse by the WAFF-48 anchors – 'Running high, are you kiddin' me? The dude broke into my window, he used a garbage can to climb up through the window, he broke into the window, and started snapping pictures away.' He also takes up Antoine Dodson's argument-advancing rhetorical strategies: 'We have a stalker out here in Gramercy Park.' Like other bed intruder–themed parodies that display departures of voice and mood, the context of this parody is taken from its creator's lived experience and personal knowledge of home invasion, but revoiced at an empathetic and ethical remove from the actual experiences reported by the Dodsons.

Second, while both the broadcast and testimonial bury (Emmott & Alexander 2014) explicit reference to race, the broadcast nonetheless visually foregrounds this world-defining element. Whiteness, as represented by Gentle and Thornhill, is associated with the WAFF-48 broadcast space – and by extension its viewers. Whiteness is positioned at a remove from Lincoln Park – with the exception of a white crime scene investigator who, like Gentle, is present metonymically in that space in an official capacity. Blackness, on the other hand, is restricted to Lincoln Park. It is foregrounded by the physical presence of the Dodsons and WAFF-48's frequent depiction of unidentified black bystanders. In addition to race, space is emphasised through periodic glimpses of the red brick buildings associated with government-sponsored housing projects and reinforced by multiple references (including a visual map) to the Dodsons' address. These visual aspects of the broadcast, combined with the broadcast's discourse, link blackness, poverty, home invasion, and attempted rape to 'the 500 block of Webster Drive' and at an ontological remove from the whiteness of the discourse-world participants.

This visual representation obscures aspects of experience foregrounded in the Dodsons' narrative. For example, their testimonial emphasises the communal or shared ('we') threat presented by the intruder. Even Kelly Dodson's 'I'-centric discourse highlights a shared spatial existence 'out here in the Projects'. Although race may be inferred by Antoine Dodson's comments, his characterisation of the intruder foregrounds his localness over his race – such as his reference to the intruder as 'homeboy'. This African American Vernacular English term privileges the relational over the racial aspects of a connection. Despite emphasising the localness of the intruder, both Dodsons set the intruder apart from the rest of the community psychologically – he is 'some idiot' who is 'so dumb ... for real'. The broadcast's linguistic burying of race is in contradistinction to its visual foregrounding of race. Making race a salient feature of the broadcast is a misrepresentation and misevaluation of the Dodsons' testimonial narrative that has the potential to impact viewers' mind-modelling (Stockwell & Mahlberg 2015) and empathetic engagement with the Dodsons' message of communal threat. The broadcast's details about race and space may restrict mind-modelling for some viewers; they enable others to engage in perspective-taking and 'imaginatively construct' (Whiteley 2011, p. 32) a response to the Dodsons' claims.

A highly viewed reimagining, 'The REAL Bed Intruder speaks out on Antoine Dodson' (OMGTv 2010, 321,057 views) opens with a black man seated against a bare wall and wearing a mock prison uniform. The parody revoices and responds to the Dodsons' claim to victimisation – 'It was said I had climbed into somebody's window, into somebody's house. And I tried to rape them ... rape they kids or something' (OMGTv 2010). The intruder demonstrates 'interpretive, affective and/or ethical distance' (Phelan 2017, p. 98) between himself and the Dodsons and their claims by treating as unreliable any inference of Kelly Dodson's innocence and sexual appeal or Antoine Dodson's ability to pursue him.

9.5.2 *Rhetorical Departures*

Several rhetorical departures figure into the broadcast's structure. First, the narrative order of the live reporting and the voice-over narration echo the chronological presentation of the Dodsons' combined testimonial narrative – 'a man broke in ... tried to rape ... brother went in ... man got away leaving ... evidence' (para. 2). However, this narrative ordering – or retelling – of events departs from the testimonial's world-building elements of temporalities, entities, and objects.

While the live reporting and voice-overs mostly adopt a reporting narrative time, the testimonial draws upon temporal expressions that flash back ('I was attacked'), evoke the present ('now') and historical present ('he's climbing'), and flash-forward to desired ('y'all need to hide'), negated ('you don't have to come and confess'), and unrealised ('we gon' find you') temporalities. The reporting as a whole retells the Dodsons' victimisation in ways that misrepresent ('terrifying *moments*') or that initially reference ('early this morning') but then fail to mark ('when ...') the duration or passage of time. Finally, the reporting, in particular, the voice-overs, nominates entities and objects from the victim narrative that have differential semantic relationships. Whereas the language featured in the reporting draws upon general and more abstract descriptors, the descriptors taken up by the Dodsons are more specific and/or hold semantic value on the level of the local – 'attacker' versus 'rapist', 'little girl' versus 'kids', 'perp' and 'whoever' versus 'idiot' or 'homeboy'. These departures misrepresent and background aspects about the event that could influence viewers' mind-modelling with the Dodsons' experience.

World-building departures in time, entities, and objects appear in a number of bed intruder–themed parodies. Termini's (2012, 1,442,320 views) animated parody features such departures. Inspired by the US animated series *South Park* (Parker & Stone 1997), the parody opens with a chronological retelling of the home invasion and attempted rape (by a white intruder). The parody follows this retelling of the Dodsons' victimisation by a chronological retelling of the broadcast. This second retelling, however, features several rhetorical departures from the original broadcast. For example, the parody depicts Antoine Dodson climbing up a ladder into the Dodsons' home, rushing into his sister's bedroom, and shouting in a stereotypical African American Vernacular voice, 'get off my sister'. In addition, Antoine Dodson is depicted carrying a gun (instead of a rolled-up sheet of paper) as he utters the statements, 'You don't have to come and confess, we' looking for you' (para. 12). Finally, although Termini visually inserts Kelly Dodson in the animation, he linguistically erases her voice and Gentle's voice-overs introducing her speech from the retelling. These departures present a deceptive retelling of the Dodsons' victimisation.

Second, in Termini's parody, Gentle's voice-over narration echoes the Dodson's rhetorical use of repetition and parallelism ('tried to rape ... tried to help'), lists ('garbage can and the windowpane and ledge'), hyperbolic irony ('whoever is responsible'), semantic categorical deviation ('got loose ... went out ... leave behind'), and name-calling ('the perp'). Gentle adopts these rhetorical strategies primarily for scene or plot-advancing purposes, whereas the Dodsons work to establish a narrative argument – 'we have a rapist in Lincoln Park ... so ... hide ... hide ... hide ...' (para. 8). While Gentle's voice-overs highlight the select use of these rhetorical elements, the Dodsons' testimonials emphasise the argumentative work to which these elements are employed on behalf of the testimonial claim.

This echo and departure in rhetorical strategies is observed in parodic retellings that emphasise the Dodsons' rhetorical style. AfricanoBoi (2010, 3,130,000 views) presents one such retelling. This parody echoes the hyperbole, repetition, and parallelism of Antoine Dodson's discourse, yet it departs from the discourse' argumentative work through amplification – 'So you need to hide your dogs, hide your fishes, hide your wife, hide your girlfriends … hide your mistresses …' (AfricanoBoi 2010). Amplification creates an impossible world of objects to hide and of objects left behind – 'you left your fingerprints, you left us your portrait, you left us your shoes … you think you Cinderella?' (AfricanoBoi 2010). Like Gentle's voice-over narration, this parody echoes the select use of Antoine Dodson's rhetorical style, but with hyperbolic and ironic distortion, trivialising the rhetorical argument that underlies his testimonial.

Last, although the live reporting and voice-overs echo the experiences recounted by the Dodsons (attacking, trying to rape, leaving evidence), these experiences are (re)keyed (Goffman 1974) differently. The live reporting and voice-overs draw upon language that portrays the Dodsons and the intruder as doers of material and behavioural actions that are associated with violent and chaotic activity – the intruder 'broke into', 'tried to rape', 'got away'; Kelly 'screamed', 'struggled', 'knocked over'; Antoine 'heard scream', 'rushed in', 'ran to help'. In addition, verbal process clauses precede clausal complements (Ho et al. 2019) that project viewers into modal text-worlds of hearsay ('Dodson says …').

In contrast, the Dodsons' argument-advancing propositions draw upon material verbs where the intruder – rather than the Dodsons – fills the grammatical role of Actor and the Dodsons that of Goal ('He tried to pull'). Unlike the voice-over narration, there are no epistemic verbal activities, only modalised processes of obligation – 'need to hide', negated 'have to confess', and the ambiguous 'can run and tell'. Finally, the Dodsons draw upon relational verb processes that identify ('from out here in the Projects', 'in Lincoln Park') and characterise ('so dumb', 'homeboy') in ways that reflect social proximity. Ultimately, the departure between the broadcast's reporting and voice-overs reflects a foregrounding of the external world of doings and happenings in the 500 block, while the Dodsons advance propositions around the remote and unverifiable inner, mental, and relational state of being victimised.

Rhetorical departures based on rekeying feature prominently in the Gregory Brothers' widely viewed 'Bed Intruder Song' (Autotune the News 2010, 150 million views). Consisting of two contrastive halves, the first half of this video parody superimposes a pop track over a reordered version of Antoine

Dodson's three and Kelly Dodson's first direct-speech discourses, turning their speech into song lyrics. The Gregory Brothers rekey the discourse using Autotune technology. This alters the intonation and pitch of the voices with a mechanised, almost robotic sound. However, the true rekeying takes place in the second half of the video. In this half, one of the Gregory Brothers performs a stylised jazz remix of the song on piano, slowing down the performance of the discourse-turned-lyrics and smoothing out the intonational rises and falls of the delivery. The remix provides a tempered rhetorical performance that retells, revoices, and rekeys the Dodsons' discourse with echoic irony. This departure alters the texture of and creates dissonance with the Dodsons' original testimonial claim.

9.5.3 Implications

While the broadcast's live reporting and voice-over endorsements of the Dodsons' testimonial may increase for the authorial audience 'the appeal and persuasiveness of the ideas expressed' (Phelan 2017, p. 99) by these reporting elements, narratorial departures between these elements can 'restrict' (Phelan 2017, p. 232) or 'interfere' (Leech & Short 2007, pp. 260, 268) with the narrative received by the audience. Narratorial departures can restrict or interfere with narrative by retelling, revoicing, rekeying, and reimagining the world-building elements and function-advancing propositions of the discourse in ways that are 'intratextually deficient' – that is, in ways that create tension or violate the 'terms set by [a work's] own larger narrative' (Phelan 2017, pp. 236–237).

Such tension marks the beginning of the broadcast's reporting with spatial and temporal distinctions that set the reporters and the audience at an ideological remove from the Dodsons. This tension continues across the voice-over narrations where Gentle's non-specific identification of discourse enactors contrasts with the labelling and name-calling adopted by the Dodsons. These perceptual and rhetorical departures have interpretative or point-of-view effects (McIntyre 2006). They reframe the narrative being told by foregrounding different entities, objects, and function-advancing propositions. Reframing can hinder mind-modelling in viewers by making narrations restrictive, unreliable, even deceptive (Phelan 2017), the effect of which is to create empathetic distance and challenges viewer identification with the Dodsons' discourse. Even as textual cues and inferences made by viewers promote their transportation or perspective-taking into the discourse, the dissonance, distortions, and distance evoked by the departures in the telling may inhibit mind-modelling and emotional identification with the victimisation depicted by the testimonial discourse.

Moreover, these departures influence the 'interpretative, affective, or ethical distance between the narrator and the authorial audience' (Phelan 2017, p. 100). By echoing or endorsing these departures, the viewing public signal their ethical judgement against the Dodsons and their victim testimonial through the bed intruder–themed video parodies that surface on YouTube. The video parodies reflect this judgement by echoing key departures between the authorial reporting and voice-over narrations and the Dodsons' testimonial narrative. The parodies alter and distort the temporal structure of the broadcast's structure (Termini 2012); they foreground an African American 'we' and 'you' (OMGTv 2010) or they create and project some fantasy 'other' (UrbanoTV 2011); and they imply the Dodsons have violated a shared understanding of rhetorical decency by endorsing through echoic mention and then distorting through irony their use of name calling (Autotune the News 2010).

9.6 Conclusion

In difference to some of the other chapters in this volume that highlight crime and the criminal, this chapter addresses the victim, victimisation (see also Chapters 5 and 6 by Gregoriou and Ibrahim/Tabbert, respectively), and the public negotiation of victim status mediated through broadcast media. Through a text-world analysis of a decade-old broadcast, 'The Bed Intruder', it is possible to explore (1) the viewer projection and identification with the Dodsons' claims and (2) the empathetic and ethical effects that departures between the broadcast's narrative telling – its live reporting and in particular the voice-over narrations – and the victim testimonial create for viewers. The scope of this work is limited to correlating the empathetic and ethical effects of the broadcast as reflected through exemplar bed intruder–themed parodies. It deliberately ignores other potential sources of data that might shed light on this phenomenon, such as news articles, radio and television interviews and commentaries. Nonetheless, the present work speaks to the impact of media production techniques on the public uptake and reception of victim claims. The mediation of the Dodsons' claim through a voice-over narration that endorses and then departs from their testimonial narrative has point-of-view effects. These effects have ethical implications for viewer identification with the Dodsons and their claims. The ethical implications are evident in the bed intruder–themed video parodies where a lack of empathy and failure to highlight the attempted rape and perpetrator responsible contribute to a secondary victimisation of the Dodsons through the public's failure to accord them and their claim to victimhood compassion, respect, and social concern.

References

AfricanoBoi (2010). 'Woman Wakes Up to Find Intruder in Her Bed (SPOOF)'. www.youtube.com/watch?v=tLgF_ZjFD9I.

Autotune the News (2010). 'Bed Intruder Song'. Recorded by the Gregory Brothers. www.youtube.com/watch?v=hMtZfW2z9dw.

Bakhtin, M. M. (1981). *The Dialogic Imagination*. Austin: University of Texas Press.

Crazy Laugh Action (2012). 'Antione Dodson Hide Yo Kids, Hide Yo Wife original interview'. www.youtube.com/watch?v=EzNhaLUT520.

Cruickshank, T., & Lahey, E. (2010). Building the Stages of Drama: Towards a Text World Theory Account of Dramatic Play-Texts. *Journal of Literary Semantics*, 39(1), 67–91.

Culpeper, J. (2011). *Impoliteness: Using Language to Cause Offence*. Cambridge: Cambridge University Press.

Emmott, C., & Alexander, M. (2014). Foregrounding, Burying and Plot Construction. In P. Stockwell & S. Whiteley, eds., *The Cambridge Handbook of Stylistics*. Cambridge: Cambridge University Press, pp. 329–343.

Gavins, J. (2005). (Re)thinking Modality: A Text-World Perspective. *Journal of Literary Semantics*, 34(2), 79–93.

  (2007). *Text World Theory: An Introduction*. Edinburgh: Edinburgh University Press.

Gavins, J., & Simpson, P. (2015). *Regina v John Terry*: The Discursive Construction of an Alleged Racist Event. *Discourse & Society*, 26(6), 712–732.

Gentle, E. (2010, July 28). Television broadcast. WAFF-48 News. Huntsville, AL: National Broadcasting Company.

Gibbons, A. (2016). Building Hollywood in Paddington: Text World Theory, Immersive Theatre, and Punchdrunk's *The Drowned Man*. In J. Gavins & E. Lahey, eds., *World Building: Discourse in the Mind*. London: Bloomsbury, pp. 70–89.

  (2019). *Using Life* and Abusing Life in the Trial of Ahmed Naji: Text World Theory, *Adab* and the Ethics of Reading. *Journal of Language and Discrimination*, 3(1), 4–31.

Gibbons, A., & Whiteley, S. (2021). Do Worlds Have (Fourth) Walls? A Text World Theory Approach to Direct Address in Fleabag. *Language and Literature*, 30(2), 105–126.

Giovanelli, M. (2010). Pedagogical Stylistics: A Text World Theory Approach to the Teaching of Poetry. *English in Education*, 44(3), 214–231.

Goffman, E. (1974). *Frame Analysis*. New York: Harper & Row.

Halliday, M. A. K., & Matthiessen, C. (2004). *An Introduction to Functional Grammar*, 3rd ed. New York: Oxford University Press.

Ho, Y., Lugea, J., McIntyre, D., Xu, Z., & Wang, J. (2019). Text-World Annotation and Visualization for Crime Narrative Reconstruction. *Digital Scholarship in the Humanities*, 34(2), 310–334.

Hutcheon, L. (2000). *A Theory of Parody: The Teachings of Twentieth-Century Art Forms*. Champaign: University of Illinois Press.

Lahey, E. (2005). Text-World Landscapes and English Canadian National Identity in the Poetry of Al Purdy, Milton Acorn and Alden Nowlan. PhD thesis, University of Nottingham.

Lahey, E. (2016). Author-Character *Ethos* in Dan Brown's Langdon-Series Novels. In J. Gavins & E. Lahey, eds., *World Building: Discourse in the Mind*. London: Bloomsbury, pp. 33–51.

Leech, G., & Short, M. (2007). *Style in Fiction: A Linguistic Introduction to English Fictional Prose*, 2nd ed. Harlow: Pearson Education.

Lugea, J. (2016). *World Building in Spanish and English Spoken Narratives*. London: Bloomsbury.

McIntyre, D. (2006). *Point of View in Plays: A Cognitive Stylistic Approach to Viewpoint in Drama and Other Text-Types*. Amsterdam: John Benjamins.

Nuttall, L. (2017). Online Readers between the Camps: A Text World Theory Analysis of Ethical Positioning in *We Need to Talk about Kevin*. *Language and Literature*, 26(2), 153–171.

OMGTv (2010). 'The REAL Bed Intruder Speaks Out on Antoine Dodson'. www.youtube.com/watch?v=X7Bqsl0HzSI.

Parker, T., & Stone, M. (Executive producers). 1997. *South Park*. Comedy Central.

Phelan, J. (2007). Rhetoric/Ethics. In D. Herman, ed., *The Cambridge Companion to Narrative*. Cambridge: Cambridge University Press, pp. 203–216.

(2017). *Somebody Telling Somebody Else: A Rhetorical Poetics of Narrative*. Columbus: Ohio University Press.

Sorlin, S. (2014). Ideological Crossings: 'You' and the Pragmatics of Negation in Jamaica Kincaid's *A Small Place*. *E'tudes de Stylistique Anglaise*, 7, 11–25.

(2015). Person Deixis and Impersonation in Ian Banks's *Complicity*. *Language and Literature*, 24(1), 40–53.

Stockwell, P. (2009). *Texture: A Cognitive Aesthetics of Reading*. Edinburgh: Edinburgh University Press.

Stockwell, P., & Mahlberg, M. (2015). Mind-Modelling with Corpus Stylistics in *David Copperfield*. *Language and Literature*, 24(2), 129–147.

Termini, V. (2012). 'Bed Intruder on South Park'. www.youtube.com/watch?v=sFZOmT1-whw.

UrbanoTV (2011). 'John Leguizamo's Bed Intruder'. www.youtube.com/watch?v=Um42JhAaINI.

Van der Bom, I. (2016). Speaker Enactors in Oral Narrative. In J. Gavins & E. Lahey, eds., *World Building: Discourse in the Mind*. London: Bloomsbury, pp. 91–108.

van Dijk, J. M. (2009). Free the Victim: A Critique of the Western Conception of Victimhood. *International Review of Victimology*, 16(1), 1–33.

Werth, P. (1999). *Text Worlds: Representing Conceptual Space in Discourse*. London: Longman.

Whiteley, S. (2011) Text World Theory, Real Readers and Emotional Responses to *The Remains of the Day*. *Language and Literature*, 20(1), 23–41.

10 Realising Betrayal
A Multimodal Stylistic Analysis of a Scene from the TV Series The Sopranos

Simon Statham

10.1 Introduction

This chapter analyses a scene from the HBO organised crime drama *The Sopranos*, produced by David Chase, examining the interaction between dialogue and cinematic techniques as it dawns on mob boss Tony Soprano that one of his top lieutenants is in the pay of the authorities. This chapter demonstrates how audiovisual techniques operate in tandem with conversational tactics employed in the dialogue of characters engaged in 'crime talk'.

Whilst Richardson (2010, p. 22) notes the almost total absence of dialogue-based analysis in major works in television studies, the stylistic analysis of dramatic dialogue in telecinematic discourse has gained significant momentum in recent years. So whilst television theorists have focussed but little on language, instead concentrating on elements of theme and characterisation, stylisticians have established the importance of dialogue in the analysis of telecinematic texts. Stylistic work on film and television discourses is also noteworthy for its embracing of techniques to examine meaning beyond the spoken word. Montoro (2015, p. 361) acknowledges the adoption of multimodal approaches as a way in which stylistics has 'felicitously diversified from its traditional take on texts by reassessing style as encoded by non-verbal as well as verbal signs'.

The type of multimodal stylistic analysis presented in this chapter is aligned with recent work in the stylistics of drama which approaches film and television dialogue by examining how meaning is constructed by multimodal aspects of language. In his analysis of the HBO television drama *The Wire*, for example, Toolan (2011) demonstrates that the interplay of visual and verbal modes is crucial for viewers in interacting with dialogue which is often 'impenetrable' to them. McIntyre and Bousfield (2011) examine the paralinguistic and kinesic actions of a range of characters in a scene from the Martin Scorsese classic *Goodfellas* (1990), while Montoro (2011) analyses how characters' gestures and cinematography are used to encode mind style in the 2004 film adaptation of Ian McEwan's novel *Enduring Love* (1997).

Statham (2015) employs the participation framework of Goffman (1981) and the conversational maxims of Grice (1975) to analyse the linguistic strategies used by cooperators to elicit incriminating conversations with criminal targets and the resisting tactics used by these targets in crime talk in *The Sopranos*. This chapter extends this focus by analysing visual aspects alongside verbal tactics in a scene from the first series of the drama, involving a cooperator and a criminal target, and specifically the realisation of the latter of his associate's betrayal.

The Sopranos, which comprised eighty-six episodes in a six-season run between 1999 and 2007, focuses on the eponymous fictional New Jersey crime family led by Tony Soprano, played by the late James Gandolfini. Alongside storylines which dramatise the criminal activities of the gang, one of the major themes throughout the series is the efforts of the FBI to investigate these crimes. As well as placing surreptitious listening devices in the meeting places and homes, and on the telephone lines, of the gang, the operations of the Organised Crime Taskforce rely on confidential informants and cooperating witnesses who are prepared to elicit testimony from criminal targets, usually under threat of prosecution.

Crime talk interactions in the organised crime world in which *The Sopranos* is set are marked by the expectation of additional conversational vigilance. First, it is usually considered unacceptable to openly discuss criminal operations given the fear amongst the characters that these could be recorded; second, there are rules in place about who can discuss 'business' with the boss. Tony Soprano instead prefers to limit his exposure to potential wiretaps by issuing orders through a select group of trusted lieutenants.

Given that criminal characters exercise a level of caution in their interactions which has implications for conversation cooperation and that adherence to Grice's (1975) conversational maxims is affected by the divergent tactics of cooperators and criminal targets, dialogue from *The Sopranos* can be examined using Grice's seminal model. The maxim of Relation and the second maxim of Quantity – 'do not make your contribution more informative than is required' (Grice 1975, p. 45) – for example, are usually strictly adhered to in the cautious interactions of *The Sopranos*. In instances where crime talk is instigated in the course of ostensibly cooperative conversations by cooperating witnesses who fail to fulfil these maxims, Tony regularly opts out of fulfilling the cooperative principle. This tactic of essentially shutting down conversational exchanges proves useful on several occasions throughout the series, as exemplified by Scene 1.

In this scene cooperating witness Salvatore 'Big Pussy' Bompensaro attempts to elicit and record incriminating talk from Tony Soprano on the subject of the murder of Soprano family associate Matthew Bevelloqua, who has been shot to death by Tony in an earlier episode.

Scene 1: City restaurant

1 PUSSY: So how's your mom, Tony?
2 TONY: Same. But my ex-goomar's cousin, I got her coming in to take care of her. Russian girl.
3 PUSSY: Who was it telling me about the Bevelloqua kid? You know that family has money from construction?
4 TONY: Fucking Matthew was never any good.
5 PUSSY: He sure cried like a baby that night. I think the family was relieved he got taken out.
6 TONY: What are you going to eat? Hey waiter!

(Season 3, Episode 1, 'Mr. Ruggerio's Neighborhood')

Initially, the conversation in this scene is about Livia Soprano, Tony's mother. Enquiring after the often troublesome Livia, such as Pussy does in Turn 1 here, is a conventional and fairly regular question in the series. His question in Turn 3, however, violates the maxim of Relation, abruptly introducing a new topic in attempting to turn a conversation about Tony's mother into one about a murdered associate. Having received an acknowledgement of the change of topic from Tony in Turn 4, Pussy attempts an elaboration in Turn 5, which violates the strict adherence to the second maxim of Quantity as it operates in crime talk in *The Sopranos*. Tony immediately opts out and shuts down the conversational exchange.

Scene 2 further demonstrates the effectiveness of the opt-out strategy when expected conversational vigilance is not adhered to. In this scene Richie Aprile, a gangster newly released from a long prison sentence and somewhat unfamiliar with the strict conversational control which holds sway in modern crime talk encounters, is eager to discuss restarting his loansharking business with Tony.

Scene 2: Satriale's pork store

1 RICHIE: I want to get my Shy business back up and running, I keep getting these calls from ...
2 TONY (interrupting): ... Sil
3 RICHIE: Where the fuck are you going?
4 TONY (leaving): I'll talk to you later Richie.
5 RICHIE (to Silvio): You want to tell me what the fuck just happened?
6 SILVIO: No more talking business with the skipper directly.
7 RICHIE: Are you fucking with me?
8 SILVIO: You can talk to him. But not now. And never here.

(Season 2, Episode 2, 'Do Not Resuscitate')

The second maxim of Quantity operates very strictly in crime talk in *The Sopranos* given the criminals' awareness of the constant possibility of them being recorded. In referring to illegal activity and almost mentioning a name in

Turn 1 Richie is saying far too much. Tony's immediate reaction is to cut off Richie and physically depart the scene. The new rules are explained by Silvio to a somewhat confused Richie, who has been in prison whilst other members of the Soprano family have been adapting to the wiretap tactics of the authorities.

In each of these examples Tony opts out of the cooperative principle, refusing to acknowledge the incriminating conversational topic of Pussy in the first scene and cutting off Richie entirely in the second. The opt-out strategy utilised by Tony Soprano is an effective counter-measure against incriminating recordings, shutting down potentially dangerous conversational exchanges by providing neither confirmation nor acknowledgement of the information contained in the turns of Pussy and Richie and not proffering any additional information of his own.

Whilst cooperating witnesses violate the maxims of Quantity and Relation, their criminal targets opt out as a conversational counter-measure. Criminal targets in crime talk in *The Sopranos* also rely on the tactic of flouting the maxims to generate conversational implicature. Given the level of surveillance targeted at organised crime families, especially electronic wiretaps on the gang's telephones, criminal characters in *The Sopranos* often strategically utilise ambiguity in order to make their interactions as inaccessible as possible to potential overhearers. Rather than avoid obscurity of expression as set out by the maxim of Manner, criminal characters embrace ambiguity to generate implicature which can be worked out by interlocutors who possess relevant contextual information but which will not be fully comprehended by an eavesdropping FBI agent. Should the implied meaning be realised by the authorities at a later date, for example, the obscure nature of the language greatly restricts their ability to convincingly offer these interactions as evidence.

Scene 3: Telephone

1 TONY: Hello.
2 PAULIE: It's done. And it's the biggest refrigerator you've ever seen.
3 TONY: What about the other thing?
4 PAULIE: Juan Valdez has been separated from his donkey. (Hangs up)
(Season 1, Episode 10, 'A Hit Is a Hit')

In Scene 3 gang member Paulie telephones Tony to report on the successful robbery and murder of a Colombian drug dealer; both participants correctly assume that Tony's telephone is bugged. Paulie's first turn appears to infringe the maxim of Manner given the obscurity of expression at the beginning of a telephone conversation. Paulie is not opting out of the cooperative principle, however; he is not infringing the maxim by accidentally being obscure or attempting to mislead Tony through obscurity by violating the maxim. In this case Paulie generates a conversational implicature which flouts the maxim of Manner, successfully implying that the robbery has been successful. Tony is aware of the plan for the robbery, that the loot would be concealed in an empty refrigerator box, and he draws on this contextual knowledge to work out the implicature. In Turn 4 here, 'Juan Valdez has been separated from his donkey', the stereotypical reference and his background knowledge of the plan allow him to infer that the drug dealer has been killed. Again Paulie flouts the maxim of Manner by being ambiguous rather than explicit so that no talk of evidentiary usefulness to the authorities can be recorded in this exchange.

In terms of Goffman's (1981) framework to account for the alternating relationship between hearers and speakers in a conversation, the FBI agents usually fill the role of unratified eavesdroppers, 'bystanders' to a conversation of which they are not an intended recipient (or at least not intended by all but their cooperating witness). They engage in what Goffman terms 'collusive sideplay' when they evaluate and editorialise upon the conversations to which they are surreptitiously privy. Cooperating witnesses who provide this access fulfil a somewhat more complex dual conversational role. They are ratified hearers in that they are addressed participants in the dominant conversation, but they also perform a conflictual unratified communication role because they engage in interactive strategies to accommodate the eavesdropping authorities. Cooperating witnesses perform a specialised conversational role which joins 'collusive crossplay' and collusive sideplay. Collusive crossplay is achieved by the tactics used by collaborators in attempting to elicit incriminating talk for the authorities, and they engage in collusive sideplay in later scenes when they meet with these handlers to discuss and clarify parts of the recorded conversations (Statham 2015, p. 329).

10.2 Scene for Analysis: Tony and Jimmy

Scene 4 is from the first season episode 'Nobody Knows Anything'. Tony has been given information by a corrupt police officer that one of his most trusted associates, Salvatore 'Big Pussy' Bompensaro, has begun working for the authorities. Whilst this information is later revealed to be accurate, the focus at the conclusion of this episode centres instead on Tony's discovery that a different associate, Soprano family *capo* Jimmy Altieri, is also an informant. Following the same robbery and murder of the Sopranos' Columbian rival referred to by Paulie in Scene 3 above, Jimmy's club is raided by the authorities, and a number of Soprano family associates are arrested. During a search of the premises a cache of weapons is discovered concealed inside a pool table. In Scene 4 Jimmy has just been released from police custody and pays a visit to Tony's house to report on his arrest and questioning.

Scene 4 will be analysed below in terms of both dialogue and audiovisual features, demonstrating how the interplay between verbal and non-verbal elements enhances the involvement of the viewing audience in Tony's discovery. Often the audience is aware before the characters are of who is cooperating with the authorities in *The Sopranos*; in the case of Jimmy Altieri, however, his betrayal is revealed to the audience and Tony simultaneously in Scene 4. For those watching the series and not understanding Tony's discovery of Jimmy's betrayal, clarification is provided in the next scene of the episode.

Owing to the vigilance which operates in *The Sopranos*, Tony Soprano rarely discusses criminal operations in his home; however, he will occasionally receive his associates in the basement, assuming that noise from the air conditioning fans will disrupt any potential recording. This scene hence takes place in the basement of the Soprano home, lasting seventy seconds. The transcript has been produced by directly viewing the episode.

Scene 4: Soprano home

1 JIMMY: You got a problem.
2 TONY: Yeah I know, I'm working on it.
3 JIMMY: Working on what?
4 TONY: Why? What were you going to say?
5 JIMMY: You better lay low with that safe house money.
6 TONY: What are you talking about?
7 JIMMY: They were asking me a lot of questions in there you know. If I know anything about the dead Columbian, the apartment and all that.
8 TONY: Well you look good.
9 JIMMY: Thanks, I wasn't gone that long.
10 TONY: Yeah, yeah I know.
11 JIMMY: My lawyer told them, 'Eh he doesn't own the building, he's not responsible for what's in the building.' I told them, 'The pool table was there when I first rented the joint.'
12 TONY: Good thinking. Missed your calling – should've been a lawyer.
13 JIMMY: Please. Enough people hate me. So ah ... what are you going to do about the Columbian money?
14 JIMMY: They were putting the screws to me like I was a school kid, telling me the money was marked, they were even saying there's a new fingerprinting technique that lifts it right off the bills.

(Season 1, Episode 11, 'Nobody Knows Anything')

In the next scene Tony visits his *consigliere* Silvio Dante where it is confirmed that he has uncovered Jimmy's betrayal, commenting, 'New fingerprint technique – I should have killed him right in my fucking basement.' This scene makes it clear that the conversation in Scene Four has revealed to Tony that Jimmy has been turned by and is now cooperating with the authorities.

10.3 Dialogue in the Tony and Jimmy Scene

In Goffman's terms both Tony and Jimmy are ratified participants in the talk, with speaker and hearer roles alternating between them. By way of the concealed microphone worn by Jimmy, the FBI are also conversational participants, filling an unratified eavesdropper role, their presence known to Jimmy but not initially to Tony. Jimmy engages in collusive crossplay with these eavesdroppers in several of his turns in Scene 4, attempting to accommodate the FBI by eliciting incriminating information-carrying turns from Tony. Tony becomes conversationally uncooperative as early as Turn 4 – 'Why? What were you going to say?' – when it begins to occur to him that the traitor in the family might be Jimmy.

'Working on what?' in Jimmy's second turn instigates an immediate reaction from Tony, who offers little of evidentiary potential for the authorities for the remainder of the scene. Turns 1 and 2 establish shared knowledge between the ratified participants; Turn 3 is Jimmy's attempt to elicit Tony to explicitly name the 'problem' for the purposes of the tape. Given the shared knowledge established by Turns 1 and 2, however, Turn 3 is over-informative and violates the maxim of Quantity. Shared knowledge between two interlocutors can often render conversations inaccessible to eavesdroppers as it is unnecessary for ratified participants to continually name and define conversational themes. Whilst 'I'm working on it' (Turn 2) might appear to infringe the maxim of Manner in being vague, the assumption of shared knowledge at this point makes naming the 'it' unnecessary. Tony assumes that Jimmy, a senior figure in the organisation who knows about the robbery and who has been arrested alongside other gang members earlier in this episode, is referring to the spotlight being placed on the gang by the authorities following the heist. Jimmy's request for a specific statement of this would be over-explicit in conventional conversation, and borders on the taboo in crime talk interactions in *The Sopranos*. Jimmy's question in Turn 3 would be plausible in this interaction if it were uttered by a third interlocutor who joins the conversation after the initial exchanges, which obviously does not occur in this scene. It is uttered by Jimmy in an attempt to accommodate the eavesdropping FBI, but rather than elicit an incriminating contribution from Tony – talk which elaborates upon or even acknowledges the robbery – it makes Tony suspicious.

As Tony realises Jimmy's betrayal throughout Scene 4, he pays only lip service to conversational cooperation, offering non-committal and uninformative turns for the remainder of the conversation. It can also be said that following Turn 3, when Tony assumes the potential presence of an FBI eavesdropper, his communication is uncooperative on two levels. His strategy of avoidance in the main interaction with Jimmy communicates to the FBI that he will not incriminate himself on tape. In this way his non-fulfilment of the maxim of Relation in 'Well you look good' (Turn 8), for example, operates as a flout of the maxim, implying his lack of cooperation to the unratified eavesdropper. Whilst this is obviously an instance of indirect communication, on this level it can be offered as an example of collusive crossplay between Tony and the FBI agents he assumes are present in the conversation.

The only incriminating talk in Scene 4 is contained in the turns of Jimmy. In a strategy defined as 'saturation' by the forensic linguist Roger Shuy (2005) the cooperating witness refers constantly to the alleged crime (in this case, the same robbery and murder of the Columbian drug dealer reported to Tony in Scene 3 above). The explicit content of Jimmy's talk, such as the violation of Quantity in Turn 7, embraces none of the ambiguity which the criminal characters in this drama often use as a strategy to frustrate potential eavesdroppers, when they flout the maxim of Manner in the way that Paulie does in Scene 3 above. In Turn 4 – 'Why? What were you going to say?' – and Turn 6 – 'What are you talking about?' – Tony does not offer any of the information desired by Jimmy but appears to simply request clarification. His fourth contribution in Turn 8 is markedly less cooperative and demonstrates a strategy used frequently by the character throughout the series:

7 JIMMY: They were asking me a lot of questions in there you know. If I know anything about the dead Columbian, the apartment and all that.
8 TONY: Well you look good.

'Well you look good' fails to fulfil the maxim of Relation and opts out of the cooperative principle which governs talk in Grice's framework. This opt-out tactic operates to guide a conversation away from incriminating subjects considered too risky to discuss in an unplanned location, and in many cases can signal the conclusion of the exchange, such as in Scene 2. As pointed out above, Turn 8 also operates as flouting the maxim of Relation as an implied signal to the FBI, who Tony by now assumes are listening, that he does not intend to proffer incriminating information.

In the case of Scene 3, Jimmy acknowledges the subject change with 'Thanks, I wasn't gone that long' (Turn 9). Turn 10 from Tony – 'Yeah, yeah I know' – operates as a seemingly innocuous conversational placeholder; however, given that Tony's suspicions are now aroused the acknowledgement that Jimmy's release seems to have been achieved very quickly is significant. By not explicitly stating these suspicions Turn 10 flouts the maxim of Quantity; the implicature generated communicates, perhaps particularly to the FBI eavesdroppers, that Tony suspects Jimmy has 'flipped' and become a cooperating witness. The explanation offered by Jimmy for the short duration of his incarceration in Turn 11 – 'My lawyer told them, "Eh he doesn't own the building, he's not responsible for what's in the building." I told them, "The pool table was there when I first rented the joint"' – signals that Jimmy has inferred that Tony is suspicious of how quickly he has been released. Turn 11 is Jimmy's attempt to address this suspicion. Turn 13, 'So ah ... what are you going to do with the Colombian money?' may indicate that Jimmy is reassured by the attempt at light humour from Tony in Turn 12, 'Good thinking. Missed your calling – should have been a lawyer.' However, any reassurance is likely coloured by the fact that Jimmy feels under a certain amount of pressure to deliver information to his FBI handlers; after all, cooperating witnesses usually 'flip' only under threat of indictment. In reintroducing the subject of the money confiscated from the Columbian gang Jimmy violates the second maxim of Quantity as he again attempts to draw Tony into an incriminating interaction.

Turn 14 – 'They were putting the screws to me like I was a school kid, telling me the money was marked, they were even saying there's a new fingerprinting technique that lifts it right off the bills' – is also over-informative. For the audience, and indeed for Tony, Turn 14 perhaps seems desperate, not to mention increasingly risky given the punishment for collaborators. The fact that Turn 13 is followed by silence from Tony, not to mention his lack of cooperation from Turn 4 onwards, may have established for Jimmy that his strategies in this scene will be ultimately unsuccessful. In this case Turns 13 and 14 are likely more relevant to Jimmy's collusive crossplay with the FBI, communicating that he is doing all he can to record something incriminating from Tony. We cannot assume that he knows that Tony has realised his betrayal in this scene because several scenes in subsequent episodes involve Jimmy attempting to elicit incriminating talk from Tony and other senior members of the Soprano family. Furthermore, when Jimmy is confronted with his betrayal and duly executed in the Season 1 finale 'I Dream of Jeannie Cusamano' his horror at having been discovered is genuine. In Scene 4 therefore he is sufficiently reassured by Tony's upbeat delivery of Turn 12 that this betrayal is unexposed. Whilst it is increasingly unlikely that Tony will yield an incriminating turn at this point, Jimmy takes the opportunity to further communicate his cooperation to the FBI with these turns; they primarily communicate that his efforts are genuine to the eavesdropping authorities.

From the perspective of an eavesdropping FBI participant in Scene 4, Tony Soprano has provided nothing that could be used in the building of a criminal case against him.

10.4 Multimodal Analysis of the Tony and Jimmy Scene

Section 10.3 demonstrates that by utilising the conversational maxims of Grice (1975) alongside conversational roles in the participation framework of Goffman (1981) dramatic dialogue can be analysed to demonstrate the divergent conversational intentions of interlocutors. In Scene 4 Jimmy's turns fail to observe the maxim of Quantity, especially as it operates in the vigilant context of crime talk in *The Sopranos*, in trying to elicit incriminating responses from Tony. The suspicions which Jimmy's talk provoke in Tony prompt him to be careful and noncommittal in his replies; on another level these uninformative responses flout the maxims of Relation and Quantity as Tony collusively communicates to the FBI that he will not allow incriminating talk to be recorded in this exchange. For the audience, who hear the dialogue whilst additionally observing the scene visually, Tony's realisation of Jimmy's treachery is simultaneously communicated through multimodal aspects of the scene.

This section of the chapter complements and strengthens the dialogue discussion above by analysing Scene 4 in terms of camera shot, gaze and any action undertaken by the speakers as the dialogue is delivered. Camera shot is hugely important for audience perception of a scene as it can 'generate a sense of being involved in the fictional world' (McIntyre & Bousfield 2011, p. 120). McIntyre (2008, p. 323) notes that camera movement in close-up shots, for example, can cause 'an increase in our psychological closeness' to a character. There are thirteen distinct shots in Scene 4. Camera position provides the audience with a certain point of view which can operate to create an allegiance with or divergence from the perception of a character in the text world of the series.

Directors throughout the six-season run of *The Sopranos* often shoot scenes from Tony Soprano's viewpoint, none more famous or indeed more controversial than the final scene in the series finale 'Made in America' in which Tony may or may not have been executed. The episode 'Nobody Knows Anything' of which Scene 4 forms a part uses a range of camera shots and positions in tandem with what is being spoken through dialogue to draw the audience vicariously into Tony's moment of realisation of Jimmy's betrayal. Given that the theme of this scene is basically one of duplicity, the gaze of the characters is also important. James Gandolfini and Joseph Badalucco Jr., who play Tony and Jimmy respectively, do not necessarily hold eye contact at all times throughout, despite there being no additional ratified participants in the exchange. Additional actions, physical as well as paralinguistic, interplay with the other visual aspects of the scene and with elements of the dialogue discussed above. In the shot-by-shot analysis below shot number is indicated in **bold** alongside the relevant turns of dialogue.

1 1 JIMMY: You got a problem.
1 2 TONY: Yeah I know, I'm working on it.
1 3 JIMMY: Working on what?

These first three turns of dialogue are contained within the first shot of the scene, a medium close-up on Jimmy with Tony in the left foreground which is held for twelve seconds; the viewer sees the side profile of his upper body as he faces towards Jimmy. This shot is maintained in Turn 2 when Tony speaks; the salient focus remains on Jimmy. The actions of the characters and the props with which they interact within the setting of the scene form part of the overall mise en scène. In Scene 4 action interplays with dialogue, gaze and camera shot to enhance important elements of the dialogue. Turn 3 – Jimmy's over-explicit 'Working on what?' – is the moment when Tony's suspicions become aroused, and the camera cuts to Shot 2 to highlight the importance of his reaction.

Also at the end of Shot 1 Jimmy is observed to disconnect the eye contact with Tony which has been consistent for the first twelve seconds of the scene; immediately after delivery of Turn 3 he turns away to avoid Tony's direct gaze. The effect of this disconnection at the beginning of Shot 2 is enhanced by Jimmy's beginning to fidget with the label attached to the water tank in the Soprano basement where his right hand is placed throughout Shot 1. The combined effect of the change of physical action and gaze highlights the importance of the over-explicit dialogue in 'Working on what?'; Jimmy's nervousness in this opening moment of conversational strategy, violating the maxim of Quantity, is also communicated visually to the audience and potentially to Tony, whose gaze remains unaltered despite the discontinuation of eye contact.

The water tank in Tony's basement is an important prop and indeed the basement itself is an important setting in *The Sopranos* series overall. In 'Mr. Ruggerio's Neighborhood', the opening episode of the third season, the same water tank explodes, impeding the FBI's attempt to place a concealed microphone in the only part of the home where Tony might engage in crime talk. The lamp in which the microphone is eventually placed is later removed from the basement by Tony's daughter, a fact about which he ironically complains in a later episode. The basement is the central setting of crime talk in the Soprano home and the focus of the FBI's attempts to eavesdrop on these interactions. The props in this setting play a recurring role in the law and order theme which runs throughout the series. A full analysis of the role of settings and props in *The Sopranos*, which operate anaphorically and cataphorically throughout the series, is obviously beyond the scope of this chapter; however, the basement of the Soprano home as a central setting for the FBI's pursuit of Tony can be said to begin with Scene 4.

This second shot of the Scene 4 lasts for three seconds with Tony delivering the fourth turn – 'Why? What were you going to say?' – which signals the initial arousal of his suspicions of Jimmy's betrayal. Tony, shot in centre frame in a medium close-up, is the sole occupier of the frame in Shot 2. The importance of his reaction to Jimmy's 'Working on what?' (Turn 3) is captured by this cut to Tony after delivery of the over-explicit dialogue. The audience get a direct perspective on Tony, viewing his reaction to Jimmy and his delivery of Turn 4.

We cannot say that Jimmy shares the audience's point of view on Tony in Shot 2 as he has pointedly diverted his gaze away from Tony to focus on the label on the water tank as soon as he delivers the first of his suspiciously over-explicit questions in Turn 3. Point of view provides the audience with vicarious access to a scene; the viewer can possess the same perspective as a character (either looking upon the speaker or the listener in a scene like Scene 4) or can instead view the scene from a less local perspective, being shown both characters and the setting in shot as an interaction proceeds. In Scene 4 the audience largely share an alternating point of view between that of Tony and that of Jimmy. Kress and van Leeuwen (1996) differentiate between the viewpoints of represented participants – the characters in a scene – and the interactive viewpoint of the audience. The interactive viewpoint of Tony's first moment of suspicion in Shot 2 is centred solely on Tony in a medium close-up with no other characters or props in the shot, so audience attention is solely on his reaction to 'Working on what?' and his delivery of 'Why? What were you going to say?' which signals the commencement of his counter-strategies in this scene.

Shot 3 is an over-the-shoulder shot focussed on Jimmy from Tony's point of view; the interactive participant and the represented participant share the same viewpoint. In Shot 3 Jimmy delivers the fifth turn of dialogue, 'You better lay low with that safe house money', attempting to elicit even an acknowledgement from Tony about the robbery and murder. For the purposes of this elicitation Jimmy re-establishes eye contact with Tony; given his increasingly perilous position he presumably thinks that it is too risky to continue to not engage visually with his interlocutor. Jimmy's discomfort is maintained, however, as he continues to fidget with the label on the water tank. This eye contact is maintained in Shot 4, shot from Jimmy's point of view with Tony centre frame in a medium close-up; the visual focus of the audience is on Tony as his suspicions rise further and he delivers the uncooperative sixth turn of dialogue – 'What are you talking about?' – which signals to Jimmy, the FBI and the external audience that he will resist attempts to elicit incriminating talk.

Shot 5 contains the seventh and eighth turns:

5 7 JIMMY: They were asking me a lot of questions in there you know. If I know anything about the dead Columbian, the apartment and all that.
5 8 TONY: Well you look good.

Tony's ultimate moment of realisation comes in this thirteen-second shot, in which Jimmy is the main speaker. As Turn 7 commences the side of Tony's head occupies part of the foreground in an over-the-shoulder shot – the audience share Tony's point of view. As this five-second turn proceeds Jimmy moves from his position at the water tank in the right of the shot across the basement and out of the shot. Given that Jimmy is the sole speaker here, one standard way of shooting the scene at this point would be to employ a tracking shot, following Jimmy as he moves and continues to speak. Instead the camera remains stationary; Tony therefore becomes the sole occupier of the frame. Tony's gaze remains fixed on Jimmy's former position at the water tank for two seconds. This indicates contemplation as Jimmy speaks and directs the audience's visual attention to Tony's reaction. By keeping the camera stationary the director indicates that Tony's reaction to Jimmy's words here is at least as important as the words themselves.

Between twenty-three and thirty seconds into the scene, the last seven seconds of Shot 5 (Turn 8 – 'Well you look good' – is delivered at thirty seconds), Jimmy's betrayal is fully realised by Tony. Over these seven seconds Tony turns 180 degrees; the interactive participant views him turn through the shot as the camera moves into a close-up of his face. The director utilises the stationary camera position and the close-up technique to increase to its highest point the psychological closeness between character and audience at this moment of realisation. This close-up commences and Tony begins to turn around as soon as Turn 7 ceases; as the character moves and the camera zooms, the dialogue is suspended for seven seconds, exclusively focussing the audience's attention on the visual delivery of the scene at this point. In Turn 7 the audience has witnessed Jimmy's third and most elaborate violation of the maxim of Quantity so far. By foregoing dialogue for silence and using the close-up in the following seconds, the director draws the audience into the realisation of this moment for Tony. When Tony's conversationally uncooperative eighth turn, opting out of the cooperative principle for Jimmy and flouting the maxim of Relation for the eavesdropping FBI, is delivered, the close-up shot on Tony is maintained and he looks directly at the new position occupied by Jimmy, still out of shot until Turn 9 commences.

Having shared Tony's realisation, the audience and the character experience the remainder of the scene with this new awareness of Jimmy's betrayal. When the medium close-up shot which dominates the scene is restored in Shot 6, the audience has now vicariously shared Tony's realisation of Jimmy's treachery. Dramatic tension is also raised from this point onwards. The game of conversational elicitation and avoidance between Jimmy and Tony is played for higher stakes now that Tony accepts that his earlier suspicions have been accurate. Tony's awareness is evident in the remaining dialogue; conversational turns are increasingly dominated by Jimmy as his attempts to incriminate Tony intensify whilst Tony's already high conversational vigilance is heightened further.

In Shots 6 and 7, Turns 9 and 10 are delivered:

6 9 JIMMY: Thanks, I wasn't gone that long.
7 10 TONY: Yeah, yeah I know.

In each of these turns there is correlation between dialogue, and camera shot and gaze. Shots 6 and 7 are each shot in medium close-up with the speaker in centre frame; the eye contact between the characters means that the audience and hearer share the same point of view for the six seconds over which these turns are delivered. Shot 8 contains most of Turn 11, with the exception of the last three words, which are contained in Shot 9:

8   11 JIMMY: My lawyer told them, 'Eh he doesn't own the building, he's not responsible for what's in the building.' I told them, 'The pool table was there when I first rented the joint.'
9   12 TONY: Good thinking. Missed your calling – should've been a lawyer.

From Shot 9 onwards then Tony's visual presence in this scene relative to the dialogue increases, reinforcing the importance of his reaction to Jimmy's turns. Throughout Scene 4, when Tony is speaking he is the sole occupant of the shot, usually centre frame in a medium close-up. This is not always the case for Jimmy, however. Shot 8 cuts to Shot 9 prior to the conclusion of Jimmy's conversational turn, so we have a medium close-up of Tony, the audience and Jimmy sharing the point of view, at the end of the turn. The focus is on Tony whilst Jimmy is still speaking, placing the visual attention of the interactive participant on one represented participant and the aural attention on the other, indicating again for the audience the importance of Tony's reaction. Visual attention alternates back to Jimmy in Shot 10. He fidgets with a punch bag with a similar effect to his fidgeting with the label on the water tank in Shots 1 and 3 and turns away from Tony, the disconnection of eye contact and physical action again signalling heightened nervousness at moments of high conversational risk. He is shot in a medium close-up in centre frame, the audience and Tony sharing the point of view, as Turn 13 is delivered:

10   13 JIMMY: Please. Enough people hate me. So ah what are you going to do about the Columbian money?
11   14 JIMMY: They were putting the screws to me like I was a school kid, telling me the
12   money was marked, they were even saying there's a new fingerprinting technique that lifts it right off the bills.

Shot 11 comprises the beginning of Turn 14, whilst this is still Jimmy's conversational turn – five seconds of silence follows Turn 13 before Jimmy tries again to elicit an incriminating contribution from Tony – the shot cuts to a medium close-up of Tony, who stares at Jimmy throughout Shot 11 but does not offer the verbal acknowledgement Jimmy hopes for.

The increased visual attention on Tony later in Scene 4 is reinforced by his facial expressions and gesticulation. The importance of facial expression and gesture is demonstrated by Shots 10 and 11 in particular. As discussed above, in response to Jimmy's 'So ah what are you going to do about the Columbian money?' Tony offers no verbal contribution, hence not even acknowledging his awareness of the topic to the eavesdropping FBI. Instead Tony purses his lips, shrugs his shoulders and shakes his head in response to Jimmy's question. Gesture and expression allow Tony to pay lip service to conversational cooperation for the ratified participant, but nothing is recorded which might accommodate the eavesdropping authorities. Kendon (2004, p. 225) states that speakers 'use gestures as part of the way in which they "do things" with utterances'. For Tony Soprano in Scene 4 physical gestures are used to take the place of utterances he wishes to avoid making verbally. He is able to signal uncertainty as an answer to Jimmy's question without offering anything of evidentiary usefulness to the FBI, who have no visual access to the conversation. As a potential verbal response such as 'I don't know' could be construed as acknowledgement that he is aware of the 'Columbian money', Tony instead signals a response to Jimmy by an emblematic gesture which cannot be recorded by a concealed microphone. These gestures are classified as 'emblems' by McNeill (2000), in that meaning is communicated without the obligation of speech. The tape at this point captures only the lengthy five-second pause before Jimmy commences Turn 14.

The pause in the dialogue at this point operates in a similar way to the seven-second pause in Shot 5; the audience is focussed solely on Tony's reactions during this period. Multimodal analysis accommodates a fuller realisation of the importance of these pauses than can be achieved by an analysis which focuses exclusively on verbal elements of the scene. The medium close-up with Tony centre frame in Shot 11 reinforces the importance of his reactions in this scene. The accompanying action demonstrates to the viewer that Tony is offering an acknowledgement of Jimmy's question, but not one which can be recorded.

When Turn 14 commences the camera remains trained on Tony. The importance of his reaction to Jimmy's lying strategy – as noted above Jimmy's turns are becoming more elaborate, flying in the face of the maxims which govern crime talk in *The Sopranos* – is emphasised; again the interactive participant views the hearer rather than the speaker as the dialogue proceeds. This technique reinforces for the audience that how Tony reacts to Jimmy's dialogue is as relevant as the obvious significance of the words themselves. A multimodal stylistic focus therefore offers a more fully meaningful examination of the scene. Tony's realisation of Jimmy's betrayal is clearly as important as the betrayal itself.

Shot 12 cuts back to Jimmy. He begins to walk from the left foreground as the remainder of Turn 14 is delivered; the director uses a tracking shot to follow Jimmy's movement, but only until he reaches where Tony is standing. The tracking discontinues at this point and the camera focuses on Tony in a medium close-up as Jimmy continues to move across the foreground, eventually exiting shot right. Again the audience's visual attention is directed to Tony as Jimmy is speaking, reinforcing for a final time in Scene 4 the significance of his reaction to Jimmy's betrayal.

The multimodal stylistic analysis of this chapter focuses appropriate attention on central visual elements of televisual discourse, demonstrating the level of interplay between dialogue and camera shot, gaze and action.

Psychological closeness between the interactive viewing audience and represented participant Tony Soprano is achieved by medium close-ups which move into enhanced close-ups at crucial moments of the scene. The effect of this enhanced close-up is intensified in Shot 5 by a lengthy seven-second pause. In this period when all dialogue and action is suspended, Jimmy's treachery is vicariously experienced by the audience. The use of tracking shots is also employed to reinforce the salience of Tony. When the speaking Jimmy begins to move from one side of the basement to the other in Shot 5, the camera remains focussed on Tony before moving into the close-up discussed above. Whilst the audience might ordinarily expect the camera to track the main speaker, the focus at this crucial moment remains trained on Tony. When tracking is employed in Shot 12, as Jimmy moves back towards the right of the shot, the camera movement ceases when Tony comes into the shot, focussing on a medium close-up of Tony and allowing Jimmy, still speaking, to exit to the right of the frame.

The salience of Tony in this scene is captured by the connection of the camera shot with the dialogue. When Tony speaks he is always shot in a medium close-up in the centre of the frame for the duration of his dialogue; the audience's point of view parallels Jimmy's. In several of Jimmy's conversational turns, however, the camera cuts to the next shot before his dialogue has concluded, focussing exclusively on Tony's reaction as Jimmy speaks. This technique shifts the audience's point of view at significant moments in the scene. The meaning of the dialogue is therefore enhanced by focussing the audience's attention not just on the content of Jimmy's dialogue but also on Tony's reaction to these turns.

The gaze of the speakers also corresponds with important elements of the dialogue. Direct eye contact is conventional in intensive one-to-one conversational encounters, and so it is unsurprising that this prevails throughout much of this scene. Breaking direct eye contact therefore foregrounds moments of significance in Scene 4: when direct visual contact between the participants is broken, crucial messages are signalled to the audience. This is borne out in Turn 3; for example, after asking the over-explicit question 'Working on what?', the point at which Tony Soprano begins to suspect his dishonesty, Jimmy immediately turns his head downwards to the right, now focussing on the water tank prop. Bluntly discontinuing direct gaze between speakers recalls the conventionalised perception of 'looking one in the eye' when telling the truth, whilst verbal dishonesty will often be accompanied by an avoidance of eye contact. Jimmy's very explicit diverting his gaze away from Tony after he delivers 'Working on what?' in the first shot indicates the importance of this turn in the context of the scene.

In Shot 5, when the dialogue contains Jimmy's elaborate attempt to elicit at least an acknowledgement from Tony 'about the dead Columbian, the apartment and all that', he moves across the foreground and eventually out of shot as the camera moves into the psychologically important close-up of Tony. At this moment of heightened verbal strategy, Jimmy again disengages direct visual contact with Tony, delivering the dialogue as he passes Tony's stationary position and looking straight ahead. The audience observe Tony's gaze as unaltered in this shot. Rather than watching Jimmy as he speaks and moves, Tony's gaze, much like that of the camera position, does not track the speaker but remains fixed. Tony is acquiring more realisation of Jimmy's betrayal as the scene progresses, and in Shot 5 his gaze remaining fixed on Jimmy's previous position rather than tracking the speaker indicates to the audience that he is working out that Jimmy has turned collaborator and is now attempting to elicit incriminating information for the eavesdropping FBI.

Jimmy disengages the eye contact which marks the previous five shots again in Shot 10. The over-explicit 'So ah what are you going to do about the Colombian money?' question in Turn 13 prompts him to focus his attention on a punch bag, with which he fidgets much like he does with the label attached to water tank prop in Shot 1. In the moments where Jimmy flies in the face of the conversational conventions of crime talk in *The Sopranos* his gaze also alters and his physical focus turns to a particular prop in the basement setting, paralleling the movement of his visual focus away from his target.

A multimodal stylistic focus which addresses audiovisual elements of televisual discourse adds much to an analysis of dramatic dialogue by the pragmatic model of conversational cooperation. In Scene 4 camera shot, gaze and action interact with the dialogue of Tony and Jimmy to heighten the audience's participation in Tony's realisation of betrayal. In Shot 12 all of these features combine as Jimmy attempts a final time to record incriminating talk from Tony. The dialogue comprises Jimmy's lying strategy as he grows more desperate to accommodate the FBI eavesdroppers, whilst the camera tracking of Jimmy ceases when he passes Tony, maintaining a medium close-up on Tony and reinforcing that the importance of this scene is not only Jimmy's betrayal but also Tony's realisation of it, which has implications for the storyline of *The Sopranos* beyond Scene 4. Jimmy's direct visual engagement with Tony is broken as he begins to walk from right to left of the shot, action and gaze again interacting with camera shot and dialogue. The multimodal approach to this scene allows the analyst to demonstrate that findings based on pragmatic models like those of Grice (1975) and Goffman (1981) can be integrated with considerations of how meaning is simultaneously encoded by non-verbal signs, producing a significantly more robust analysis of an example of telecinematic discourse.

10.5 Conclusion

The dialogue of crime talk in *The Sopranos* has proven particularly amenable to pragmatic models of talk given the often divergent conversational intentions of a range of interlocutors. Cooperating witnesses, their handlers and their targets fulfil different participant roles and employ a range of conversational strategies in crime talk. The specialised merging of collusive crossplay and collusive sideplay performed by the cooperating witness is realised by conversational contributions which fail to fulfil conversational maxims as they operate in crime talk scenarios in *The Sopranos*. Targets often violate the maxim of Relation in attempting to steer conversations away from the specifics which cooperating witnesses are attempting to record for their eavesdropping FBI handlers and flout the maxim of Manner to strategically exclude overhearers from crime talk.

Scene 4 features Jimmy Altieri, 'wired for sound' in the lion's den of Tony Soprano's house, as he attempts to elicit from the boss of the Soprano crime family an admission of his knowledge of and involvement in the murder of a rival criminal. The extreme danger in which Jimmy has placed himself is manifested in his gaze and actions in Scene 4, whilst his talk exposes his ultimate conversational intention. This extreme danger is eventually realised when Jimmy is executed in the season finale.

For his part, Tony's conversational turns offer nothing which might incriminate him whilst he utilises gesture to maintain the appearance of cooperation with Jimmy. His questions in Turns 4 and 6 pay lip service to the cooperative principle whilst ultimately providing neither verbal acknowledgement nor information for the eavesdropping authorities. 'Well you look good', failing to fulfil the maxim of Relation in Turn 8, signals the moment which confirms his realisation that Jimmy has betrayed him. The audience share in this moment of realisation in Shot 5 when the camera moves into a close-up of Tony within a lengthy seven-second pause in the dialogue. The effect of these silences in Shots 5 and 11 is critical to the scene and a stylistic analysis must approach the scene from a multimodal perspective to fully address their importance. A multimodal analysis also focuses on the gestural actions which are used by Tony to ostensibly adhere to the cooperative principle in terms of ratified participant Jimmy, by nodding, smiling and shrugging his shoulders, but to explicitly frustrate access to the interaction for the eavesdropping FBI, who do not have visual access to the interaction. The verbal analysis in the opening section of this chapter demonstrates that Tony's dialogue in Scene 4 often operates on two levels: in his refusal to be drawn into incriminating himself to Jimmy he is simultaneously implying to the FBI that their attempts to record compromising talk will be unsuccessful.

In focussing on camera shot, gaze and the actions of the characters alongside the dialogue of Scene 4 this chapter dovetails with other analyses within the stylistics of drama which address audiovisual alongside textual elements of film and television dialogue. The vicarious participation of the interactive audience in Tony's realisation of betrayal in Scene 4 would be difficult to analyse thoroughly by focussing on models for the analysis of dialogue alone. An analysis which addresses this dialogue by established stylistic parameters demonstrates how the divergent intentions of the participants are realised by various deviations from Grice's conversational maxims. Through the shot-by-shot analysis in the fourth section of this chapter these findings are strengthened considerably by assessing how features of the dialogue interact with camera shot, gaze and action. The multimodal approach demonstrates how the audience are psychologically drawn into the fictional world of the drama and share in Tony's ultimate moment of realisation. In most cases the audience are aware that a character has 'flipped' in *The Sopranos* before their treachery is discovered by other characters; in the case of Jimmy Altieri a multimodal stylistic analysis demonstrates how his betrayal is only exposed to the audience in the same scene that it becomes clear to Tony Soprano himself.

References

Goffman, E. (1981). *Forms of Talk*. Oxford: Blackwell.
Grice, H. P. (1975). Logic and Conversation. In P. Cole & J. L. Morgan, eds., *Syntax and Semantics, vol. 3: Speech Acts*. New York: Academic Press, pp. 41–58.
Kendon, A. (2004). *Gesture: Visible Action as Utterance*. New York: Cambridge University Press.
Kress, G., & van Leeuwen, T. (1996). *Reading Images: The Grammar of Visual Design*. London: Routledge.
McIntyre, D. (2008). Integrating Multimodal Analysis and the Stylistics of Drama: A Multimodal Perspective on Ian McKellen's *Richard III*. *Language and Literature*, 17(4), 565–577.
McIntyre, D., & Bousfield, D. (2011). Emotion and Empathy in Martin Scorsese's *Goodfellas*. In R. Piazza, M. Bednarek & F. Rossi, eds., *Telecinematic Discourse: Approaches to the Language of Films and Television Series*. Amsterdam: John Benjamins, pp. 105–123.
McNeill, D. (2000). *Language and Gesture*. Cambridge: Cambridge University Press.
Montoro, R. (2011). Multimodal Realisations of Mind Style in *Enduring Love*. In R. Piazza, M. Bednarek & F. Rossi, eds., *Telecinematic Discourse: Approaches*

to the Language of Films and Television Series. Amsterdam: John Benjamins, pp. 69–84.

(2015). The Year's Work in Stylistics 2014. *Language and Literature*, 24(4), 355–372.

Richardson, K. (2010). *Television Dramatic Dialogue: A Sociolinguistic Study*. Oxford: Oxford University Press.

Shuy, R. (2005). *Creating Language Crimes: How Law Enforcement Uses (and Misuses) Language*. Oxford: Oxford University Press.

Statham, S. (2015). 'A guy in my position is a government target ... You got to be extra, extra careful': Participation and Strategies in Crime Talk in *The Sopranos*. *Language and Literature*, 24(4), 322–337.

Toolan, M. (2011). 'I don't know what they're saying half the time, but I'm hooked on the series': Incomprehensible Dialogue and Integrated Multimodal Characterisation in *The Wire*. In R. Piazza, M. Bednarek & F. Rossi, eds., *Telecinematic Discourse: Approaches to the Language of Films and Television Series*. Amsterdam: John Benjamins, pp. 161–183.

11 'Nossa Vida é Bandida'
Reading Rio Prohibited Funk from a CDA Perspective

Andrea Mayr

Rio funk (*funk carioca*) has arisen in the context of conflict and violence in Brazil's favelas and is as complex and multi-faceted as the reality it stems from. An important part of Rio de Janeiro's popular culture, it has fused American soul, funk and hip-hop with aspects of life in favelas. Rio funk has evolved into a rich musical experience, but its connection to irregular armed groups inside favelas means that it is widely associated with criminality. This is particularly true of its main subgenre, *proibidão*, a kind of underground 'gangster' funk that praises these armed groups in many of its lyrics. It is therefore often perceived as an anti-social and dangerous phenomenon that challenges the state's authority. This limiting way of looking at funk *proibidão*, however, largely occludes the social, cultural and political processes that underlie its creation and existence. It also undermines a consideration of its cultural and political potential.

This chapter offers a different assessment of Rio funk and explores how funk *proibidão* in its lyrics addresses and recontextualises the imbrications of state and criminal violence, which are often left unsaid in media and public discourses about favelas.

To do so, I employ a critical discourse analytical approach combined with ethnographic insights in the form of participant observation at funk parties (*baile funks*) and informal interviewing. I argue that funk (*proibidão*) is not merely a demonstration of unlawful powers, but rather a fundamental counter-cultural expression that amounts to a local form of 'insurgent citizenship' (Holston 2008) through which favela residents define and redefine their socio-spatial identities under the political, economic and symbolic constraints they face.

11.1 Introduction

Rio funk is a fusion of African American soul, funk beats and Afro-Brazilian rhythms. The question of its exact origin is not settled, but it appears to have emerged from the 1970s club culture of the impoverished peripheries of Rio de Janeiro as well as its more middle-class counterparts, where local DJs transformed records coming from the United States to create a style of their own (Vianna 1988; Palombini 2010). While Rio funk at first drew its inspiration from Miami Bass, a subgenre of American hip-hop, it has since become a distinctly Brazilian electronic type of music with its own dance styles, slang and modes of dress.[1] Rio funk is now firmly rooted in favelas and has become their most significant, if criminalised, cultural practice. This is because of its customary association with criminal factions inside favelas which sponsor and pay for large-scale outdoor funk parties, known as *bailes funk*. These events are performed by sound system crews that include DJs who play funk tracks from vinyl, CDs, a drum machine or a laptop, and one or several MCs[2] who sing/rap live.

Rio funk is the result of 'the creative appropriation of cheap technology by people with no formal musical training who produce music for segregated segments of the population' (Palombini 2014, p. 320). Musically, it typically consists of a blend of pre-recorded beats and diverse *samples*, that is, extracted portions of sound, which may include digitally enhanced voices, radio and TV sound bites and/or machine-gun shots. The lyrics, which are composed by the MCs, often contain graphic and violent imagery, particularly in funk *proibidão* ('strictly forbidden funk'), which is demonised for supposedly valorising gang warfare and extolling the exploits of favela drug dealers. Often dismissed by the state, its police forces and the media for 'advocating' crime (*fazer apologia ao crime*),[3] *proibidão* is more adequately described as dealing with

life on the retail end of the illicit substance trade, narrated with specific ethical concerns, *from the perspective of those who experience its problems*, according to a particular aesthetics of composition, performance, and musical and phonographic production. (Palombini 2013, p. 1; my emphasis)

Proibidão is therefore deeply embedded in the cultural and physical space in which it is produced and performed. This makes it an important tool for underprivileged youth to articulate their sense of identity as well as the marginality that comes with it. In so doing, *proibidão* does allude to the violence inherent in structural inequalities, although it is not as politically charged as Brazilian hip-hop. As the quote above suggests, it is also an

---

[1] Miami Bass is based on the electro-funk sound pioneered by Afrika Bambataa. In the early 2000s, a new beat, *tamborzão* ('big drums'), a driving drum machine breakbeat, replaced the previously imported Miami Bass, which has more identifiable Brazilian beats, but also maintains the heavy bass characteristic of the Miami bass (Sá 2007, p. 13).

[2] MC ('Master of Ceremonies') is a term usually applied in hip-hop, but also Rio funk. True MCs use skills that are often ignored in hip-hop today. These skills include wordplay, punchlines, metaphors, similes, multis, flow and switch ups (www.rapdict.org/MC).

[3] The Portuguese term *apologia* means defending or advocating a certain idea or cause. Funk *proibidão* is regulated by two articles of the Brazilian penal code: Article 286 prohibits inciting violence and Article 287 makes it illegal to defend crime (*apologia*) (Sneed 2003).

aesthetic practice which finds its expression not only in lyrics and sound but also in the active and creative use of distinctive dance moves, clothing and hair styles (see Mizrahi 2011). Hence, Rio funk articulates discourses of power, exclusion and resistance as well as identity, belonging and style.

One of the ways in which exclusion of favelas and *baile funks* manifests itself is through their representation in the media. Reports about drug trafficker violence in favelas frequently dominate the news in Brazil, and sensationalist reporting divides actors into distinct categories of legality and criminality that preclude further interrogations of the dynamics of urban violence, the social realities that underlie much of it and the social actors who are involved in it (Penglase 2007; Biazoto 2011). Those who are commonly labelled *traficantes* ('drug dealers'), *marginais* ('delinquents') and *bandidos* ('outlaws') have their 'multifaceted subjectivities' obscured by simplistic portrayals of them as enemies of the state (Robb-Larkins 2015, p. 163; see also Hall 1997).

However, the (violent) actions of drug traffickers and the discourses used to describe them in funk become meaningful when set within cultural understandings of violence (Whitehead 2004; Penglase 2005). As Whitehead (2004, p. 74) argues, 'forms of violence are not produced by the febrile excess of savage or pathological minds, but are cultural performances whose poetics derive from the history and socio-cultural relationships of the locale'. The meaning of violence has to be appreciated for the way it is also a fundamental cultural expression.

Violence is 'poetic' in the sense that it goes beyond the merely instrumental and involves competence in the strategic and creative use of signs and symbols. This means that violence needs to be analysed as a discursive process which produces new meanings, practices and symbols. Funk *proibidão* is such a practice, whose complex symbols, codes and language have developed out of the de facto rule of favelas by drug gangs. Brazil's two main gangs, the Comando Vermelho (CV) and the Primeiro Comando da Capital (PCC) have proved skilful in the 'poetic' use of the notion of violence, using a 'vocabulary of motive' (Mills 1940) through which they justify the violence in the favelas under their control as legitimate. These vocabularies are recontextualised in funk, when MCs construct positive identities for drug traffickers, providing ways for listeners to understand and appreciate their (violent) conduct. Analysing violence as a discourse practice therefore provides insights into cultural meanings of violence from the standpoint of insiders. It also allows us to interpret and not simply condemn violence.

So while funk *proibidão* can be regarded as a demonstration of the territorial power of drug dealers who exercise a 'politics of presence' (Oosterbaan 2009) inside favelas, it is more importantly a tool for MCs and favela youth to construct and voice identities whose references lie in the sharing of the experiences of armed, structural and symbolic violence under conditions of social exclusion and class disparity. In this respect, Gramsci's (1971) concept of 'organic' intellectuals and their emancipatory potential provides a useful framework for understanding funk. According to Gramsci, 'organic intellectuals emerge from within (and in immediate response to) the political energies, pressures, and contradictions of marginalised and oppressed social groups' (Strine 1991, p. 159). Conscious of their exclusion, favela funksters act as organic intellectuals who circulate counter-discourses, formulating oppositional interpretations about the identities, values and actions of drug dealers and their own. In this sense, funk *proibidão* functions as an 'antilanguage' (Halliday 1978), a language of social conflict that is used by its creators as a moderate form of counter-power.

With these considerations in mind, this chapter calls for a more contextualised analysis of funk *proibidão*. It rejects the view that *proibidão* is merely a celebration of criminal gang membership and instead aims to illustrate that it is a valuable subcultural expression that provides a discourse to explore those cultural values and norms that inform important aspects of life in Rio's favelas. Rio funk has already been analysed from sociological, anthropological, historical and musicological perspectives, all of which have produced valuable insights into its evolution and potential as a subcultural practice (e.g. Vianna 1988; Yúdice 1994; Herschmann 2000; Sneed 2003, 2008; Palombini 2010, 2013; D'Angelo 2015). Several of these studies have focused on funk *proibidão* and its lyrics, notably Sneed (2003, 2008) in his ethnographic study of funk and drug gangs and Palombini (2013, 2014) in his musicological accounts of the genre, but they have not looked at the finer linguistic details that tell us *how* the lyrics are used to promote certain themes and values. This chapter contributes to and expands on the existing literature by exploring the more subtle discursive processes through which funk *proibidão* functions as a site of contestation that challenges the dominant social and cultural order by constructing (violent) social identities and counter-hegemonic discourses that legitimise the rule of gangs in favelas.

In so doing, my analysis does not necessarily treat the lyrics as more or less accurate reports of drug gangs and their actions. Bearing in mind that lyrics can range from 'truths to exaggerated fantasies' (Keyes 2002, p. 4), they are both real and imaginary, sometimes at the same time. The lyrics are seen here as discursive actions that construct an 'interpretive environment' (Kubrin 2005, p. 366) for describing violent identities and behaviour as appropriate and acceptable. Funk artists not only portray, but also *create* cultural understandings of life in favelas that render violence, danger and unpredictability normative. Hence they represent the social world of favelas as much as they are constitutive of it. This makes funk *proibidão* particularly worthwhile for an ethnographically informed critical discourse analysis that aims at exposing unfamiliar aspects of a sociocultural environment. The question addressed here will be: How do the MCs communicate their respective themes and values and how do they align their audience with these values? In other words, how do they use language interpersonally?

11.2 Analytical Approach

The discourse paradigm adopted here is in the tradition of Critical Discourse Analysis (CDA) and Systemic Functional Linguistics (Halliday 1978; Martin 1992) and uses Martin's (2000) Appraisal Theory for the analysis of funk *proibidão* lyrics. Appraisal is designed to identify evaluation in language and provides a systematic account of language resources for expressing emotions and attitudes. This discourse-analytical approach is combined with ethnographical insights from participant observation at funk events and informal interviews with funk insiders. An ethnographic perspective is essential when we want to understand texts taken from a specific subculture.

CDA primarily studies how dominance and inequality are produced and reproduced in discourses of the powerful and aims to 'understand, expose, and ultimately resist social inequality' (Van Dijk 1998, p. 352). The focus of this chapter, however, is not so much on the discourses of the powerful, but on the productive uses of discourse by members of subordinated groups. This heeds Martin's (2004, p. 186) injunction that in CDA a complementary focus on community is needed that takes into account 'how people get together and make room for themselves in the world'. In this respect a combined discourse-analytical and ethnographic angle can shed light on 'parallel discursive arenas where members of subordinated social groups invent and circulate counter-discourses', helping to 'expand discursive space' (Fraser 1990, p. 67). The *baile funk* therefore is here understood as a stage for a 'subaltern counter-public' (Fraser 1990, p. 67), a site that brings to the fore issues that have been overlooked, ignored or suppressed by dominant public spheres of production and communication practice.[4] It is also the site where the legitimation of drug traffickers is enacted and reproduced.

In order to show how these social actors are legitimated in *proibidão* lyrics and how the audience is meant to identify with them, Martin and White's (2005) system for evaluation, Appraisal, is instructive as it is concerned with 'how writers/speakers approve and disapprove, enthuse and abhor, applaud and criticise, and with how they position their readers/listeners to do likewise' (Martin & White 2005, p. 1). It therefore offers an effective framework for revealing interpersonal meanings and attitudes, which, according to Halliday

---

[4] In liberal democracies, the 'public sphere' has been identified as a deliberative space between the state and society in which social actors come together as citizens in order to debate common affairs on mutually agreed grounds (Habermas 1989).

(1978), realise the relationship between writer and reader and, in the case of funk, between singer and listener (see Caldwell 2008; Križan 2013). Here I will focus only on Appraisal's subsystem of Attitude, as it covers the semantic resources used for describing emotions, judgments and evaluations as well as the polarity of these evaluations and their targets. The funk songs below will therefore be analysed first and foremost according to their expression of Attitude. Those findings are then used to show how they function as a form of localised 'insurgent citizenship' (Holston 2009a).

In expanding discursive space, the *baile funk* counterpublic MCs appropriate and transform or 'recontextualise' discourses. The concept of 'recontextualisation' (Bernstein 1990) has been adapted in CDA to capture the strategies and processes that occur as practices are turned into discourses (e.g. Van Leeuwen 1996; Richardson & Wodak 2009). Recontextualisation is a specific intertextual practice that involves taking a textual element from a specific context and inserting it into a new one, where it acquires (partly) new meaning (Reisigl & Wodak 2009). Recontextualisation also entails an *evaluation* and *legitimation* of the social practice and its social actors; hence, it can be usefully combined with the Appraisal framework. As pointed out above, Rio funk is a creative appropriation and hence recontextualisation of African American musical styles originally imported from the United States. In this sense, it constitutes an 'intertextual artifact' (Herschmann 2000, p. 163). Songs have been shown to be particularly interesting to consider with regard to recontextualisation because of the ways that lyrics, themes and motifs, melodies and entire songs are reworked and rearranged (see Machin 2010; Richardson 2017; Way 2017). In the case of Rio funk, it is stereotyping mainstream media discourses about favelas, funk and drug gangs as well as the drug gangs' discourses of 'legitimate violence' that are recontextualised in a genre-adequate way through verbal features (lyrics) and musical elements (sampling, re-mixing).

Three funk songs have been chosen for analysis. In line with the ethnographic approach that informs the linguistic analysis, the songs were selected on the basis of the themes that funk insiders (*funkeiros*) said were common in *proibidão* funk: reflecting on a life of crime, praising courageous criminals and criticising the 'war on drugs' of which favelas bear the brunt. The lyrics are in Brazilian Portuguese, so have been given an English version. Linguistic analysis of translated texts is not without its problems, but has been used in CDA (e.g. Wodak & Weiss 2005; Way 2017). Bearing this in mind, my analysis has therefore taken careful consideration of the meaning of the original lyrics, which I discussed with favela residents who are immersed in funk culture and therefore understand the intricacies of the meanings conveyed. Hence, my translation of the songs is based on their interpretation of the meaning of the originals. Language is of course 'always embedded within other semiotic systems, particularly music and dance' (Pennycook 2007, p. 98). This means that, ideally, an analysis of funk should also take into account other semiotic resources, such as the actual music or visual imagery (as in video clips) in order to explore how these interact with each other and connect to macro-level discourses (see, e.g., Machin 2010; Helland 2018). That said, lyrics are central to funk and their function as an 'interpretative resource' (Kubrin 2005) becomes particularly apparent through the language that is used to express the projected emotions, evaluations and values of the MCs, the drug gangs and the culture they are part of. In CDA, social, political and historical context is considered essential in analysing discourse. For an analysis of funk *proibidão* it is therefore necessary to place it in the sociopolitical and historical settings which gave rise to its articulation. The following section therefore offers an account that situates funk and its ongoing criminalisation within wider developments of Brazil's 'dangerous, hybrid space of citizenship' (Holston 2009b) and the rise of its criminal gangs (*comandos*).

11.3 The Criminalisation of Rio's Funk Culture

Rio de Janeiro is classed as one of the most violent and unequal cities in the world, with large numbers of its population subjected to waves of urban violence, much of it drug-related. Physical violence notwithstanding, it is symbolic violence (Bourdieu & Wacquant 2001) that affects the lives of Rio's poor just as pervasively. Symbolic forms of violence can be expressed in hegemonic discourses that often appear 'as socially conceived categories that are naturalised and put into action in complex ways' (Araújo 2010, p. 218). In the case of Rio funk, this happens through the delegitimisation of a cultural manifestation that comes from 'below'. The cultural criminalisation of funk goes hand in hand with the 'socio-spatial stigmatisation' and the historical depreciation of favela residents as second-class citizens (Fernandes & Rodriguez 2015, p. 5).[5] Many of the negative reactions against funk and *proibidão* in particular therefore stem from existing biases against favelas and their residents, which are endemic throughout Brazilian society. As Caldeira (2000, p. 79) has put it,

[F]avelas ... are considered unclean and polluting.... Excluded from the universe of the proper, they are symbolically constituted as spaces of crime, spaces of anomalous, polluting, and dangerous qualities. Predictably inhabitants of such spaces are also conceived of as marginal.... Their behaviour is condemned: they are said to use bad words, to be immoral, to consume drugs, and so on. In a way, anything that breaks the patterns of propriety can be associated with criminals, crime, and its spaces.

---

[5] Rio's favela population makes up approximately 23% of the city's 6,32 million inhabitants (World Bank 2012).

The social construction of favelas as areas of lawlessness and neglect has given rise to public security approaches which treat favelas first and foremost as spaces that need to be controlled and disciplined (Dias & Eslava 2013; Mayr 2015). Favela dwellers are regarded as 'matter out of place' in Mary Douglas's (1966) words, which violate the 'proper' organisation of Rio's space. To this day, Rio's urban poor hold what Holston (2008) has described as Brazil's 'disjunctive citizenship', which is characterised by an extremely unjust distribution of and access to wealth and space and an often indiscriminate and disproportionate use of violence against the poor. A rapid expansion of neo-liberal economic policies since the end of the country's dictatorship in 1985 has made social inequalities even worse. According to Holston (2009a, p. 261), it is Brazil's 'entrenched regime of a differentiated citizenship' that has produced high levels of criminal and police violence and in response to these 'a set of social and artistic practices in those poor peripheries that are also aggressive'. Holston (2008, p. 274) refers to these practices as instances of an 'insurgent citizenship', which resists and 'erodes entrenched practices of domination'. Funk *proibidão* does so by actively celebrating favela culture and its criminal actors. It is central to 'current reimaginings of Brazilian citizenship' (Avelar & Dunn 2011, p. 109).

Funk *proibidão* therefore has to be seen in the context of the rise of Rio's powerful drug gangs (*comandos*) and their presence in favelas. As a result of the repressive role of the state and its failure to provide social services, an informal form of social order took hold in favelas, in which drug gangs began to play a central role from the late 1980s onwards. Before that, favela criminals were engaged in minor illicit activities, such as the illegal lottery and dealing in marijuana. The gangs mainly spread into the favelas in Rio's north, as these offered them autonomy and anonymity due to their sheer size and local distrust of the police. The most prominent gang to do so was the Comando Vermelho (CV), which still controls most favelas in Rio and is revered in many funk songs.[6] Its origins go back to the final years of the dictatorship, when groups of common criminals (mostly bank robbers) were imprisoned with left-wing political prisoners and went on to form an alliance against the brutal prison conditions (Dowdney 2003, p. 29). In their joint fight, the political prisoners inspired the common criminals to politicise their work, creating a gang that had both criminal and political knowledge and strategies. Originally named the Falange Vermelho (Red Phalanx), the gang was later dubbed the Comando

---

[6] Gangs have a long history in Brazil, going back to the nineteenth-century *maltas* that congregated in Rio de Janeiro's port, as well as the music-centred *galeras cariocas* and *quadrilhas* of the 1970s and 1980s. Since the beginning of the 1990s, the Brazilian gang scene has been dominated by more violent drug gangs, the *comandos* (Rodgers & Baird 2015). The most prominent and oldest gang in Rio de Janeiro is the Comando Vermelho.

Vermelho (Red Command) by the press. As the gang then spread into Rio's poor neighbourhoods, building its criminal networks for drug distribution and sale, it also set up its own system of government, providing informal employment and social services to inhabitants long excluded from Brazilian society. It thereby embedded itself deeply into the social fabric of favela communities, shoring up the support of many.

In time, the funk parties became a symbolic marker of the territorial rule of the drug gangs. While they still took place across the city during the 1980s, the practice came to an end after a key event in 1992, the so-called *arrastões*, or 'drag-net' robberies. These consisted of coordinated beach-side muggings in Rio's wealthy south zones of Copacabana and Ipanema, which were blamed by the media on teenage funk fans from favelas. Funk was presented as inherently violent and 'alien', despite an intervention from Rio's foremost expert on funk at the time, anthropologist Herman Vianna (Penglase 2009). Media reports linked the funk fans to Rio's two main gangs at the time, the Comando Vermelho and the Terceiro Comando, prompting the police to ban many funk parties. Crucially, this drove funk back into the favelas and allowed the drug gangs to establish themselves as organisers and financiers of funk parties, resulting in their glorification in funk songs (Vianna 2005). The *arrastões* also marked a decisive shift in (media) discourses about crime and violence in Rio. Young people from the poor northern parts of the city were reported by the press as 'invading' the city's wealthier parts, using the language of war ('This *army* was drawn from the two million frequenters of funk').[7] The following excerpts from the newspaper *Jornal do Brasil* are revealing in that respect:

[They] took to the Zona Sul the *battle* of one of the *wars* that they have faced since birth – the *war* between communities. Yesterday the Zona Sul (South Zone) of Rio became a *battle zone* with arrastões carried out by gangs of adolescents from the slums of the suburbs.... The Military Police, with 110 guards armed with revolvers, machine guns and rifles, had difficulty in putting down the violence of the various groups involved in the *attack*. (*Jornal do Brasil*, 19 October 1992; my emphasis)[8]

In the end, despite the media panic, hardly any robberies were reported and police confirmed that there were no official victims (Penglase 2009). However, the metaphorical conceptualisation of urban conflict as 'war' in those media discourses has since justified a militaristic approach to interventions in Rio's favelas, with criminals gaining 'the status of enemy troops' (Ramos & Paiva 2007, p. 57). Metaphors of war have been shown to act as a 'principle of division' (Chilton 1996, p. 147) that paves the way for actions which accord to

---

[7] *Jornal do Brasil*, 23 October 1992; quoted in Yúdice (1994, p. 201)
[8] *Jornal do Brasil*, 19 October 1992; quoted in Yúdice (1994, pp. 200–201).

these metaphors. In the case of Rio, they clearly helped to cement the opposition of 'hill' (favela) versus 'asphalt' (formal city) and 'bandits vs. police' (Leite 2000; Penglase 2009).

This is the urban and sociopolitical landscape that informs (*proibidão*) funk and its lyrical content. Favela gangs, for their part, also resort to a rhetoric of violent warfare. This rhetoric is recontextualised in funk songs, as we shall see in Section 11.5, although the equation between drug gangs and violence is reversed. In funk, drug gangs such as the Comando Vermelho bring not violence and danger, but greater security and safety. This logic can be explained by the fact that the CV in the past has used the political language of civil rights to justify its intentions and deeds, typically through public pronouncements during a prison rebellion, city assault or police operation. An excerpt from one CV communique, released by the gang to the press in 2003 after its city-wide shutdown of commerce in the name of justice for the people, demonstrates this strategy:

> No longer are criminals (*bandidos*) from the favelas or behind prison bars. The people one finds living in a favela or behind prison bars are simply humble and poor people.... Is there greater violence than robbing the public treasury and killing people without a decent minimum salary, without hospitals, without work, and without food? Will this violence succeed in ending violence? Because violence generates violence. Among those imprisoned in this country is there one person who has committed a crime more heinous than killing a nation with hunger and misery? (quoted in Penglase 2005, p. 6)

By stating that there is no worse violence than the violence of the state against the poor, the CV could be said to resort to a common 'technique of neutralisation' (Sykes & Matza 1957, p. 30), that is, 'condemning the condemners'. The gang justifies using violence, combining a discourse of crime with that of citizen's rights for favela residents. This may be one reason why the gang continues to have support in favelas.

Finally, another important, but more recent development that has contributed to the criminalisation of funk was the introduction of the 'Pacifying Police Units' (UPPs) in many favelas from 2008 onwards, partly in preparation for Rio's 2014 World Cup and the 2016 Olympics. The much-lauded UPPs marked a shift away from violent policing and the hard-line 'war on drugs' strategy, focusing instead on reclaiming favelas from the control of drug gangs by driving them out, while also curtailing or prohibiting funk parties that had formerly been organised by the gangs.[9] The suppression of funk has

---

[9] Despite initial favourable results between 2009 and 2012 with a marked decrease in killings by police, shoot-outs and robberies, many favela residents lost faith in the UPP Programme due to serious incidents of violence against residents from the UPP's own ranks (see Mayr 2018). The drug gangs have also begun to fight back and have regained territorial control in some formerly pacified favelas, so that the UPP strategy has now all but collapsed (Ramos & Ucko 2017).

jeopardised both its economic and sociocultural potential. First, the *baile funk* subculture has become an autonomous and independent informal economy within favelas, partly facilitated by the drug gangs, who provide many temporary jobs and incomes to DJs, MCs, record labels, sound systems, dancers, producers and distributors of CDs as well as to the many informal sellers of food and drink at the funk parties. The *baile funk* underground economy illustrates how the gangs and favela residents respond creatively to the structural disadvantages they face as result of state neglect and Brazil's wider neoliberal context with its attendant forms of structural and symbolic violence. By organising *baile funks*, traffickers also reinvest at least some of their gains into the favelas' infrastructure and maintenance. Second, despite its persistent denigration, Rio's funk culture has undeniable sociocultural significance for thousands of socially excluded youth.[10] According to Sneed (2008), it has at its core a 'utopian impulse' which elevates them emotionally above the harshness of their lives. Rio funk therefore communicates group and socio-spatial identity, but, as we shall see below, it also produces and reproduces boundaries between different groups of people in relation to the cityscape of the favela (Oosterbaan 2009). In the following section I will describe the favela complex where I attended *baile funks*.

11.4 The Maré Favela Complex

The favela cluster Complexo da Maré, situated in Rio's northern periphery (Zona Norte), is home to some 132,000 people spread across sixteen communities, making it one of the largest favela complexes of the city.[11] Two of these communities, Nova Holanda and Parque União, are well-known for staging *baile funks*. This is where I gained my ethnographic experience, attending several of these funk parties, which usually take place at weekends.

The residents of Maré share their space with a military police battalion and two rival drug factions, the Comando Vermelho (CV) and the Terceiro Comando Puro (TCP; 'Third Pure Command'), who fight over territorial control. In their often violent disputes over favela territory, the two gangs

---

[10] In response to the criminalisation of funk, favela-based activists and *funkeiros* (i.e. MCs, DJs, singers and all those who participate in Rio's funk culture) organised demonstrations, events and online petitions to legitimise funk. In 2009, *funkeiros* created the Association of Professionals and Friends of Funk (APAFUNK) and in the same year funk gained legal recognition as a form of popular culture by the Assembleia Legislativa do Estado do Rio de Janeiro, the State Legislative Assembly of Rio de Janeiro.

[11] The arrival of the first residents in the 1940s was influenced by the opening of the Avenida Brazil and later the state government policy of favela eradication in the 1960s (when residents evicted from favelas in southern Rio were transferred to Maré), as well as Brazil's rural to urban migration in the second half of the twentieth century, notably that from the north-east of the country (Alvito & Velho, 1996, p. 273).

restrict the movements of residents, limiting access to schools and other public services. The drug commands therefore 'self-define real and imaginary boundaries for circulation and sociability' (Araújo 2006, p. 294). This means that residents of one favela or favela area usually cannot enter an area controlled by an enemy command, even for delivering goods or visiting friends, for fear of being attacked or worse. The gangs also have high numbers of poorly educated and disenfranchised boys and young men to recruit from, as formal unemployment in Maré is extremely high, forcing many residents into precarious and illicit markets. It is estimated, however, that only about 1 per cent of Rio's favela population is directly implicated with the drug gangs, which would mean about 1,200 members in Maré (Dowdney 2003; Wilding 2010).

In addition to the danger of debilitating physical violence from the two rival drug factions and from sporadic military police operations that target them, Maré residents were also subjected to a fifteen-month occupation by the army before and during the FIFA World Cup of 2014. One negative effect of this militarisation of favela life was the attempted, but ultimately unsuccessful, suppression of its musical production and outdoor funk dances. Nor did the army manage to dislodge the drug factions. Due to its sheer size, there was also no attempt to 'pacify' Maré through the UPP police forces, who often ban funk events in the favelas under their control for public security reasons. Although both the gangs and the police are responsible for most of the violence occurring inside Maré, resident attitudes towards them differ. People I spoke to acknowledged the gangs' 'good' sides as well as their disposition towards violence. Attitudes to police have been shown to be more consistently negative, as the police are held responsible for reproducing criminality, more so than the actual criminals. The following comment by a Maré resident is instructive: 'Policing ... instead of helping the residents, actually makes them take the traffickers' side' (quoted in Wilding 2010, p. 731).

Because of Maré's association with drug gangs and public security issues, it is one of Rio's most visible and most stigmatised favelas. However, apart from a funk culture that is thriving, Maré has also been successful in many other areas of culture and education, often without government support. It has a history of community organisation, its own museum as well as a number of newspapers, television and radio stations, which represent residents' views and interests and challenge stereotypical mainstream media discourses. Finally, a renowned photography school has turned many of its local students into successful photojournalists (see Baroni & Mayr 2017).

11.5 Entering the Favela Funk Scene

I went to Brazil four times between 2014 and 2017, spending a total of twelve months in Rio de Janeiro. Even though I did not stay immersed in the field for more than three months at a time, I had ample opportunity to observe the relationship of funk with drug gangs and security forces in the two favelas where I lived and conducted fieldwork (see Baroni & Mayr 2017; Mayr 2018). By experiencing day-to-day elements of life in favelas I was able to make connections and develop an understanding of the *baile funk* culture that would never have been possible with only short visits. The particular outdoor funk event I describe here took place on a Saturday night in January 2016 in Parque União in Maré, which is well-known for staging *baile funks* that regularly attract more than 2,000 people. The area is under the control of one of the two main gangs in Maré, the Comando Vermelho (CV), which organises and pays for the *bailes* as well as for the MCs and DJs who perform at them. The MCs are usually locals and may sympathise with the gang in their area, but by and large are not commissioned by the gang to compose songs for them (Washington, personal communication; see also Sneed 2003). I was accompanied by my local contact, Washington, who led me through the labyrinth-like alleyways inside the favela to the event, making sure I was safe and would not get lost. Once near the venue, I was asked not to take photos, so as not to attract unwanted attention from the CV. The funk event was sprawled over a roughly one-mile-long stretch of one of the narrow bustling main streets, which was blocked on both ends by buses. I was told these had been provided by a bus company located inside the favela on orders of the CV, so as to prevent police from entering the street in armed vehicles. The street itself was lined with hundreds of food and drink stalls and with massive walls of loudspeakers and sound crews (*equipes de som*), whose MCs and DJs performed funk songs to a deafening and reverberating bass sound. Most revellers were young African Brazilians from Maré and neighbouring favelas. The music consisted mainly of *funk proibidão* and *funk putaria*,[12] which was recorded on bootleg CDs. Usually, the music is distributed right at the *baile funk*, at radio stations inside the favela or on websites and blogs created by the DJs and MCs. Because of their often laudatory tone towards criminals and criminal behaviour, the funk songs can be performed and recorded only at the dances. From time to time during that night, members of the CV appeared among the huge crowds, holding their weapons up high in a ritualistic display of their strength and marking of territory. Through their presence they made sure that the event, despite the masses of people attending it, remained orderly, but they also made their presence a spectacle to behold. Their weapons are empowering adornments that excite 'by attesting to a purpose that transcends

---

[12] Funk *putaria* ('porn funk'), the other contemporary sub-genre of funk, contains sexually explicit lyrics revolving around non-romantic sexual encounters. Its main protagonists are now often female MCs who challenge the male dominance of the genre in their funk songs (see Moreira 2017).

the material utility of power' (Katz 1988, p. 106). Hence Rio's drug traffickers confirm Katz's (1988) assertion that display and performance are an essential element of criminality.

11.6 Analysis

As established in the introduction, the aim of this chapter is to explore how funk *proibidão* lyrics construct favela identities and justify the rule of drug dealers as legitimate, appropriate and just. Using Appraisal as the main framework, the lyrics of three songs are analysed in terms of how participants, their actions and the settings in which they operate are recontextualised through certain linguistic strategies. The main focus of the analysis is to show how attitudinal resources are used to express emotions, judgements and evaluations and how they attempt to align the audience. The patterns that are revealed about the relationship between MCs, drug dealers and the audience can thus be key to a deeper understanding of the song messages and their potential ideological meanings. The analysis also addresses how the songs articulate discourses that can be seen as emblematic of an 'insurgent citizenship'.

11.6.1 Song 1: 'É o Império da Nova Holanda'

With its praise for the favela and its criminal actors, the first song analysed here, 'É o Império da Nova Holanda', offers a quintessential expression of funk *proibidão*:

'É o Império da Nova Holanda'	'The Empire of Nova Holanda'
1. *Só cachorro grande e as tropa dos cria*	Only Big Dogs and the troops of locals
2. *Motoboy, MK, o Sheikh e o Brita*	Motoboy, MK, Sheik and Brita
3. *Máximo respeito aos ronca da NH*	Maximum respect for the hard men of NH [Nova Holanda]
4. *O L, o Gão, Chupadedo, e o MK*	for L, Gão, Chupadedo and MK
5. *Conquistamos um império, grana, fama e poder*	We conquered an empire, money, fame and power
6. *Seguimos sem trepidação os fundamentos do CV*	We follow without trepidation the tenets of the CV
7. *E só armas esclusivas vindo das Forças Armadas*	And only exclusive weapons coming from the Armed Forces
8. *Glock, Uzi, G3, AK fuzil e granada*	Glock, Uzi, G3, AK rifle and grenades
9. *Pensa que invadir e fácil tenta sorte experimenta*	You think invading is easy, try your luck, give it a go
10. *Na frente a ponto 30 ta na laje a ponto 50*	Ahead a .30 caliber and on the roof a .50 caliber pistol
11. *Quer K.O. vai ter K.O.*	You want trouble you will get trouble
12. *Pode vim que tem é o império da Nova Holanda*	Come who may this is the empire of Nova Holanda
13. *que não rende pra ninguém.*	And it does not surrender to anyone.

The lyrics to this song construct favela gang leaders as the legitimate rulers and defenders of their favela territory, a portrayal which is common to many *proibidão* songs. This is expressed in the strong 'war frame' (Semino 2008) that permeates the entire song and which includes social actors or participants ('troops'), processes or actions ('conquer', 'invade', 'surrender', 'fight'), places where war occurs ('empire', Nova Holanda) and instruments with which this 'war' is carried out ('exclusive weapons', 'AK rifle', 'grenades', 'Glock', 'Uzi', etc.). I will now analyse these features in turn.

In order to show how these social actors are evaluated, let us now turn to Martin and White's (2005) system of Attitude. Attitude has three basic subtypes: *Affect*, *Judgment* and *Appreciation*. Affect is used for making assessments based on emotion; Judgment for making moral assessments of human behaviour and social norms; and Appreciation for making aesthetic evaluations. Within the system of Judgment, the two main distinctions are *Social Sanction* and *Social Esteem*. Social Esteem is further subdivided into *Normality* (how unusual somebody is), *Capacity* (how capable somebody is), and *Tenacity* (how resolute they are). Judgments of Sanction in turn have to do with *Veracity* (how truthful somebody is) and *Propriety* (how ethical somebody is). The final subsystem of Attitude, *Appreciation*, is organised around evaluation of objects, products, events and human appearance rather than behaviour. Appreciation is to do with reaction and the degree to which a product or performance captures our attention (reaction: impact) or the emotional effect it has (reaction: quality). Evaluation is *inscribed* when the meaning is explicitly expressed in a lexical item or *invoked* when the meaning is more implicit and needs deduction. All categories can carry a positive (+) or negative value (−), depending on context. Whether evaluative meanings are positive or negative is therefore locally contingent, not universal.

The following patterns of Attitude emerge from Song 1 (numbers refer to song lines):

1. Only **big dogs** and the **troops of locals** [+Social Esteem: capacity; Appreciation: quality]
3. **Maximum respect** [Appreciation] for **the hardmen of NH** [+Social Esteem: capacity]
5. **We conquered an empire** [+Social esteem: capacity; +Appreciation: impact]
   Money fame and power [+Social esteem: capacity]
6. We follow the tenets of the CV **without trepidation** [+Social esteem: tenacity]
7. And only **exclusive weapons** from the Armed Forces [+Appreciation: reaction: quality]

8. **Glock, Uzi, G3, AK rifle** and **grenades** [+Social esteem: capacity]
10. Ahead **a .30 caliber** and on the roof **a .50 caliber pistol** [+Social Esteem: capacity]
11. **You want a fight you will have a fight** [+Social Esteem: Capacity]
12. Come who may and the **empire of Nova Holanda** (+Social Esteem: Capacity; +Appreciation: reaction: impact)
13. **Does not surrender to anyone** [+Social Esteem: tenacity]

The analysis of Attitude in Song 1 shows that there is a strong occurrence of positive Judgements of Social Esteem throughout, with seven subcategories of capacity and two of tenacity. Appreciation is less common, but does occur four times. All evaluations of Nova Holanda (which is not just a favela, but an 'empire'), its drug traffickers, the CV gang and the (criminal) locals bestow legitimacy upon the favela. Some of the evaluative expressions contain more than one Attitude category: 'the empire of Nova Holanda' can be said to express both positive Social Esteem in terms of capacity as well as positive Appreciation (impact). In other words, it can be understood as an expression of the capacity or skill of the social actors in Nova Holanda as well as the product of that skill, which is the 'empire'. These 'hybrid realisations' (Martin & White 2005, p. 61) can occur as a result of co-text, varying cultural backgrounds and different reading positions. This is where my ethnographic perspective and participant observer status was essential. All codings were discussed with my main favela contacts in order to avoid imposing my evaluative codings, which may not be shared by those immersed in funk culture.

Recontextualisations of social practices include participants or social actors, activities and settings (Van Leeuwen & Wodak 1999). As for the social actors in the song, the main drug traffickers are named by being given the admiring categories of *cachorro grande* (big dogs) and *ronca* (hard men), two examples of positive Appreciation (quality) and/or Social Esteem (capacity). *Cachorro grande* is a common slang term to refer to the main drug dealer(s) in a favela. They are then listed individually by their given nicknames or initials, starting with the local leader of the CV, Motoboy, followed by the names of other well-known local traffickers (MK, Sheikh, Brita, etc.). These strategies of 'informal nomination' and 'individualisation' (Van Leeuwen 1996, p. 53) are recontextualisations by 'substitution' (Van Leeuwen & Wodak 1999) which here serve to personalise and humanise the drug dealers and foreground the familial and 'heroic' traits of their identities, while backgrounding their other, perhaps less savoury, characteristics.

According to Sneed (2003), as a discourse, funk *proibidão* operates the ideological strategy of 'unification' (Eagleton 1991). Therefore the discursive construction of the drug dealers as part of one big family is significant in building the gang's legitimacy. This strategy is evident from the beginning:

'*Only* Big Dogs and the troops of locals (as tropa dos *cria*)'. The construction of drug dealers as 'tropa dos *cria*' (troops of *locals/family*) is significant. *Cria* is short for *filho de criação* (foster child) and in traditional usage stands for the informal adoption of a poor (favela) orphan into a wealthy family, often to be used as cheap labour (Penglase 2014). In favela usage, however, the term *cria* has been reclaimed to mean somebody born in the favela, changing its meaning of a person of no status to somebody with status, here through positive Social Esteem of their capacity as 'troops'. A *cria* then is, metaphorically speaking (here I refer to Chapters 2 [by Kövecses and Douthwaite], 3 [by Fludernik] and 13 [by Ponton and Canepa] for in-depth exploration of metaphor), somebody who has been adopted and raised by the favela as a whole. Hence, by referring to themselves as *cria*, the drug dealers become as much part of the kinship ties and social networks of the favela as any other resident. They share the same upbringing and culture and are always somebody's relatives or friends. This partly explains why they are tolerated by many residents.

Looking at settings, one of the strongest characteristics of the unity of the people living under the rule of the drug traffickers is, not surprisingly, their common geographic identity. Representations of space in music occupy a central role in defining social identity and practice and have also been found to play a key role in expressing resistance (see, e.g., Forman 2002, p. 3; Mazierska & Gregory 2015; Way 2017). Hence the ideological importance that is placed on geographic space in the discourse of funk. In the song discussed here, the physical and social space of the favela of Nova Holanda is elevated to an 'empire' in a kind of 'semiotic inversion of the geopolitical map of the city' (Sneed 2008, p. 138), giving it positive Appreciation. This rhetoric of pride in local place and in defending that space against outsiders in the form of positive Judgements of capacity and tenacity of the drug traffickers and their arsenal of weapons has been crucial to how the gang constructs its authority and legitimises its rule (Penglase 2008).

As for actions, we can see another unification strategy operating in the song where first-person plural verbs are used in lines 5 and 6: *Conquistamos* um império (*we* conquered an empire); *Seguimos* os fundamentos do CV (*we* follow the tenets of the CV). These verbs imply an 'inclusive we', identifying the 'in-group' of drug dealers and locals as opposed to an out-group that remains unnamed. This strategy positions the addressees in the same space, time and social category as the speaker and as sharing the same social values. Through this ideological strategy, familiarity with the listeners is constructed, based on the assumption that they should also share the same sense of belonging. At the same time, the use of second-person verbs places social actors in social categories separate to the speaker and with different social values. This strategy is used twice, first in line 9, where the unnamed outsiders or enemies of the favela are addressed tauntingly through a second-person verb and two imperatives: '*Pensa* invadir e fácil *tenta* sorte *experimenta*' (*You* think invading is easy, *try* your luck, *give* it a try), and in line 11, '*Quer K.O. vai ter K.O.*' (You want trouble you will have trouble), which exhibits semantic and grammatical parallelism.

Besides glorifying the CV, the song also briefly alludes to state corruption in line 7: 'And only exclusive weapons coming from the Armed Forces'; it does so by way of Appreciation of the weapons' exclusivity and Positive Social Esteem of the capacity of the gang to secure these weapons. This line is an oblique reference to the common practice of drug dealers buying weapons from corrupt police who in this way supplement their low salaries (Monken 2012).

Not everything in a social practice is represented; what is represented depends on the goals, values and priorities of the presenters, that is, the MCs and drug traffickers. Hence, there is no mention of the fact that the relationship between drug dealers and residents is often fraught with tension and ambivalence, despite the (grudging) respect they receive. This is because the gangs take on roles that are traditionally performed by the state, thereby solidifying their claim to authority in the favela. In so doing they apply what is known throughout Rio's favelas as the *lei do morro* (law of the hillside). Under this law, murder, rape, child abuse, theft and domestic violence are strictly forbidden. In exchange for providing a degree of safety, conflict resolution and assistance, the gangs demand silence. They operate on a system of 'forced reciprocity' (Dowdney 2003), which ensures that residents support or turn a blind eye to drug gangs in exchange for social assistance and a veneer of law and order imposed by their gang. The song resolves this tension between favela residents and the gang members by substituting their violent activities through 'abstractions' and 'generalisations' (Van Leeuwen & Wodak 1999), leaving complexities and details of actions of drug dealers vague: 'We conquered an empire' is a glorifying abstraction that glosses over the human toll of fighting over favela territory. Where the gang members pledge their allegiance to the CV ('We follow the tenets of the CV without trepidation') in line 6, the song recontextualises the political rhetoric of the CV as a gang that 'defends' its community against outsiders and against abusive state authority, again constructing legitimacy for itself, here encoded through positive Social Esteem in terms of tenacity. The tenets include protecting the weak, operating as a collective and destroying the gang's enemies (Washington, personal communication). However, these rules are now more a remnant from the time when the CV was more political and able to create a romantic 'Robin Hood mystique' around it (Perlmann 1976). As it became drugs-based, militarised and ruthless, the CV also began to prey upon its communities (see Arias & Rodrigues 2006). Still, its inherited identity as a former politicised prison faction makes itself felt in favelas to this day.[13] Sometimes described by favela residents as 'a way of thinking and acting' (*um modo de pensar e agir*), the CV should be considered as more than just a criminal organisation profiting from the sales of drugs (Penglase 2008, p. 140). According to Penglase, it is the 'unintended and undesired offspring' of Brazil's dictatorship, globalisation and neo-liberal political and economic reform. So while the CV may still exhibit traces of a revolutionist ideology, it has also adopted mainstream cultural values associated with money and the notoriety that comes from being a drug dealer. This is evident in the song in line 5: 'We conquered an empire, *money, fame* and *power*.' The identification with money and fame can be seen primarily as a reaction to the exclusion traffickers (and non-trafficking youth) face from other mainstream signifiers of power and status, such as regular employment or an education. It also shows that some of the values that underpin funk *proibidão* are the by-product of broader consumer culture. Despite their poverty and exclusion drug traffickers are part of this globalised culture to which they aspire.

11.6.2 Song 2: 'Vida Bandida'

The following funk song, 'Vida Bandida' (Bandit's Life) tells the story of one of Rio's well-known drug dealers, which is a common trope in funk *proibidão*. In mainstream media discourses the figure of the 'bandit' is racialised and constructed as 'back-ward, aggressive, and primitive or uncivilised in nature, qualities that their geographical position on the urban periphery supposedly reflects' (Goldstein 2004, p. 12). 'Bandido' is a very loaded term in mainstream media and popular crime discourses. Unlike the more neutral term *criminoso* (criminal), *bandido* is more potent and has connotations of 'evildoer' (Goldstein 2004, p. 12). In funk *proibidão*, on the other hand, the word *bandido* carries romantic notions of the outlaw and 'social bandit' (Hobsbawm 1959), an image some drug dealers like to project of themselves for reasons regarding their legitimacy, already discussed above (see also Sneed 2003; Penglase 2014). Favela drug dealers command the respect of many youth because they threaten the government's monopoly on the use of force. They both outrage and thrill with their seeming ability to stand outside the law

---

[13] Brazil's two main gangs, the Rio-based Comando Vermelho (CV) and Sao Paulo's Primeiro Comando da Capital (PCC), were both formed inside prisons in defence against the state's brutal prison system.

and to make their own laws instead. It is these 'subromantic gestures' (Caterson 2001, p. 21) that are eulogised in funk *proibidão* and that contribute most to the mythologisation of these social actors. The song below is a good illustration of this:

'Vida Bandida'	'Bandit's Life'
1. *Partia pros bailes de briga*	He went to the fight dances
2. *Pegava carona e roupa emprestada*	He took lifts in borrowed clothes
3. *Era um dos mais falados*	He was one of the most talked about
4. *Era brabo na porrada*	He was good with his fists
5. *Mas ninguém vive de fama*	But nobody lives off fame
6. *Queria grana, queria poder*	He wanted money, he wanted power
7. *Se envolveu no artigo doze pela facção CV*	He got involved in Article 12 for the Red Command faction
8. *Ninguém lhe dava nada*	Nobody gave him anything
9. *Tá fortão na hierarquia*	He is very strong in the hierarchy
10. *Abalando a mulherada*	Messing with women
11. *É o rasante do falcão em cima da R1*	He is the gliding falcon on his Yamaha R1
12. *A grossura do cordão*	His thick gold necklace
13. *Está causando zum zum zum*	is causing rumours
14. *Mas é varias mulher*	And he has various women
15. *Vários fuzis à sua disposição*	And various guns at his disposal
16. *O batalhão da área comendo na sua mão.*	The police battalion in the area is eating out of his hand
17. *Ele tem disposição para o mal e para o bem*	He has a disposition for the bad and the good
18. *Mesmo rosto que faz rir*	The same face that makes you laugh
19. *É o que faz chorar também*	also makes you cry
20. *Nossa vida é bandida*	Ours is a bandit's life
21. *E o nosso jogo e bruto*	And our game is tough
22. *Hoje somos festa,*	Today we party
23. *Amanhã seremos luto*	Tomorrow we will be mourning
24. *Caveirão não me assusta!*	The Big Skull does not scare me!
25. *Nós não foge do conflito*	We don't run away from conflict
26. *Nós também somos blindados*	We are also armoured with the blood
27. *No sangue de Jesus Cristo*	of Jesus Christ

A good part of the song (lines 1–19) is taken up with praising the drug dealer, charting his life from humble beginnings to a life as a famed drug lord who is adored by women and has the local police at his beck and call. The Attitude analysis of Song 2 reveals the following picture (numbers refer to song lines):

1. **He went to the fight dances** [+Social Esteem: capacity]
2. **Taking lifts in borrowed clothes** [+Social Esteem: tenacity]

3. He was **one of the most talked abou**t [+Appreciation: reaction: impact]
4. He was **good with his fists** [+Social Esteem: capacity; +Appreciation: reaction: impact]
5. But **nobody lives off fame** [+Social Esteem: normality]
6. He **wanted money, he wanted power** [+Social Esteem: tenacity/+ Social sanction: propriety]
7. **He became involved in article 12 for the *CV*** [+Social Esteem: capacity]
8. **Nobody gave him anything** [+Social Esteem: tenacity]
9. **He is very strong up in the hierarchy** [+Social Esteem: capacity/ +Appreciation: reaction: impact]
10. **Exciting all the women** [+Social Esteem: capacity/+Appreciation: reaction: quality]
11. **He is the falcon gliding on his R1 motorbike** [+Appreciation: reaction: quality]
12. **The thickness of his necklace causes rumours** [+Appreciation: reaction: impact]
14. **He has several women** [+Social Esteem: capacity]
15. And **several guns at his disposal** [+Social Esteem: capacity]
16. **The police battalion in the area eating out of his hand** [+Social Esteem: capacity/+Appreciation: reaction: impact]
17. **He has a disposition for the bad and the good** [– and +Social Sanction: propriety]
18. **The same face that makes you laugh also makes you cry** [+ and – Affect: happiness and unhappiness]

The mythologisation of the criminal is expressed mainly through positive Social Esteem in the form of capacity (7) and tenacity (3) and also through positive Appreciation in terms of impact (5) starting with the song telling us that FB attended *bailes de briga* (literally 'fight dances'), where he excelled as a fighter: 'he was good with his fists'. The notorious fight dances of the 1980s and 1990s involved two large teams of young men from different favelas lining up on the dance floor on opposite sides, forming a 'corridor' and attempting to conquer dancers from the opposite side by bump-dancing into and hitting them. FB made a name for himself at these dances; hence the Judgment of positive Social Esteem in terms of capacity and the positive Appreciation (impact). But then there comes the realisation in line 5 that 'nobody lives off fame' (Social Esteem: normality) and that 'he wanted money, he wanted power', which in this song receives a *positive* Judgment of tenacity. The result was that 'he got involved in Article 12 for the CV' (line 8), which is a reference to the article in the Brazilian Criminal Code which makes drug dealing a criminal offence. The line is a euphemistic way of saying that FB became a drug dealer for the CV, a decision which would provoke negative Social Sanction on the part of the media and the state, but which is valued positively in the song through positive Social Esteem in terms of capacity. In lines 8 and 9, admiration or positive Social Esteem for him is expressed in terms of tenacity ('nobody gave him anything') and capacity ('he is very strong in the hierarchy'), although the latter can also be classed as positive Appreciation (impact). This is followed by another positive Appreciation (quality) in line 11, where he is judged in aesthetic terms: 'He is the falcon gliding on his R1 motorbike,' with the metaphor of the falcon connoting strength and skill. Line 12, 'The thickness of his necklace causes rumours,' is also a positive Appreciation of impact in the sense that the thicker the (gold) necklace, the greater the power of the drug trafficker. This song illustrates perfectly the recontextualisation of the marginal 'drug trafficker' into a 'protagonist' (Pardue 2010, p. 441) and essentially a positive figure who should command our respect. In so doing, the song also makes reference to what Katz (1988) calls the 'sensual nature' of crime that draws people into it because it is seductive and thrilling. At the subjective level, Katz argues, crime can be exciting and liberating and offer a sense of 'self-transcendence' for the criminal, a means of overcoming the mundanity of daily routines. The 'thrill' of a criminal life-style in the song is conveyed through positive Appreciation and Social Esteem of material wealth (the gold necklace), sexual conquest ('*various* women') and the possession of 'various guns'. The latter is a result of him being in control of the police battalion, expressed in a metaphor of the police 'eating out of his hands'. As we saw in Song 1, Rio funk does not necessarily feel obliged to dissociate itself from materialism (such as has been made popular in US hip-hop) or to necessarily avoid such a position in its lyrics. What the song points to instead is that in favela culture, drug traffickers are seen as ambivalent figures who 'combine welfare and predation' (Davis 2008, p. xi). This can be seen through the evaluative semantic binary opposites that are used to describe the character traits of the gang leader: he has 'a disposition for the *bad* and the *good*' and a face that 'makes you *laugh* and *cry*'. The entire song builds up oppositional meanings through grammatical and semantic opposites (Davies 2008; Jeffries 2010). Parallelism is another important contrast-generating device in the song, with several examples of syntactic and semantic parallelism: '*Era* um dos mas falados – *era* brabo na porrada' (He was one of the most talked about – he was good with his fists); '*queria grana* – queria *poder*' (He wanted money – he wanted power); '*varias* mulher – *varios* fuzis' (several women – several guns); '*faz rir – faz chorar*' (makes you laugh – makes you cry). As Short (1996, p. 15) points out, 'parallelism not only foregrounds part of a text, but also makes us look for parallel or contrastive meaning'. Finally, the use of alliteration (*Partia pros bailes;*

Pegava corona; era, era), nós não foge, nós também somos blindados no sangue do Jesus Cristo fulfils the functions alliteration in songs usually has; that is, it creates rhythm and makes the lyrics easier to remember.

Moving on to the refrain, the following picture emerges:

20. **Ours is a bandit's life** [+Affect/+Social Esteem: normality]
21. **And our game is tough** [+Affect/+Social Esteem: tenacity]
22. **Today we party** [+Affect/ +Social Esteem: normality]
23. **Tomorrow we will mourn** [−Affect/+Social Esteem: normality]
24. The **Big Skull** [−Affect] does **not scare me** [+Affect]
25. **We don't run away from the fight** [+Social Esteem: tenacity]
26. **We are also armoured with the blood of Jesus Chris**t [+Affect/+Social Esteem: capacity]

Whereas from lines 1–19 the Appraiser tells us about of the life of the drug dealer in third-person narration, he switches to first-person plural narrative in line 20. Here he includes himself in the 'bandit's life' (*Ours* is a bandit's life), talking from the position of those subjected to and/or inflicting violence and giving an insider perspective of what it means to be a 'bandit'. As in the previous song, the choice of inclusive personal pronoun 'we' and possessive pronoun 'our' is of significance here as it is an effective way of aligning the listener. In line 24, an example of negative Affect ('mourn'), he briefly switches to talking about himself: 'The Big Skull does not scare *me*.' This personal and individualised comment is one of only two instances of first-person narration in all three songs (the other example occurring in Song 3 below). First-person narrative appears to be a feature that is uncommon in Rio funk, perhaps because the lyrics are concerned with constructing the favela and its social actors as a collective (Washington, personal communication). 'Big Skull' is a metonymic expression for the tank used by the Elite Force of the Military Police, BOPE, in its incursions into favelas, evoking negative Affect. The tank derives its name from BOPE's infamous emblematic symbol, a skull flanked by two crossed pistols, which is emblazoned on all its vehicles and acts as a potent symbol of police brutality in favelas (see Mayr 2015). As we have seen so far, funk songs cast (drug-related) crime as a way of life, but they also refer to 'the collective trauma of losing a brother, a father, a friend' (Palombini 2011, p. 80), praising those who may die as a result of getting involved with a criminal faction. The use of grammatical parallelism and semantic opposition (the contrast between 'today' and 'tomorrow') further enhances the positive and negative Affect that is already created through the two contrasting emotive verbs 'party' and 'mourn', respectively: '*today* we *party*, *tomorrow* we will *mourn*'. The suddenness implied by the change in the temporal deictics from 'today' to 'tomorrow' heightens the dramatic effect. The life of crime is referred to metaphorically as a 'game' (*jogo*); however, this game is 'tough' (*bruto*). There are two metaphors at play here: one, a metaphor of crime as a game, and the other a religious metaphor of war ('We are also *armoured* with the *blood of Jesus Christ*'). The inclusion of six instances of positive and one of negative Affect indicates the attitudinal stance taken by the MC and is another effective strategy for positioning the listeners and aligning them into sympathy with those involved in a bandit's life. Essentially, the song is concerned with those young men who live in the precarious illegal job market of drug trafficking. These 'flip-flop bandits' (Fernandes 2014) are the most fragile members of the drug trade network, and they are the first to be arrested and the first to die in police operations ('Today we party, tomorrow we will *mourn*'). Such conditions are hidden in mainstream media portrayals of the generic 'drug dealer', which construct these young men as dangerous, rather than as vulnerable and in need of protection. The song suggests that an early death through the police (or rival gang members) is seen as a normal consequence of being caught up in the 'war on drugs'. This is also conveyed through the use of the simple present tense (lines 21–27), which presents a life of crime as something that is normal, generally happens, and will happen in the future. The song hereby recontextualises the hyper-masculine 'warrior ethos' ('Our game is tough') that is instilled in gang members from an early age, which means that their average lifespan often does not surpass their late twenties (Zaluar 2000). Corrupt and demoralising police behaviour is another reason for some young men's propensity towards criminal activity, and the decision to take up guns is sometimes due to their experiences of police brutality. The massive numbers of casualties of mainly young men from poor and black backgrounds, however, are met with indifference by many Brazilians. This attitude is succinctly expressed in a popular saying in Brazil, *Bandido bom e bandido morto* ('A good bandit is a dead bandit'). In the lyrics above, however, these social actors are given worth and Social Esteem, as the Attitude categories demonstrate. Positive Affect is further evoked when their military strength is conveyed through a religious metaphor ('We are also armoured with the *blood of Jesus Christ*'), which casts them as invincible. This metaphorical expression is common in the discourse of (neo-)Pentecostal churches, which increasingly dominate the religious landscape in favelas, gradually replacing the Catholic Church. Part of the appeal of Pentecostals is that they valorise a 'spiritual war' between good and evil, which fits well with the war ethics of drug dealers and also offers them a spiritual way out of the violence towards a clear (religious) order (Zaluar 2000). Young gang members often see these favela churches as potential saviours from a constantly looming violent death (Lanz 2016).[14]

11.6.3 Song 3: 'Tá Tudo Monitorado'

Given that favelas are implicated in a futile government-imposed 'war on drugs', it is not surprising that this 'war' is often recontextualised in funk *proibidão*. The following funk song is a critical interrogation of media coverage that usually does not address the structural problems underlying drug trafficking (see, e.g., Zaluar 2000; Arias 2006; Arias & Rodrigues 2006), but relies on de-contextualised and sensationalist coverage instead. In the song, drug dealing inside the favela is presented as an activity that is controlled and adheres to ethical rules. The song carries a clear message against favela stigmatisation and the complicity of the media in it. As the other two songs, this one strikes a clear note of defiance, this time by laying the blame for problems in favelas at the door of the media.

'Tá Tudo Monitorado'	'It's All Monitored'
1. *Traz o boldo e traz o lança mas preste atenção*	Bring the dope bring the poppers but pay attention
2. *Use longe das crianças pra não ter complicação*	Use it away from the kids to avoid complications
[Reportagem Globo]	[TV report by O Globo]
3. *Aqui fica a nova cracolândia do Rio de Janeiro*	Here is Rio de Janeiro's new crackland
4. *Do outro lado da pista, a favela Parque União*	On the other side of the road the favela Parque União
5. *Onde existem pontos de venda da droga*	Where there are drug selling points
[Refrain: Traz o boldo ...]	
6. *Mas o bagulho tá monitorado*	But the stuff [drug dealing] is monitored
7. *O que se passa vai sair no radio*	Everything that happens will be on the walkie-talkie
8. *Passou crackudo na televisão*	There was a crackhead on TV
9. *A mídia quer prejudicar os irmão*	The media wants to harm the brothers
10. *Mas nessa vida nunca vou me abalar*	But in this life I will never be shocked
11. *No que pode acontecer ou no que pode rolar*	by what will happen or come about
12. *A vida passa não cai na ilusão*	Life is passing don't have any illusions
13. *Tu vê sorriso, crime não é bom não*	You see smiles, crime is not good
[several lines omitted]	
14. *Pra ta na Nova tem que tá ligado*	To be in Nova [Holanda] you have to be clued up
15. *Pra não pisar em lugar errado*	To not step into the wrong place

---

[14] While Pentecostal pastors regard drug dealing as 'evil', they do not exclude drug dealers, attempting instead to convert them (Lanz 2016). It is not uncommon for drug dealers to adhere to the Pentecostal faith or indeed for former drug dealers to turn into evangelical pastors.

(cont.)

'Tá Tudo Monitorado'	'It's All Monitored'
16. *Até então bagulho aqui tem divisão*	Even the 'stuff' here has its division
17. *Nós daqui tudo vermelho e do outro lado os Alemão*	We here all reds and on the other side the 'Germans' [enemies]
...	
18. *Pam, pam, pam, pam pam*	Pam, pam, pam, pam, pam
19. *Nóis tá aqui não é atoa defendendo*	We are here not for nothing defending
20. *A favela as criança ta de boa*	The favela the kids are fine
21. *E pam, pam, pam, pam pam*	And pam pam pam pam
22. *Se brota você se complica*	If you come here you complicate things
23. *Tu tá ligado nóis aqui é tudo cria.*	You get it here we are all family.

In this song, we find the following Attitude patterns:

1. Bring the **dope**, bring **the poppers** [+Social Sanction: propriety] but pay attention [+Social Sanction: propriety]
2. Use it away from the kids to avoid complications [+Social sanction: propriety]
3. Here is Rio de Janeiro's new **crackland** [–Social Sanction: propriety; –Appreciation: reaction: quality]
4. On the other side of the road the favela Parque União
5. Where there are **drug selling points** [–Social Sanction (of media): propriety and veracity]
6. But the stuff is monitored [+Social Sanction: propriety]
7. 7. What happens will be on the walkie-talkie [+Social Sanction: propriety]
8. There was a **crackhead** on television [Affect; –Social Sanction: propriety]
9. **The media wants to harm the brothers** [–Social sanction (of media): veracity; –Affect for 'harm'; +Affect for 'brothers'
10. But in this life **I will never be shocked** [+Affect]
12. Life is passing [–Appreciation: reaction: quality], don't have any illusions
13. You see smiles **crime is not good** [–Social Sanction: propriety]
14. To be in Nova **you have to be clued up** [+Social Esteem: capacity]
15. **To not step into the wrong place** [–Social Sanction: propriety]
16. Even here the stuff has its division [–Social Esteem: normality]
17. We here all **reds** [+Affect/+Social Sanction: propriety]
    On the other side the **Germans** [–Affect/–Social Sanction: propriety]
19. **We are here not for nothing** [+Social Sanction: propriety]
    Defending the favela [+Social Esteem: capacity]
20. **The kids are fine** [+Appreciation: reaction: quality]
21. If you come here **you complicate things** [–Social Sanction: propriety]
22. You get it here **we are all family** [+Appreciation: reaction: quality]

In this song, the favela is constructed as a site of order ('Everything is monitored'), which is in contrast to media discourses which portray favelas as chaotic environments. The violence meted out by drug dealers is recontextualised as productive of a sense of order, not as a destructive force, as expressed in lines 19 and 20 through positive Social Sanction of their propriety ('We are not here for nothing'), positive Social Esteem of their capacity ('defending the favela') and positive Appreciation ('the kids are fine'). The lyrics thereby reverse the simplistic equation of favelas as sites of violence and disorder, a myth that has also been debunked by several academics (e.g. Perlman 1976; Araújo & Grupo Musicultura 2010; Arias & Barnes 2016). Gangs are often highly effective in preventing violence and crime. In extended fieldwork in Maré (see Sections 11.3 and 11.4 above) conducted by Arias and Barnes (2016), dozens of interviewed gang members revealed that they frequently resolve disputes and ensure public order.

The song starts by stating an unwritten rule in favelas, which is not to use drugs in front of children, in the form of positive Social Sanction of propriety. The drugs the song mentions are 'boldo', which is a slang expression for marijuana, and 'lança' or 'lança-perfume', a mixture of chloroform and methyl alcohol, which is popular both at Carneval and funk parties. There is no mention of crack here, which can have a devastating effect on individuals and communities, but which is not commonly used in favelas. The first two lines of the song are therefore also meant to illustrate that the favela is not a space of indiscriminate and irresponsible drug use. This is stressed again in lines 6 and 7 through positive Social Sanction of propriety of the actions of drug dealers: 'But everything is monitored, what happens will be on the walkie-talkie.' The walkie-talkies are used by the lookouts (*olheiros*) in favelas to warn the dealers of the police or a rival drug faction approaching.

The song then moves to criticising sensationalist media reporting of drug problems in Maré (lines 3–5) by imitating the reporting style of TV anchors from O Globo (Brazil's main television and news network) on the 'crackland' in Parque União: 'Here is Rio de Janeiro's new crackland. On the other side of the road [is] the favela Parque União, where there are drug selling points.' From a news reporting perspective, these words would be negative Social Sanctions of the favela in terms of propriety, expressed through evaluative lexis ('crackland'; 'drug selling points'). However, by impersonating a news reporter, the song socially sanctions the media in terms of veracity and propriety; that is, it basically accuses the media of misrepresentation and lying. This intertextual reference functions as a recontextualisation, criticising and parodying the simplistic media condemnation of a phenomenon that is marked by complexity. The existence of a criminal society in favelas and the very sale of drugs that sustains it are only symptoms of more complex issues related to social exclusion. As Souza (1996) points out, drug trafficking in favelas is the very end of a complex network that involves two interconnected subsystems, the import-export-wholesale; and the retail system. While 'white collar' criminals operate in the first sub-system, favela criminal groups operate in the retail sub-system. It is, however, the generic favela dealer who is most exposed, which adds to the wider process of 'socio-symbolic homogenisation', negative labelling and targeting of favela residents (Fernandes 2014). The song also challenges the stereotypical mainstream media construction of drug traffickers as dangerous criminals by referring to them instead as 'brothers': 'The media wants to harm the *brothers.*' This substitution in the form of 'relational identification' (Van Leeuwen 1996) is yet another example of how drug dealers are humanised in funk and how the media are condemned for presenting a 'crackhead' on television. This condemnation is further enhanced by the negative Affect expressed though the verb 'harm'. Both sides use attitudinally loaded lexis to present their story. Line 11 contains the only first-person reference of the song: 'But in this life nothing will shock *me*,' creating Affect. In lines 12 and 13 the song very briefly reflects on a life of crime and its contradictions and concedes that it is not worth it ('Life is passing, don't have any illusions'; '*Crime is not good*'), directly addressing the listener. This expression of negative Social Sanction in terms of propriety may be an attempt to dissuade young people from entering a life of crime.

Finally, like funk Songs 1 and 2, this song also uses binary semantic opposites and spatial deixis to express the division between the CV and the rival drug faction in Nova Holanda (the 'Germans') in lines 22 and 23: '*Us here* all *reds* and *on the other side* the *"Germans"*'; 'If *you* come here *you* complicate things; You get it *here we* are all *family.*' Using the spatial deictic 'here' conveys emotional attachment to the locale, whereas use of the spatial deictic 'on the other side' implies the opposite. 'Reds' is obviously judged positively, whereas 'Germans' receives negative Social Sanction. In favela slang, '*Alemão*' (literally, 'German') means 'enemy' and is applied to police as well as enemy drug factions. It is a reference to US films on the Second World War (Washington, personal communication).

As we saw in the lyrics of all three songs, the language used to refer to drug traffickers is ambivalent, drawing variously upon a rhetoric and imagery of warfare and attitudinal lexis that glorifies and romanticises them. This illustrates one legacy of the rule of Rio's drug dealers: a linguistic culture where reality is often opaque and ambiguous. As Penglase (2008) has pointed out, the way drug trafficking affects the language used also reshapes perceptions of reality inside favelas. These are of course functions that have long been associated with criminal slang (Halliday 1978; Mayr 2012). For example, the literal meaning of *bagulho* in the song is 'stuff', but it is also used as a reference to marijuana or drug dealing in general (Washington, personal communication). *Bagulho* is therefore an example of a metonymic expression that allows speakers to gloss over responsible, involved or affected actors and to keep them in the background (Reisigl & Wodak 2001, p. 58).

Funk *proibidão* breaks not only with social and aesthetic but also with linguistic conventions. The slang (*gíria*) used by favela residents is commonly understood to be a less 'civilised' way of speaking and is commonly linked to blackness and criminality (Roth-Gordon 2007), which only exacerbates the largely negative perception of funk.

11.7 Discussion

As Martin (2004, p. 326) points out, Appraisal 'positions us to feel – and through shared feelings to belong'. This, according to Martin, makes Appraisal 'a source for negotiating solidarity'. How then, do the Attitude meanings revealed in the analysis above enact relationships between MCs, gangs and favela residents? The prevailing Attitude categories in all three songs are those of positive Judgement. The songs show how the MCs who have composed them use the songs to recontextualise the violence that all too often surrounds young men from favelas. All three songs also use a theme of 'condemning the condemners' (Sykes & Matza 1957), meaning that in funk those who condemn favelas are in turn 'judged or condemned' for their actions and attitudes. The composers of the songs, the MCs, counter the many negative Judgments they receive with positive Judgements of the favela and its drug traffickers. This allows the listeners to build 'solidarity' with the MCs and the drug dealers and gives the wider (non-trafficking) favela community a tool to challenge their oppression, if largely in a symbolic way. The feeling of solidarity between MC and listeners is also constructed through the almost exclusive positive Judgements of Social Esteem in terms of normality, capacity and tenacity of the criminal social actors. Another strategy is the use of inclusive 'we' through which both speaker and listener are constructed as belonging to the same cultural and social community and identifying with the same 'discourse world' (Simpson 2004, p. 91). The analysis also reveals the complex nature of the Appraisal items which at times allow for hybrid realisations that work together to create the desired meaning. Most examples of Judgement are inscribed through use of attitudinally loaded lexis, although there are also instances where they are invoked.

Despite favelas being regarded as areas of poverty, the songs are not about necessity or lack but about *power*. They are about the power of the favela to sustain itself and the power of the criminal factions who make this possible.

The Attitude categories further show that all three songs allude to the city's split state and the socio-spatial distinction between favela and 'asphalt' (as the paved city outside the favela where better-off people live is called). The funk songs analysed here lay bare the ongoing polarisation between rich and poor areas of Rio de Janeiro (see also Ventura 1994). They describe this polarisation again mainly through the use of positive Judgement of Social Esteem of drug traffickers (Songs 1 and 2) and negative Judgement of Social Sanction of the media (Song 3), and of the police and the wider city (Song 2). The analysis also reveals how the lyrics emphasise the worth that is given to these armed actors which goes beyond their capacity for violence. This may have to do with the fact that, unlike the police, who are perceived as an arbitrary force, drug traffickers are seen as adhering at least to certain rules when administering violence (Soares 2000, p. 40). As I have attempted to establish, funk *proibidão* subverts the logic of dominant media discourses concerning members of drug factions as 'enemy combatants' and places them at the centre of the narrative as human characters with codes of conduct. As the Attitude categories suggest, funk *proibidão* does not 'believe' in the culture of inclusion, race mixing and consensus that is propagated, for example, in *samba* and *carnival.* Instead, funk becomes 'an antidote to the ideology of subaltern integration' (Palombini 2014, p. 317).[15] In this sense, funk is an expression of a localised 'insurgent citizenship' (Holston 2008) that disrupts these ideologies of universal inclusion that blur inegalitarian distributions and race and class relationships. In other words, and as the small sample of songs analysed here has shown, funk implicitly 'questions the fantasy of access to social space for the underprivileged', elevating the space of the favela instead (Yúdice 1994, p. 197). Funk must take possession of space through the display of symbolic force in the shape of violent language (and sampled gunshots in its music). Excluded from wider society, favela drug dealers and favela youth are opting for a favela-centric funk culture that actively celebrates favelas. The *baile funk* can therefore be read as an innovative attempt by favela people to 'clear a space of their own' that offers temporary freedom from the oppression of favela life through the construction of an 'alternative space of invention and *agency*' (Holston 2009a, p. 249). Hence, by being personally subjected to the simultaneously oppressive yet also *enabling* effects of ruling class power, the MCs and DJs that perform at *baile funks* become organic intellectuals who rebuke dominant

---

[15] Samba rose from being outlawed in the 1930s, partly because of lyrics that then praised the ghetto hustlers or *malandro*, to become an icon of Brazilian unity, offering the black and the poor *symbolic* compensation for material exploitation.

discourses about favela violence by producing discourses of oppositional violence. One could of course argue that by ostensibly 'glorifying' drug traffickers, funk *proibidão* risks being caught up in hegemonic media discourses that stigmatise favelas as spaces of violence and little else, which might void its political potential. That may be the case, but even by glorifying the drug gangs, MCs still implicitly condemn the inadequacy and corruption of the state, the poverty and the marginalisation. We also need to remind ourselves that funk lyrics may not always be literal accounts, but also contain fictive elements and make use of linguistic devices 'in the pursuit of aesthetic value' (Bramwell 2017, p. 10). This does not mean that funk songs are devoid of an explanatory value; but neither are they deterministic nor do they 'cause' violence.

It is true that, unlike politically conscious hip-hop, the lyrical content and the 'idiosyncratic, body-oriented musical culture' (Lanz 2013, p. 35) of Rio funk resists a clearly defined and coherent political ideology. Funk therefore represents an attempt to resolve *symbolically* concrete problems that confront many young favela residents. Its politics is 'subpolitical' and is expressed through subversion and provocation rather than a clear political theme. Funk is a resistance practice, but its resistance has to be understood as 'partial, fragmented, temporary, and transgressive rather than revolutionary and totalising' (Di Placido 2019, p. 5). Funk *proibidão* talks back insolently to the experience of being socially excluded and it does so in a way that is intentionally raw and disruptive. Its significance lies more in the fact that it has enabled stigmatised youth to create *self-determined* discursive and cultural modes of expression and identity creation (Lanz 2013). As MC Leonardo, a well-known funk artist from Rio has put it,

We are underground and that's our strongest weapon.... Funk is democratic and that's why it is dangerous. We upset the market, because it is we who compose, we who produce, we who distribute, we who buy and we who sell.

Funk therefore functions as an alternative medium that creates music and culture outside a capitalist-controlled music industry. The quote also hints at the possibility of some funk artists to be able to move beyond the structural conditions imposed on them and to occupy different spaces of the city and become political as well as aesthetic agents. Despite being stigmatised as an 'aesthetically inferior culture of poverty' (Lanz 2013, p. 23), funk, including its prohibited version, has begun to penetrate Rio's wealthy areas and club venues, affording some funk artists opportunities to perform. It is ironic that it is precisely the discourses of the marginal and the peripheral that have been taken up by youth from upper social classes who 'consume' the cultural expressions of funk as rebellion and transgression. However, for some favela residents the spread of this part of their culture to exclusive social clubs they cannot frequent themselves represents nothing short of 'black cultural dispossession by white appropriation' (Comelli et al. 2018; see also Harvey 2004).

11.8 Concluding Remarks

This chapter has placed the emergence of Rio funk, a creative appropriation of African American music by marginalised groups in Rio de Janeiro, in the context of acts of physical, structural and symbolic violence that many favela residents experience, sometimes on a daily basis. It has not looked at funk as an *aesthetic* practice, which would be equally important, as pleasure and Affect can be also be mobilised to challenge authority. Instead, the analysis has sought to draw attention to how one of its main subgenres, *proibidão*, recontextualises this violence, making visible what is often left unsaid in hegemonic (media) discourses about urban violence in Rio. While funk *proibidão* is employed to legitimise favela criminals, at the same time it acts as an implicit form of condemnation of the civil injustices facing many favela inhabitants. To this day, Brazil's black and mixed-race youth have no proper citizenship rights. They are not protected by a police force that at best harasses and often kills them with impunity. I have pointed to complex representations of violence and violent actors in funk which contest simplistic portrayals of drug traffickers as savage 'others'. Rather, funk demonstrates how traffickers' violence is intertwined with and part of state violence and that the latter allows drug traffickers to play such a fundamental social role in favelas, one of which is financing funk events. Traffickers are not drawn into drug dealing because of an inherent attraction to violence, but because they have to sell their labour to survive in a capitalist system, and this is one of the few options available to them. Favela drug dealers should therefore be seen as responding creatively (if often violently) to larger forces such as neo-liberalism and changing patterns of state repression and tolerance. It is these larger structural factors that (re) produce criminal economies in the first place. It has been argued here that even by glamorising and naturalising Rio's drug gangs, funk nevertheless opens a window into patterns of inequality and social exclusion that disproportionately affect Brazil's young black poor. The Appraisal analysis of a small sample of *proibidão* lyrics has demonstrated that this is conveyed through a language which reveals the dynamics of a discourse of insurgent citizenship that challenges stigmatisation and structural constraints and at the same time positively values favelas and their cultural vibrancy.

Although my analysis has only scratched the surface of the cultural politics of funk *proibidão*, I would argue that funk offers vital clues for how disenfranchised people deal with patterns of exclusion and 'make room for themselves in the world'. Despite its sometimes openly laudatory tone towards drug traffickers or perhaps precisely because of it, *proibidão* is a necessary instrument for understanding and, in the long run, tackling urban violence. Funk should therefore not be seen as anti-social, criminal and dangerously provocative, but first and foremost as a subcultural expression that plays a decisive role in defining and redefining the socio-spatial identities of favela youth under the economic, political and symbolic constraints they face on a daily basis. Funk needs to be understood as an aspect of the reality of thousands of socially excluded youth and as a dimension where this reality is constructed, reflected and commented upon. It needs to be welcomed, not vilified, for holding up a mirror to the dynamics and politics of urban violence and state neglect. This is particularly true in Brazil's current political climate with its openly declared state agenda of violent and lethal persecution of its urban outcasts.

References

Alvito, M., & Velho, G. (1996). *Cidadania e Violência*. [Citizenship and Violence]. Rio de Janeiro: Editora UFRJ.
Araújo, S. (2006). 'Conflict and Violence as Theoretical Tools in Present-Day Ethnomusicology: Notes on a Dialogic Ethnography of Sound Practices in Rio de Janeiro'. *Ethnomusicology*, 50(2), 287–313.
Araújo, S., & Grupo Musicultura (2010). 'Sound Praxis: Music, Politics and Violence in Brazil'. In J. O'Connell & S. El-Shawan Castelo-Branco, eds., *Music and Conflict*. Urbana: University of Illinois Press, pp. 217–231.
Arias, E. D. (2004). 'Faith in Our Neighbours: Networks and Social Order in Three Brazilian Favelas'. *Latin American Politics & Society*, 46(1), 1–38.
  (2006). *Drugs and Democracy in Rio de Janeiro: Trafficking, Social Networks, and Public Security*. Chapel Hill: University of North Carolina Press.
  (2013). 'The Impacts of Differential Armed Dominance of Politics in Rio de Janeiro, Brazil'. *Studies in Comparative International Development*, 48(3), 263–284.
Arias, E. D., & Barnes, N. (2016). 'Crime and Plural Orders in Rio de Janeiro, Brazil'. *Current Sociology*, 65(3), 448–465.
Arias, E. D., & Rodrigues, C. D. (2006). 'The Myth of Personal Security: Criminal Gangs, Dispute Resolution, and Identity in Rio de Janeiro's Favelas'. *Latin American Politics and Society*, 48(4), 53–81.
Avelar, I., & Dunn, C. (2011). *Brazilian Popular Music and Citizenship*. Durham, NC: Duke University Press.
Baroni, A., & Mayr, A. (2017). 'Community (Photo)journalism and Political Mobilisation in Rio de Janeiro's Favelas'. Special Issue of *Journalism Practice*: Mapping Citizen Journalism: in Newsrooms, Classrooms and Beyond, pp. 285–301.
Bernstein, B. (1990). *Class, Codes and Control, vol. 4: The Structuring of Pedagogic Discourse*. London: Taylor and Francis.
Bourdieu, P., & Wacquant, L. (2001). 'New Liberal Speak: Notes on the New Planetary Vulgate'. *Radical Philosophy*, 105, 2–5.

Bramwell, R. (2017). 'Freedom within Bars: Maximum Security Prisoners' Negotiation of Identity through Rap'. *Identities: Global Studies in Culture and Power*, 25(4), 475–492.
Biazoto, J. (2011). 'Peace Journalism Where There Is No War: Conflict-Sensitive Reporting on Urban Violence and Public Security in Brazil and Its Potential Role in Conflict Transformation'. *Conflict & Communication Online*, 10(2), 1–19.
Caldeira, T. P. R. (2000). *City of Walls: Crime, Segregation, and Citizenship in São Paulo*. Berkeley: University of California Press.
Caldeira, T. P. R., & Holston J. (1999). 'Democracy and Violence in Brazil'. *Comparative Studies in Society and History*, 41(4), 691–729.
Caldwell, D. (2008). 'Affiliating with Rap Music: Political Rap or Gangsta Rap?'. *Novitas-Royal*, 2(1), 13–27.
Caterson S (2001). 'Chopping into Literature: The Writings of Mark Brandon Read'. *Australian Book Review*, 236, 19–21.
Chilton, P. (1996). *Security Metaphors: Cold War Discourse from Containment to Common House*. Frankfurt: Peter Lang.
Comelli, T., Anguelovski, I., & Chu, E. (2018). 'Socio-spatial Legibility, Discipline, and Gentrification through Favela Upgrading in Rio de Janeiro'. *Analysis of Urban Change, Theory, Action*, 22 (5–6), 633–656.
D'Angelo, S. (2015). 'Sampling the Sense of Place in Music'. In E. Mazierska & G. Gregory, eds., *Relocating Popular Music: Pop Music, Culture and Identity*. London: Routledge, pp. 44–62.
Davies, M. (2008). *Opposition and Ideology in News Discourse*. London: Bloomsbury.
 (2008). 'Foreword'. In J. Hagedorn, *A World of Gangs: Armed Young Men and Gangsta Culture*. Minneapolis: University of Minnesota Press, pp. xi–xvii.
Di Placido, M. (2019). 'Between Pleasure and Resistance: The Role of Substance Consumption in an Italian Working-Class Subculture'. *Societies*, 9(58), 1–21.
Dias, M. C., & Eslava, L. (2013). 'Horizons of Inclusion: Life between Laws and Developments in Rio de Janeiro'. *University of Miami Inter-American Law Review*, 44(2), 177–218.
Douglas, M. (1966). *Purity and Danger*. London: Ark.
Dowdney, L. (2003). *Children of the Drug Trade: A Case Study of Children in Organised Armed Violence in Rio de Janeiro*. Rio de Janeiro: Editora 7 Letras.
 (2008). *Neither War nor Peace*. Rio de Janeiro: Viva Rio/COAV/IANSA.
Eagleton, T. (1991). *Ideology: An Introduction*. London: Verso.
Fairclough, N. (1992). *Discourse and Social Change*. Cambridge: Polity.
Fernandes, F. (2014). 'The Construction of Socio-political and Symbolical Marginalisation in Brazil: Reflecting the Relation between Socio-spatial Stigma and Responses to Violence in Rio de Janeiro'. *International Journal of Humanities and Social Science*, 4(2), 52–67.
Fernandes, F. L., & Rodriguez, A. (2015). 'The "Lost Generation" and the Challenges in Working with Marginalised Groups. Learnt Lessons from Brazilian Favelas'. *Radical Community Work Journal*, 1(1), 1–21.
Forman, M. (2002). *The 'Hood Comes First: Race, Space, and Place in Rap and Hip-Hop*. Hanover, NH: Wesleyan University Press.
Fraser, N. (1990). 'Rethinking the Public Sphere: A Contribution to the Critique of Actually Existing Democracy'. *Social Text*, 25–26, 56–80.

Gay, R. (2015). *Bruno: Conversations with a Brazilian Drug Dealer*. Durham, NC: Duke University Press.
Goldstein, D. (2004). *The Spectacular City: Violence and Performance in Urban Bolivia*. Durham, NC: Duke University Press.
Gramsci, A. (1971). *Prison Notebooks: Selections*. London: Lawrence and Wishart.
Habermas, J. (1989). *The Structural Transformation of the Public Sphere: An Inquiry into a Category of Bourgeois Society*. Trans. T. Burger with the assistance of F. Lawrence. Cambridge: Polity Press.
Hall, S. (1997). *Representation: Cultural Representations and Signifying Practices*. London: Sage in association with the Open University.
Halliday, M. A. K (1978). *Language as Social Semiotic*. London: Arnold.
Harvey, D. (2004). 'The New Imperialism. Accumulation by Dispossession'. *Actuel Marx*, 25(1), 71–90.
Helland, K. (2018). 'Mona aka Sad Girl: A Multilingual Multimodal Critical Discourse Analysis of Music Videos of a Japanese Chicana Rap Artist'. *Discourse, Context &Media*, 23, 25–40.
Herschmann, M. (1997). *Abalandao os Anos 90: Funk e Hip Hop, Globalização, Violência e Estilo Cultural*. [Shaking the 1990s: Funk and Hip-Hop, Globalisation, Violence and Cultural Style]. Rio de Janeiro: Rocco.
   (2000). *O Funk e o Hip Hop Invadem a Cena*. [Funk and Hip-hop Invade the Scene]. Rio de Janeiro: Editora UFRJ.
Hobsbawm, E. (1959). *Primitive Rebels: Studies in Archaic Forms of Social Movement in the 19th and 20th Centuries*. Manchester: Manchester University Press.
Holston, J. (2008). *Insurgent Citizenship: Disjunctions of Democracy and Modernity in Brazil*. Princeton, NJ: Princeton University Press.
   (2009a). 'Insurgent Citizenship in an Era of Global Urban Peripheries'. *City & Society*, 21(2), 245–267.
   (2009b). 'Dangerous Spaces of Citizenship: Gang Talk, Rights Talk, and Rule of Law in Brazil'. *UC Berkeley CLAS Working Papers*, pp. 1–23.
Jeffries, L. (2010). *Opposition in Discourse: The Construction of Oppositional Meaning*. London: Continuum.
Katz, J. (1988). *Seductions of Crime: Moral and Sensual Attractions in Doing Evil*. New York: Basic Books.
Keyes, C. (2002). *Rap Music and Street Consciousness*. Chicago: University of Illinois Press.
Križan, A. (2013). 'Getting the Message Across: Attitudinal Analysis of the Popular Songs "Like Toy Soldiers" and "Toy Soldiers"'. In V. Kennedy & M. Gadpaille, eds., *Words and Music*. Newcastle upon Tyne: Cambridge Scholars Press, pp. 50–64.
Kubrin, C. (2005). 'Gangstas, Thugs, and Hustlas: Identity and the Code of the Street in Rap Music'. *Social Problems*, 52(3), 360–378.
Lanz, S. (2013). 'On the Move: Globalizing Subcultures in Rio de Janeiro's Favelas'. In C. Irazábal, ed., *Transbordering Latin Americana: Liminal Places, Cultures, and Powers (T)here*. London: Routledge, pp. 23–39.
   (2015). 'Large-Scale Urbanisation and the Infrastructure of Religious Diversity in the Favelas of Rio de Janeiro'. *New Diversities*, 17(2), 87–101.
   (2016). 'The Born-Again Favela: The Urban Informality of Pentecostalism in Rio de Janeiro'. *International Journal of Urban and Regional Research*, 40(3), 541–558.

Leite, M. P. (2000). Entre o Individualismo e a Solidariedade: Dilemas da Política e da Cidadania no Rio de Janeiro. [Between Individualism and Solidarity: Dilemmas of Politics and Citizenship in Rio de Janeiro]. *Revista Brasileira de Ciências Sociais*, 15(44), 73–90.

Machin, D. (2010). *Analysing Popular Music: Image, Sound and Text*. London: Sage.

Martin, J. R. (1992). *English Text: System and Structure*. Amsterdam: John Benjamins.

(2000). 'Beyond Exchange: APPRAISAL System in English'. In S. Hunston & G. Thompson, eds., *Evalation in Text*. Oxford: Oxford University Press, pp. 142–176.

(2004). 'Mourning: How We Get Aligned'. *Discourse & Society*, 15(2–3), 321–344.

Martin, J. R., & White, P. (2005). *The Language of Evaluation: Appraisal in English*. London: Palgrave Macmillan.

Martinez, T. (1997). 'Popular Culture as Oppositional Culture: Rap as Resistance'. *Sociological Perspectives*, 40, 265–286.

Mayr, A. (2012). 'Prison Language'. In *The Encyclopedia of Applied Linguistics*. Wiley Online Library. https://onlinelibrary.wiley.com/doi/10.1002/9781405198431.wbeal0954.

(2015). 'Spectacles of Military Urbanism in Online Media Representations of the Elite Squad of the Military Police of Rio de Janeiro: A Multimodal Approach'. *Social Semiotics*, 5, 533–557.

(2018). 'Social Media Activism by Favela Youth in Rio de Janeiro'. In C. Hart & D. Kelsey, eds., *Discourses of Disorder: Riots, Strikes and Protests in the Media*. Edinburgh: Edinburgh University Press, pp. 175–194.

Mazierska, E., & Gregory, G. (2015). *Relocating Popular Music: Pop Music, Culture and Identity*. London: Palgrave Macmillan.

Mills, C. W. (1940). 'Situated Actions and Vocabularies of Motive'. *American Sociological Review*, 5, 904–913.

Mizrahi, M. (2011). 'Brazilian Jeans: Materiality, Body and Seduction at a Rio de Janeiro's Funk Ball'. In D. Miller & S. Woodward, eds., *The Global Denim Project*. Oxford: Berg, pp. 103–126.

Monken, M. (2012). 'Os Negócios Ilegais de PMs no Rio: Venda de Armas e Drogas ao Tráfico'. [The Illegal Dealings of Military Police Officers: Selling Arms and Drugs to the Drug Trade]. *Ultimo Segundo*, 30 May. http://ultimosegundo.ig.com.br/brasil/rj/2012-05-30/osnegociosilegais-de-pms-no-rio-venda-de-armas-e-drogas-ao-tra.html.

Moreira, R. (2017). '"Now that I'm a whore, nobody is holding me back!": Women in Favela Funk and Embodied Politics'. *Women's Studies in Communication*, 40(2), 172–189.

Oosterbaan, M. (2009). 'Purity and the Devil: Community, Media and the Body. Pentecostal Adherents in a Favela In Rio de Janeiro'. In B. Meyer, ed., *Aesthetic Formations: Media, Religion and the Senses*. New York: Palgrave Macmillan, pp. 53–70.

Palombini, C. (2010). 'Notes on the Historiography of Música Soul and Funk Carioca'. Historia Actual Online 23, 99–106.

(2011). 'Musicologia e Direito na Faixa de Gaza' [Musicology and Rights in the Gaza Strip], in B. Batista, ed., *Tamborzão: Olhares sobre a Criminalização do*

Funk [Tamborzão: Perspectives on the Criminalisation of Funk]. Rio de Janeiro: Editora Revan, pp. 133–170.

(2013). 'Funk proibido'. In L. Avritzer, F. Filgueras & H. Starling, eds., *Dimensões Políticas da Justiça* [Political Dimensions of Justice]. Rio de Janeiro: Civilização Brasileira, pp. 647-657.

(2014). 'Funk Carioca and Música Soul'. In D. Horn & J. Shepherd, eds., *The Bloomsbury Encyclopedia of Popular Music of the World, Volume IX . Genres: Carribbean and Latin America*. London: Bloomsbury, pp. 317–323.

Pardue, D. (2010). 'Performing Attitude: An Imposing Space and Gender by Brazilian Hip Hoppers'. *The Journal of Latin American and Caribbean Anthropology*, 15(2), 434–456.

Penglase, B. (2005). 'The Shutdown of Rio de Janeiro: The Poetics of Drug Trafficker Violence'. *Anthropology Today*, 21(5), 3–6.

(2007). 'Barbarians on the Beach'. *Crime, Media, Culture*, 3(3), 305–325.

(2008). 'The Bastard Child of the Dictatorship: The Comando Vermelho and the Birth of Narco-Culture in Rio de Janeiro'. *Luso-Brazilian Review*, 45(1), 118–145.

(2009). 'States of Insecurity: Everyday Emergencies, Public Secrets, and Drug Trafficker Power in a Brazilian *Favela*'. *Political and Legal Anthropology Review*, 32 (1), 47–63.

(2010). 'The Owner of the Hill: Masculinity and Drug-Trafficker Power in Rio de Janeiro, Brazil'. *The Journal of Latin American and Caribbean Anthropology*, 15(2), 317–337.

(2014). *Living with Insecurity in a Brazilian Favela: Urban Violence and Daily Life*. New Brunswick, NJ: Rutgers University Press.

Pennycook, A. (2007). *Global Englishes and Transcultural Flows*. London: Routledge.

Perlman, J. (1976). *The Myth of Marginality: Urban Poverty and Politics in Rio de Janeiro*. Berkeley: University of California Press.

Ramos, S., & Paiva, A. (2007). Mídia e Violência: Novas Tendências na Cobertura de Criminalidade e Segurança no Brasil [Media and Violence: New Tendencies in the Coverage of Crime and Security in Brazil]. Rio de Janeiro: IUPERJ.

Ramos, C., & Ucko, D. H. (2017). 'Beyond the *Unidades de Polícia Pacificadora*: Countering Comando Vermelho's Criminal Insurgency'. *Small Wars & Insurgencies*, 29 (1), 38–67.

Reisigl, M., & Wodak, R. (2001). *Discourse and Discrimination*. London: Routledge.

(2009). 'The Discourse-Historical Approach'. In R. Wodak & M. Meyer, eds., *Methods of Critical Discourse Analysis*. London: Sage, pp. 63–93.

Richardson, J. (2017). 'Recontextualisation and Fascist Music'. In L. Way & S. McKerrell, eds., *Music as Multimodal Discourse*. London: Bloomsbury, pp. 71–94.

Richardson, J., & Wodak, R. (2009). 'Recontextualising Fascist Ideologies of the Past: Right-Wing Discourses on Employment and Nativism in Austria and the United Kingdom'. *Critical Discourse Studies*, 6(4), 251–267.

Robb-Larkins, E. (2015). *The Spectacular Favela: Violence in Modern Brazil*. University of California Press.

Rodgers, D., & Baird, A. (2015). 'Understanding Gangs in Contemporary Latin America'. In S. Decker & D. Pirooz, eds., *Handbook of Gangs and Gang Responses*. New York: Wiley, pp. 478–502.

Rodrigues, R., (2014). 'The Dilemmas of Pacification: News of War and Peace in the "Marvellous City"'. *Stability: International Journal of Security and Development*, 3(1), Art. 22. http://doi.org/10.5334/sta.dt.

Roth-Gordon, J. (2007). 'Youth, Slang and Pragmatic Expression: Examples from Brazilian Portuguese'. *Journal of Sociolinguistics*, 11(3), 322–345.

Sá, S. (2007). 'Funk Carioca: Música Eletrônica Brasileira?' *Revista E-Comps 10*.

Sansone, L. (2001). 'The Localisation of Global Funk in Bahia and in Rio'. In C. Perrone & C. Dunn, eds., *Brazilian Popular Music and Globalisation*, Gainesville: University Press of Florida, pp. 136–160.

Semino, E. (2008). *Metaphor in Discourse*. Cambridge: Cambridge University Press.

Short, M. (1996). *Exploring the Language of Poems, Plays and Prose*. London: Longman.

Simpson, P. (2004). *Stylistics: A Resource Book for Students*. London: Routledge.

Sneed, P. (2003). 'Machine Gun Voices: Bandits, Favelas and Utopia in Brazilian Funk'. PhD dissertation, University of Wisconsin-Madison. http://beatdiaspora .blogspot.com. br/2006/10/machine-gun-voices.html.

(2007). 'Bandidos de Cristo: Representations of the Power of Criminal Factions in Rio's Proibidão Funk'. *Latin American Music Review* 28(1), 220–241.

(2008). 'Favela Utopias: The *Bailes Funk* in Rio's Crisis of Social Exclusion and Violence'. *Latin American Research Review*, 63(2), 57–97.

Soares, L. E. (2000). *Meu Casaco de General* [My General's Coat]. Rio de Janeiro: Companhia das Letras.

Souza, M. L. de (1996). 'Redes e Sistemas do Tráfico de Drogas no Rio de Janeiro: Uma Tentativa de Modelagem' [Nets and Systems of Drug Trafficking In Rio de Janeiro: A Tentative Model]. *Anuário do Instituto de Geociências, Rio de Janeiro*, 19, 45–60.

Strine, M. (1991). 'Critical Theory and "Organic" Intellectuals: Reframing the Work of Cultural Critique'. *Communication Monographs*, 58, 195–201.

Sykes, G., & Matza, D. (1957). 'Techniques of Neutralisation: A Theory of Delinquency'. *American Sociological Review*, 22, 664–670.

Van Dijk, T. (1998). *News as Discourse*. London: Routledge.

Van Leeuwen, T. (1996). 'The Representation of Social Actors'. In C.-R. Caldas-Coulthard & M. Coulthard, eds., *Texts and Practices: Readings in Critical Discourse Analysis*. London: Routledge, pp. 32–70.

(2012). 'The Critical Analysis of Musical Discourse'. *Critical Discourse Studies*, 9(4), 319–328.

Van Leeuwen, T., & Wodak, R. (1999). 'Legitimising Immigration Control: A Discourse-Historical Analysis'. *Discourse Studies*, 1(1), 83–118.

Ventura, Z. (1994). *Cidade Partida* [Divided City]. Rio de Janeiro: Companhia das Letras.

Vianna, H. (1988). *O Mundo Funk Carioca* [The Rio Funk World]. Rio de Janeiro: Jorge Zaluar Editora.

(2005). 'Entregamos o Ouro Ao Bandido' [We throw the baby out with the bath water]. *Revista Raiz*, 1, 20–21.

Way, L. (2017). *Popular Music and Multimodal Critical Discourse Studies: Ideology, Control and Resistance in Turkey since 2002*. London: Bloomsbury.

Whitehead, N. (2004). 'Rethinking Anthropology of Violence'. *Anthropology Today*, 20(5), 1–2.

Wilding, P. (2010). '"New Violence": Silencing Women's Experience in the *Favelas* of Brazil'. *Journal of Latin American Studies*, 42(4), 719–747.

Wodak, R., & Weiss, G. (2005). 'Analysing European Union Discourses: Theories and Applications'. In R. Wodak & P. Chilton, eds., *A New Agenda in Critical Discourse Analysis*. Amsterdam: John Benjamins, pp. 121–135.

World Bank (2012). 'Bringing the State Back into the Favelas of Rio de Janeiro'. Document of the World Bank, October 2012. documents1.worldbank.org/curated/en/255231468230108733/pdf/760110ESW0P12300Rio0de0Janeiro02013.pdf.

Yúdice, G. (1994). 'The Funkification of Rio'. In T. Rose & A. Ross, eds., *Microphone Fiends: Youth Music and Youth Culture*. New York: Routledge, pp. 193–217.

Zaluar, A. (2000). 'Perverse Integration: Drug Trafficking and Youth in the Favelas of Rio de Janeiro'. *Journal of International Affairs*, 53(2), 653–670.

12   Deviant Mind Style of a Schizophrenic Offender

Ulrike Tabbert

This chapter sets out to identify the linguistic patterns that are indicative of the mind style of an offender with schizophrenia I will call John Doe.[1] He published an account of his criminal offence on his freely accessible web page.[2] When analysing his writings it is not my intention to prove by means of stylistic analysis that John Doe suffers from schizophrenia, since such a diagnosis falls into the realm of other disciplines. Furthermore I want to avoid circular reasoning as, for example, that John Doe has schizophrenia and that linguistic evidence proves this. For such a circular conclusion Demjén was criticised in relation to her book on Sylvia Plath, who suffered from depression and eventually committed suicide (Demjén 2015; Williams 2017).

The discerning diagnosis John Doe offers in his reflections and which I take for granted gives rise to a document which is probably the result of his mental disorder and which consequently illustrates a 'deviant understanding of the world' (Semino & Swindlehurst 1996, p. 145). The document thus constitutes the starting point for identifying by means of stylistic analysis 'distinctive and striking textual patterns' (Boase-Beier 2003, p. 254) in John Doe's account which can shed light on how he, as an individual, conceptualises reality (Bockting 1994, p. 159). In other words, my objective is to identify his mind style. This chapter therefore presents a forensic linguistic perspective on the writings of someone who exhibits deviant behaviour in contrast to analysing writings on the person with deviant behavior.

12.1   Mind Style

The term 'mind style', first coined by Fowler (1977, p. 103), 'captures those aspects of world views that are primarily personal and cognitive in origin, and which are peculiar to a particular individual, or common to people who have the same cognitive characteristics (for example as a result of a similar mental illness)' (Semino 2002, p. 97). Mind style is, therefore, according to Nuttall

---

[1] Name changed out of respect for John Doe's privacy.
[2] http://contra-supermarkt.de/index.html, accessed 16 June 2017.

(2018, p. 16), to be regarded as 'a specific manifestation of a wider narrative phenomenon of point of view'.

Although mind style was developed with a focus on the fictional character, there is no reason that hinders its application to the writings of a real person, John Doe. This, I argue, has two reasons: First, in the text world of his written account John Doe is conceptualised as an enactor (Gibbons 2019, p. 8) in the same way a fictional character in the text world of a novel is. The difference between an enactor and a character is that the former is a conceptual entity with 'multiple versions of the same designated character/person' (Gibbons 2019, p. 8) such as, for example, character Henry in Audrey Niffenegger's novel *The Time Traveler's Wife* who exists as 'many different textual versions', for example, as a young boy and as an adult (Gavins 2007, p. 42). The reader conceptualises John Doe as enactor in the same way, the only difference being that enactor John Doe has a counterpart in the real world, whereas Henry does not. The second reason for applying the notion of mind style to John Doe's writing is authenticity. Much attention is being paid in literary texts to make them authentic as, for example, the portrayal of a boy with autism in *The Curious Incident of the Dog in the Night-time* (Haddon 2003) or character Benyi, who has learning disability, in Faulkner's (1929) *The Sound and the Fury*. The text under scrutiny shows language use by a real person facing mental challenges and is thus a non-fictional text. It therefore depends on the contextual knowledge the reader possesses to know that John Doe's writings are not fiction. Herman (2011, p. 9) thus rightly claims that real and fictional minds 'can be more or less directly encountered or experienced – depending on the circumstances'.

The concept of mind style has been investigated in several studies mainly looking at literary texts and dates back to the seminal identification of transitivity patterns in Golding's novel *The Inheritors* (Halliday 1971). Although the novel's main character Lok apparently does not suffer from any mental disorder, his limited vision due to restrained experience and knowledge is indicated by a predominance of intransitive verbs and an intransitive use of verbs as Halliday demonstrated. It should be noted, however, that the term 'mind style' for such a phenomenon was introduced only later, namely, by Fowler (1977). Since then, linguists have developed an interest in those mind styles which are 'most noticeable and interesting interpretatively', namely, those that deviate from normal assumptions. Linguistic patterns of deviant mind styles have been identified for various literary characters such as the aforementioned Benjy (Bockting 1994) (see also Semino's [2014] study of three characters with autism), the character Bromden, with paranoid schizophrenia, in Kesey's *One Flew over the Cuckoo's Nest* (Semino & Swindlehurst 1996), Aleko in de Bernières' *Captain Corelli's Mandolin* as well as Frederick Clegg in Fowles's *The*

Collector (Semino 2002) or Christopher Boone, who suffers from Asperger's syndrome, in the aforementioned Haddon novel (Gregoriou 2011b; Semino 2007, pp. 8ff.). More recently, work on mind style has been undertaken by Dore (2017), Dorst (2019), Giovanelli (2018), Gregoriou (2007a, 2007b, 2011a, 2011b, 2020), Hermann (2016), Hoover (2004), Lugea (2016), Montoro (2011), Nuttall (2015, 2018, 2019), Rundquist (2020) and Whiteley (2020), to name but a few. Mind style analysis is not limited to literary texts, though, nor to characters with mental disorders but has also been conducted on American writer Sylvia Plath's journals (Demjén 2015), on the conceptualisation of the minds of serial killers in Berry-Dee's *Talking with Serial Killers: The Most Evil People in the World Tell Their Own Stories* (Gregoriou 2007b) or on the eccentric character of Miss Shepherd, who suffers from paranoia in Bennett's *The Lady in the Van*, based on an autobiographical memoir (McIntyre 2005). Pillière (2013, pp. 69f.) even argues that 'the theory of mind style is indeed relevant for all kinds of texts' and that 'by focusing on mind styles that reflect limited cognitive skills, the concept of mind style has become far more limited than its original authors intended'. In her article, Pillière focuses on character Stevens in Kazuo Ishiguro's *The Remains of the Day* and, to a lesser extent, the character Smith in *The Loneliness of the Long-Distance Runner* by Alan Sillitoe.

In summarising this varied linguistic research, mind style can be evoked by various linguistic patterns ranging from the use of personal pronouns, transitivity patterns, metaphors, syntactic and sentence structure through to preferred semantic fields or a character's idiosyncratic use of inductive logic. In other words, the linguistic patterns indicative of a mind style are as varied as the different possible mind styles themselves. Closest to the research at hand, however, comes Semino and Swindlehurst's (1996) analysis: the character they analysed, Bromden, the Indian chief, is apparently diagnosed with schizophrenia as well. The authors found that Bromden perceives the world around him in terms of machinery, exhibited by his frequent use of metaphors with machinery as source domain. This does not contradict findings from neurolinguistics that found a correlation between schizophrenia and a deficit in understanding metaphors, because understanding and producing metaphorical expressions are two different things. Also close to the topic at hand is Hens' (2000) analysis of the poems of the Austrian Ernst Herbeck, who was diagnosed with schizophrenia. Hens concludes that Herbeck 'takes cues for the extension of his text from the preceding lines only' (p. 43), which proves that Herbeck's disorder limits the room for creativity and Hens' analysis allows for assertions about the nature and aesthetics of schizophrenic speech.

In identifying the linguistic patterns that constitute John Doe's mind style I wish to provide closer insight into the reasons behind his crime. Despite the crime committed being petty (spitting), the material is extremely rich, lends itself to a deep and revealing stylistic analysis and epitomises perfectly a deviant mind style, namely, how a person with mental disturbance perceives his criminal act. My research is thus placed at the intersection between forensic linguistics, cognitive science and also narrative criminology (Presser 2009), a relatively young branch of criminology looking at criminals' narratives, which will be introduced in brief later in this chapter. Before I get there I will introduce research into the connection between language and the human mind.

12.2   Language and the Unconscious

A connection between the unconscious and language was first argued for by Sigmund Freud (1901), who examined paraphrases (slips of the tongue). Jacques Lacan (1968) later suggested, based on insights from psychoanalysis, 'that the unconscious asserts itself through language', which leads Pennebaker et al. (2003, p. 560) to state that a linguistic analysis of a patient's speech sample allows for this patient to be classified in a diagnostic group, such as schizophrenia. These insights from psychology and psychiatry[3] relate to a basic linguistic and particularly stylistic assumption, namely, that language use bears 'an element of choice over *how* to say something' (Jeffries & McIntyre 2010, p. 25), which includes conscious as well as subconscious choices. This 'element of choice' follows from language providing 'finite means but infinite possibilities of expression' (Chomsky 1966, p. 29). Both psychology as well as stylistic analysis make use of this 'element of choice', the former to identify 'marker of personality' (Groom & Pennebaker 2002) and the latter to identify style and, more relevant to the topic at hand, 'mind style' (Fowler 1977, p. 103).

Psychologists Groom and Pennebaker (2002, p. 615) claim that 'linguistic style' is determined by 'particles or function words (e.g., pronouns, articles, and prepositions)' in contrast to content words such as nouns or (not auxiliary) verbs which, according to them, do not yield 'many consistent social or psychological effects' (Pennebaker et al. 2003, p. 570). However, Pennebaker et al.'s definition of 'linguistic style', which is in fact limited to semantic but not syntactic choices, is different from the understanding of the term 'style' in stylistics, a sub-discipline of linguistics that is concerned with the study of style in its widest sense. In the latter, 'style' is regarded as a 'motivated choice from the set of language or register inventions or other social, political, cultural and contextual parameters' (Nørgaard et al. 2010,

---

[3] The distinction between both fields is of no relevance for this chapter.

p. 156) and thus goes beyond an examination of word choice and sentence structure while certainly including these. As both sciences explore different trajectories and with the research presented in this chapter being situated at their intersection, particular attention has to be paid to clarify the terminology used as well as the aim of the research conducted, which I will shortly be expounding.

A substantial body of relevant research exists in the fields of psychology, psychiatry/psychoanalysis, neurolinguistics, cognitive stylistics and narrative criminology which provide the basis for the investigation presented in this chapter.

For a cursory overview, I first wish to mention the work of Weintraub (1989), an American psychoanalyst who, for example, examined the speeches of American presidents after the Second World War and linked their language patterns to personality traits. He focused on linguistic features such as the use of the personal pronouns 'I', 'me' and 'we' as well as others which he named (non)personal reference, direct reference, evaluators, adverbial intensifiers, explainers, expressions of feeling, qualifiers, retractors and negatives. Although the features which he analysed do not fully overlap with linguistic categories (e.g. noun, verb, determiner, pronoun, negators, etc.), he reaches interesting results (although rather in terms of personality traits than mental disorder traits with regard to American presidents). Examining John F. Kennedy, for example, he states that the president's 'little use of "emotional" verbal categories ... enhanced the impression of a cool, detached leader' and that the 'moderate use of *qualifiers* and *retractors* reflects the personality of a leader who could make decisions and reconsider them without yielding to impulse. A moderate *negatives* score suggests that Kennedy was not oppositional or stubborn and approached questions of state in a positive way.... His use of the pronouns *I*, *we* and *me* reflects a healthy ego, an ability to work with others and an absence of strong passive strivings' (p. 136).

However, my interest reaches beyond personality traits and extends to traits of mental disorders, in the case of John Doe, schizophrenia. Mental disorders are classified in two different ways predominantly used in westernised countries like the United Kingdom or Germany: first, in Chapter V of the International Classification of Diseases (ICD-10), published by the World Health Organization, and second, in the *Diagnostic and Statistical Manual of Mental Disorders* (DSM-5), published by the American Psychiatric Association. Although these two are not congruent, they allow us to distinguish between mere (non-pathological) personality traits and mental disorder traits by drawing a line where a mental characteristic is actually regarded as constituent of a mental disorder such as schizophrenia.

The term 'schizophrenia' is generic and, according to ICD-10, refers to a group of severe mental disorders in which a person has trouble telling the difference between real and unreal experiences, thinking logically, having normal emotional responses to others, and behaving normally in social situations. Symptoms include seeing, hearing, feeling things that are not there, having false ideas about what is taking place or who one is, nonsense speech, unusual behavior, lack of emotion, and social withdrawal.[4]

One per cent of the world's adult population is affected by this disorder (Kuperberg 2010, p. 576) or, in absolute figures, 51 million people (Mitchell et al. 2015, p. 12). Schizophrenia is regarded to be 'one manifestation of an underlying schizophrenic phenotype', or 'schizotype'. Schizotypal individuals can, when exposed to stress or other environmental factors including drug abuse, experience a schizophrenic breakdown. However, not all schizotypal individuals develop schizophrenia (Kiang 2010, p. 194; Rado 1953) which is regarded as a heterogeneous disorder,[5] meaning that two persons diagnosed with this disorder might display 'different subsets of symptoms' (Kuperberg 2010, p. 577). This explains why when examining John Doe's narration we cannot draw on a supposedly fixed pattern of language use established for patients with schizophrenia and see whether we re-encounter this in Doe's writings. In other words, there is no established mind style for people suffering from schizophrenia, but based on insight from previous research John Doe's mind style needs to be explored individually in order to see how he perceives the world.

Symptoms of schizophrenia are divided into three groups: positive, negative and cognitive symptoms. Positive symptoms refer to an excess or distortion of normal functions and can include hallucinations, delusions, positive thought disorder (disorganised language output) or disordered thinking and moving. Negative symptoms are those that display an absence of characteristics that typically appear in healthy individuals, such as lack of voluntary behaviour/ motivation, apathy, flat/inappropriate affect or negative thought disorder (poverty of speech and language). Third, cognitive symptoms refer to a poor ability to understand information and make decisions as well as having trouble focusing (Kuperberg 2010, p. 576; Mitchell et al. 2015, p. 12). Based on their impaired self-monitoring abilities (Kircher & Leube 2003, p. 665) following from a 'disturbance of self' (Klein et al. 2013, p. 276), persons suffering from schizophrenia tend to wrongly interpret events (or non-events) in the real world, leading to (re)actions perceived as strange or abnormal by others, as

---

[4] www.icd10data.com/ICD10CM/Codes/F01-F99/F20-F29/F20-/F20, accessed 17 August 2016.
[5] Some even argue that the concept of schizophrenia is coming to an end and will be replaced by a concept of a 'psychosis spectrum disorder' (McCarthy-Jones 2017) because the reasons for and symptoms of schizophrenia are manifold.

was my first impression when reading John Doe's account of events. Another common feature of schizotypal individuals is their inability to experience pleasure (Rado 1953), which we will also encounter in Doe's writings. Research into verbal output of patients with schizophrenia shows a knowledge progress about this disorder over time. Whereas France and Muir (1997, pp. 12ff.) stated that 'only the highest levels of language processes are impaired in schizophrenia', later research proved that abnormalities can also occur at the level of single words (structure and function of lexico-semantic memory), sentence (impaired use of different types of linguistic context) and discourse (abnormal relationships between sentences) (Kuperberg & Caplan 2003, p. 459). However, the reason for the inability of persons with schizophrenia to understand higher levels of language use such as pragmatics or metaphors is rooted in their Theory of Mind deficit (Champagne-Lavau & Stip 2010, p. 285). Theory of Mind (ToM) from cognitive science means the human ability to attribute mental states both to others and to oneself (Heider & Simmel 1944). A distinction is made between cognitive and affective ToM: the former refers to the ability to construct other people's cognitive status, their beliefs, thoughts or intentions; the latter to constructing other people's affective states, emotions and feelings (Compère et al. 2016, p. 52). The link between a ToM deficit and pragmatic impairments in patients with schizophrenia forces itself upon the reader at this stage of the chapter already: pragmatics being considered a 'mind-reading exercise' means that understanding pragmatic meaning in language use involves inferences concerning the speaker's mental status (Grice 1969), which is hindered by the ToM deficit in a person with schizophrenia.

After this brief introduction to insight from cognitive science the question arises as to how we as linguists can make use of the existing body of knowledge on schizophrenia and contribute what is rightfully within our realm of expertise, namely, linguistic analysis. The aforementioned psychologist Pennebaker states that 'people's linguistic styles provide far richer psychological information than their linguistic content' (2002), which correlates with the fact that 'people are more consistent in how they talk than in what they say' (Groom & Pennebaker 2002, p. 618). For us as linguists (in particular, stylisticians), this means that we can provide linguistic analysis of verbal output of people with schizophrenia that yields insight into their unique world view and allows us to understand how people suffering from this disorder make sense of the world around them as shown in their language use (as done by Spitzer et al. [1992], Schmidt-Knaebel [1998] and McKenna and Oh [2005]). The notion of mind style has been proved useful for this undertaking, as it is able to capture and explain deviant ways to understand the world exhibited in the language used and is a contribution to the existing body on language of people with schizophrenia.

Last in this cursory overview of relevant research I turn to narrative criminology and its declared interest in offender's narratives and what these *do* rather than what they *reveal* (Presser 2016, 139). Coined by Presser (2009) and 'grounded in a narrative understanding of self-making, narrative criminology analyses stories about crime not as accounts of "what really happened", but as examples of the performative work individuals do on themselves and their surroundings, and the effects these have'.[6] Although offender's narratives have been of interest for criminologists for some time (Bennett 1981), in narrative criminology they are positioned centre stage. Presser (2009, p. 178) acknowledges that offenders' narratives are 'a factor in the motivation for and accomplishment of crime and criminalization' in that they direct harmful behaviour. Obviously not limited to offenders with mental disorders, Presser (2013, p. 131) and later Sandberg & Ugelvik (2016, p. 131) identify a combination of capability ('the licence to do harm') and compulsion ('the logic of powerlessness') leading towards harmful behaviour. Although Presser (2009, p. 178) claims that 'narrative criminology attends to discourse, not minds', compulsion (if not capability to some extent as well) is a product of a cognitive process. Such cognitive processes can be identified by analysing John Doe's narration to answer the question of what inspired/motivated his crime and how he uses his narration to make 'sense of harm' (Presser & Sandberg 2015, p. 1).

An offender's point of view which manifests itself in their narrative allows the offender to show 'the evolution of misconduct from identifiable and culturally intelligible causes' and them to be positioned 'as less bad or wrong than ascribed labels suggest (e.g. "offender")' (Presser 2009, p. 179). As Presser (2009, p. 178) argues, narratives affect the narrator (whom she calls the 'actor') as well. It has to be noticed that because John Doe has been diagnosed as having schizophrenia, he has been acquitted on grounds of lack of criminal responsibility. He is thus not a convicted criminal, whose verbal outputs were studied by O'Connor (2000, 2015) or Lynn (2019). Nevertheless, John Doe's narrative lends itself for analysis, even though he cannot be punished for his offence due to a lack of *mens rea* ('Schuldfähigkeit' in the German Criminal Code).

12.3 John Doe's Account of Events

One problem with using narratives from offenders with schizophrenia is confidentiality. The present author in her capacity as a public prosecutor is not allowed to use material from potential court files on John Doe for the

---

[6] www.jus.uio.no/ikrs/english/research/projects/networkfornarrativecrim/events/second-narrative-criminology-symposium.html, accessed 15 June 2017.

research at hand but has to rely on publicly available content. Further, publicly accessible texts from people with well-known mental disorders such as the former German Reich Chancellor Adolf Hitler in his book *Mein Kampf* are less than ideal, as editing processes might have altered Hitler's original verbiage, thus damaging the precision of the results. However, in the case of John Doe, he himself published his account of events on his web page where he also states that he was diagnosed with schizophrenia and that a court trial took place over his offence. The connecting question then arises over whether John Doe displayed psychotic symptoms at the time of writing (meaning in an acute schizophrenic episode) or was medicated and therefore not exhibiting many symptoms. On the basis of the information on schizophrenia provided so far in this chapter together with the following examples from John Doe's writings, the reader is in a position to judge by themselves whether this question is relevant here.

The entire content of John Doe's web page was copied into a .txt file which provides the basis for the analysis that follows and which I named the John Doe Text (JDT). To give the reader an impression of how John Doe thinks, acts and, most importantly, justifies his crime, a lengthier extract from the JDT was chosen in which he narrates the events leading up to the criminal act as well as the crime itself. It gives an impression how John Doe justifies his crime (spitting), which is disturbing not so much in itself but as an indicator of his mental state. It also allows for a brief introduction to the language he uses, which will later be analysed in detail. John Doe wrote in German and I analysed the German text (as shown in the Appendix at the end of this chapter). However, as not all readers are familiar with German, I provide my own English translation of the core piece (i.e., the crime and the events leading up to it) to allow the reader to get their own first impression and to follow my argument later on.

Example 1 (extract from JDT)
My Adventure in a Supermarket
  Summer 2009 I constantly noticed a young female shop assistant. She constantly stung out of the corner of my eyes but only noticed who it was, who stood out when I looked who it was again. I was totally annoyed in the supermarket by this one woman (want to mention here that this never happened to me before that a woman so annoyed me and wanted to have my peace as I was in the garden all day at that time and also stayed overnight.
  ...
  Then, end of October/November 2009, several young very attractive women started working in the supermarket (not all on the same day) and strangely were flirting with me though. I wasn't interested however, because I, as I noticed then, had achieved something in the garden which I hadn't known till then....
  The women were continually flirting. One of the women was constantly looking me in the eyes and, unfortunately, I her also although I didn't know why, somehow it didn't

matter to me. This woman touched me not just accidently when giving change but she was stroking my palm with the back of her hand. This also left me indifferent and I think the shop assistances could sense that.

Then one day in December 2009, I still had no interest in flirting in the supermarket, I was standing alone at the till, there the shop assistant (strangely not one of the women who had been flirting with me previously) was stretching herself over the back of her chair thus far backwards that I only saw her breasts (I didn't even see her head anymore) and she was sticking them out to me for 2 to 3 seconds, maybe longer. I was so perplexed that I didn't know what this was now again. Arriving at home I unfortunately was getting hot because I fancy breasts. Unfortunately, I kept seeing the breasts bouncing on TV for three days and I had to think of this woman who had stuck out her breasts to me....

I thought that when I'm hot anyway and the women were flirting with me anyway I could ask one of them if we want to go out. I chose another blonde woman who had also been flirting with me, though not the one who had been looking me in the eyes and stroking me excessively. When I was in the supermarket again this woman came towards me and I greeted her friendly and she greeted me back friendly. Then I stood at the till and this woman suddenly stood behind me, I turned around towards her but didn't know what this meant, whether I should do something or whether she merely wanted to give me a sign. But then I noticed that the cashier who was cashiering at that time was looking at me and this other shop assistant alternately and appeared to be very nervous. Five seconds later the shop assistant behind me was gone again.

Arriving home again I wanted to know now where I stood and I took heart and decided to go to the supermarket again to approach this one woman. So I went to the supermarket again and it didn't take long and she came towards me, but what happened next I didn't expect this way. I asked her if I could have a quick word with her and then whether she wanted to go out with me. She merely stopped and only threw a cold 'Nö' towards me. I didn't expect it this way. The sound makes the music [it's not what you say, but how you say it]. I then bought myself a little something and when I was standing at the till I saw how this woman went to the information while looking at me again and grinning insultingly. Everybody can possibly imagine how I felt then. The strange thing is that this was also the last day she worked at the supermarket, she has possibly noticed afterwards that it was her mistake to stand behind me [at the till] because there is one witness now who saw that this woman had stood behind me at the till.

I then approached another woman who flirted with me but who had been working at the supermarket for longer, but she too replied to me with the same words 'Nö'. After two rebuffs I then didn't feel like it anymore because I actually indeed hadn't been really interested anyway. I actually only asked these women because I wanted to know where I stood. What would have happened had I approached them. I have asked this myself repeatedly when I didn't dare.
...

I decided to not put up with this any longer and then I remembered the one young women in the supermarket who I had noticed repeatedly. Should she have initiated all this or even instigated her friends to this. Because my suspicion grew even more

I decided to claim back part of my dignity and humaneness. I therefore decided to spit at her when she would be sitting at the till next time. Because such a woman who does such a thing only deserves to be spit at in my opinion. I couldn't think of anything else at that time. A word and a blow. I spat at her but then from intuition: some piece of paper fell off her hand and when she picked it up I said to her: 'And pass on my best greetings to your friends.' When she was still crouching and wanted to pick up her piece of paper she nodded with her head and mumbled 'Mhm' as if she knew what this was about. When she rose and stood at the till her hands were trembling. It was clear to me that I was possibly right and she had just given herself away. One or two days [later] I called her 'slut' when walking past although I don't know why I said that.

This extract reveals what is characteristic for John Doe due to his mental disorder: he tends to wrongly interpret the shop assistants' behaviour based on his Theory of Mind deficit. It is not, however, that John Doe is unable to attribute mental states (both cognitive and affective ToM) to the shop assistants at all as, for example, the following passage from Example 1 illustrates: 'When she rose and stood at the till her hands were trembling. It was clear to me that I was apparently right and she had just given herself away.'

It is rather that he reaches wrong conclusions based on his (correct) observations paired with perceiving himself at centre stage. In the passage cited, John Doe assumes that the trembling he observes proves his suspicion instead of considering that the trembling could be a reaction to his recent spitting and that the shop assistant most certainly had been completely unaware of his feelings up to this point.

What further catches the eye is John Doe's frequent use of modal expressions (e.g. 'could', 'possibly'), mental cognition processes (e.g. 'I was so perplexed') and references to self (I-talk) as well as infrequent metaphor use. We will put these four initial observations to test in the following sections using the JDT and begin with John Doe's use of first-person singular pronouns.

12.4 John Doe's Use of First-Person-Singular Pronouns

The JDT consists of 13,144 word tokens (total number of words) and 2,169 word types (number of different words, not the same as lemmas). A starting point for a systematic way to explore the JDT is a word list which lists all the word types in the JDT sorted according to their frequency. To create a word list I use the freely available software package AntConc[7] (Anthony 2014); those who have little familiarity with corpus analysis may consult McIntyre and Walker (2019) or Tabbert (2016, pp. 56ff.).

---

[7] For this chapter I use AntConc 3.4.4m, downloaded from www.laurenceanthony.net/software/antconc/, accessed 16 June 2017.

The JDT word list tells us that the most frequently used word in the corpus by far is 'ich' ('I' personal pronoun, 710 occurrences), followed by 'und' ('and' conjunction, 293) and 'die' ('the' female singular or plural determiner, 273). While the frequency of the conjunction and of the definite article are standard in German (in language use in general), 'ich' ('I') is not only the most often used word in the text but its occurrence number also strongly contrasts against the other two and thus calls for closer examination. Frequent use of first-person pronouns has, for example, been linked in the literature to a high degree of self-involvement (Stirman & Pennebaker 2001), lower social status (Kacewicz et al. 2014), to people experiencing physical or emotional pain (Rude et al. 2004) or to depression (Weintraub 1981, 1989) and suicide (Pennebaker & Lay 2002). This shows that the implications of this phenomenon taken on its own can be manifold and that it is not exclusively linked to schizophrenia (if at all). However, the question arises of whether this perceived overuse in the JDT is actually statistically significant or merely proof of the established fact that '[s]peakers telling life-story narratives use "I"-centred discourse' (O'Connor 2000, p. 39).

Statistical significance can be calculated using log-likelihood ratio or chi-square.[8] In order to establish statistical significance, the frequency of the target word 'ich' ('I') in the JDT has to be compared with its occurrence in other corpora, preferably also personal narrations of the same kind as John Doe's. Suitable figures for comparison are offered by Pennebaker et al. (2001, 2015), in a manual accompanying their software package called Linguistic Inquiry and Word Count (LIWC). LIWC is able to 'read' a target text, to extract words found in the target text matching the words in the software's built-in English dictionary and to calculate statistical figures for the occurrence of these words in the target text. LIWC's speciality is that the incorporated dictionary has the words in it assigned to 'psychologically meaningful categories' (Tausczik & Pennebaker 2010, p. 24), ranging from standard linguistic dimensions (e.g. pronouns, articles, auxiliaries), psychological processes (e.g. emotion, anxiety, anger), personal concern categories (e.g. work, home, leisure) to informal language markers (e.g. swear words, fillers) to name but a few. The aim of this approach to texts is guided by psychological insight, namely, that the words people use 'provide rich information about their beliefs, fears, thinking patterns, social relationships, and personalities' (Pennebaker et al. 2015, p. 1), or, as Pennebaker et al. stated elsewhere, it allows for 'classifying patients into diagnostic groups, such as schizophrenia, depression, paranoia, or somatisation disorder' (2003, p. 560). In its manual, LIWC 2015 provides percentages for the occurrence of words belonging to the relevant category of '1st person

---

[8] Those who have little familiarity with these statistical tools may consult McIntyre and Walker (2019, pp. 154ff.) or Tabbert (2015, pp. 84ff.).

singular' (e.g. 'I', 'me' or 'mine') in blogs, expressive writing, novels, natural speech, the *New York Times* and Twitter. Although the software package in its entirety is unsuited to use as the JDT is in German, these percentage figures together with the total number of words in each listed genre are suitable to use for testing whether John Doe's overuse of first-person singular pronouns is statistically significant.

From the description Pennebaker et al. (2015, pp. 9f.) provide for each of these text types, expressive writing, blogs and, to a certain extent, natural speech as well come closest to John Doe's text in terms of genre and are thus suited for comparison despite the language difference. In order to match LIWC's category '1st person singular', I extended the word types from the JDT belonging to this category to include possessive pronouns as well. The following word types and figures were extracted from the JDT: 'ich' ('I') 710, 'mir' ('me' third case) 232, 'mich' ('me' fourth case) 151, 'meinen' ('my') 36, 'meine' ('my') 34, 'mein' ('my/mine') 28, 'meinem' ('my') 26, 'meiner' ('my') 22. The total number of words in this category in the JDT is thus 1,230.

The comparison is shown in Table 12.1. Log-likelihood ratio and chi-square figures indicate a statistically significant overuse of first-person pronouns in the JDT when compared with the LIWC 2015 figures, even in the LIWC

Table 12.1. *Calculating statistical significance for first-person-singular pronoun use in JDT compared with LIWC 2015*

	John Doe Test	LIWC 2015 expressive writing	LIWC 2015 blogs	LIWC 2015 natural speech
Total number of words in category/Test	13,144	2,526,709	119,449,058	2,566,446
Number of words from first-person singular category	1,230	218,813	7,907,527	180,421
Percentage	9	8.66	6.62	7.03
Log-likelihood ratio when compared with John Doe Test		7.86	142.37	98.86
Chi-square when compared with John Doe Test		8.05	159.36	108.26
Chi-square with Yates correction		7.96	158.92	107.9
Statistically significant? (*p*-value 0.01, threshold of statistical significance: 6.63)		yes, statistically significant	yes, statistically highly significant	yes, statistically highly significant

2015 category of expressive writing. In describing the sort of texts that went into this category and their authors, Pennebaker et al. (2015, p. 10) state that these texts were written by people 'from all walks of life – ranging from college students to psychiatric prisoners to elderly and even elementary-aged individuals' on 'deeply emotional topics'. This category of texts comes thus closest to John Doe's account of events, also a piece of highly personal and emotional writing.

The overuse of first-person pronouns has thus been identified as a 'distinctive and striking textual pattern' (Boase-Beier 2003, p. 254) in the JDT and is thus relevant for John Doe's mind style. It shows that he is overly self-aware and self-focused.

12.5 John Doe's Use of Mental Processes

It might be hypothesised that Doe's preferred use of mental processes links with his frequent I-talk. This can be witnessed in sentences such as, 'Summer 2009 I constantly noticed a young female shop assistant' (mental cognition) from Example 1. Both I-talk and mental processes can be seen as indicators of his self-directed focus.

An analysis of process types (transitivity analysis) was conducted manually for all 710 concordance lines of 'ich' ('I'), namely, all clauses/sentences in which this personal pronoun occurred. The concordance list was created by AntConc. Out of a total of 710 concordance lines, 197 (27.7%) exhibited mental cognition processes, followed by 169 (23.8%) instances of material action intention, 76 (10.7%) instances of mental processes perception and 70 (9.8%) instances of mental processes reaction.[9] This demonstrates John Doe's preference for mental process types with a total of 48.2% which the reader might have already noticed when glancing through the extract above. The following example from the JDT illustrates this phenomenon further.

Example 2
Seit ich versuche mein Denken zu verändern verändert sich auch wieder mein Bewusstsein, die Stimmen werden weniger und es geht mir immer besser ‚der normale Alltag so wie vor Dez 2009 kehrt immer mehr zurück.

(Since I try to change my thinking, my consciousness changes again, the voices become less and I [mir/me in German] feel increasingly better, the normal daily routine such as before Dec[ember] 2009 is returning more and more.)

This sentence contains four instances of mental processes and one material action event (the returning of the daily routine). The striking thing about this sentence is that John Doe thinks he can work with his mind to achieve a

---

[9] Note that the analysis was conducted on the German data, not the translated text.

change and in doing so he claims success. Whether this progress is real or imagined is of no relevance for the study at hand as is also the fact that his mentioning voices correlates with a positive symptom of schizophrenia, namely, delusion. Instead, the focus lies on the identification of consistent linguistic choices John Doe makes (consciously or subconsciously) which portray his mind style (Semino & Swindlehurst 1996, p. 144). The high percentage of mental processes show how much John Doe listens inwardly, but not only that, he also 'works' with his mind, which reminds us of the character Bromden and his machinery metaphors in Semino and Swindlehurst's (1996) study.

Inwardly directed perception in the case of John Doe goes as far as *coenaesthesis*, a phenomenon meaning an abnormal or bizarre body experience 'in the borderland between *soma* and *psyche*' (Fuchs 1995, p. 103). An example thereof is the following passage from the JDT.

Example 3
Mir war damals schon klar das mit dem Duft aus den Handrücken konnte nicht real sein, da ich schon vorher (seit 2011) immer mal eigenartige Düfte in der Nase hatte die aber einfach so auftraten. hat wohl eher was mit den Chakren zu tun oder so. Ich hab mir dann mal Einkaufstüten um die Hände gebunden. Der Duft wurde etwas abgeschwächt, aber ich hatte das Gefühl daß ich noch etwas Duft wahr nehmen würde. Das kann ja aber nicht sein da der Duft nicht durch die Tüten kann. Also muß das Einbildung gewesen sein.

Das ganze wahr wohl Suggestion vom feinsten. Der Duft aus den Händen kam 2009 übriegens wieder denn da fing mir auch wieder das Herz an zu schmerzen, diesmal aber nur für ein paar Tage dann wars wieder vorbei. (Spelling and grammatical mistakes in the original)

(It was clear to me then that the scent out of the back of my hands couldn't have been real, because before that I had strange scents in my nose on and off which just so happened. Has probably rather something to do with chakras or so. I wound shopping bags around my hands. The scent lessened but I had the feeling that I would still perceive some scent. This cannot be because the scent cannot get through the bags. Therefore it must have been imagination.

The whole [thing] must have been suggestion at its best. The scent out of the hands came back in 2009 by the way, then my heart began to hurt, this time only for a few days then it was over again.)

The experience of scent coming from the back of his hands as well as pain from his heart are coenaesthesic phenomena. It means that these people experience body feelings that go beyond other people's body experiences and develop out of an extreme form of focus on the own body while at the same time enhancing this inwardly directed focus. To witness this phenomenon in the text is thus another facet of John Doe's deviant mind style. Notice that although he has his suspicions about the scent and therefore conducts a 'test', the delusive sense perception remains against his own better judgement, which illustrates that for people suffering from coenaesthesia feelings, such as the ones described by John Doe, they feel real.

The presence of material action processes serves to reinforce the predominance of mental processes since the actions John Doe reports are generally directly connected to his cognitive states and mental processing. Hence, in Example 3, the material action reported ('I wound shopping bags around my hands') serves as a 'test' of his mental perception (the scent) on the basis of his suspicion that the scent might not be real. The same applies to Example 1 where the spitting as a material action follows after and is grounded in mental processes of perception and cognition such as 'She constantly stung out of the corner of my eyes ...' (perception) and 'Because such a woman who does such a thing only deserves to be spit at in my opinion' (cognition). Other than being a material action process, the spitting could also be perceived as a mental (evaluative) reaction and thus underlines the pattern already identified of a prevalence of mental process types in the JDT. John Doe's preference for this process type is another building block in constructing his mind style.

12.6   John Doe's Use of Modality

In line with his inwardly directed focus as already indicated by his frequent use of I-talk and mental processes stands his preference for epistemic modality. To reach this conclusion, the same 710 concordance lines for 'ich' ('I') were analysed for modal expressions. Epistemic modality occurs in 221 concordance lines, boulomaic in 82 and deontic in 46. Examples of epistemic modality are provided in the following extract.

Example 4 (taken from Example 1)
When she was still crouching and wanted to pick up her piece of paper she nodded with her head and mumbled 'Mhm' as if she knew what this was about. When she rose and stood at the till her hands were trembling. It was clear to me that I was possibly right and she had just given herself away.

The three sentences in Example 4 contain three instances of epistemic modality: (1) 'as so she knew what this was about' (conditional), (2) 'it was clear to me' (high degree of certainty) and (3) 'that I was possibly right' (lesser degree of certainty). Here, John Doe speculates about the shop assistant's thoughts by trying to read her mind (which Stockwell and Mahlberg [2015, p. 133] call 'mind-modelling' born out of ToM). The relevant part of this theory for the study at hand is that 'we do not assume a "blank slide" when a person is imagining others ... instead we assume a template of selfhood [i.e. the self as a basis] that is already quite richly filled out'; incoming information is perceived as 'cues' used 'to alter their self-template in order to differentiate it away from that self and towards the other person' (Stockwell & Mahlberg 2015, p. 133).

Example 4 displays a factual inability on John Doe's part to understand the shop assistant's 'Mhm' correctly, which might correlate with the already stated fact that persons with schizophrenia exhibit pragmatic impairments in co-occurrence with a ToM deficit (Champagne-Lavau & Stip 2010, p. 285). Supposing John Doe heard the shop assistant's utterance correctly, the shop assistant in this situation of recent assault probably wants to de-escalate by not contradicting him and rather gives a neutral response or even fakes consent depending on the intonation of her utterance. Seen from John Doe's perspective, he (probably correctly) observes a nodding of her head, a verbal utterance 'Mhm' and a trembling of her hands. Despite his correct perceptions, he then fails to process this information correctly. He perceives the crouching shop assistant based on a template of his own self including his thoughts about her, in particular, his detestation of her because following from his erroneous mind-modelling she initiated his exposure through rejection. The crouching shop assistant has no chance to understand the sarcastic undertone in his earlier request, 'And pass on my best greetings to your friends' (see Example 1 for context), which can be understood only if his utterance is placed in context with his absurd mind-modelling. Seen from his point of view, he had to take two rebuffs despite earlier various and repeated flirtation. The crux is, however, that the flirting he perceived was in fact another misinterpretation of the shop assistant's behaviour which was probably not even directed at him (the stretching) or just ordinary social interaction between shop assistant and customer in a supermarket (the look in the eyes or the brief touch of hands when returning change). Seen in context of his mind-modelling he is bound to take her utterance 'Mhm' as affirmation and thus in a reassuring sense. Such a positive affirmation is particularly important in his understanding of events because through the insulting act of spitting he has, to his mind, resolved a perceived power imbalance (Presser 2013, p. 87): he had been fooled by the shop assistants, and the crouching shop assistant he spat at acts as proxy.

Whereas in Example 3 John Doe's world knowledge tells him that there cannot be a scent coming from the back of his hands, he does not question his mind-modelling in Example 4 but instead perceives confirmation from the crouching shop assistant's reaction. The difference between Examples 3 and 4 is that in Example 3 he questions himself, whereas in Example 4 he mind-models other people. However, it needs to be mentioned that the third instance of modal expression in Example 4 indicates some doubt (modal adverb 'wohl'/ 'probably'). Despite this doubt concerning mind-modelling, he fails to pursue any remaining doubts further.

Another example clearly exhibits his deficits in social encounters despite his constant mind-modelling.

Example 5 (taken from Example 1)
Then I stood at the till and this woman suddenly stood behind me, I turned around towards her but

[1] didn't know what this meant,
[2] whether I should do something or
[3] whether she merely wanted to give me a sign.

Here again, three epistemic modal expressions (indicated by numbers 1–3) reveal John Doe's inability to interpret the fact that the shop assistant was queuing behind him correctly. The second instance contains a deontic expression ('solle'/'should') beside the epistemic ('ob'/'whether') and relates to a social conventions of politeness (Leech 2014). This example indicates that whereas in Example 1 he took his time for mind-modelling and acted only once he felt he had reached a conclusion, here in Example 5 an almost spontaneous mind-modelling result is required from him, which he is unable to produce.

An analysis of John Doe's use of modal expressions allows revealing access to his mind and to his mind-modelling processes and allows for understanding his motives for the crime, namely, a misinterpretation of his presumably correct observations. It also shows to what extent epistemic modality is intertwined with John Doe's mind-modelling and is thus another building block towards his mind style. I-talk, mental processes and epistemic modality have been identified so far as consistent linguistic patterns across the text, and the 'cumulative effect of these linguistic choices' eventually leads to 'the creation of a deviant mind style' (McIntyre 2005, p. 25).

The next example indicates how John Doe uses modal expressions for hedging purposes.

Example 6 (taken from Example 1)
... da ich ja eigentlich eh nicht wirklich interessiert war.
... because I actually indeed hadn't been really interested anyway.

This clause contains four modal words used both epistemically and for hedging. All four soften the assertion that John Doe had not been interested in making personal contact with the shop assistants: (1) 'ja'/'indeed', (2) 'eigentlich'/'actually', (3) 'eh'/'anyway' and (4) (nicht) 'wirklich'/(not) 'really'. Given the context of this clause (see Example 1), the other results presented so far and the fact that the word 'frauen'/'women' is the highest-ranking content word in the JDT word list (rank 30, 81 occurrences), it might be safe to suggest that John Doe actually means the opposite of what he says and that this utterance thus contains implied meaning. To categorically state that he was interested in going out with a shop assistant right from the start but failed to arrange a date although the shop assistants were flirting with him would be face-threatening (Brown & Levinson 1987) to the self. He therefore has to maintain his reasoning throughout the entire text, including this clause, so he does not contradict himself and give away his (secret) wishes. In order not to lose face he can only implicitly (and not openly) state that he was, in fact, interested. The full implied meaning of this utterance, however, cannot be explored without taking into account the negation it contains. I therefore continue on Example 6 in the next section.

12.7   John Doe's Use of Negation

Out of the 710 sentences analysed, 164 contain negation which has the potential to produce 'a hypothetical version of reality' (Jeffries 2010). Leaving the modal adverbials in Example 6 to the side for a moment, two scenarios are evoked by the clause and the negator in it, namely, (1) John Doe had been positively interested and (2) he 'hadn't been' (negative particle 'nicht'/'n't'). Both scenarios are constructed in opposition to each other following from the oppositional character of negation, namely, between presence and absence of an event, a state or an existence (Nahajec 2009, p. 109). In detail, the state of not being interested is opposed to the 'non-state' (ibid.) of being interested. The pragmatic presupposition arising from this negated utterance (the clause and its context) is that the reader might have expected John Doe to be actually interested. At this stage of interpretation the modal adverbials become relevant which, because there are so many and they all work on the same trajectory of meaning, flout the Gricean cooperation maxims of quantity (this contribution is over-informative) and manner (contribution is not brief and orderly) (Grice 1975, p. 47). Arising from this flout is an implicature, namely, the implicit negation of the negator, which turns the assertion into a positive one: John Doe had, in fact, been interested. The oppositional 'non-state' of positive interest becomes thus the only alternative left after the 'state' of no interest becomes obsolescent.

Another example illustrating John Doe's use of negation is the following.

Example 7
Für mich ist Fakt ich will keine Freundin mehr und auch Freunde können mir gestohlen bleiben denn auch hier in dieser Stadt hatte ich noch keine Freunde, verzichte ich echt drauf, da geh ich lieber in die Psychiatrie.

(For me it's a fact I want no girlfriend anymore and also friends can go hang because also here in this town I have had no friends yet, I really relinquish, I instead rather go to the psychiatry [psychiatric ward].)

This sentence contains four instances of negation, two expressed by a content verb ('gestohlen bleiben'/'go hang'; 'verzichte'/'relinquish') and two adjectival negators ('keine'/'no'). All negation relates to girlfriend/friends whom John Doe does not have and claims he has no wish for. These negations pragmatically presuppose that the reader might have expected John Doe to have a wish for friends or a girlfriend. Here again, an extensive use of negation (an overkill) turns the assertion into its opposite and implies that John Doe really does wish for social contacts. One might even go as far as to state that he might feel lonely, which stands in line with the fact that persons with schizophrenia suffer from social withdrawal. Assertions like those in Examples 6 and 7 can be regarded as a (sub)conscious expression of emotional needs, if not a cry for help. Following from his misinterpretations and thus his deficient mind-modelling, other people perceive his reactions at least as strange, which then leads to his social exclusion where his wishes for acceptance, friendship and companionship remain unanswered.

12.8   John Doe's Use of Metaphorical Expressions

This section on metaphors concludes the analysis of the JDT for patterns of mind style. So far we have identified a statistically significant overuse of first-person-singular pronouns, indicating an almost exclusive focus on the self, which is reaffirmed by his preference for mental processes, mainly perception and cognition. Material action intention processes are also frequent but serve in a supportive role to allow the narrative to move forward and bring about more mental processes. In line with this is John Doe's use of epistemic modal expressions, which fully exposes his dilemma. Although he spends a lot of time on mind-modelling, he fails to interpret his accurate and detailed observations of other people's behaviour according to social norms and conventions. His erroneous interpretations, in particular, of the flirting, lead to various stages of mind-modelling, taking into account new observations, and eventually to a perceived inferiority of the self. As this contradicts his understanding of the self, he finds the situation unbearable and takes action (the spitting) to resolve the perceived power imbalance. Although John Doe clearly exhibits a ToM deficit, he uses higher levels of language such as implicatures or metaphors; the latter will be explored in this section. Whether he is able to understand implicatures and metaphors when used by others cannot be examined with this kind of data. An indication that he does not might be his frequently inaccurate mind-modelling, witnessed in his misinterpretation of the shop assistant's 'Mmh' as affirmation.

The employment of conceptual metaphors or, more generally, figurative language 'usually requires more cognitive resources' (Bohrn et al. 2012, p. 2681) compared with the use of words or the construction of sentences as metaphorical meaning arises from an expression and its context. Detecting conceptual metaphors in the JDT means carrying out manual analysis of the data, as automatic metaphor detection software is still under development

(Sardinha 2010). An examination of the metaphors used by John Doe will, for reasons of space constrains, focus on those occurring in the German text as translated in Example 1.

Equal to the already mentioned fictional character Bromden in *One Flew over the Cuckoo's Nest* (Semino & Swindlehurst 1996), John Doe appears to prefer source domains which can be related to the human body and its sensory abilities. This stems from the long-standing belief that metaphorical meaning 'arises from the mapping of bodily source domain knowledge onto different domains of experience' because the human body is 'assumed to be purely physical and completely non-metaphorical'.[10] This means that John Doe makes sense of the world around him by relating everything to his own body. In relation to his mind style it is of interest which overarching metaphor themes he uses. An analysis of the metaphors in Example 1 shows three groups of metaphorical expressions which all have a source domain relating to the human body.

The first group of metaphorical expressions in Example 1 can be assigned to the conceptual metaphor ABSTRACT CONCEPTS ARE TANGIBLE OBJECTS. Into this category fall expressions like 'mir ein Stück Würde und Menschlichkeit wieder zurückzuholen'/'retrieve a piece of dignity and humanness' like retrieving a lost object or 'schmiß mir nur ein kaltes "Nö" entgegen'/'only threw a cold "Nö" at me' as if a verbal response can be thrown like a ball. Further, his rejection ('2 Körben'/'2 baskets') and the mental act of him working up courage ('fasste mir ein Herz'/'took heart') are perceived as tangible objects (like the heart) he can touch with his hands. Last, 'ein Zeichen geben'/'to give a sign' is also understood as if a gesture is an object that can actually be handed over to somebody else.

The second group of metaphorical expressions John Doe uses can be summarised with the conceptual metaphor MENTAL PERCEPTION/COGNITION IS BODILY EXPERIENCE. Into this category fall the expressions 'nerven'/'to annoy/to get on one's nerves', 'stach mir aus den Augenwinkeln hervor'/'stung out of the corner of my eyes', 'ließ mich kalt'/'left me indifferent/cold', 'wurde scharf'/'getting hot/spicy'. All these examples are mental perceptions which he in fact perceives with his body. The already mentioned concept of coenaesthesis is related to this category, as it is evidence of hyper-sensation towards (imagined) body experiences.

The third group can be given the headline INITIATING IS MANUAL LABOUR. Into this category fall 'anbaggern'/'flirting/digging' as well as 'in die Wege geleitet'/'initiated/guided'. The physical act of 'digging' is used to describe

---

[10] As mentioned by Gibbs in an interview (2019) where he also contests this belief and instead argues that 'bodily sensations and actions are often infused with metaphorical symbolic meaning', p. 5.

'flirting' in colloquial terms, thus John Doe perceives 'flirting' in terms of manual labour. In the phrase 'Sollte sie das alles in die Wege geleitet haben' (Should she have initiated/conducted all this) the mentioned woman is constructed as guiding the actions, again a material action done by a women, similar to 'digging'.

The expression 'die Brüste im Fernseher hüpfen sehen'/'to see the breasts bouncing on TV' is not metonymy as the breasts do not stand for the entire female body in a figurative relationship, nor meronymy because of a lack of semantic relationship. John Doe actually means this expression literally and what he claimed to have seen on TV might in fact have been a delusion.

The expression 'Der Ton macht die Musik'/'The tone makes the music' is a German idiomatic expression based on a meronymical sense relation between music consisting of tones which, in a metaphorical sense, relates tone in talking (variation in the pitch of language) to music.

This examination of John Doe's overarching metaphor themes underlines two things, namely, that they are not to be regarded as innovative (which correlates with an inability to master higher levels of language) and, second, that his exclusive use of body-related metaphors underlines his inwardly directed focus if not even reveals his dilemma where his last resort of trust is his own body (which, due to his disorder, is not trustworthy either – see Example 3). Doe cannot trust other people, for example, the shop assistants, who, according to his understanding, were flirting with him and then suddenly changed their minds and even made fun of him when he approached them.

12.9   Conclusion

In summary, John Doe's mind style is characterised by an almost exclusive and seemingly compulsive focus on the self as well as impaired mind-modelling, both leading to social exclusion. The language patterns identified are an overarching body-related theme in his use of metaphors as well as the already summarised first-person-singular pronoun use paired with the predicator, predominantly exhibiting mental processes as well as his preference for epistemic modal expressions which also serve as hedges. These four consistent linguistic patterns exhibit John Doe's mind style, characterised by constant observing, both of the self and of other people's behaviour. His narrative as published on his website provides him with an opportunity to conceptualise the self by making sense of his own feelings as well as of other people's behaviour towards him. His social exclusion, it might be claimed, is at least partially brought about by his erroneous mind-modelling results, which lead to mental cognitions such as a self-perceived inferior position against which he rebels. His subsequent actions such as spitting then draw him further into seclusion and perpetuate a vicious circle from which he cannot break free.

References

Anthony, L. (2014). *AntConc(3.4.4w)* [Computer Software]. Tokyo: Waseda University. www.laurenceanthony.net/.

Bennett, J. (1981). *Oral History and Delinquency: The Rhetoric of Criminology.* Chicago: University of Chicago Press.

Boase-Beier, J. (2003). Mind Style Translated. *Style*, 37(3), 253–265.

Bockting, I. (1994). Mind Style as an Interdisciplinary Approach to Characterisation in Faulkner. *Language and Literature*, 3(3), 157–174.

Bohrn, I. C., Altmann, U., & Jacobs, A. M. (2012). Looking at the Brains behind Figurative Language: A Quantitative Meta-Analysis of Neuroimaging Studies on Metaphor, Idiom, and Irony Processing. *Neuropsychologia*, 50, 2669–2683.

Brown, P., & Levinson, S. C. (1987). *Politeness: Some Universals in Language Usage.* Cambridge: Cambridge University Press.

Champagne-Lavau, M., & Stip, E. (2010). Pragmatic and Executive Dysfunction in Schizophrenia. *Journal of Neurolinguistics*, 23, 285–296.

Chomsky, N. (1966). *Cartesian Linguistics.* New York: Harper & Row.

Compère, L., Mam-Lam-Fook, C., Amado, I., Nys, M., Lalanne, J., Grillon, M.-L., ... Piolino, P. (2016). Self-Reference Recollection Effect and Its Relation to Theory of Mind: An Investigation in Healthy Controls and Schizophrenia. *Consciousness and Cognition*, 42, 51–64.

Demjén, Z. (2015). *Sylvia Plath and the Language of Affective States: Written Discourse and the Experience of Depression.* London: Bloomsbury.

Dore, M. (2017). Narrative Strategies and Mind Style in Emma Donoghue's Room. In D. Montini, ed., *Fictions*. Studi sulla narratività XVI. Style and Stories: Contemporary Stylistics and Narrativity. Pisa: Fabrizio Serra Editore.

Dorst, A. G. (2019). Translating Metaphorical Mind Style: MACHINERY and ICE Metaphors in Ken Kesey's *One Flew over the Cuckoo's Nest. Perspectives*, 27(6), 875–889.

Faulkner, W. (1929). *The Sound and the Fury.* London: Jonathan Cape and Harrison Smith.

Fowler, R. (1977). *Linguistics and the Novel.* London: Methuen.

France, J., & Muir, N., eds. (1997). *Communication and the Mentally Ill Patient.* London: Jessical Kingsley Publishers.

Freud, S. (1901). *Psychopathology of Everyday Life.* New York: Basic Books.

Fuchs, T. (1995). Coenästhesie: Zur Geschichte des Gemeingefühls. *Zeitschrift für klinische Psychologie, Psychopathologie und Psychotherapie*, 43, 103–112.

Gavins, J. (2007). *Text World Theory: An Introduction.* Edinburgh: Edinburgh University Press.

Gibbons, A. (2019). Using Life and Abusing Life in the Trial of Ahmed Naji: Text World Theory, Adab and the Ethics of Reading. *Journal of Language and Discrimination*, 3(1), 4–31.

Gibbs, R. W., Jr. (2019) The Metaphor Column/Interviewer: C. Rasse. RaAM Newsletter November 2019.

Giovanelli, M. (2018). 'Something happened, something bad': Blackouts, Uncertainties and Event Construal in *The Girl on the Train. Language and Literature*, 27(1), 38–51.

Gregoriou, C. (2007a). *Deviance in Contemporary Crime Fiction*. Basingstoke: Palgrave Macmillan.

(2007b). The Stylistics of True Crime: Mapping the Minds of Serial Killers. In M. Lambrou & P. Stockwell, eds., *Contemporary Stylistics*. London: Continuum, pp. 32–42.

(2011a). *Language, Ideology and Identity in Serial Killer Narratives*. London: Routledge.

(2011b). The Poetics of Deviance in *The Curious Incident of the Dog in the Night-time*. In M. Effron, ed., *The Millennial Detective*. Jefferson, NC: McFarland & Company, pp. 97–111.

(2020). Schematic Incongruity, Conversational Power Play and Criminal Mind Style in Thomas Harris' *Silence of the Lambs*. *Language and Literature*, 29(4), 373–388.

Grice, H. P. (1969). Utterer's Meaning and Intentions. *Philosophical Review*, 78, 147–177.

(1975). Logic and Conversation. In P. Cole & J. Morgan, eds., *Syntax and Semantics, vol. 3: Speech Acts*. New York: Academic Press, pp. 41–58.

Groom, C. J., & Pennebaker, J. W. (2002). Words. *Journal of Research in Personality*, 36, 615–621.

Haddon, M. (2003). *The Curious Incident of the Dog in the Night-time*. Oxford: David Ficklings Books.

Halliday, M. A. K. (1971). Linguistic Function and Literary Style: An Inquiry into the Language of William Golding's *The Inheritors*. In S. Chatman, ed., *Literary Style: A Symposium*. London: Oxford University Press, pp. 330–368.

Heider, F., & Simmel, M. (1944). An Experimental Study of Apparent Behaviour. *American Journal of Psychology*, 57, 243–259.

Hens, G. (2000). What Drives Herbeck? Schizophrenia, Immediacy, and the Poetic Process. *Language and Literature*, 9(1), 43–59.

Herman, D. (2011). Introduction. In D. Herman, ed., *The Emergence of Mind: Representations of Consciousness in Narrative Discourse in English*. Lincoln: University of Nebraska Press, pp. 1–42.

(2016). Building More-than-Human Worlds: *Umwelt* Modelling in Animal Narratives. In J. Gavins & E. Lahey, eds., *World Building: Discourse in the Mind*. London: Bloomsbury.

Hoover, D. L. (2004). Altered Texts, Altered Worlds, Altered Styles. *Language and Literature*, 13(2), 99–118.

Jeffries, L. (2010). *Critical Stylistics: The Power of English*. Basingstoke: Palgrave Macmillan.

Jeffries, L., & McIntyre, D. (2010). *Stylistics*. Cambridge: Cambridge University Press.

Kacewicz, E., Pennebaker, J. W., Davis, M., Jeon, M., & Graesser, A. C. (2014). Pronoun Use Reflects Standings in Social Hierarchies. *Journal of Language and Social Psychology*, 33(2), 125–143.

Kiang, M. (2010). Schizotypy and Language: A Review. *Journal of Neurolinguistics*, 23, 193–203.

Kircher, T. T. J., & Leube, D. T. (2003). Self-Consciousness, Self-Agency and Schizophrenia. *Consciousness and Cognition*, 12, 656–669.

Klein, S. B., Altinyazar, V., & Metz, M. A. (2013). Facets of Self in Schizophrenia: The Reliability and Accuracy of Trait Self-Knowledge. *Clinical Psychological Science*, 1(3), 276–289.

Kuperberg, G. R. (2010). Language in Schizophrenia Part 1: An Introduction. *Language and Linguistics Compass*, 4(8), 576–589.

Kuperberg, G. R., & Caplan, D. (2003). Language Dysfunction in Schizophrenia. In R. B. Schiffer, S. M. Rao, & B. S. Fogel, eds., *Neuropsychiatry*, 2nd ed. Philadelphia: Lippincott Williams and Wilkins, pp. 444–466.

Lacan, J. (1968). *The Language of the Self: The Function of Language in Psychoanalysis*. Baltimore: Johns Hopkins University Press.

Leech, G. (2014). *The Pragmatics of Politeness*. New York: Oxford University Press.

Lugea, J. (2016). Spanglish Dialogue in You and Me: An Absurd World and Seile Mind Style. In J. Gavins & E. Lahey, eds., *World Building: Discourse in the Mind*. London: Bloomsbury.

Lynn, V. (2019). Prison Autobiographical Narratives: Making Sense of Personal and Social (Racial) Transformation. *Crime Media Culture*, 17(1), 65–84.

McCarthy-Jones, S. (2017). The Concept of Schizophrenia Is Coming to an End – Here's Why. The Conversation. http://theconversation.com/the-concept-of-schizophrenia-is-coming-to-an-end-heres-why-82775.

McIntyre, D. (2005). Logic, Reality and Mind Style in Alan Bennett's *The Lady in the Van*. *Journal of Literary Semantics*, 34, 21–40.

McIntyre, D., & Walker, B. (2019). *Corpus Stylistics: Theory and Practice*. Edinburgh: Edinburgh University Press.

McKenna, P. J., & Oh, T. M. (2005). *Schizophrenic Speech*. Cambridge: Cambridge University Press.

Mitchell, M., Hollingshead, K., & Coppersmith, G. (2015). Quantifying the Language of Schizophrenia in Social Media. Paper presented at the 2nd Workshop on Computational Linguistics and Clinical Psychology: From Linguistic Signal to Clinical Reality, Denver, Colorado.

Montoro, R. (2011). Multimodal Realisations of Mind Style in Enduring Love. In R. Piazza, M. Bednarek, & F. Rossi, eds., *Telecinematic Discourse: Approaches to the Language of Films and Television Series*. Amsterdam: John Benjamins.

Nahajec, L. (2009). Negation and the Creation of Implicit Meaning in Poetry. *Language and Literature*, 18(2), 109–127.

Nørgaard, N., Busse, B., & Montoro, R. (2010). *Key Terms in Stylistics*. London: Continuum.

Nuttall, L. (2015). Attributing Minds to Vampires in Richard Matheson's *I Am Legend*. *Language and Literature*, 24(1), 23–39.

  (2018). *Mind Style and Cognitive Grammar*. London: Bloomsbury.

  (2019). Transitivity, Agency, Mind Style: What's the Lowest Common Denominator? *Language and Literature*, 28(2), 159–179.

O'Connor, P. (2000). *Speaking of Crime: Narratives of Prisoners*. Lincoln: University of Nebraska Press.

  (2015). Telling Moments: Narrative Hot Spots in Accounts of Criminal Acts. In L. Presser & S. Sandberg, eds., *Narrative Criminology: Understanding Stories of Crime*. New York: New York University Press.

Pennebaker, J. W. (2002). What Our Words Can Say about Us: Toward a Broader Language Psychology. *Psychological Science Agenda*, 15, 8–9.

Pennebaker, J. W., Boyd, R. L., Jordan, K., & Blackburn, K. (2015). *The Development and Psychometric Properties of LIWC2015*. Austin: University of Texas at Austin.

Pennebaker, J. W., Francis, M. E., & Booth, R. J. (2001). *Linguistic Inquiry and Word Count (LIWC): LIWC 2001*. Mahwah, NJ: Erlbaum.

Pennebaker, J. W., & Lay, T. C. (2002). Language Use and Personality during Crises: Analyses of Mayor Rudolph Giuliani's Press Conferences. *Journal of Research in Personality*, 36, 271–282.

Pennebaker, J. W., Mehl, M. R., & Niederhoffer, K. G. (2003). Psychological Aspects of Natural Language Use: Our Words, Our Selves. *Annual Review of Psychology*, 54, 547–577.

Pillière, L. (2013). Mind Style: Deviance from the Norm? *Études de Stylistique Anglaise*, 4, 67–80.

Presser, L. (2009). The Narratives of Offenders. *Theoretical Criminology*, 13(2), 177–200.

  (2013). *Why We Harm*. New Brunswick, NJ: Rutgers University Press.

  (2016). Criminology and the Narrative Turn. *Crime Media Culture*, 12(2), 137–151.

Presser, L., & Sandberg, S., eds. (2015). *Narrative Criminology: Understanding Stories of Crime*. New York: New York University Press.

Rado, S. (1953). Dynamics and Classification of Disordered Behavior. *American Journal of Psychiatry*, 110, 406–416.

Rude, S., Gortner, E. M., & Pennebaker, J. W. (2004). Language Use of Depressed and Depression-Vulnerable College Students. *Cognition Emotion*, 18(8), 1121–1133.

Rundquist, E. (2020). The Cognitive Grammar of Drunkenness: Consciousness Representation in *Under the Volcano*. *Language and Literature*, 29(1), 39–56.

Sandberg, S., & Ugelvik, T. (2016). The Past, Present and Future of Narrative Criminology: A Review and an Invitation. *Crime Media Culture*, 12(2), 129–136.

Sardinha, T. B. (2010). A Program for Finding Metaphor Candidates in Corpora. *The ESPecialist*, 31(1), 49–67.

Schmidt-Knaebel, S. (1998). *Sprache und Schizophrenie: Eine kommentierte Bibliographie zur Schizolinguistik*. Hamburg: Helmut Buske Verlag GmbH.

Semino, E. (2002). A Cognitive Stylistic Approach to Mind Style in Narrative Fiction. In E. Semino & J. Culpeper, eds., *Cognitive Stylistics: Language and Cognition in Text Analysis*. Amsterdam: John Benjamins, pp. 95–122.

  (2007). Mind Style 25 Years On. *Style*, 41(2), 153–203.

  (2014). Pragmatic Failure, Mind Style and Characterisation in Fiction about Autism. *Language and Literature*, 23(2), 141–158.

Semino, E., & Swindlehurst, K. (1996). Metaphor and Mind Style in Ken Kesey's *One Flew over the Cuckoo's Nest*. *Style*, 30(1), 143–166.

Spitzer, M., Uehlein, F., Schwartz, M. A., & Mundt, C., eds. (1992). *Phenomenology, Language & Schizophrenia*. New York: Springer-Verlag.

Stirman, S. W., & Pennebaker, J. W. (2001). Word Use in the Poetry of Suicidal and Nonsuicidal Poets. *Psychosomatic Medicine*, 63, 517–522.

Stockwell, P., & Mahlberg, M. (2015). Mind-Modelling with Corpus Stylistics in *David Copperfield*. *Language and Literature*, 24(2), 129–147.

Tabbert, U. (2015). *Crime and Corpus: The Linguistic Representation of Crime in the Press*. Amsterdam: John Benjamins.
(2016). *Language and Crime: Constructing Offenders and Victims in Newspaper Reports*. London: Palgrave Macmillan.
Tausczik, Y. R., & Pennebaker, J. W. (2010). The Psychological Meaning of Words: LIWC and Computerized Text Analysis Methods. *Journal of Language and Social Psychology*, 29(1), 24–54.
Weintraub, W. (1981). *Verbal Behavior: Adaptation and Psychopathology*. New York: Springer.
(1989). *Verbal Behavior in Everyday Life*. New York: Springer.
Whiteley, S. (2020). Interpreting (Autistic?) Mind Style: Categorisation and Narrative Interrelation in Reading Group Discussions of *The Universe versus Alex Woods*. *Anglistik: International Journal of English Studies*, 31(1), 71–89.
Williams, S. (2017). Review of *Sylvia Plath and the Language of Affective States: Written Discourse and the Experience of Depression*, by Zsófia Demjén, 2015. London: Bloomsbury Publishing. *Discourse & Society*, 28(3), 319–320.

Appendix

An extract from John Doe's account of events, taken from his web page, including spelling and grammatical mistakes (translated in Example 1).

Mein Erlebnis im Supermarkt

Sommer 2009 fiel mir immer eine junge Verkäuferin auf. Sie stach mir immer aus den Augenwinkeln hervor sah aber erst wer es war wer da so auffiel als hin schaute wer das denn wieder ist. Ich war total genervt im Discounter von dieser einen Frau (möchte an dieser Stelle auch mal anmerken daß ich so etwas noch nie hatte daß eine Frau so nervt) und wollte meine Ruhe haben da ich zur Zeit den ganzen Tag im Garten bin und auch dort übernachte. Die Frau stach aus den Augenwinkeln hervor ich wußte aber zu der Zeit noch nicht warum das so ist. Es war einfach nur nervig.

. . .

Dann Ende Oktober/November 2009 fingen mehrere (nicht alle an einem Tag) junge sehr attraktive Frauen an im Supermarkt zu arbeiten an und baggerten mich aber eigenartigerweise an. Ich war aber nicht interessiert da ich wie ich jetzt feststellte mir im Garten etwas erarbeitet habe was ich bis dahin nicht kannte.. . .

Die Frauen jedoch baggerten fleißig weiter. Eine der Frauen schaute mich immer in die Augen ich ihr leider auch aber warum wußte ich eigentlich nicht irgendwie war mir das auch egal. Diese Frau berührte mich nicht mal ebenmal zufällig beim Wechselgeld sondern sie streichelte meine Handinnenfläche mit ihrem Handrücken. Auch das ließ mich kalt und ich denke das konnten die Kassiererinnen auch spüren.

Dann eines Tages im Dezember 2009, ich hatte immer noch kein Interesse an Flirtereien im Supermarkt, stand ich allein an der Kasse, da streckte sich die

Kassiererin (komischerweise war es keine der Frauen die mich zuvor angebaggert hatten) über ihre Stuhllehne sehr weit nach hinten so daß ich nur noch ihre Brüste sah (ihren Kopf sah ich schon gar nicht mehr) und streckte mir diese für mind. 2–3 Sekunden vielleicht auch länger entgegen. Ich war so perplex daß ich gar nicht wußte was das denn nun wieder war. Zu hause angekommen wurde ich dann leider scharf da ich nun mal auf Brüste stehe. Leider sah ich dann auch noch 3 tage im Anschluss die Brüste im Fernseher hüpfen und mußte immer an diese Frau denken die mir ihre Brüste entgegengestreckt hatte....

Ich dachte mir wenn ich schon mal scharf bin und die Frauen mich eh anbaggern dann könnte ich ja auch mal eine ansprechen ob wir uns mal verabreden wollen. Ich suchte mir eine andere blonde Frau aus die mich ebenfalls anbaggerte, also nicht die die mir immer in die Augen schaute und mich übertrieben streichelte. Als ich wieder im Supermarkt war kam mir diese eine Frau entgegen und ich grüßte sie freundlich und sie grüßte freundlich zurück. Dann stand ich an der Kasse und diese Frau stand plötzlich hinter mir ich drehte mich zu ihr um wußte aber nicht was das nun bedeutet, ob ich irgendwas machen solle oder ob sie mir nur ein Zeichen geben wollte. Aber da bemerkte ich daß die Kassiererin die zu der Zeit kassierte mich und diese andere Kassiererin abwechselnd ankuckte und sehr nervös schien. Nach 5 Sekunden war die Kassiererin hinter mir wieder weg.

Wieder zu Hause angekommen wollte ich nun wissen woran ich bin und fasste mir ein Herz und habe beschlossen nochmal zum Supermarkt zu gehen um diese eine Frau anzusprechen. Ich gin also nochmal zum Supermarkt und es dauerte nicht lange da kam sie mir auch schon entgegen, was dann aber passierte habe ich so nicht erwartet. Ich fragte sie ob ich sie kurz sprechen kann und dann ob sie Lust hätte mal mit mir auszugehen. Sie blieb aber kaum stehen und schmiß mir nur ein kaltes 'Nö' entgegen. So hatte ich das nicht erwartet. Der Ton macht die Musik. Ich kaufte mir dann noch eine Kleinigkeit und als ich anderen Kasse stand sah ich wie diese Frau in die Info ging schaute mich dabei nochmal an und grinste frech. Wie es mir da ging kann sich wohl jeder denken. Das komische ist daß dies auch der letzte Tag war an dem sie im Supermarkt arbeitete, sie hat wohl hinterher gemerkt daß das ein Fehler von ihr war sich hinter mich zu stellen denn so gibt es ja jetzt eine Zeugin die gesehen hat daß sich diese Frau hinter mich gestellt hat an der Kasse.

Ich sprach dann noch eine weitere Frau an die mich anbaggerte die aber schon länger im Supermarkt arbeitete, aber auch die entgegnete mir mit dem gleichen Worten 'Nö'. Nach 2 Körben hatte ich dann keine Lust mehr da ich ja eigentlich eh nicht wirklich interessiert war. Eigentlich habe ich diese Frauen auch nur gefragt weil ich wissen wollte woran ich bin. Was wäre gewesen wenn ich sie angesprochen hätte. Das habe ich mich schon oft gefragt als ich mich nicht traute.

...
Ich beschloss mir das nicht gefallen zu lassen und da erinnerte ich mich wieder an die eine junge Frau im Supermarkt die mir immer aufgefallen war. Sollte sie das etwa alles in die Wege geleitet haben wenn nicht sogar ihre Freundinnen dazu angestiftet haben. Da sich bei mir der Verdacht immer mehr bestätigte beschloß ich mir ein Stück Würde und Menschlichkeit wieder zurück zu holen. Also beschloß ich sie anzuspucken wenn sie das nächstemal an der Kasse sitzt. Denn so eine Frau die so etwas macht gehört meiner Meinung nach nur angespuckt. Mir fiel zu dem Zeitpunkt auch nichts anderes ein. Gesagt getan. Ich spuckte sie an aber dann aus der Intuition heraus: Ihr fiel irgendein Zettel aus der Hand und als sie ihn aufhob sagte ich zu ihr: 'Und grüße deine Freundinnen schön von mir.' Noch als sie in der Hocke saß und ihren zettel aufheben wollte nickte sie mit dem Kopf und murmelte 'Mhm' so als wenn sie wüsste worum es geht. Als sie wieder aufstand und wieder an der Kasse stand zitterten ihre Hände. Für mich war klar daß ich wohl richtig liege und sie sich grade verraten hatte. 1 oder 2 Tage sagte ich dann noch zu ihr 'Schlampe' im Vorbeigehen, wobei ich nicht weiß warum ich das sagte.

13 Narrower or Broader Ground? The Role and Function of Metaphors in Legal Discourse

Douglas Mark Ponton and Marco Canepa

13.1 Introduction

Metaphors are a fundamental resource of both formal and informal legal discourse, as many recent studies testify (Smith 2007; Houbert 2008; Morra 2010; Richard 2014; etc.). In non-technical discourse about legal topics, metaphor serves as a means of conceptualising processes which are frequently abstract or hard to comprehend. Justice may exploit the source domain of machines ('to oil the wheels of justice', Cognitive Metaphor JUSTICE IS A MACHINE) or that of roads ('the paths of justice', Cognitive Metaphor LIFE IS A JOURNEY). (On the theory of Cognitive or Conceptual metaphor, see Kövecses 2010 and also Chapters 1 and 2 in this volume.) It may call on 'light' in the darkness, it may conceive of justice as a commodity with a 'price', as a 'game', and so on.

These linguistic practices are long-established; Shakespeare's 'the insolence of office' may sound metonymical to modern ears, but 'the law's delay' is clearly metaphorical.[1] Thus, metaphor is an important resource for the layman to conceptualise justice, to permit discussion of its complexities. Turning to the professional use of legal language, the contribution made by metaphor is far stronger, and this constitutes the topic of our chapter. Our fundamental aim is to show that metaphor is closely involved in the formation and delineation of precise legal concepts, and in the discursive processes by means of which they become accepted or applied, modified, and so on.

In a traditional, 'Aristotelian', conception of the functions of metaphor, they are seen as a component of good verbal style, and as part of the verbal resources of 'forensic rhetoric'. Aristotle thought of metaphor as a compressed form of analogy, which gave aesthetic pleasure because of its 'clarity and sweetness and strangeness' (Aristotle 2007, p. 200). He saw it, at least partly, as a means of conceptualising the unfamiliar in terms of the familiar (Kirby 1997, pp. 541–542). One of his metaphorical analogies, old age as the sunset of life (Aristotle 1997, p. 151), exemplifies this; the source domain or 'sunset'

---

[1] Both quotes are from Hamlet's 'to be or not to be' soliloquy.

is a familiar, repetitive experience for all, while no one can fully comprehend what old age (the target domain) is like until it happens to them.

Modern perspectives in cognitive metaphor theory, such as Lakoff and Johnson's (2003) influential model, relegate to a secondary position what was probably key for Aristotle: the aesthetic/pleasurable dimension to metaphor and its role in winning arguments. From being seen as just another among many rhetorical devices, a central role is claimed for metaphor in human language development, in cognition, and in the evolution and structuring of human thought (Lakoff & Johnson 2003, p. 202). Recent studies of legal language are in harmony with cognitive approaches to the point that it has been argued (Klinck 1992, in Richard 2014) that legal reasoning is itself metaphorical and that metaphor may constitute an intrinsic feature of the law itself (Philippopoulos-Mihalopoulos 2016).

In this chapter, we suggest that legal metaphors are vital resources for legal specialists, on many fronts. They have a function in rhetoric, an obligatory continuation of the ancient business of forensic rhetoric, where *ars bene dicendi*, a wide-ranging concept that includes the skilful deployment of metaphors, may help win cases. However, as we shall see, they also play a vital role in the processes through which laws are made and debated, commented on by legal specialists, revised, redrawn, commented upon again, and so on. In other words, they are central to the legal system's understanding of itself, to its 'cognitive' functioning (to state the matter, appropriately enough, metaphorically).[2] Philippopoulos-Mihalopoulos (2016, p. 50) claims that the law is 'understood through metaphors', indeed, that one 'can no longer talk of law and legal metaphors as mere symbolic entities, but as a shared surface between the semiotic and the material'.

In this chapter we first review some of these theoretical issues, which have formed part of the debate within legal philosophy. We then focus on legal metaphors as they appear in the British online legal journal, *Cambridge Law Journal* (CLJ hereafter), which contains articles characteristic of the 'Case and Comment' genre; that is, they describe recent cases from criminal or administrative law and comment on the decisions. Thus, we focus on legal discourse that is freely available and frequently shares the same rhetorical/persuasive aims as the more directly interactive kind found in courtrooms. The comments are generally not neutral; it is usual for the commentator to have a particular point of view, sometimes in favour of the decision, sometimes critical. Thus, there is an implicit argumentative dimension to this discourse, as the writer attempts to engage with possible pro and contra

---

[2] See Dee (2009), for instance, who shows how the 'penumbra' metaphor has shaped judicial thinking in a number of different American contexts. We discuss her paper at some length in the Conclusion.

opinions, and construct support for a particular view. Since contributors to CLJ and its readers are legal professionals of one kind or another, it is plain that such discourse about current cases is highly relevant to the formation and application of current laws.

13.2 Courtroom Discourse: Applying a Syllogism or Developing an Argument?

We must first explore some background issues in the nature of courtroom discourse; in particular, it is necessary to distinguish between a view of justice that sees it as the application of an all-inclusive legal code, and one which instead privileges interpretation and conviction through verbal processes.

Metaphor and analogy, arguably, are rhetorical figures rather than tools for logical reasoning, even though they may be used in legal argumentation to solve problems and justify judicial decisions. They may be, on the one hand, a means of explaining complicated or abstract concepts, but, on the other, they can be used by an able counsel to influence the opinions of judge and jury.

To attempt to draw a line between logic and rhetoric, in legal reasoning, is to refer to a long-standing issue within legal philosophy, which has practical implications for the daily business of courtroom practice (see, e.g., Tarello 1989, 2013; Siltala 2000). The question is whether the law is to be viewed as something which needs to be interpreted by jurists or only applied. The former of these positions entails the use of rhetorical tools by counsels, judges, and many other social actors involved in the legal process. Legal discourse, in this perspective, is inherently persuasive. From the latter point of view, by contrast, the law is a more static entity, a body of rules and judgements which, potentially, covers every possible offence and simply needs to be applied.

Clearly, if law needs to be interpreted, the interpreter is also acting, to a certain extent, as a *lawmaker*, because interpretation assumes that a given legal text can convey different meanings, and hence, different norms may emerge from cases trying to apply it. Interpretation is, per se, a guarantee that dialogical processes, persuasive discourse, and rhetorical figures will be involved in the effort to win a particular case.

To give a concrete example: if there is a sign at the entrance of a children's playground reading 'dogs are not allowed', what does this really mean? Would it be possible to enter with a lion? Or a snake, a cat, a turtle? This, it will be seen immediately, involves interpretation. If an analogy is used (and metaphor, from one perspective, is a figurative form of analogy, as we shall see below), a certain argument can be advanced (*lex minus dicit quam voluit*[3]) that would

---

[3] Translation: 'the law has said less than it would have liked'.

exclude such an extension. In other words, it would be argued that, in its ruling on dogs, the law implicitly intended to include other domestic animals, as well as – by analogy – other potentially dangerous animals such as lions or snakes.[4] Such discursive processes are implicit in the Latin term *ratio*. On the other hand, consider the contrary argument (*a contrariis*), which would result from the application of the concept *ubi lex voluit dixit ubi noluit tacuit*.[5] According to this principle, it can be argued, if the law prohibits dogs it may be assumed to prohibit only dogs and nothing else. This argument prevents inclusion of the cases not expressly and clearly included, and makes for a narrow interpretation of the law.

Even such an apparently simple example as the above, then, illustrates the issue. If the law is simply seen as a formal code to be applied, then a multiplicity of signs will be necessary in front of every park, specifying explicitly which animals are not permitted entry. If interpretation is permitted, then rhetorical figures and persuasive discourse instantly become central features of the legal process.

This distinction, between the law as something to be interpreted, on the one hand, and as an all-inclusive code requiring only to be perfected and then applied, on the other, was a matter of major concern for the legal philosopher Giovanni Tarello (1934–1987), the founder of so-called legal realism as opposed to 'legal positivism'. According to his doctrine, interpretation of the law is a creative process. A given law, expressed as a legal statement, might have several meanings, and these very meanings in themselves constitute different norms expressed by the same text (see Tarello 1989, 2013). As a consequence, figures of legal speech are seen as rhetorical tools rather than logical devices. It is up to the interpreter to use these tools in order to justify norms based on legal statements.

As a matter of fact, as Tarello says, 'the line between interpretation of pre-existing norms and the "creation" of new rules is anything but clear cut'. This applies particularly to modern criminal legal systems such as those of the United Kingdom or United States that are, on principle, adversarial. In such contexts, the judicial decision-maker has no previous opinion or knowledge regarding the facts of the case, and the parties (counsels for defence and prosecutor) bring evidence to the trial and present it to the judge or jurors

---

[4] Grice's Quantity maxim – give as much information as needed and no more – explains why the sign does not specify the whole range of possibly dangerous animals to be excluded from the park, but rather takes the dog as symbolising these. In terms of relevance theory (Sperber & Wilson 1986), it is not necessary to specify many of these, since the world knowledge assumed as shared between the writer of the sign and users of the park will exclude animals such as tigers and poisonous snakes, mostly unknown in a British park.

[5] Translation: 'what the law has wanted, it has said; what the law has not wanted, it has not indicated'.

(i.e. the decision-makers). Counsels make extensive use of rhetorical figures in presenting their cases, in the examination and counter-examination of witnesses, and in closing statements.

Contrast the above picture with the more traditional model, in which deductive reasoning in judicial decisions was thought to hinge on Aristotelian syllogism, the application of perfect logic. The importance of this deductive position was particularly stressed in the age of Enlightenment, when most philosophers of the positive school thought that the application of law, especially if carried out by judges, was a logical and potentially perfectable process. They thought it possible to achieve perfect codification, by following rational thought or natural law. Hence, legal positivism (see Siltala 2000; Alexy 2002) is a doctrine of law that emphasises the search for norms drawn up by the legislator (in civil law systems); in common law models, these are considered to be common law or case law.

These norms and codifications were supposed to be clear, complete, with no faults or contradictions, without antinomy, and, hence, also without any need for interpretation. In consequence, when applying the law, the relevant discursive device was the Aristotelian syllogism. Montesquieu, in this context, speaks of the judiciary as not really a power but 'only the mouth which proclaims the formulation of law' (Montesquieu, in Siltala 2000, p. 3), while Voltaire said that interpretation was always a corruption of the text. Such ideas were common among jurists in the European Enlightenment and most lawmakers in the seventeenth and eighteenth centuries. The picture has changed in the modern period, with the consolidation of practices involving legal argumentation and the use of rhetorical techniques, including metaphor.

13.3 More on the Interpretation of Metaphors

Most accounts of metaphor, including Aristotle's, devote attention to the question of similarity; indeed, metaphor has traditionally been thought of as an *elliptical simile* (Fogelin 1988, p. 27), and the following discussion adopts this perspective, seeing it essentially as a type of *figurative comparison* (p. 32). Searle (1979a, p. 105) says, 'Where an utterance is defective if taken literally, look for an utterance meaning that differs from sentence meaning', and it is this defectiveness, or apparent deviation from Grice's truthfulness maxim (Grice 1989), that alerts listeners to the figurative nature of the language used. 'Blind justice', for example, has to be figurative, since there is no literal sense in which justice, which is basically a set of social and discursive processes, can 'see'; and if it cannot see, then of course it cannot be 'blind'. The hearer will therefore engage in a series of automatic cognitive processes in order to identify the grounds of comparison between the source domain (Lakoff & Johnson 2003), blindness, and the target domain, the law. Interpretation usually involves the dimension of *salience* (Oakes et al. 1994), where possible attributes are considered, before one is selected as the most probable. Giora (2003, p. 10) states that this involves a search through the 'coded meanings foremost on our mind due to conventionality, frequency, familiarity, or prototypicality'. Some typical associations of blindness, for example, would be loss of vision/short-sightedness (as in the case of a political decision, for example), helplessness, darkness, limitation, misfortune, and so on.

It may appear rather strange that, among all possible meanings, that of impartiality has been settled on, by convention, as the most suitable for this metaphor. It is not obvious, for example, why a blind person should be more impartial than a seeing one. Indeed, the interpretation is paradoxical, because one could argue that those engaged in the activities of justice ought to possess unusually clear vision, in order to correctly assess the rights and wrongs of a case. However, when interpreting a metaphor, knowledge of the context in which it occurs is always a necessary inclusion. In this case, knowledge of the legal context, and especially of the quasi-universal principle that 'the law is equal for all', may conjure up a mental picture of a blindfolded judge, indifferent to the fine clothes or pauper's rags worn by the prisoner, who gives judgement solely on the merits of the case, unmoved by these extraneous circumstances. In the words of David Hills (2017), what happens next is as follows:

When they think they've hit on such a possible adjustment, listeners promptly implement it: they reinterpret the comparison in accord with the adjusted canon of similarity, and take the resulting adjusted content to be what the speaker intended to get across all along.

The ideal of the impartiality of legal proceedings has produced, over time, an uncontroversial understanding of the 'meaning' of this particular metaphor. It has become by now a conventional metaphor, like the other mentioned above, 'the long arm of the law', which is generally taken to indicate the power of justice to apprehend even well-hidden criminals. Let us take the following example, from our CLJ data, of an innovative metaphor (Deignan 2005, in Douthwaite 2009, p. 84), to see if the same mechanisms may produce a satisfactory interpretation. In one of the cases, we find:

Lord Hughes acknowledged that dishonesty is not a defined concept but, <u>like an elephant</u>, will be recognised when encountered.[6]

---

[6] Cambridge Law Journal 1977(01): 19. Technically, this would be defined as a 'simile' rather than a 'metaphor'. However, for our purposes the figures are similar enough that Griffiths' (2006, p. 86) words apply: 'we should regard similes as metaphors, which happen to contain like or some other explicit marker of similarity'.

The immediate co-text gives some clues to interpretation here, as it indicates that the salient features of the elephant are to be sought not in the hearer's 'list' of potential characteristics (*greyness, size, mnemonic capacity*, etc.), but rather in the area of *recognisability*. However, we then have to ask in what respect the recognisability of the elephant is different from that of any other real-world object, such as a post office or a palm tree. These things are equally recognisable. Here proverbial or cultural associations, expressed in phrases such as 'the elephant in the room' or indeed 'the elephant never forgets', may be invoked to explain why Lord Hughes chose this object for his metaphor. The 'elephant in the room' is usually a taboo subject for those present, which resonates with a notion of guilty or possibly criminal secrets, while criminals have records for their past actions, which live long in the memory of the law. As Sperber and Wilson (2008) note, the onus is on the listener to infer the intended meaning of any metaphor, drawing on the perceived relevance of the 'sights, sounds, utterances, thoughts, memories, suppositions' (p. 88) that are evoked by the words used.

To illustrate the operation of metaphors within the legal process itself, as opposed to their operation at the level of popular culture, consider the well-known proposition that 'a man is innocent until proven guilty', a concept familiar enough at the level of common knowledge today. Less well-known is a metaphor relating to it, that of the 'Golden Thread', first mentioned in 1935 by Lord Sankey, who said:

Throughout the web of the English Criminal Law one golden thread is always to be seen, that it is the duty of the prosecution to prove the prisoner's guilt. (De Saulles 2017)

In making this claim, he was taking issue with Lord Justice Avory, who, in rejecting the prisoner's right to appeal, had been guided by the following passage in Foster's Crown Law:

the law presumeth the fact to have been founded in malice, until the contrary appeareth

To a degree, then, until Sankey's pronouncement, the onus was on the prisoner to prove their innocence, rather than the contrary. Sankey's metaphor sums up centuries of debate that had centred on this point, and represents a landmark in its acceptance within the British legal system. The episode is made richer, in the terms of our study, by the fact that Sankey used other metaphors alongside that of the thread.[7] First, he characterises the law as a 'web', then proceeds to mix metaphors, by claiming:

---

[7] To a degree, Sankey appears to propose an instance of 'extended metaphor' (Mulholland 2005, p. 183), as he proceeds to refer to the 'web' of the law. Here, the 'golden thread' would, presumably, constitute part of a spider's web. However, he also blends domains, as it is arguably more plausible to view the 'golden thread' in question as part of the diachronic 'tapestry' of legal discourse.

that the prosecution must prove the guilt of the prisoner is part of the common law of England and no attempt to <u>whittle it down</u> can be entertained.

The metaphors here, put in Lakoff and Johnson's (2003) form for what they call 'conceptual metaphors' are, respectively: THE LAW IS A WEB, and THE LAW IS A PIECE OF WOOD. Among the threads of the web is a golden one; hence, of great value compared with the rest. The metaphor does not necessarily also include the presence of a spider; however, applying the interpretative processes outlined above, the hearer will consider the associations of the keyword. A criminal, for example, may become 'entrapped' in the law like a fly in a web; the law itself, like a spider, is waiting to visit punishment on the criminal. Each legal case and individual sentence form part of the web, which builds up through time into a complete structure. Part of the web is its golden thread; in the position of entrapped fly, the prisoner will find comfort in the fact that at least one of the threads in which they are caught is a source of hope, and may in the end constitute grounds for release. The second conceptual metaphor (THE LAW IS A PIECE OF WOOD) compares the law to a structure, something solid, substantial, which would be weakened by 'whittling down'.

To extrapolate the meaning of such metaphors in this way cannot be seen as unduly 'poetic' or fanciful. On the contrary, it is precisely these interpretative associations that may explain not just the surface meaning of the metaphor but arguably its deeper levels of appeal, its functioning as a persuasive resource, and even its place as an element in the normative power of the law itself. The 'golden thread' was to become, over time, a fundamental component in the cognitive as well as argumentative resources of barristers, justices, and other legal agents, a way of conceptualising the laws they seek to apply.

We have touched on the operation of metaphors within legal discourse, but a further point remains to be made. It is that if metaphor constitutes, as we suggest, a fundamental resource through which the business of justice is carried out, then we must also accept that there are limitations to the so-called objectivity of the law (Stavropoulos 1996), in the terms of the above discussion. The law, in this perspective, is not simply a system of codes, or rules that citizens must observe. Nor is justice to be thought of in terms of the dispassionate, objective enforcement of these rules, with clear, unequivocal sentences and utterly predictable punishments. The Aristotelian syllogism is not the basic discursive instrument of legal process. Rather, the law is viewed more as a developing organism, each case progressively adding layers of interpretation, adjustments to the system; and negotiation, of which verbal persuasion and rhetorical devices are at the heart, becomes a central feature of the process.

Since metaphors have to be interpreted, and since a range of interpretations are standardly possible, their use in a legal context means that there is generally an element of subjectivity in legal proceedings, at the very least at the discursive level, where a great proportion of such activity takes place. The process of establishing legal meaning involves negotiation of opinions and ideologies, which foregrounds the exercise of argumentation through rhetoric. The application of the law, therefore, requires the exercise of persuasive verbal techniques (Pawlowski 1980, pp. 65–72; Amsterdam & Bruner 2000, pp. 178–179; Heffer 2005, p. 95; etc.); in sum, as Heffer (2005, p. 84) declares, though both naturally have a role, the practice of law is more concerned with the use of rhetorical skills than the syllogistic application of pre-established norms. In our chapter, we focus on the circulation of legal opinions in an influential legal journal, where the writers present recent sentences and discuss them, thereby engaging in implicit dialogue with colleagues in the profession, and thus carrying forward debate that may shape future legal practices.

13.4   Data and Methodology

The data consists of thirty papers, taken from volumes of the *Cambridge Law Journal* (CLJ) from 2016 to 2019, which were analysed in order to identify instances of metaphorical language. The focus of this qualitative study is on the functional role of metaphors as components of legal argumentation, and only those instances were selected where the metaphor could be seen as playing some role in this sense. As an example of this, consider this contribution from Swain (2019) on employment law, where the title contains a metaphor that encapsulates some of the issues dealt with in this chapter: 'A Historical Examination of Vicarious Liability: A "Veritable Upas Tree"?' On the first page, we find:

In his forthright and, at times, rather eccentric critique written in 1916, Thomas Baty likened vicarious liability to the Upas tree. The Upas tree (antiaris toxicaria), ... is a traditional source of poison for arrows and blow darts. (Swain 2019, p. 1)

The Upas tree metaphor characterises a particular domain of legal practice, vicarious liability, which has proved notoriously difficult for legal specialists to define. The poison arrows are metaphorically associated with the legal problems encountered in the past by lawyers attempting to apply the doctrine. The paper goes on to argue that clarity in this area would be extremely desirable, and the metaphor, by stressing the dangerous potentialities of the law in its current state, underlines the argument and adds to its persuasive force. This is indeed the kind of metaphor we are concerned with. Equally relevant is Denning's metaphorical term for employees, from the same paper:

If he takes the benefit of a machine like this he must accept the burden of seeing that it is properly handled. (Swain 2019, p. 16)

The argument here is that, since the employee is a kind of 'machine', any misdeeds committed by him in the exercise of his functions are his 'handler's' responsibility, and the employer rather than the employee should be held legally liable for them.[8] To the extent that the metaphor is felt to be an apt one, the force of the argument will be augmented (see, e.g., Charteris-Black 2006; Lakoff 2014).

These metaphors are of central interest because of the dialogical work they engage in; they can be situated within an implicit argumentative structure in which the speaker/writer attempts to persuade the hearer/reader that their view is correct and should therefore be adopted. This interpretation supports Charteris-Black's (2004, p. 7; 2005, p. 15) view of metaphor, that its chief pragmatic characteristic resides in the domain of persuasion. In the example just given, the writer reports the words of a prominent judge, Denning, who is both giving grounds for a specific decision and simultaneously arguing that his position on vicarious liability is the correct one. Arguably, then, Denning engages in an implicit process of argumentation with other legal specialists, pre-empting objections and warding off contrary positions.

Metaphors that have been in the language a long while may be seen as conventional or dead (Searle 1979b; Closs Traugott 1985; Black 1993); a dead metaphor is one whose metaphorical nature, as Leech (1969, p. 147) puts it, has become 'institutionalised' through many appearances in dictionaries. In Nöth's words, 'through multiple recurrence, metaphors can themselves finally become conventionalized and therewith a part of the language norm' (Nöth 1985, p. 6). Here are some examples of such conventional metaphors, from our CLJ data:

> In this regard, A and B provides a tentative roadmap (CLJ 2017 76, s. 3)
> sow the seeds for new disputes (CLJ 2017 76, s. 3)
> The rule has deep roots (CLJ 2018 77, s. 1)
> the most adventurous steps were taken in XYZ (CLJ 2018 77, s. 1)
> thus buttressing the case for reform (CLJ 2018 77, s. 1)

Nöth (1985) uses the term 'demetaphorization' to apply to such terms as these, at one time 'creative metaphors' but which have become, through repeated use, part of the lexicon.

However, the notion of how dead such metaphors really are has been a focus for research (Lakoff 1987, Müller 2008), and it is plain that metaphors of this type may also play a role in argumentation, as in the final instance, above, 'buttressing the case for reform'. In this fragment of text, an implicit

---

[8] For a discussion of the Conceptual Metaphor PEOPLE ARE MACHINES, see Douthwaite (2009, p. 97).

argumentation pattern may be identified, and put in the standard form (Sinnott-Armstrong & Fogelin 2009, p. 55) as follows:

> SINCE: It is a good thing that the doctrine of benefit and burden should be strong,
> (and since) the weakness of the current system has been exposed
> THEREFORE: there is a strong need for reform

It should be noted that the metaphor plays a significant role in this argumentative structure, adding rhetorical strength to the conclusion, and we shall have more to say about the pragmatic force of metaphor in argumentation below. The metaphor also underlines the notion of this doctrine, and by extension, the law itself, as a kind of structure (buttresses are found almost exclusively on ancient buildings such as cathedrals). Such associations also contain evaluative positions and ideologies, the latter term comprising what Simpson (1993, p. 161) describes as 'cultural assumptions, political beliefs and institutional practices'. The writer implies a type of conservative attitude and at the same time a range of persuasive notions, connected to possible *collapse*, to the need for *preservation*, to the law as a *venerated institution*, and so on.

Conventionalised or dead metaphors, then, may also play an important role in construing implicit argumentation. Our basic approach to metaphors, however, in this chapter, does not consider whether a metaphor is conventionalised, dead, or innovative. Rather, we focus principally on the function the metaphor plays, within an implicit argumentative structure, as in the following instances:

in enforcing copyright online, 'the right balance' between that freedom and the interests of copyright holders must be struck (CLJ 2017 76. s. 3)

This reasoning came to be known as the 'narrower ground' ... to be distinguished from the explanation of Lord Griffiths, known as the 'broader ground' (CLJ 2017 76, s. 3)

taking account of the promisee's intention avoids him receiving an undeserved windfall (CLJ 2017 76, s. 3)

Concern has been expressed of a judicial abdication of proper duty (CLJ 201877, s. 1)

a hollow doctrine teetering on unstable legal footings (CLJ 2018 77, s. 1)

In these cases, the metaphor is the crucial element in an implicit argument; it can be seen to concentrate a series of deontological propositions and covertly advance a specific position on the case under discussion. This is so in each of the above instances, and also in the *buttress* example, as we have seen. To better understand this point, something of the legal contexts, in each case, must be appreciated. Consider the following example:

taking account of the promisee's intention avoids him receiving an undeserved windfall

To understand this, we need to know that the case concerns an award of damages, and the 'intention' refers to the litigant's plan to spend the money on making good the damage suffered. For example, let us presume the court awards a complainant a large sum to repair faulty building work. The complainant may decide, in the interim period between bringing the action and receiving the award, that they no longer need the proposed building, and decide to spend the money on something else. Through the metaphor, the money is compared to a windfall apple, that is, something good which appears in one's way, purely by chance and without one having done something to merit it. This may appear paradoxical; after all, we are talking about money which belongs to the complainant, who should arguably be free to decide what they spend their money on. Nevertheless, from the legal point of view, it is money which the court has awarded for a specific purpose, and the complainant is not free to decide what it should be spent on (at least, in the view of the legal agent[s] represented in the text).

The text, especially the evaluative pre-modifier 'undeserved' and the semantics of the verb 'to avoid', suggests that 'a windfall' is a bad, unjust, or unfair thing: this is the crux of the persuasive attempt. To frame the scenario just outlined – where a litigant is awarded money to repair a wall, for example, and instead spends it on a world cruise – as a 'windfall' is part of a persuasive line of reasoning that aims to convince the reader that it is a bad thing and should not be allowed. Behind this, arguably, are a set of quasi-religious attitudes, of the Weberian kind, that typify the Anglo-Saxon culture from which this particular instance has emerged (Weber 2001). This is strongly suggested by the semantics of the modalising qualifying adjective 'undeserved'; it is simply 'not fair' that the complainant should enjoy the possible pleasures afforded by a large sum of money, and fairness is well-known as an important, quasi-legal, social value for the British (Mullan 1975).

Space considerations prohibit the explication of more than a few of these instances, and the rest of our chapter concerns a case study in greater depth of one of these metaphors, exploring its functioning and role in legal argumentation.

13.5   Case Study: The Question of the Narrower Ground

One of the primary functions of metaphor is that it enables us to comprehend – or at least to have the illusion that we comprehend – matters that are intrinsically too complicated for 'ordinary' understanding. This is implicit in much of Lakoff and Johnson's writings on metaphor (e.g. Lakoff 1993; Lakoff & Johnson 2003), and at times explicitly spelled out:

When we are suffering substantial economic losses due to complex economic and political factors that no one really understands, the INFLATION IS AN ADVERSARY metaphor at least gives us a coherent account of why we're suffering these losses. (Lakoff & Johnson 2003, p. 34)

Though the domains of law and economics are widely different conceptually, this reflection may provide a clue about the importance of metaphor in the legal context. Like economic texts, legal language is notoriously complex, and consists of labyrinthine stretches of prose that are beyond the grasp of the layman. In this section we present an illustration of the functions of argumentative metaphor, showing how it not only clarifies the issues for the uninitiated, but also facilitates practical argumentation among specialists. The metaphor in question is that LEGAL ARGUMENTS ARE GROUNDS, which assimilates the domains of spatial logic and abstract reasoning. The grounds may be broad – of wide, general application – or narrow, in which case they will apply in specific circumstances only.

The case is that of *Linden Gardens Trust Ltd* v *Lenesta Sludge Disposals Ltd, 1994*. The *Cambridge Law Journal* lays out the circumstances thus:

The promisee, the lessee of a plot of land, engaged the promisor, a building contractor, to develop the land. For tax reasons, the promisee later assigned its interest in the land to a third party. It also purported to assign the full benefit of the construction contract but the assignment was invalid. Certain aspects of the work were discovered to be defective and the third party incurred remedial costs of around £800,000. (Rowan 2017, p. 624)

The problem was, essentially, identifying the party who was entitled to claim damages. The original lessee had ceded his interest in the property to a third party, so apparently had no interest in claiming. However, since the third party's letting contract had a technical fault that rendered it invalid, that party had no legal right to make the claim. This situation was described by another vivid metaphor, a 'legal black hole' (Rowan 2017, p. 624), and the House of Lords were called on to resolve the impasse.

Their solution, which became known as 'the narrower ground', was to propose an exception to the rule that damages could be claimed only by the actual landowner. Lord Griffiths (who was in favour of a 'broader ground' solution) opposed this, arguing that it was sufficient that damage had been suffered for a claim to be advanced. However, Lord Griffiths placed a strong emphasis, in arguing that damages should be awarded, on the intention of the third party to actually make good the damages:

the court will of course wish to be satisfied that the repairs have been or are likely to be carried out (Rowan 2017, p. 625)

This requirement was not present in the alternative solution proposed by the House of Lords. This led to the observation, which was noted in *Chitty on Contracts*, the principal reference work for contract law, that

Table 13.1 *The narrow ground versus the broad ground*

The narrower ground (House of Lords)	The broader ground (Griffiths)
The law states that 'the injured party can recover damages only in respect of his own loss'	'Not receiving the promised performance was itself loss to the promisee, entitling him to claim substantial damages'
Griffiths also adds a condition: No mention of repair work or intention to have it done	'damages should depend on the remedial work <u>having been done</u> or the promisee <u>intending to do the work</u> subsequently'

paradoxically, this makes the narrower ground broader than the broader ground (Rowan 2017, p. 626)

For the layman, one would suppose that it is quite challenging to follow even the simple outline of the case provided above, let alone enter into its merits on one side or another; however, it is possible for anyone to appreciate the force of the above conclusion, once the matter has been transported onto a metaphorical plane. For the legal specialist, meanwhile, the development of such a metaphorical frame is a crucial resource in the business of negotiating, and shaping, the law itself. The metaphor becomes a key element of argumentation, which can be appreciated from Table 13.1.

We can see that the opinion of the House of Lords is the 'narrower' position, since it rules out a claim by the third party – only the actual owner of the land can make a claim for damages. Griffiths waives this, and is therefore appropriately seen as occupying a broader position. However, his requirement about remedial work is significantly more restrictive than the position of the House of Lords. Thus, a metaphor of this kind (broader, narrower ground is the conceptual metaphor INTERPRETATION/APPLICATION OF THE LAW IS SPATIAL DIMENSION) plays a role in an implicit argumentative structure, as follows:

SINCE
It is clearly absurd that the narrow ground be broader than the broad ground
(and since)
   The House of Lords are conceding more liberty to the claimant than their supposedly liberal adversary

THEREFORE
The House of Lords should also include a requirement for intention to make good the damage

The metaphor forms a key component of the basic premise (Allen 1995) of the argument. In this example, the argumentation remains at an implicit level

(Van Eemeren & Grootendorst, 2004; Van Eemeren et. al. 2014). In this instance, the metaphor is seen to occupy a central place in legal argumentation: not only does it bring legal concepts within the purview of the layman, but it makes abstract concepts concrete, permitting specialists to debate the points involved, and thereby shape the law.

13.6 Conclusion

Our study focused on written discourse; it would be useful to conduct further research, for example, to explore the role of metaphor in spoken language in courtrooms or in other contexts of legal interaction, where it may be used to debate the issues involved.

The study followed lines similar to those of Dee (2009), who explores the impact of a particular metaphor, the 'penumbra', on American legal discourse. She writes:

> A metaphor, of course, is a rhetorical device. It is not a legal rule or principle. But spatial metaphors, perhaps because they give the illusion of being 'concrete' amid abstract legal principles, sometimes take on a life of their own in the sense that they provide a legal 'shorthand' so pervasive that even Supreme Court justices themselves sometimes accept these spatial metaphors as postulates without question. (Dee 2009, p. 55)

It will be observed here how heavily the writer herself leans on the expressive power of metaphor. Metaphors are 'concrete', they have 'a life of their own', they provide a 'shorthand', and so on. Dee's case study concerned an episode in which it was ruled that the actions of the United States tax authorities, who used wiretapping in a case of liquor importation in 1928, in the era of prohibition, had not infringed the defendants' rights under the fourth and fifth constitutional amendments. A dissenting judge argued:

> I am not prepared to say that the penumbra of the fourth and fifth amendments covers the defendant.. but I think ... that apart from the Constitution, the government ought not to use evidence obtained and only obtainable through a criminal act.

The judge in question, Oliver Wendell Holmes, was in this case quoting from an earlier work of his own, in which he had used the metaphor to explore the formation of legal precedent:

> The distinction between the groups [of opposing case decisions] ... is philosophical, and it is better to have a line drawn somewhere in the penumbra between darkness and light, than to remain in uncertainty. (Holmes, cited in Greely 1989, p. 253)

These instances illustrate what we have been suggesting in this chapter, that the role of metaphor is not confined to influencing the jury in a courtroom harangue; stated differently, its impact is not solely at the level of verbal rhetoric. Rather, it is closely involved in the formation and delineation of precise legal concepts, on the one hand, and in the real-world dialogical contexts in which the law progressively emerges, on the other. The penumbra is the zone of twilight that occurs during an eclipse, between the zone of complete darkness or shadow that exists where the sun's light is completely cut off, and the zone of light outside the eclipse's influence. We can also observe the presence of implicit metaphors here (LIGHT IS GOOD, DARK IS BAD, LIGHT IS UNDERSTANDING/KNOWLEDGE, SEEING IS UNDERSTANDING), which arguably guide the judge's thinking. 'The justice system is the sun', and this recognition also helps us unpack the significance of the penumbra metaphor. In an ideal world, cases would be black and white; the light of justice would fall on a criminal, whose offence would be immediately discernible, together with the appropriate punishment. Such idealistic conceptions of the legal process recall the discourse of legal positivism in the age of Enlightenment, discussed above. However, it is noticeable that, as an individual judge, conceptualising the law, Holmes' thinking was intrinsically metaphorical. Moreover, when it came to the business of applying and developing the law, in the day-to-day business of negotiating in the courtroom, Holmes used the metaphor as a central component of his argument. Dee (2009, p. 56) cites three other judges who subsequently used the penumbra metaphor, to refer to the 'shadowy, unsettled areas of law in which judges struggle to find the correct place to draw legal lines'. The rest of her paper offers ample proof of the role which this particular metaphor was to play in American legal discourse throughout the twentieth century and into our own time.

The idealistic, positivist vision of justice discussed above rests on a conception of the law that is static, whose most appropriate discursive form is the Aristotelian syllogism. Fundamentally, the ideal conception may be reduced to a three-step process:

- 'fact finding' (the collection of relevant facts concerning the offence and assembly of a convincing case against the accused)
- 'law finding' (the task of the legal process was to find an appropriate norm for the offence which had been committed)
- 'law applying' (the sentence, which would match offence and rule and decide on appropriate punishment).

In an Aristotelian perspective, therefore, applying a syllogistic model, the major premise is represented by the proposition of law involved, the minor premise is the proposition of fact concerning the crime committed, and the judgement the conclusion. As we have suggested above, the ideal model leaves little scope for the exercise of any rhetorical processes, nor for the work of interpretation. There may be some scope for the sophist's skills of forensic rhetoric at various stages of a trial, especially during cross-examination and the final harangue. However, as soon as more dynamic models of legal systems prevail, and the function of interpretation becomes an integral part of the process, the centrality of rhetorical processes, and metaphor, becomes apparent.

The position we have been advocating is not universally accepted. Rideout (2010), for instance, as well as discussing the role of the penumbra metaphor, explores the general history of legal metaphor in the United States, providing other episodes such as the 'wall of separation between church and state' (Rideout 2010, p. 156), and suggesting that the explicit use of such metaphors in legal discourse could be controversial. Some judges, he suggests, would prefer counsel to use 'the simple language of the Constitution' (p. 156).

However, despite such contrary voices, our thesis – in line with ordinary language philosophy and cognitive linguistics – is that metaphor is not just widely recognised as a component of legal discourse of all kinds, but rather is an essential feature, a sine qua non, a means both of talking about the law and of making the law, without which it is hard to imagine how the legal profession would get on at all.

References

Alexy, R. (2002). *The Argument from Injustice: A Reply to Legal Positivism*. Oxford: Oxford University Press.

Allen, D. (1995). Assessing Basic Premises. In F. H. Van Eemeren, R. Grootendorst, J. A. Blair, & C. A. Willard, eds., *Proceedings of the Third ISSA Conference on Argumentation*. Amsterdam: Sic Sat: International Centre for the Study of Argumentation, 2, pp. 218–225. https://scholar.uwindsor.ca/cgi/viewcontent.cgi?article=1853&context=ossaarchive.

Amsterdam, A. G., & Bruner, J. (2000). *Minding the Law*. Cambridge, MA: Harvard University Press.

Aristotle (1997). *Aristotle's Poetics*, trans. G. Whalley. Montreal: McGill-Queen's University Press.

  (2007). *On Rhetoric: A Theory of Civic Discourse*, trans. G. A. Kennedy. New York: Oxford University Press.

Black, M. (1993). More about Metaphor. In A. Ortony, ed., *Metaphor and Thought*. Cambridge: Cambridge University Press, pp. 19–41.

Charteris-Black, J. (2004). *Corpus Approaches to Critical Metaphor Analysis*. New York: Palgrave Macmillan.

  (2005). *Politicians and Rhetoric: The Persuasive Power of Metaphor*. New York: Palgrave Macmillan.

  (2006). Britain as a Container: Immigration Metaphors in the 2005 Election Campaign. *Discourse and Society*, 17(5), 563–581.

Closs Traugott, E. (1985). 'Conventional' and 'Dead' Metaphors Revisited. In W. Paprotte and R. Dirven, eds., *The Ubiquity of Metaphor: Metaphor in Language and Thought*. Amsterdam: John Benjamins, pp. 17–57.

Dee, J. (2009). Shedding Light or Casting Shadows? The Penumbra Metaphor, Privacy and Privileged Communication. *Free Speech Yearbook*, 44(1), 55–63.

Deignan, A. (2005). *Metaphor and Corpus Linguistics*. Amsterdam: John Benjamins.
De Saulles, D. (2017). On Law and Litigation. https://dominicdesaulles.wordpress.com/2017/04/03/the-golden-thread-burden-of-proof-woolmington-v-dpp-1935-a-c-462-hl/.
Douthwaite, J. (2009). Pragmatic Patterning in the Deployment of Conceptual Metaphor and Communication. In C. Marcato & V. Orioles, eds., *Studi Plurilingui e Interlinguistici in Ricordo di Roberto Gusmani*. Udine: Forum, pp. 83–119.
Fogelin, R. J. (1988). *Figuratively Speaking*. New Haven, CT: Yale University Press.
Giora, R. (2003). *On Our Mind: Salience, Context and Figurative Language*. Oxford: Oxford University Press.
Greely, H. T. (1989). A Footnote to 'Penumbra' in *Griswold v. Connecticut*. *Constitutional Commentary*, 6, 251–265.
Grice, H. P. (1989). Logic and Conversation, Lecture 2. In *Studies in the Way of Words, Cambridge*. Cambridge, MA: Harvard University Press, pp. 22–40.
Griffiths, P. (2006). *An Introduction to English Semantics and Pragmatics*. Edinburgh: Edinburgh University Press
Heffer, C. (2005). *The Language of Jury Trial: A Corpus-Aided Analysis of Legal-Lay Discourse*. Basingstoke: Palgrave Macmillan.
Hills, D. (2017). Metaphor. In E. N. Zalta, ed., *The Stanford Encyclopedia of Philosophy* (Fall 2017), https://plato.stanford.edu/archives/fall2017/entries/metaphor/.
Houbert, F. (2008). Caught in the Web of the Law: Le traducteur juridique face à la métaphore. www.initerm.net/post/2011/05/18/Les-metaphores-juridiques.
Kirby, J. T. (1997). Aristotle on Metaphor. *The American Journal of Philology*, 118(4), 517–554.
Klinck, D. R. (1992). *The Word of the Law: Approaches to Legal Discourse*. Ottawa: Carleton University Press.
Kövecses, Z. (2010). *Metaphor: A Practical Introduction*. Oxford: Oxford University Press.
Lakoff, G. (1987). The Death of Dead Metaphor. *Metaphor and Symbolic Activity*, 2(2), 143–147.
  (1993). The Contemporary Theory of Metaphor. In A. Ortony, ed., *Metaphor and Thought*. Cambridge: Cambridge University Press, pp. 202–251.
  (2014). *Don't Think of an Elephant! Know Your Values and Frame the Debate*. White River Junction, VT: Chelsea Green Publishing.
Lakoff, G., and Johnson, M.(2003). *Metaphors We Live By*. Chicago: University of Chicago Press.
Leech, G. (1969). *A Linguistic Guide to English Poetry*. London: Longman.
Morra, L. (2010). New Models for Language Understanding and the Cognitive Approach to Legal Metaphors. *International Journal for the Semiotics of Law/ Revue internationale de Sémiotique juridique*, 23(4), 387–405.
Mullan, D. J. (1975). Fairness: The New Natural Justice? *The University of Toronto Law Journal*, 25(3), 281–316.
Müller, C. (2008). *Metaphors Dead and Alive, Sleeping and Waking*. Chicago: University of Chicago Press.
Mulholland, J. (2005) *Handbook of Persuasive Tactics: A Practical Language Guide*. London: Routledge.

Nöth, W. (1985). Semiotic Aspects of Metaphor. In W. Paprotte & R. Dirven, eds., *The Ubiquity of Metaphor: Metaphor in Language and Thought*. Amsterdam: John Benjamins, pp. 1–17.

Oakes, P. J., Haslam, A., & Turner, J. C. (1994). *Stereotyping and Social Reality*. Oxford: Blackwood.

Pawlowski, T. (1980). *Concept Formation in the Humanities and the Social Sciences*. Dordrecht: Springer.

Philippopoulos-Mihalopoulos, A. (2016). Flesh of the Law: Material Legal Metaphors. *Journal of Law and Society*, 43(1), 45–65.

Richard, I.(2014). Metaphors in English for Law: Let Us Keep Them! *Lexis Online*: 8. https://journals.openedition.org/lexis/251.

Rideout, J. C. (2010). Penumbral Thinking Revisited: Metaphor in Legal Argumentation. *Journal of the Association of Legal Writing Directors*, pp. 155–198.

Rowan, S. (2017). Cost of Cure Damages and the Relevance of the Injured Promisee's Intention to Cure. *Cambridge Law Journal*, 76(3), 616–641.

Searle, J. (1979a). *Expression and Meaning: Studies in the Theory of Speech Acts*. Cambridge: Cambridge University Press.

(1979b). Metaphor. In A. Ortony, ed., *Metaphor and Thought*. Cambridge: Cambridge University Press, pp. 83–111.

Siltala, R. (2000). *A Theory of Precedent: From Analytical Positivism to a Post-Analytical Philosophy of Law*. Oxford: Hart Publishing.

Simpson, P. (1993). *Language, Ideology and Point of View*. London: Routledge.

Sinnott-Armstrong, W., & Fogelin, R. J. (2009). *Understanding Arguments: An Introduction to Informal Logic*, 8th ed. Belmont: Wadsworth Publishing.

Smith, M. R. (2007). Levels of Metaphor in Persuasive Legal Writing. *Mercer Law Review,* 58(3), 919–948.

Sperber, D., & Wilson, D. (1986). *Relevance: Communication and Cognition*. Oxford: Basil Blackwell,

(2008). A Deflationary Account of Metaphors. In R. W. Gibbs Jr., ed., *The Cambridge Handbook of Metaphor and Thought*. Cambridge: Cambridge University Press, pp. 84–105.

Stavropoulos, N. (1996). *Objectivity in Law*. Oxford: Oxford University Press.

Swain, W. (2019). A Historical Examination of Vicarious Liability: A 'Veritable Upas Tree'? *The Cambridge Law Journal*, 78(3), 640–661.

Tarello, G. (1989). Interpretazione ed Evoluzione del Diritto. In S. Castignone, ed., *L'Opera di Giovanni Tarello nella Cultura Giuridica Contemporanea*. Bologna: Mulino, pp. 321–330.

(2013). *La Interpretación de la Ley*, trans. Diego Dei Vecchi. Lima: Palestra Editores.

Van Eemeren, F. H., & Grootendorst, R. (2004). *A Systematic Theory of Argumentation: The Pragma-dialectical Approach*. Cambridge: Cambridge University Press.

Van Eemeren, F. H., Garssen, B., Krabbe, E. C. W., Snoeck Henkemans, A. F., Verheij, B., & Wagemans, J. H. M. (2014). *Handbook of Argumentation Theory*. Dordrecht: Springer.

Weber, M. (2001). *The Protestant Ethic and the Spirit of Capitalism*, trans. Talcott Parsons [1930]. London: Routledge.

14 Condemning the Condemners
The Portrayal of Regulators in UK News about Corporate Crime

Ilse A. Ras

14.1 Introduction

Sykes and Matza (1957) note that one of the ways delinquents 'neutralise' their delinquent acts is by 'condemning the condemners'. In doing so, the delinquent, 'in effect, [changes] the subject of the conversation in the dialogue between his own deviant impulses and the reactions of others; and by attacking others, the wrongness of his own behaviour is more easily repressed or lost to view' (Sykes & Matza 1957, p. 668). In other words, delinquents neg(oti)ate the legitimacy of condemning parties so as to shift blame to these parties and/or diminish their own blame. Other portrayals of condemning parties may instead work to emphasise this legitimacy and emphasise the (moral and/or legal) wrongness of the condemned act and condemned actor.

This chapter examines how British newspapers have written about regulators and investigators in reporting on corporate fraud between 2004 and 2014, focusing also on the portrayal of the two leading regulatory agencies, the UK-based Financial Services Authority (FSA) and the US-focused Securities and Exchange Commission (SEC). The FSA, empowered by the UK Financial Services and Markets Act 2000, was tasked with regulating financial markets, with four regulatory objectives under the FSMA 2000:

1. Market confidence
2. Public awareness
3. The protection of consumers, and
4. The reduction of financial crime.

In its last objective, the FSA had a preventative function, rather than responsive. As the UK Financial Services and Markets Act 2000 implies, the FSA's responsibilities covered UK financial markets. This Act was amended in 2012 by Part 2 of the UK Financial Services Act 2012, which split the FSA into the Prudential Regulation Authority and the Financial Conduct Authority, following the heavy criticisms it received in the aftermath of the global financial crisis.

The SEC, like the FSA, supervises and regulates the market, albeit in the United States, with a particular focus on ensuring public companies communicate meaningfully, transparently and truthfully with investors and the broader public (SEC 2013).

The question is whether (and how) the newspapers included in this study (*The Guardian*, *The Times*, *The Daily Telegraph*, *The Financial Times*, *The Daily Mail*, *The Sun*, and *The Mirror*) broadly work to (de)legitimise these institutions and their work. To examine the reporting on these institutions, this chapter focuses on the top twenty-five collocates by frequency, further informed by MI-score and LL-ratio, both of which are measures for the strength of the collocation (Gablasova et al. 2017), for each of these institutions.

14.2 Corporate Fraud

Corporate fraud must be considered an umbrella term, referring to all

those cases in which a corporation or a (number of) employee(s) or member(s) of a corporation, for the benefit and on behalf of said corporation, act(s) in a manner that conceals, falsely represents, or misrepresents the status or situation of a good, service or case, to their unjust advantage, resulting in negative consequences for other individuals, legal persons or for society as a whole, including injuring their rights. (Ras 2017, p. 23)

Punch indicates that corporate fraud has the capacity to undermine 'political legitimacy' (Punch 1996, pp. 66–7) and, by extension, democracy. Corporate wrongdoing also disrupts the market, as unchecked criminal behaviour gives the delinquent corporation an unfair competitive advantage and diminishes trust in markets (Punch 1996, pp. 67–8).

There is also financial harm. For instance, governments and taxpayers can be victimised (Punch 1996, p. 66) through tax shortfalls. The tax gap (the difference between the tax that should have been collected by Her Majesty's Revenue and Customs [HMRC], which is the British tax collection authority, and what has actually been collected) of large businesses was estimated by HMRC (2018) to be £7.0 billion and of small and medium enterprises (SMEs) to be £13.7 billion. Of the total tax gap (£33bn), £5.3 billion is lost through evasion, a further £1.7bn through avoidance, £3.4bn through simple non-payment, and £5.3bn through the potentially euphemistically titled 'legal interpretation', which is, as HMRC puts it, where HMRC and the tax-liable person have a difference of opinion in how to interpret tax law (HMRC 2018). To compare, the 2017 spring budget for the UK government detailed expected public sector receipts (from various taxes and National Insurance contributions) to be £744bn (HM Treasury 2017). In other words, the total estimated tax gap is 4.44 per cent of expected total tax receipts for 2017, and that part of the tax gap that is explicitly attributed to corporate tax avoidance is 2.78 per cent. A further comparison can be made with the estimated total social and economic cost of crime in Britain, which is £58.8 billion but does not appear to include estimates for the cost of corporate wrongdoing (Heeks et al. 2018).

14.3 Media Reporting of Corporate Fraud

The media remain an important channel for negotiating the legitimacy of law enforcement (Chermak & Weiss 2005; Gray 2009), as shown empirically by Povey (2001), Callanan and Rosenberger (2011) and Graziano, Shuck and Martin (2010). An appropriate level of public trust in policing institutions, and the perception of their legitimacy, is one of the key factors in the continued functioning of law enforcement and regulatory institutions, as trust affects people's willingness to offer witness statements and report crimes (Povey 2001; Wood 2009). However, there appears to be limited research into the portrayal of those agencies tasked with regulating and investigating the potentially illegitimate (financial) activities of companies.

Newspapers have generally been found to deny corporate responsibility (see Sykes & Matza 1957), by constructing corporate wrongdoing as 'disasters' (Jewkes 2011, p. 24; Mayr & Machin 2012, p. 203; McMullan & McClung 2006), and are reluctant to 'socially construct corporate violence as a crime' (Wright et al. 1995). Generous interpretations of this tendency to not assign blame, at least not until the authorities have done so, are possible. However, Wright et al. (1995, p. 34) argue that this reluctance to report corporate crime as 'real crime' reflects 'larger power structures in society', in the sense that corporations are generally much more powerful than individuals. As is also the argument made by Sutherland (1949), white-collar criminals are in a much better position to influence mainstream norms than 'common' criminals. Furthermore, given the deep pockets of corporations, harsh reporting on corporate wrongdoing is more likely to have negative consequences for the reporting newspaper and journalist than harsh reporting on individual crime, and is therefore unlikely.

14.4 Critical Discourse Analysis and Corpus Linguistics

This study examines the portrayal of law enforcement and regulatory agencies using Critical Discourse Analysis (CDA), which assumes that language shapes and is shaped by social structures (Fairclough 2015; Wodak 2001). As such, it is a highly suitable approach for a study into newspaper writing on what Sutherland (1949) would classify as a 'crime of the powerful'.

Fairclough's (2015, pp. 48–50) CDA assesses 'what is' in a text, and explores the differences between this 'what is' and 'what should be'. The findings are then used to determine the necessary action to 'change reality for the better' (Fairclough 2015, p. 48). Given this explicit political aim, CDA is a contested approach. It is often accused of cherry-picking (see, e.g., Baker 2012; Jeffries 2010, 2014; Widdowson 2004), especially as, in the past, many Critical Discourse Analyses focused on limited amounts of data (Widdowson 1995, 2004). As such, Widdowson (2004) promotes the use of corpora and corpus linguistic methods to guard against cherry-picking, given that corpora generally contain many more articles and are thus often more representative of the specific topic, genre, time period, source, and so on under investigation. Similarly, Toolan (1997), Orpin (2006), Poole (2010), and Jeffries (2014; Jeffries & Walker 2012) express great enthusiasm for the possibilities corpus linguistic methods offer traditionally qualitative approaches. A particularly noteworthy study that combines CDA with corpus methods is Baker et al.'s (2008) examination of a 140-million-word corpus containing 'discourses of refugees and asylum seekers in the UK press 1996–2006' (p. 274).

14.4.1 The Corpus

This particular study into UK newspaper reporting on investigators and regulators in cases of corporate fraud, reported between 2004 and 2014, uses a corpus of corporate fraud news containing 90,443 articles: the corpus has 53.8 million tokens, 184,151 types; see Table 14.1 for a breakdown by newspaper.

To create this corpus, an initial set of search terms, including 'corporate fraud' and a number of famous cases of corporate fraud, such as the US's Enron scandal, were entered into the Lexis Nexis database of news articles. Search results were then evaluated on a case-by-case basis, determining

Table 14.1. *Overview of articles and words per newspaper in corporate fraud corpus*

	Number of articles	Number of words
Broadsheets	76,154	46,947,302
The Financial Times	32,072	17,347,148
The Guardian	13,172	9,978,745
The Telegraph	12,278	7,139,887
The Times	18,632	12,481,522
Tabloids	14,289	6,885,556
The Daily Mail	9,465	5,110,358
The Mirror	2,705	1,086,217
The Sun	2,119	688,981
Totals	**90,443**	**53,832,858**

whether the article indeed covered a case of corporate fraud, using the definition of corporate fraud reproduced in section 2 as a guide. For a full list of search terms, see Ras (2017).

14.4.2 Analysis

A key point of CDA in examining the portrayal of concepts, people and items is the choice of words used to refer to them. Richardson (2007, p. 49), for instance, reflects on an author's choice of words as being indicative of the identity imposed by the creator of the text on a person, object or situation, thereby foregrounding certain aspects and obscuring others. In this regard, however, we must also pay attention to the context of these words; Fowler (1991, p. 84) writes that whilst some words have a very strong meaning and connotation of their own, others are 'coloured by their contexts'. As such, this study primarily focuses on the top collocating content words by frequency to *regulator|regulators, FSA* and *Securities # Exchange Commission.* The items *regulator* and *regulators* are separated by the |-mark, which functions, in AntConc (Anthony 2019), as an operator signalling 'OR', while # functions as a wildcard in AntConc that allows any one words to be placed between 'Securities' and 'Exchange' – this is because the SEC is referred to both as the *Securities and Exchange Commission* and the *Securities & Exchange Commission.*

To ensure that these content words were indeed statistically significant collocates for the target phrases *regulator|regulators, FSA* and *Securities # Exchange Commission,* both MI scores and log-likelihood scores were calculated and are presented. One known issue with MI scores is that collocates with very low frequencies, such as, in this corpus, misspellings and names, tend to have high MI scores that are not reliably indicative of the strength of the collocation of the target word and the collocate (Gablasova et al. 2017). For this reason, log-likelihood scores are also included. Nonetheless, MI scores are reported due to their prevalence in corpus studies, and so this inclusion enables comparisons across studies.

As this corpus includes reporting that spans over a decade, it must also be considered that a simple list of top frequent collocates may be skewed toward a particular year. As such, the top frequent collocates for each target noun (phrase) were checked against a list of constant collocates (see Gabrielatos & Baker 2008) for these targets. A constant collocate is a collocate that has a minimum frequency per year in at least a minimum number of years. In this study, a collocate was counted as constant if it had a minimum frequency of five per year in at least seven out of eleven years. As such, each table shows the number of years in which a collocate had a minimum frequency of five, or whether dispersion was such to be able to call that collocate 'constant'.

14.5 The Portrayal of Regulators

Let us now turn then to the question of how these regulators are actually represented in this corpus of British news on corporate fraud.

14.5.1 Who Are the Regulators?

Table 14.2 first shows, through the identification of the semantic domain of the top twenty-five collocations of *regulator* and *regulators* by frequency according to the UCREL [University Centre for Computer Corpus Research on Language, at Lancaster University] Semantic Analysis System (USAS) (function words and verbs excluded), that regulators, in this corpus, are primarily associated with Money and Business, and that, given the associations with Government and Power, they have some sort of authorisation to work in the financial field. What they do is, presumably, Investigate.

Agencies

But who are these regulators? One can recognise in Table 14.2 those agencies tasked with regulating financial institutions in the United Kingdom and United States: the ('new') *Financial Conduct Authority*; the *Financial Services Authority* or *FSA*, and the American *Securities and Exchange Commission*. Indeed, the n-grams presented in Table 14.3 also show that in this corpus, the primary use of the words 'financial', 'authority', 'services', 'commission', 'securities', 'exchange' and 'conduct' is to indicate one of these agencies. Table 14.4 shows the top twenty-five most frequent constant collocates of *FSA* and *Securities # Exchange Commission*, which are the agencies that were active for the majority of years covered by the corpus.

Note that 'FSA' collocates with *FSA*; a brief survey of concordances shows that this repetition is generally due to first introducing the agency, and then printing a direct speech representation of a statement made on behalf of the *FSA*:

1. In a statement yesterday, the FSA said: 'The FSA is committed to ensuring consumers are protected and the firm treats its customers fairly.'

Another large share of this repetition is made up of a combination of sentences in which the first ends with 'Financial Services Authority (FSA)' and the second begins with 'The FSA', as in the following example:

2. The police spokesman said the business is in liquidation and is no longer authorised by the Financial Services Authority (FSA). The FSA has described mortgage fraud as a 'serious and widespread problem'.

In the above two examples, the *FSA* is personified, able to make statements and offer descriptions that are reported in Direct Speech, as though the person who

Table 14.2. *Top twenty-five collocates of regulator|regulators, sorted by frequency*

Rank	Collocate	Frequency	Years Freq. > 5	MI score	LL score	Semantic domain (USAS[a])
1	financial	6,129	11	6.71	45,185.07	Money generally
2	city	2,941	11	7.58	25,325.66	Places/business: generally
3	uk	2,079	11	5.75	12,543.45	Geographical names
4	authority	1,949	11	7.10	15,444.45	Power, organizing
5	new	1,718	11	5.24	9,169.42	Time: old and new
6	bank	1,638	11	4.56	7,234.67	Money generally
7	services	1,533	11	5.96	9,693.59	Helping
8	market	1,446	11	5.24	7,711.39	Business: selling
9	banks	1,390	11	5.14	7,224.37	Money generally
10	fsa	1,337	11	5.61	7,804.25	Other proper names
11	commission	1,178	11	6.13	7,719.83	General actions, making etc./ government etc.
12	securities	1,155	11	6.57	8,288.62	Industry
13	industry	963	11	5.74	5,798.33	Industry
14	investigation	897	11	5.69	5,340.73	Investigate, examine, test, search
15	exchange	868	11	5.93	5,449.06	Getting and giving
16	european	856	11	6.31	5,833.35	Geographical names
17	year	813	11	3.70	2,674.83	Time: period
18	chief	787	11	4.78	3,711.31	Power, organizing
19	banking	758	11	5.35	4,156.90	Money: affluence
20	investors	709	11	4.70	3,063.01	Money: affluence
21	rules	701	11	5.75	4,228.53	Power, organizing
22	companies	693	11	4.20	2,734.93	Money: affluence
23	government	674	11	4.48	2,904.34	Government etc.
24	conduct	615	11	6.98	4,766.59	Social actions, states and processes
25	company	582	11	3.41	1,701.62	Business: generally

[a] USAS: UCREL [University Centre for Computer Corpus Research on Language, at Lancaster University] Semantic Analysis System.

spoke these utterances is identified as the *FSA* itself, rather than, presumably, a spokesperson for this institution. Whilst the personification of institutions is common, captured in the legal context that creates institutions as legal persons, and presumably often also done for space-saving reasons, it does have the effect of limiting the responsibility of the individual who acts on behalf of the institutions. Similarly, it tars the entire institution with the same brush if an individual makes a mistake. This tendency is worthy of further examination in a format in which it can fully be done justice.

Table 14.3. *Top five n-grams for financial, authority, services, commission, securities, exchange and conduct*

Rank	Financial	%	Authority	%2	Services	%3	Commission	%4	Securities	%5	Exchange	%6	Conduct	%7
1	Financial services authority	35.5	Financial services authority	60.68	Services authority	34.99	Exchange commission	33.20	Securities and exchange	44.64	Exchange commission	39.26	Conduct authority	40.19
2	Financial conduct authority	7.67	Financial conduct authority	13.78	Services to	9.31	The commission	16.83	Securities & exchange commission	1.74	Exchange for	3.84	Conduct of	7.01
3	Financial ombudsman service	3.12	Prudential regulation authority	1.90	Services and	3.07	Competition commission	9.34	Securities fraud and	0.58	Exchange and	2.45	Conduct a	3.89
4	Financial services industry	2.96	And markets authority	1.35	Services industry	2.99	European commission	8.60	Securities and futures	0.54	Exchange's	1.87	Conduct and	2.88
5	Financial services compensation	1.88	Advertising standards authority	0.69	Services group	2.36	Trading commission	2.53	Securities in the	0.49	Exchange rates	1.77	Conduct an	2.32

Table 14.4. *Top twenty-five collocates for FSA and Securities # Exchange Commission, sorted by frequency*

	FSA							Securities # Exchange Commission					
Rank	Collocate	Frequency	Years Freq. > 5	MI score	LL score	Semantic domain (USAS)	Rank	Collocate	Frequency	Years Freq. > 5	MI score	LL score	Semantic domain (USAS)
1	Financial	4,973	11	5.05	25,349.34	Business: generally	1	Commission	12,403	11	9.27	139,123.06	General actions, making etc.
2	Services	3,695	11	5.85	22,975.05	Business: generally	2	Exchange	12,394	11	9.48	143,406.07	Getting and giving
3	Authority	3,637	11	6.65	26,775.27	Government etc.	3	US	4,576	11	6.25	30,784.64	Geographical names
4	Bank	1,689	10	3.27	4,659.53	Money generally	4	Filing	904	11	8.64	9,228.87	Paper documents and writing
5	UK	1,431	10	3.84	4,976.61	Geographical names	5	SEC	838	11	6.11	5,481.65	Time: period
6	Rules	1,366	11	5.33	7,489.56	Power, organizing	6	Chairman	620	11	5.08	3,176.40	Power, organizing
7	Chief	1,358	9	4.18	5,336.37	Power, organizing	7	Yesterday	449	10	4.14	1,736.11	Time: general: past
8	Director	1,290	11	5.27	6,972.33	Power, organizing	8	Investigation	355	11	4.11	1,358.77	Investigate, examine, test, search
9	FSA	1,276	10	4.17	5,000.23	Other proper names	9	Former	323	11	3.65	1,044.08	Time: beginning and ending
10	Investigation	1,267	11	2.97	6,034.33	Investigate, examine, test, search	10	Department	276	11	5.18	1,448.46	Groups and affiliation
11	Year	1,236	11	2.92	2,867.17	Time: period	11	Justice	273	11	5.34	1,492.20	Crime, law and order
12	New	1,233	10	3.38	3,567.62	Time: old and new	12	Financial	264	11	1.96	325.61	Money generally
13	Enforcement	1,211	10	7.14	9,788.67	General actions, making etc.	13	America	241	11	5.00	1,207.25	Geographical names
14	Chairman	1,167	11	4.85	5,631.36	Power, organizing	14	Charges	239	9	3.93	857.03	Money: Price / Crime, law and order
15	Regulator	1,113	10	5.07	5,711.26	Objects generally	15	Fraud	235	10	3.59	739.30	Crime, law and order
16	Executive	1,041	10	3.89	3,685.08	Power, organizing	16	Civil	232	10	5.86	1,434.10	Government etc. / Crime, law and order

309

Table 14.4. (cont.)

		FSA						Securities # Exchange Commission					
Rank	Collocate	Frequency	Years Freq. > 5	MI score	LL score	Semantic domain (USAS)	Rank	Collocate	Frequency	Years Freq. > 5	MI score	LL score	Semantic domain (USAS)
17	Report	1,030	10	4.65	4,693.47	Speech acts	17	Filings	231	10	8.18	2,194.80	Paper documents and writing
18	Banks	1,016	9	3.36	2,908.32	Money generally	18	New	211	11	1.98	265.17	Time: old and new
19	Market	935	9	3.21	2,507.18	Business: generally	19	Regulator	210	10	3.81	721.55	Objects generally
20	Yesterday	907	10	4.01	3,359.80	Time: general: past	20	Week	202	10	2.95	474.72	Time: period
21	City	899	10	4.51	3,920.66	Places / Business: generally	21	Chief	192	8	2.51	351.35	Power, organizing
22	Firms	825	9	4.67	3,778.86	Places / Business: generally	22	Rules	189	10	3.62	602.61	Power, organizing
23	Fine	785	9	5.55	4,541.19	Evaluation: Good/bad	23	Regulators	185	9	3.81	634.55	Objects generally
24	Sants	774	9	7.79	7,033.26	Unmatched	24	Settlement	167	9	5.00	837.22	Business: generally
25	Companies	743	11	2.90	1,707.61	Business: generally	25	Company	164	9	1.32	104.72	Business: generally

Concordances show that *regulator** tends to be used to explain the involvement of these specific agencies in the reported cases of corporate fraud:

3. In June the UK's Financial Conduct Authority, the City regulator, also launched an investigation into potential rigging of currency markets ....

4. If any of these banks go bust then you can claim up to £35,000 per person per bank as they are all fully authorised by the Financial Services Authority (FSA), the industry regulator.

5. The company agreed to pay £405m to settle two earlier lawsuits brought by US financial regulator the Securities and Exchange Commission.

In each of the above examples, these agencies are also the agents in Material Action Intentional (MAI) processes (Jeffries 2010); these agencies launch investigations, authorise banks and bring lawsuits. That these are not agentless passives suggests, perhaps, that it often needs to be specified who launches investigations and brings lawsuits on corporate crime; one wonders how often the police or Crown Prosecution Service is mentioned as the agent in agentive passives relating to their routine activities, for example, 'the murder trial was brought by the CPS'.

Note also the metaphor in example 3 that, through the use of the verb 'launch', 'investigation' is constructed as a vessel or missile, suggesting that the relationship between *regulators* and those who are regulated is antagonistic (For more information on metaphor see Chapters 2–5 and 13 in this volume).

Jurisdiction and Remit

Example 6 below shows a more precise description of this regulator through the modifier 'City', which in this context is a synecdoche that specifically means 'the City of London' (which is the historic centre of London, whilst 'London' more generally also refers to the area that also contains the City of Westminster and thirty-one boroughs), in which many financial institutions are located and generally refers to Britain's financial services industry more broadly (see also Chapter 13 on synecdoche). Further examples of this collocate include the following:

6. The ombudsman chairman spelled out his concerns in a formal letter to City regulator the FSA. But nearly nine months later, it has failed to respond.

Example 6 includes the verb 'failed', albeit not in a position to be counted as a collocate; we will come back to this verb later. That said, example 6 suggests, through the use of 'failed', that there is an expectation that the *FSA* should respond to a formal letter spelling out concerns. The use of the capitalized 'But' here helps create the implicature (Grice 1989) and suggests that the period of 'nearly nine months' that has lapsed is, indeed, entirely too long a period to go without response, thereby indirectly but strongly criticizing the FSA.

Further, more precise descriptions of the remit of these *regulators* are also given through the collocates 'banking', 'industry' and 'market', as well as 'financial' for the *Securities and Exchange Commission*:

7. The SEC, the American market regulator, claimed that in some cases select investors with large sums of money – such as hedge funds – were allowed rapidly to trade in and out of a portfolio, despite clear guidelines outlawing the practice in mutual fund prospectuses.

8. The Financial Services Agency, the industry regulator, will seek a response from BNP before determining what disciplinary action to take against the bank, possibly as early as this month.

9. According to new reports, a range of federal agencies, including the SEC, FBI, IRS and banking regulators, have all been investigating allegations of fraud and possibly other illegal activity at Mr Stanford's companies for at least two years and perhaps, as far back as the 1990s.

10. Five industry groups opposed to the registration of hedge funds have written to the Securities and Exchange Commission, the US financial regulator, requesting a 45-day extension of the comment period.

Note, again, in the above examples 7–10, the personification of these agencies, as well as the fact that these are MAI and Verbal processes in which these agencies perform the functional role of the agent, with the exception of example 10. Note also the use of epistemic modality, in particular in example 9, in which the certainty of whether 'fraud' and 'illegal activities' took place at 'Mr Stanford's companies', as well as the time range over which these activities took place, through 'allegations', 'possibly' and 'perhaps', is called into question. This is in keeping with a key tenet of both the US and UK legal systems, in which a legal person is presumed innocent until proven guilty, and so the use of epistemic modality here signals an adherence to that ideology.

In other words, for these agencies, it often needs to be explained why specifically they are authorised to launch investigations, authorise banks, and bring lawsuits. This illustrates that readers are generally presumed to be somewhat unfamiliar with the agencies that do, in fact, have these tasks. This is symptomatic of a greater issue, of white-collar and corporate crime being relatively underreported compared with 'typical' crimes, which are generally handled by the police and Crown Prosecution Service – people are simply presumed to be less familiar with these sorts of cases. However, imagine how patronising it would feel for readers to read a news article reporting that 'the police, *the crime prevention and investigation agency*, launched an inquiry into bicycle theft'!

In the case of the *FSA*, however, 'market' generally refers to the kind of crimes this agency is brought in to investigate and pursue:

11. The pair, one of whom continues to work in the City, faced six-figure fines and the possibility of a permanent ban after being accused of market abuse by the FSA.

12. The regulator warns this may amount to market manipulation. The FSA's markets division also points out that it would look at whether investors jumping on the back of an activist's strategy were using their own money to buy shares rather than that of the institution for which they worked.

Henceforth, the personification of institutions and the general construction of these *regulators* as agents of MAI and Verbal processes, as well as the use of epistemic modality to signal an adherence to the notion of 'innocent until proven otherwise' will no longer be commented on, only the noteworthy absence of any of these elements.

In example 11 and other examples in this chapter, those who are acted upon by these *regulators* often find themselves 'facing' regulatory action. The OED notes that the transitive meaning of 'face' is to confront or meet a danger or an enemy; as such, in line also with the use of 'launch' linked with 'investigation', the relationship between those 'facing' the *FSA* and other *regulators* remains one of hostility, rather than an attitude that acknowledges that collaboration could be the more long-term efficient behaviour.

In the above two examples, furthermore, 'six-figure fines' and a 'permanent ban' appear to be suggested as an appropriate, perhaps even somewhat harsh punishment for 'market abuse', given the use of 'face'. Similarly, the use of the word 'amount', in conjunction with the Verbal act 'warns', suggests that 'market manipulation' is a pretty serious crime. Indeed, many of the crimes referenced in the examples in this chapter are presented as at least somewhat serious; the bigger issue is the assignation of (partial) guilt to the *regulators*, thereby distracting from the individuals at the accused *companies* and *banks* that took the decision to commit an act of corporate fraud, and diffuse the responsibility for that act.

A further noteworthy metaphor concerns the 'market'; we see in examples 11 and 12 that the 'market' can be 'abused' and 'manipulated', whilst example 3 notes that 'currency markets' can be 'rigged'. In each of those examples, the 'market' is conceptualised as a concrete item; 'manipulation' and 'rigging' further suggest that it is something upon which one could lay their hands, perhaps a ship, suggested through 'rigging', that can be adjusted to go in a different direction from the one it would have gone in had it not been adjusted – if the rigger had truly a laissez-faire attitude to the 'market'.

Similarly, the *SEC* is often associated with 'fraud':

13. The Securities and Exchange Commission's fraud probe could finally be the wake-up call for its clients.

Note again the personification in the above example, which goes slightly further by suggesting that the (corporate) clients of the *SEC* are sentient beings capable of being asleep – humans, most likely, given that the context of wake-up calls tends to be common in hotels.

Other modifiers to *regulators* include 'UK' and 'European', which specifically refer to the geographical jurisdiction of these *regulators*, and specifically the *FSA*, whilst the *SEC* collocates with its own jurisdiction, *US*, and *new*, partially for *New York*:

14. They were still hit for a total of £1.1bn, the largest penalty ever imposed by the UK regulator.

15. Handed the task of drawing up a new remuneration code, the UK's Financial Services Authority (FSA) was slammed from all sides last weeks as accusations rained down that it was being too soft on the City in its latest proposals to crack down on bonuses.

16. European regulators have also stepped up their activity since an Organisation for Economic Co-operation and Development convention on combating bribery was passed in 1997.

17. The Securities and Exchange Commission, the US financial regulator, is to take legal action against Hollinger International to determine whether the media group should be punished over the 'alleged unauthorised transfers of assets of at least $32m [pounds 17.8m] to corporate insiders and related entities'.

18. Leaks from the Securities and Exchange Commission, America's financial watchdog, suggest Shell knew two years ago it had overstated some reserves by up to 20 per cent.

19. Shell is already facing investigations from the Securities and Exchange Commission in New York, and the Financial Services Authority in London.

Example 15 requires particular attention, given the density of metaphors. A 'task' is a physical object, passed from person to person ('handed') – the *FSA* is again personified – and in this case contains instructions to visually create rules – perhaps 'a code' is an architectural structure. The personified *FSA* is physically attacked from all sides; accusations, then, are punches – alternatively, they could be raindrops, but given 'slammed', punches seem more likely, and 'raining punches' – itself metaphorical – is conventional. In other words, the accusations like punches have come fast and many at once and in quick succession. The actions of the *FSA*, in the meanwhile, have been more like gentle touches than of the kind that would crack hard materials – the item to be cracked is the 'City', also personified. In other words, the *FSA* has failed to break (the bones of?) the City, and has received physical punishment in return. Key in this is the fact that there are expectations of toughness, an antagonism to 'companies' and 'banks' that the *FSA* should live up to – and does not.

In example 16, 'combating' again creates a hostile, violent opposition on the part of *regulators* to bribery. The crime is, through 'combating', suggested to be a relatively serious one.

Example 17 is also heavy with over-lexicalisation: an 'unauthorised transfer of assets to corporate insiders and related entities' is, more simply put, theft. The over-lexicalisation here functions to conceal the fact that many white-collar crimes, despite their relative complexity, eventually boil down to more common, easy-to-interpret crimes; as such, the impact of these crimes is somewhat negated. Similarly, 'overstated some reserves by up to 20 per cent' in example 18 is an over-lexicalisation of 'lied, a lot (and for a long time)' to investors.

Note also the use of 'watchdog' in this example, to describe the *regulator*; this is a metaphor that occurs in many examples, primarily through the ascription of animal characteristics to the *regulators*. What a watchdog guards is usually a property or important location; this fits generally with the conceptualisation of the now-abstract marketplace as a physical location, and the significance of 'market' as a collocate to *regulator*|*regulators*.

14.5.2 Who Else Is Involved?

Collaborators

These *regulators* often act in conjunction with the (UK) 'government':

20. The UK's listing rules must be urgently redrawn by the Government and regulators to stop foreign firms with lapsed controls being presented as premium stocks, a leading shareholder has warned.

21. They have also had to cope with an unprecedented level of reviews and changes imposed by the Government, the regulator and Europe.

Similarly, the set of frequent collocates 'department' and 'justice' indicate the US Department of Justice, with which the SEC often collaborates:

22. Since the reserves shock, the group faces investigations by the US Securities and Exchange Commission and the US Department of Justice.

23. The Department of Justice and the Securities and Exchange Commission are in advanced settlement talks with ConvergEx in which the broker may admit to wrongdoing as part of a civil settlement.

It may be hypothesised that the involvement of the (UK) 'government' and the (US) Department of Justice signal the seriousness of the crimes investigated. Note, furthermore, that in example 20, the use of the strong deontic modal verb 'must' also lays the responsibility for stopping the presentation 'as premium stocks' of 'foreign firms with lapsed controls' with *regulators* and the 'government', rather than with those responsible for that presenting. Example 21, through 'cope' and 'unprecedented', suggests that the actions of the 'government' and *regulator* have been too much, have negatively affected business.

Opponents

Aside from identifying the regulatory agencies as agents, many of the examples presented in this chapter also show that the targets of these processes tend to be banks and companies. 'Banks' and 'companies' are, indeed, also close constant collocates of *regulator** and *FSA*, as are some other items in the semantic domains of 'Money' and 'Business': 'bank' and 'company', which, as shown in the examples below, also tend to be the target of the processes set in motion by *regulators* and the *FSA*, in the same way that 'firms' are affected by the *FSA*:

24. Andrew Bailey, the FSA's top regulator, accused the bank of a 'culture of gaming – and gaming us', when he appeared before MPs.

25. The FSA said the bank failed to keep proper records on the identity of customers.

26. By making it uneconomical to invest in many hedge funds, the FSA is robbing Japanese banks of the opportunity to learn the kind of sophisticated financial techniques they need to improve their performance in the years ahead, argues another.

27. The Financial Services Authority (FSA) fined companies and individuals pounds 27.3m for the year to March 31, a 514pc increase on the previous year and the most in its 12-year history.

28. Mick McAteer at the consumer group Which? is concerned that the new rules could lead to misselling if they are not implemented carefully. 'It depends very much on how the basic advice regime turns out, but at the moment we are very concerned that the FSA has given firms too much leeway to write their own selling strategies.'

29. Shell sought to limit the damage by disclosing the fines last month. But now a joint operation by Britain's Financial Services Authority and the U.S. Securities and Exchange Commission has caused the company further humiliation.

The targets, being primarily 'companies' and 'banks', are the Goals or Receivers of process types that must either be labelled MAI or Verbal, suggesting that the agencies that are the actors (or sayers) of these processes actively chose to carry out these actions. Furthermore, processes such as 'taking disciplinary action', 'bringing a lawsuit', 'investigating allegations of fraud', 'accusing' and 'fining' are all actions that, in the context of an adversarial legal system, such as that of the United Kingdom and the United States, can be considered as antagonistic. Indeed, the context of such a legal system means that these regulators and companies are inherently considered to be in opposition to one another; the question is then whose side the newspapers are on. As has been noted earlier in this chapter, many of the processes in which the *regulators* affect 'companies' are metaphorically constructed as physically violent actions. As such, the adversarial relationship between *regulators* and 'companies' becomes a metaphorical battle.

14.5.3 What Do Regulators Do?

Regulators are generally presented as the actors in processes that affect 'companies' and 'banks' as targets, suggesting that they make it a point to, as it were, strike first, instead of respond to indications of wrongdoing at these companies. In other words, through the grammar, it is suggested that *regulators* act outside their remit, and indeed unfairly. Whether this reading is accurate depends on which process types these *regulators* initiate. Table 14.5 shows the top twenty-five collocating verbs (defined as having a _v* or _m* tag after the corpus was processed using TagAnt 1.2.0 [Anthony 2015]; stats are for the untagged corpus) for *regulator|regulators*.

Given the process types of these verbs, the following groups can be distinguished: Verbal (what do the regulators say), including 'said', 'says', 'told', 'according' and 'say'; deontic modal (what should and will the regulators do), including 'will', 'would', 'should', 'may', 'must' and 'need'; MAI (what have the regulators done), including 'take', 'did', 'fined', 'found', 'make', 'settle', 'do', 'made' and 'working'; and the remainder, including 'expected', 'looking' and 'concerned'.

Modal Verbs and Expectations

In the group of deontic modals, a distinction must be made between those that communicate an externally imposed expectation (*should, must, need*) and those that more simply communicate intentions on the part of the *regulators* themselves (*will, would, may*). The presence of relatively many strong deontic modals in this top twenty-five suggests a preoccupation on the part of the newspapers with what these *regulators* are, at the moment, not yet getting right, or are expected not to get right:

30. 'The FSA as regulator should have been making sure the systems and controls were up to standard.'

Table 14.5. *Top twenty-five collocating verbs to regulator|regulators*

Rank	Collocate	Frequency	Years Freq. > 5	MI score	LL score	Process
1	said	3,962	11	5.11	20,548.31	Verbal
2	will	1,871	11	4.42	7,935.24	Modal: deontic
3	would	1,494	11	4.54	6,599.92	Modal: deontic
4	should	870	11	5.05	4,406.78	Modal: deontic
5	could	813	11	4.34	3,353.40	Modal: epistemic
6	says	620	11	4.29	2,529.09	Verbal
7	can	569	11	3.95	2,059.73	Modal: dynamic
8	take	486	11	4.68	2,226.85	Material intention
9	may	491	11	4.28	1,986.88	Modal: deontic
10	did	355	11	4.56	1,578.24	Material intention
11	fined	558	11	7.19	4,492.06	Material intention
12	found	541	11	5.57	3,122.06	Material intention
13	must	356	11	5.16	1,870.16	Modal: deontic
14	make	383	11	4.26	1,550.11	Material intention
15	expected	346	11	4.72	1,612.96	
16	told	471	11	5.08	2,425.04	Verbal
17	settle	275	10	6.85	2,093.36	Material intention
18	looking	281	11	5.59	1,643.21	Mental perception
19	according	293	11	4.61	1,315.184	Verbal
20	do	465	11	4.29	1,881.54	Material intention
21	need	397	11	4.91	1,957.45	Modal: boulomaic
22	concerned	281	11	6.33	920.85	Mental reaction/ material intention
23	say	375	11	4.83	1,783.08	Verbal
24	made	415	11	4.23	1,655.94	Material intention
25	working	250	10	5.27	1,345.06	Material intention

31. Rather, the regulator should make sure that promises are honoured, insofar as they can be, and that an institution is wound up with as little disruption as possible.

32. Now the industry and its regulator must make sure the same thing can never happen again.

33. Washington's regulators need to wake up and think about the next crisis.

34. The regulators need sharper teeth.

35. The regulator's review revealed a catalogue of appalling mistakes, leading to accusations that the FSA was 'asleep on the job'.

Several examples in this chapter have already touched on these newspapers' tendency to cast judgment on the actions of these *regulators*. Similarly, in examples 30 and 32–34, these *regulators'* ability to carry out their responsibilities are called into question: examples 33 and 34 in particular tap into a metaphorical understanding of these agencies as living beings, whose role is to be focused and aggressive. Of these two, example 34 most explicitly appears to be linked to the common synonym for *regulator*, 'watchdog'. In other words, much of the newspaper representation of *regulators* focuses on the question of whether they are (1) ineffective and/or (2) overly aggressive. Such concerns are also raised in the following examples:

36. Mr Geoghegan also raised concerns that regulators may be overzealous in their banking reforms by demanding too much capital be put aside, which could restrict lending and economic growth.

37. At every stage, regulators have been flexing their muscles more, becoming intensive, intrusive and raising the bar not just for capital and liquidity ratios for the banks, but acceptable standards around suitability of products for consumers, the management of potential conflicts of interests, anti-money-laundering, antibribery measures and risk culture in general.

'Overzealous' and 'flexing', used in the above examples, as well as 'sharper teeth' and its negation, 'toothless', are not constant collocates, nor are they particularly important collocates, as shown in Table 14.6. Note, however, their fit with the construction of *regulators* as animalistic, aggressive, antagonistic beings. Furthermore, semantically related words like 'aggressive' and 'tough' are constant and more clearly significant, as shown in Table 14.6.

Examples of this collocation are:

38. The move is a further signal that the regulator is becoming more aggressive in its attempts to combat business practices that are detrimental to consumers.

Table 14.6. *Aggressive, fail*, flexing, overzealous, teeth, toothless and tough as collocates to regulator|regulators*

Collocate	Frequency	MI score	LL score	Constant?
aggressive	87	5.57	503.91	Yes
failed	351	5.71	2,097.82	Yes
failings	104	6.57	746.65	Yes
failure	146	5.28	786.52	Yes
flexing	11	8.29	106.14	No
overzealous	11	8.49	109.56	No
teeth	42	6.91	321.13	No
toothless	29	8.55	291.25	No
tough	172	6.10	1,122.14	Yes

39. Until the regulator gets tough with these shady practices, its bite has all the ferocity of a slobbery pair of gums.

40. The French bank also warned of the potential dire consequences for the banking system if US regulators imposed an excessively tough penalty.

In example 38, 'aggressive' does not appear to be particularly bad; indeed, by focusing on the potentially negative effects that these business practices have on consumers, becoming more aggressive is presented as a desirable quality. Nonetheless, the use of 'aggressive' also fits with the metaphorical conceptualisation of *regulators* as watchdogs. Example 39 underpins the watchdog metaphor further, by focusing on 'bite' and 'a slobbery pair of gums'. In fact, many breeds of guard dogs were bred from mastiffs, which are, indeed, relatively slobbery dogs. Again, in this sentence 'getting tough' is presented as a desirable quality, especially through the opposition with the evaluative 'shady'. However, as example 40 also shows, *regulators* must also beware of being too aggressive, too tough; 'dire consequences for the banking system', presented as a likely outcome of the US regulators' proposed course of action, strongly negatively evaluates this course of action, as does the modifying 'excessively'. As such, *regulators* are expected to walk a tightrope.

The use of strong deontic modals suggests, as noted, that these *regulators* are not living up to expectations. In fact, by expecting *regulators* to be 'tough' but not 'too tough', they are set up to fail. And they do, as shown in Table 14.6. Variations on 'fail*' are significant constant collocates to *regulator|regulators*. In fact, 'failed' has a greater frequency and higher MI and LL scores than 'working' in Table 14.5; this is presumably due to the use of tags to define verbs for Table 14.5 (the reported statistics are for the untagged corpus and thus remain comparable). In other words, there is a remarkably consistent undermining of the *regulators*; they are constantly presented as simply not being up to their task.

Examples of these collocations are the following:

41. The regulator failed, rather than the regulations, but the FSA still seems not to recognise this.

42. Since then the FSA has appeared to compound its initial error in not making more of its investigation public with a series of delays that mean the final report will focus as much on the regulator's failings as it does on those at RBS.

43. Lord Turner was questioned by MPs over the regulator's failure to spot warning signs of Libor cheating early enough as well as its decision not to pursue criminal prosecutions against individual Barclays employees.

44. The failure of the regulator to sort this out is remarkable.

The Portrayal of Regulators in UK News about Corporate Crime 321

Concordance Hits	400			
Hit	KWIC			File
99	a grilling from MPs who complained that the	FSA failed to	flag up the impending credit crunch.	G75616.t
100	the chaos in our banking system which the	FSA failed to	foresee or prevent. A measure of	ST73293.t
101	ic circle was never satisfactorily proved and the	FSA failed to	get an admission of guilt from	ST25057.t
102	was safe to eat. The Food Standards Agency	(FSA) failed to	give clear guidance on which products	M73284.t
103	ial Advisers, recently told Financial Mail: OEThe	FSA failed to	mind the shop.!	DM79228
104	and could thus be bailed out. What the	FSA failed to	note was that because of the '	DM72075
105	, and among the regulators - is also crucial. The	FSA failed to	perceive the risks to financial stability.	T77323.tx
106	ommon with other regulators across the globe, the	FSA failed to	predict that liquidity would completely dry	FT72176.t
107	enrose Report clearly shows that the Treasury and	FSA failed to	protect policyholders. It strengthens our case	MS4679.t
108	r boss</TITLE> THE Financial Services Authority	(FSA) failed to	protect British savers, according to the	DT77062.t
109	es. In particular, the action group believes the	FSA failed to	protect consumers by allowing Cameron Farley	T18115.tx
110	financial services and markets tribunal says the	FSA failed to	prove mis-selling was widespread. The £1.1	G24505.t
111	ed £750,000 in 2006 for illegal trading. But the	FSA failed to	prove he deliberately committed market abuse.	FT50854.t
112	to a fall in its shares. But the	FSA failed to	prove that anyone had deliberately spread	G73368.t
113	advisers warned that, if the company and the	FSA failed to	provide more detailed information than this	DT68797.
114	ulator blamed over Dunfermline City watchdog the	FSA failed to	provide the "necessary level of supervision"	FT76455.t
115	refusing to publish a report into why the	FSA failed to	punish Fred Goodwin and other former	DM83118
116	report says. Her seventh charge is that the	FSA failed to	pursue Equitable over its failure to	FT74165.t

Figure 14.1. Collocation of FSA and 'failed'

This tendency, to focus on the failures of *regulators*, including the *FSA*, is systematic. 'Failed' is also a constant collocate to *FSA*, with a frequency of 402, an MI score of 4.55, and a log-likelihood score of 1776.07, suggesting a strong collocation of the two items. 'Failed', 'failing', 'failings' and 'failure' are all also constant collocates to *FSA*. Furthermore, 'fail*' collocates with *FSA* at a frequency of 1,040, an MI score of 8.33642 and a log-likelihood score of 4,505.75. These are also mainly the result of accusations that the *FSA* 'failed' to carry out their work as expected, as shown in Figure 14.1.

Given the apparent tendency for reporters to prefer 'negative' news (Bednarek & Caple 2012, p. 42), that failings of the *FSA* are likely to be reported is somewhat expected, but nonetheless results in a portrayal of the *FSA* as quite incompetent.

The constructed opposition in example 41 of *regulator* and *regulations* suggests that these newspapers do not necessarily have a problem with the actual regulations and laws that apply to the activities of the financial industry, but with the way they are carried out. Indeed, several of the examples given in this chapter negatively evaluate the illegal or illegitimate actions of 'banks' and 'companies'. What these newspapers do seem to have an issue with, however, is with the way these regulations are (or are not!) applied by the *regulators*. They cast aspersions on the regulators by emphasising that such wrongdoing happened not necessarily just because these 'banks' and 'companies' committed wrongdoing, but because these *regulators* either allowed wrongdoing to happen or were so tough that companies saw no other way to survive but through wrongdoing. In other words, many of the linguistic choices made in the examples presented in this chapter contribute to a

Table 14.7. *Aggressive, fail*, flexing, overzealous, teeth, toothless and tough as collocates to Securities # Exchange Commission*

Collocate	Frequency	MI score	LL score	Constant?
aggressive	4	0.90	1.28	Yes
failed	12	0.63	1.99	No
failings	2	0.70	0.41	No
failure	10	1.20	5.34	No
flexing	1	4.55	4.40	No
overzealous	0	0.00	0.00	No
teeth	0	0.00	0.00	No
toothless	0	0.00	0.00	No
tough	6	1.04	2.50	No

distraction strategy, a discursive red herring, in which attention is deflected from the arguably more important question: Why is it that, time and time again, 'companies' and 'banks' commit offences that have such a large impact (see Punch 1996)?

It must be noted, by the way, that, according to Table 14.7, the *Securities and Exchange Commission* is not generally presented as 'failing', except in a small number of cases. It is unclear why this is the case; one might hypothesise that the owners and financial journalists of UK newspapers have closer links with UK financial institutions than US ones, and as such, US *regulators* forms less of a threat to those parties that UK journalists are relatively close with.

Material Action Intention

It must be noted that 'failing' is also not something all *regulators* and the *FSA* do. Returning to Table 14.2, we still have to consider the collocates 'investigation' and 'rules'. 'Rules' are what give these agencies a justification for acting:

45. Pace Micro Technology, the digital TV set-top box maker, has lodged an appeal after being found guilty of breaching stock market rules by the City regulator.

46. The FSA made a concerted effort to crack down on insider dealing last year. The crime, which comes under the FSA rules on market abuse, is notoriously difficult to prove.

47. Its error was to ignore the rules of the US Securities and Exchange Commission on the conditions that need to be satisfied for a company to classify a find in this category.

However, it is also the *regulator* that affects 'rules', whereby the 'rules' are an explicit target. As mentioned above, there is, in the case of the *FSA*, much mention of bringing in 'new' 'rules':

48. The regulator introduced transitional rules for those borrowers who simply wanted to remortgage to get a better rate without borrowing more but were unable to meet the new affordability requirements.

49. But given the trends in place, with passive funds, particularly exchange traded funds, enjoying significant growth, perhaps active managers are worried about the impact the FSA's new rules will have on fund sales.

50. A US federal appeals court has thrown out new rules from the Securities and Exchange Commission intended to make it easier for shareholders to eject board members at listed companies.

Note that in examples 49 and 50, the 'rules' are negatively evaluated through the focus on the worries about the 'impact' on 'fund sales', and the mention that the US Federal Appeals Court has thrown these rules out.

51. A trade body representing mortgage brokers said that they were the victims of conflicting rules from regulators and that they had been unfairly singled out.

52. But now the regulator's rules have gone way too far.

53. Treasury committee chairman criticises listing rules for overseas funds.

54. Lenders also face tougher rules from the regulator as part of the FSA's clampdown on irresponsible lending.

Example 51 describes rules as 'conflicting', whilst example 52 says that they (much like *regulators*) have now 'gone way too far', and in example 53, the *rules* are criticised. It seems then that 'rules', like *regulators*, also must have the characteristics of being non-conflicting and not too tough in order to be accepted. The consequences of bad 'rules' are, as in examples 51 and 53, pretty serious: 'facing' such rules creates 'victims', in the same sense that 'banks' and 'companies' appear to be identified as victims of *regulators*' inability to act according to expectations.

Similar is the general identification of 'investigation' by the *regulators* as a cause of some other action:

55. Credit insurance group CPP has issued a fresh profits warning due to an ongoing investigation by the City regulator, causing its shares to slump.

56. When it floated the insurer was valued at £400m, but the shares halved after it was revealed in March 2011 that it was under investigation by the City watchdog and had suspended sales of identity theft cover.

57. A full investigation by the FSA would be the clearest sign yet that, far from being the trifling issue that some of the banks suggest, swap misselling to small businesses has been endemic and is the next reputational disaster awaiting the banking industry.

58. But his troubles worsened when the US Securities and Exchange Commission announced a formal investigation into the disaster.

In the above examples, the 'investigation' is given as the cause for financial issues – rather than the fact that these institutions acted in a sufficiently suspicious manner to prompt such an 'investigation'! – although example 57 does acknowledge that 'swap misselling' itself may play a part in the expected 'reputational disaster'. 'Rules' and 'investigation' then further illuminate the tightrope *regulators* are expected to walk: to be sufficiently tough to prevent corporate crime, but not so tough as to impede trade. Finding such a Goldilocks zone of regulation would, theoretically, be possible, were it not that some level of rule-breaking is generally suggested to be part and parcel of trade (see Ras 2017). A similar thing seems to be happening in the following examples, of the collocation of 'enforcement' and 'report' with *FSA*:

59. However, Mr Shankland told *The Daily Telegraph*: 'In relation to the billions that were written off by the bank, my business was relatively small,' adding he was 'hugely concerned about what could happen' with fallout from potential enforcement proceedings at the FSA.

60. Royal Bank of Scotland fell 1.43p to 20.56p after a long-awaited FSA report into the bank.

The other material processes in which *regulators* are involved are *take*, *did*, *fined*, *found*, *make*, *settle*, *do*, *made* and *working*. Some of the uses of these verbs again centre on the question of whether responses by these agencies to allegations made were adequate:

61. Lord Turner, as chairman of the Financial Services Authority was also implicated following the revelation that the City regulator failed to take action against a senior Barclays executive at the centre of the scandal.

62. But that has raised questions about why the regulator did not act sooner to demand Mr FitzPatrick's resignation.

63. Sometimes, regulators simply won't do anything – sometimes they uncover no fraud; sometimes they are overworked and understaffed; and sometimes they and lawmakers are too cushy with the company or industry in question to do what's right. When regulators do act, it is a certainty that Washington and Wall Street's clocks are not synchronized.

64. But it is uncertain whether the regulator will take any action.

'Scandal', in example 61, generally serves a euphemistic purpose in the context of corporate crime (Mayr & Machin 2012, p. 203). Note also that number 61 is a further example of the collocate 'failed'. Similarly, the *SEC* collocates significantly with 'settlement':

65. A federal judge yesterday raised fresh questions about the US Securities and Exchange Commission's settlement with Bank of America over bonus disclosures, calling the regulator's explanation for why it did not charge individuals 'puzzling'.

The above examples again call into question the capacity of these agencies to fulfil their duties; the evaluation inherent to the negation 'failed' in example 61 focuses on what these agencies have neglected to do. Similarly, examples 62 and 63 offer a negation of the expectation that the *regulator* would act. Furthermore, whilst example 64 only raises the likelihood that the *regulator* will not take any action, the fact that it does so through negated epistemic modality suggests that this is unlikely; the use of 'but' communicates implicitly that the *regulator* should take that action.

Other uses of these verbs more explicitly evaluate the *regulator*:

66. The far-reaching reforms instigated by Ms Schapiro have two prime objectives – to make the regulator both more efficient and much better able to anticipate crises before they occur.

67. What a shame the regulators make [doubting their capabilities] so easy.

68. 'We've all had to foot the bill for the mistakes made by the regulators, and so those regulators should be accountable to the British taxpayer not to Brussels. Gordon Brown should stop dithering and stop these plans in their tracks.'

Example 66 implies that until the mentioned reforms are pushed through, the *regulator* will remain inefficient and unable to anticipate crises; example 67 is even more explicit and confirms that raising doubts about the abilities of *regulators* is rather easy. Example 68, finally, associates regulators with making mistakes, and by mentioning 'footing the bill' underlines the gravity of that mistake – the 'we' in this example refers to the British taxpayer to whom regulators must be made accountable, and, throughout the newspapers included in this corpus (see Ras 2017) as well as throughout other British media, anything that costs the taxpayer money is constructed as inherently negative. Again, however, *regulators* must not go 'too far' in their responses to fraud:

69. It is also essential that regulators do not raise their eyebrows too often. Frequent usage can take a disastrous toll on the potency of forehead hair. And regulators are so risk averse that it may be that they cannot be relied on to act, or rather not act, in a suitably judicious fashion.

70. People close to the FSA insist the regulator did not force HBOS to the table.

In example 69, the personification of the *regulator* is taken pretty far. It is made the agent of the conventional 'raising their eyebrows', which literally refers to a facial expression involving negative judgement, but metaphorically refers to a mild (verbal) expression of negative judgement. However, the next sentence takes the metaphor further, also suggesting that the *regulator* has forehead hair, and that raising eyebrows too often can have negative effects on that. Presuming forehead hair to be a good thing – otherwise, what would be the point of warning against actions that may endanger it? – it may be understood as referring to the *regulators'* reputation, their public image. Given the use of 'potency' in this sentence, perhaps it is not just the public image that is threatened by 'raised eyebrows', but the impact thereof. Indeed, the next sentence again casts explicit doubt on the capabilities of the *regulators*. Example 70, meanwhile, has to explicitly negate, and do so with some force through 'insist', that the FSA used force to talk with HBOS – again, the implication is that *regulators* must never be too aggressive.

It must be noted, however, that not all processes involving *regulators* and the *SEC* must immediately be interpreted as negative:

71. Last year the FSA fined JP Morgan 633.3m for a similar offence.

72. Standard Chartered has agreed to pay £217million to settle allegations from a US regulator that it laundered £160billion for Iranian clients.

73. She also paid $1million (£635,000) to settle an SEC lawsuit which alleged that she and her relatives netted $23million (£14.6million) from illicit trades.

74. HSBC stressed it was 'working with regulators and agencies to resolve [allegations of money laundering]'.

75. The recommendations are likely to strike fear into a banking sector reeling from the US Securities and Exchange Commission's fraud charges against Goldman Sachs.

The above examples list the successes of the *regulators*, and the reported numbers appear to be relatively impressive amounts. On the other hand, the comparisons made in examples 72 ('pay £217million [for] £160billion') and 73 ('paid $1million [for] $23million') invite discussions on the impact of settlements; perhaps settlements comprising, respectively, 1/737 and 1/23 of the illegitimately earned amounts are less likely to have a deterrent effect than might, at first glance, seem. Similarly, the 633.3m reported in example 71, in the context of being a fine that was given the year before for a similar offence, suggests that such fines are not particularly effective general deterrents. This is, indeed, the view communicated in the following example of the collocation of 'fine' with *FSA:*

76. Consumer groups said tougher enforcement was needed. Peter Vicary-Smith, chief executive of Which, the consumer organisation, said: 'We believe the fine imposed by the FSA is far too lenient. If we're going to deter financial institutions from failing their customers, then fines need to be much higher.'

14.6 Conclusion

This chapter describes the findings of a corpus-assisted Critical Discourse Analysis of the portrayals of regulators in news on corporate fraud, as published by UK newspapers between 2004 and 2014, with a particular focus on the UK-based FSA and the US-based SEC and the question of whether this reporting enhances or negates the legitimacy of these agencies in regulating UK and US financial institutions. The FSA and SEC were both the most reported-on regulatory agencies, but also the leading regulators in these two economies. As this corpus contains articles from UK newspapers, a focus on the UK regulator is unsurprising; the cultural proximity (see Fowler 1991) of the United States, and the importance of the US economy to the UK one, explains why the SEC is so heavily reported on.

Throughout the corpus, regulators are personified, even metaphorically constructed as animalistic; they are watchdogs. The tendency to personify institutions requires further examination. A key finding is the constant tendency to identify these regulators as the agent of actions that often negatively affect companies and banks; such actions are, in many cases, metaphorically identified as physically violent. As such, through grammar, metaphor and the context of the common law system, the relationship between financial institutions and regulators is an antagonistic one. Because of this antagonism, regulators are expected to walk a tightrope of not intervening too aggressively, 'going too far', as doing so would impede business, and also not 'going far enough', being not too lenient, as doing so would 'let them get away with it'. Many of the examples presented in this chapter show that regulators often do not, and cannot, live up to those expectations, generally by being 'too lenient'. However, by focusing on how regulators fell short in preventing cases of corporate fraud, regulators are also made to share in the blame for these cases of fraud. This is a diffusion of responsibility and a form of 'condemning the condemners' (see Sykes & Matza 1957); no longer are those who decided to commit an act of corporate fraud the sole offenders, but so are the regulators. This implicit argument generally functions to undermine the legitimacy of the regulator; if they cannot even prevent the crimes they are supposed to prevent, then what authority do they have?

References

Anthony, L. (2015). TagAnt (Version 1.1.0) [Computer Software]. Tokyo: Waseda University. www.laurenceanthony.net/software.

(2019). AntConc (Version 3.5.8) [Computer Software]. Tokyo: Waseda University. www.laurenceanthony.net/software.

Baker, P. (2012). Acceptable bias? Using corpus linguistics methods with critical discourse analysis. *Critical Discourse Studies*, 9(3), 247–56.

Baker, P., Gabrielatos, C., Khosravinik, M., Krzyzanowski, M., McEnery, T., & Wodak, R. (2008). A useful methodological synergy? Combining critical discourse analysis and corpus linguistics to examine discourses of refugees and asylum seekers in the UK press. *Discourse and Society*, 19(3), 273–306.

Bednarek, M., & Caple, H. (2012). *News Discourse*. London: Continuum.

Callanan, V. J., & Rosenberger, J. S. (2011). Media and public perceptions of the police: Examining the impact of race and personal experience. *Policing and Society*, 21(2), 167–89.

Chermak, S., & Weiss, A. (2005). Maintaining legitimacy using external communication strategies: An analysis of police–media relations. *Journal of Criminal Justice*, 33(5), 501–12.

Fairclough, N. (2015). *Language and Power*, 3rd ed. London: Routledge.

Financial Services and Markets Act 2000. (c. 8). London: The Stationery Office.

Fowler, R. (1991). *Language in the News: Discourse and Ideology in the Press*. London: Routledge.

Gablasova, D., Brezina, V., & McEnery, T. (2017). Collocations in corpus-based language learning research: Identifying, comparing, and interpreting the evidence. *Language Learning*, 67, 155–79.

Gabrielatos, C., & Baker, P. (2008). Fleeing, sneaking, flooding: A corpus analysis of discursive constructions of refugees and asylum seekers in the UK press 1996–2005. *Journal of English Linguistics*, 36(1), 5–38.

Gray, J. M. (2009). What shapes public opinion of the criminal justice system? In J. Wood & T. A. Gannon, eds., *Public Opinion and Criminal Justice*. Cullompton: Willan, pp. 49–72.

Graziano, L., Schuck, A., & Martin, C. (2010). Police misconduct, media coverage, and public perceptions of racial profiling: An experiment. *Justice Quarterly*, 27(1), 52–76.

Grice, H. P. (1989). *Studies in the Way of Words*. Cambridge, MA: Harvard University Press.

Heeks, M., Reed, S., Tafsiri, M., & Prince, S. (2018). *The Economic and Social Costs of Crime*. [Online]. London: Home Office. https://assets.publishing.service.gov.uk/government/uploads/system/uploads/attachment_data/file/727958/the-economic-and-social-costs-of-crime-horr99.pdf (accessed 31 July 2018).

Her Majesty's Revenue and Customs (2018). *Measuring Tax Gaps 2018 Edition: Tax Gap Estimates for 2016–17*. [Online]. London: HMRC. https://assets.publishing.service.gov.uk/government/uploads/system/uploads/attachment_data/file/715742/HMRC-measuring-tax-gaps-2018.pdf (accessed 31 July 2018).

Her Majesty's Treasury (2017). *Spring Budget 2017*. [Online]. London: HM Treasury. www.gov.uk/government/publications/spring-budget-2017-documents/spring-budget-2017 (accessed 1 March 2019).

Jeffries, L. (2010). *Critical Stylistics: The Power of English*. Basingstoke: Palgrave Macmillan.

  (2014). Critical stylistics. In M. Burke, ed., *The Routledge Handbook of Stylistics*. London: Routledge, pp. 408–20.

Jeffries, L., & Walker, B. (2012). Key words in the press: A critical corpus-driven analysis of ideology in the Blair years (1998–2007). *English Text Construction*, 5(2), 208–29.

Jewkes, Y. (2011). *Media and Crime*, 2nd ed. London: Sage.
Mayr, A., & Machin, D. (2012). *How to Do Critical Discourse Analysis*. London: Sage.
McMullan, J. L., & McClung, M. (2006). The media, the politics of truth, and the coverage of corporate violence: The Westray disaster and the public inquiry. *Critical Criminology*, 14, 67–86.
Orpin, D. (2006). Corpus linguistics and critical discourse analysis: Examining the ideology of sleaze. *International Journal of Corpus Linguistics*, 10(1), 37–61.
Poole, B. (2010). Commitment and criticality: Fairclough's critical discourse analysis evaluated. *International Journal of Applied Linguistics*, 20(2), 137–55.
Povey, K. (2001). *Open All Hours: A Thematic Inspection Report on the Role of Police Visibility and Accessibility in Public Reassurance*. London: HMIC.
Punch, M. (1996). *Dirty Business: Exploring Corporate Misconduct, Analysis and Cases*. London: Sage.
Ras, I. A. (2017). A corpus-assisted critical discourse analysis of the reporting of corporate fraud by UK national newspapers, 2004–2014. PhD thesis, University of Leeds.
Richardson, J. E. (2007). *Analysing Newspapers: An Approach from Critical Discourse Analysis*. London: Palgrave.
Securities and Exchange Commission (2013). What we do. www.sec.gov/Article/whatwedo.html (accessed 10 March 2019).
Sutherland, E. H. (1949). *White Collar Crime*. New Haven, CT: Yale University Press.
Sykes, G. M., & Matza, D. (1957). Techniques of neutralization: A theory of delinquency. *American Sociological Review*, 22(6), 664–70.
Toolan, M. (1997). What is critical discourse analysis and why are people saying such terrible things about it? *Language and Literature*, 6(2), 83–103.
Widdowson, H. G. (1995). Discourse analysis: A critical view. *Language and Literature*, 4(3), 157–72.
  (2004). *Text, Context, Pretext: Critical Issues in Discourse Analysis*. Oxford: Blackwell Publishing.
Wodak, R. (2001). What CDA is about – A summary of its history, important concepts and its developments. In R. Wodak & M. Meyer, eds., *Methods of Critical Discourse Analysis*. London: Sage, pp. 1–13.
Wright, J. P., Cullen, F. T., & Blankenship, M. B. (1995). The social construction of corporate violence: Media coverage of the Imperial Food Products fire. *Crime & Delinquency*, 41(1), 20–37.

15 Ideology in Critical Crime Fiction

John Douthwaite

The full version of this chapter can be accessed online at www.cambridge.org/ LinguisticsOfCrime

Douthwaite selects the television series Inspector George Gently as an exemplification of critical crime fiction in order to lay bear the ideological workings of that sub-genre and of the linguistic techniques it employs to position readers/viewers.

The chapter is in three parts. The introduction identifies the central issue as that of ideological struggle between conservative and critical crime fiction. The claim is made that enormous differences exist in constructional techniques between the two sub-genres and such differences are determined by their differing goals.

Part two proceeds to analyse the constructional and linguistic differences and how these are linked to the underlying aim of suasion. Comparison of Gently with Barnaby is constantly engaged in to highlight the nature of those differences and connect them directly to goal.

The factors analysed to determine how a television series or a novel are constructed include: how politics influence the production and broadcasting of programmes; the intentionality of the writer/producer; the effects of the need for verisimilitude in critical crime fiction and the effects of the constraints placed on writing and production by having to respect verisimilitude, as well as the effects of the lack of such a constraint on the conservative variety; the ways verisimilitude are achieved and how these influence production; the constraints of format and of narrative technique, in addition to the effect of format on narrative technique and vice versa, (for instance, the storyline and how event-led narration differs from character-led narration and the effects this produces on depth of analysis and consequently on suasion); the general cultural and historical context and the specific context of production, and the constraints these place on production (such as the conflict between entertainment and education, or the production of 'quality' programmes); the central role of emotion - developed in depth - in critical crime fiction and the relative lack of emotion (or its superficial treatment) in the conservative sub-genre. All of these factors are interrelated and connected directly to goal.

These constructional variables are manipulated in such a way as to produce an overall effect of profundity and complexity of analysis of people and society in the critical sub-genre and superficiality and simplicity in the conservative variety. These two starkly contrasting traits are directly connected to the ideological goals of the two subgenres: to induce critical analytical thinking in the critical sub-genre, to lull into complacent serenity in the conservative subgenre.

Part three offers an extensive (but not exhaustive), in-depth stylistic, pragmatic analysis of communication in an extract each from two episodes of Gently in order to demonstrate how the factors identified in part two of the chapter work in the text and to demonstrate the depth of the critical text and the superficiality of the conservative text. One target text centres on the social aspect (gender, patriarchy, power, culture, how police attitudes and techniques affect the outcome of investigations), the other target text examines how personality, emotion and values are intimately related to ideology and how these affect the workings of 'justice'.

Index

action
   doers of; 134
adaptation
   adaptor; 151, 154–157, 159, 162
   augmentation; 150
   domestication; 159, 161, 167–168
   exoticism; 159, 161
   fidelity; 151, 156, 162, 171
   modernisation; 157, 159
   resemblance; 155, 162
   transmediation; 150
   transnational; 157
   value; 151, 156
addition; 144
alterity. *See* Otherness
analogy; 44, 282, 284–285
animate object; 126
antilanguage; 217
appraisal; 183, 218–219, 227, 242, 245
Appraisal Theory; 218, *See also* evaluation
   Attitude; 219, 228–229, 233, 237, 239, 242–243
Aristotelian; 282, 286, 289, 297
Aristotle; 18, 282, 286
ars bene dicendi; 283
atrocities; 108, 112–113, 115, 118, *see also* genocide
attitude; 52–53, 78, 91, 100, 102, 116, 154, 158–159, 178, 218, 225, 237, 242, 292–293, 313

Becker, Howard; 26–27, 34, 64
Behan, Brendan; 28, 46
Bekas, Faiq; 105
Bekas, Sherko; 105
   Bekas' poetry; 107
Borstal Boy; 28
broadcast; 159, 168, 174–176, 178–179, 184, 186–191

camera shot; 203–204, 207, 209–210, 212
categorisation; 16–19, 26, 28, 36, 40, 46

categorise; 31–33, 60, 70, 76, 78–79, 102, 128, 208, 256–257, 264, 303, 322
censorship; 111
character-accessible; 177–178
characterisation; 162–163, 169, 187, 194
class. *See* category
class (social class); 28–29, 32, 36, 52, 62, 71, 73, 79–80, 214, 217, 243
clause
   coordinate; 139–140
   relative; 133, 135, 142, 144
   subordinate; 68, 83, 125, 129–130, 139–140, 145
cognitive effect; 114
   positive; 152, 156
Cognitive grammar; 114
cognitive metaphor. *See* conceptual metaphor
collocation; 32, 35, 75, 130, 133, 140, 302, 305–306, 309, 311
collocations; 306
collusive crossplay; 198, 200–202, 211
collusive sideplay; 198, 211
Comando Vermelho (CV); 216, 221–224, 226, 232
communicative act; 156, 159
Conan Doyle, Arthur; 62, 64, 150, 156, 159, 161–163, 165, 168–170
Conrad, Joseph; 25, 49
consciousness; 23, 70, 75, 83, 266
   locus of; 23
context; 19, 28, 45, 47, 49–50, 62, 67, 79, 82, 99, 111, 113–116, 123, 126–127, 133, 143, 150–153, 155, 158–159, 167–168, 174, 177, 186, 197, 203, 210, 214, 219–221, 224, 228, 245, 254, 256, 259, 269–272, 283, 285, 287, 289, 292, 294, 296–297, 305, 307, 311, 314, 317, 324, 326–327
conversational cooperation; 200, 210
conversational vigilance; 195–196, 206
cooperating witnesses; 195, 197, 202, 211
coordinate clause; 141
corpus analysis; 263

Index 333

crime
  institutionalised; 117
  violent; 127
crime fiction; 58–59, 61–62, 88–89, 102,
    121–122, 145–146
  conservative/mainstream crime fiction;
    57–58, 60–63, 77, 80
  critical, radical crime fiction; 59, 91,
    Chapter 15 *passim*
crime talk; 194–196, 200, 203–204, 208, 210–211
criminalisation; 220, 223–224
Critical Discourse Analysis; 218, 303, 327
culture; 17–18, 28, 40, 44, 47, 51, 60, 62, 64,
    72–73, 75, 80, 94, 99, 105–107, 115,
    118, 121, 150, 156–159, 161, 166–169,
    214–217, 220, 229, 232, 242, 244–245,
    256, 260, 288, 292–293, 316, 327
  of denial; 117
  club; 214
  consumer; 232
  contraculture; 27–28
  cultural relativity; 27
  cultural relevance; 162
  favela; 221, 235
  globalised; 232
  Japanese; 169
  popular; 214, 224, 288
  Soviet; 166
  subculture; 28, 217–218, 224, 246

defamiliarisation; 21
deixis; 68, 74, 76, 82, 110, 117–118, 125,
    177–181, 183, 193, 241
  social; 131
democracy; 106
demonisation; 21, 215
  demons; 21, 95–96, 98
departures
  perceptual; 184
  rhetorical; 184, 187–188, 190
  world-building; 188
depression; 50, 264
detective fiction; 150, 159–160, 169–170
Dickens, Charles; 44, 53
Direct Writing; 127, 129
discourse
  hegemonic; 102, 117–118, 217, 220
  media; 219, 222, 225, 232, 240, 243
  media; 90
  narrator's; 126
  of funk; 230
  participant; 116, 177, 179
  political; 117
  structures of; 174
  world; 177–179, 184–185, 187, 242

discrepancy
  stylistic; 145
Diwan (by Sherko Bekas); 108
drug gangs; 216–217, 219–225, 231, 244
dual number; 128

effect
  aesthetic; 167
  dramatic; 126, 237
  ethical; 191
  iconic; 143
  point of view; 190–191
  stylistic; 134, 138
  stylistic; 132
Elementary (CBS series); 157, 168
emotion; 21, 23–24, 49–50, 73–74, 76–77,
    79–84, 108, 113, 136, 144, 155, 175,
    177–178, 190, 218–220, 224, 227–228,
    241, 257–259, 264, 266, 272
enactor; 177–180, 182, 254
ethnicity; 19, 116, 118, *See also* race
evaluation
  evaluative; 40, 64, 68, 79, 180, 182–183,
    228–229, 235, 240, 268, 292–293, 320
  negative; 20, 27, 30, 34, 58, 66, 72, 74, 94,
    99, 320–321, 323
  neutral; 18, 134, 141, 190, 232, 283, 301
  positive; 18–21, 33, 35, 44, 46, 58, 65, 72,
    80, 111, 139, 216, 229–231, 234,
    236–237, 240–242, 245
  value judgement; 71
  values; 61, 65–67, 69, 72–73, 77, 84, 109,
    118, 162, 166–167, 217–218, 220, 230,
    232, 245
exclusion; 17–18, 40, 45–47, 49, 51–52, 140,
    166, 216–217, 220, 222, 224, 232, 241,
    243–246, 272, 274
explicitation; 125, 133, 143

Favela funk scene; 225
favelas; 214–217, 219–223, 225–226, 231,
    234, 236, 238, 240–242, 245
feminism; 77
focaliser; 67–68, 88, 91–95, 98–99, 101–102,
    137–138
foregrounding; 30, 32, 72, 82, 111–113,
    115–116, 186–187, 189–190, 305
Foucault, Michel; 40
Free Direct Writing; 129
function-advancing; 184, 190
funk
  baile; 218–219, 224, 226, 243
  culture; 219, 224–226, 229, 243
  dances225. *See baile funk*
  lyrics; 244

gaze; 100, 203–207, 209–212
gender; 63, 102, 180–181
Genette, Gérard; 137
genocide; 108, 116, *see also* atrocities
genre
   crime fiction; 157, 160, 170
   detective fiction; 150, 159–160, 169–170
   fanfiction; 156
   gothic fiction; 160
   preferences; 168
   pulp fiction; 158
   sensation fiction; 160
gesture; 207, 211, 273
Gillette, William; 163–164
golden thread; 288–289
graphic novel; 155–156, 160

Halabja; 105, 115
Halliday, M.A.K.; 29, 109, 114, 217–218, 241, 254
Heart of Darkness; 25–26
Hemingway, Ernest; 105
heterotopia; 40, 45
Hogan, Patrick Colm; 16, 20, 22–23, 32, 156
Holmes, Oliver Wendell; 296
Holmes, Sherlock (character); 58, 61, 64, 81, 121, 150, 156–157, 159, 162, 166
Hound of the Baskervilles, The (1981 Russian-language made-for-television film); 157
   Livanov, Vasilij (Holmes); 161, 164, 166
   Maslennikov, Igor (director); 157, 161–162, 164–167
   Mikhalkov, Nikita (Sir Henry Baskerville); 164
   Solomin, Vitali (Watson); 161, 164
Hound of the Baskervilles, The (by Arthur Conan Doyle); 159
   Baker Street; 165, 170
   Barrymore (character); 164, 165
   Baskerville Hall; 165
   Baskerville, Sir Henry (character); 163–164, 168
   Devonshire; 165, 168
   Lyons, Laura (character); 164, 168
human trafficking; 88–90, 102
Hussein, Saddam; 105

iconicity; 145
ideal victim; 90
identification; 70, 81, 117, 136, 175, 177, 184, 186, 190–191, 232, 241, 254, 267, 306, 323

identity; 23, 27, 30, 80, 89, 96, 144, 157, 162, 167, 214–217, 224, 227, 229–230, 232, 244, 246, 305, 316, 323
ideology; 28–33, 35, 39, 44, 48–49, 57–62, 64–65, 69–70, 72, 78, 80, 96, 99, 106–109, 112, 118, 166, 186, 190, 227, 229–230, 232, 243–244, 290, 292, 312
implications; 145, 151, 153, 175, 177, 184, 191, 195, 210, 264, 284
implicature; 32, 110, 116, 151–152, 159, 197–198, 201, 271–272, 311
   conversational; 197–198
inference; 126, 136, 138–139, 187
insurgent citizenship; 245
interpretation; 153–155, 162, 165–166
   intended; 152, 155–156
   non-spontaneous; 150, 152–156, 166, 170
inversion; 135, 174, 230
Iraq; 105
irony; 35, 66, 68, 72, 76, 79, 93–94, 102, 167, 174, 181–183, 188–191, 244

Japan
   contemporary (2017); 169
   Meiji-era; 157, 159
justice; 35, 51, 61, 106, 223, 282, 284, 286–287, 289, 297, 307, 309, 315

Kimmel, Michael; 25–26
Kurdish Liberation Movement; 107
Kurdistan; 105, 108, 117–118
Kurds; 105, 118

Lakoff, George; 17, 19, 21–23, 37–38, 109, 140, 283, 286, 289, 291, 293–294
language
   source; 154
   target; 121, 123, 125, 133, 154, 157
law; 283
legal positivism; 285–286, 297
legal realism; 285

Malmkjaer, Kirsten; 123, 146
Maré Favela Complex (Complexo da Maré); 224
maxim
   conversational; 152
   of quantity; 112
McLevy, James; 157
McReynolds, L.; 158, 166
mental disorder; 253–254, 257, 263
mental processes; 266
metafunctions
   of language; 109

Index 335

metaphor; 98, 112, 282
 as rhetorical figure; 50
 animal; 20, 32–34, 36, 46, 51, 53, 70, 72, 95–96, 98, 284, 289, 315, 319, 327
 biological; 70
 black/dark; 19, 28, 89, 97–98, 282, 294
 carceral; 39–40, 50–51
 conceptual; 19–21, 24–25, 32, 36, 40, 44, 95, 98–99, 116, 272–273, 282–283, 289, 295
 dead; 31, 291–292
 down; 98
 epistemological; 47, 50
 experiential; 47
 extended metaphor; 33
 legal; 283, 298
 megametaphor; 33
 penumbra; 296–298
 religious; 237
 war; 20, 24, 32–33, 36, 219, 222, 228, 237, 241, 243
metonymy; 16, 18–19, 22, 29, 32, 34–36, 45, 48, 52, 70, 73, 100–101, 112, 126, 177, 180, 182, 186, 236, 242, 274, 282
 metonymy and the Other; 18–19
mind style; 91, 194, 253–256, 258–259, 266–267, 270, 272–274
mind-modelling; 186–188, 190, 268–270, 272, 274
mise-en-scène; 165, 169
Miss Sherlock (HBO-Asia series); 157–158, 169
 Tachibana, Wato-san (character); 158
 Takeuchi, Yūko; 169
Moby Dick; 24
modality; 30, 68, 79, 99–102, 116, 132, 145, 177, 189, 263, 269–271, 293, 313, 316–318, 320, 325
 deontic; 91, 181, 183, 316–317, 320
 epistemic; 25, 130, 177–183, 189, 268, 270, 272, 274, 312–313, 325
modern slavery; 90–91
More, Sir Thomas; 43
Murders in the Rue Morgue, The; 121–123, 128, 145
mystery; 123

naming; 91, 94, 102, 110–113, 116–117, 136
narrative strategy; 72
narrator
 first-person; 117, 123
negation; 110, 115–116, 271–272
Nepomnyashchy, C. T.; 157, 161, 164, 166–167
neurolinguistics; 255, 257
Nil by Mouth; 28

offender; 111
omission; 131, 138, 144
opposition
 binary ~; 109, 111, 117–118
Orwell, George; 52
ostensive; 153–154
Othello; 23
Otherness; 32
 alterity; 27, 71
 Alterity; 26–28
 conceptualisation of; 16–26, 35, 52, 95–96, 98, 158
 outsider; 27, 164, 230–231
 stereotyping the Other; 19, 36
 the Other; 34, 36

Paget, Sidney; 163–165, 170
parallelism; 16, 35, 43, 79, 110–111, 181, 188–189, 231, 235–236
parody; 151, 154, 186–189
participation framework; 195, 202
patriarchy; 28, 44, 47, 49
pattern
 syntactic; 126, 143
perception
 mental; 132, 268
 subjective; 144
perspective; 23, 43–44, 46, 53, 107–108, 111, 114, 140, 151, 153–154, 177, 187, 190, 202, 205, 211, 215, 218, 229, 236, 240, 253, 269, 284, 286, 289, 297, *See also* attitude, point of view, stance, standpoint, narratological. *See also point of view*
Peshmerga; 105
phrase
 nominal; 125
 prepositional; 70, 111, 125, 129, 131, 136, 138, 143
plot-advancing; 179, 188
Poe, Edgar Allan; 121–124, 150
poetry
 Kurdish; 105–107
point of view; 58, 70, 116, 122, 128, 153, 193, 203, 205, 207, 209, 254, 260, 269, 283–284, 293
presupposition; 76, 110, 116, 271
proibidão; 214–215, 217, 221, 238, 242–245
projection
 psychological; 24
pronoun
 personal; 255
 personal; 117, 134, 236, 264, 266
props; 162, 164, 204–205

Putilin, Ivan Dmitrievich (*Forty Years among Robbers and Murderers*, autobiography); 157–158

Quirk, Randolph; 130, 135, 140

race; 94, 102, 180, 186, 243, 245
racism; 20, 63, 66, 70, 77, 79, 93, 160, 170
Rathbone, Basil; 164, 170
realism; 89, 107, 164
reception; 121–122, 167, 174, 191
recontextualisation; 219, 229, 235, 240
recontextualise; 214, 216, 219, 223, 227, 231, 237–238, 240, 242, 245
recontextualisation; 35
reframing; 190
register
  formal; 131
  verb; 131
relevance theory; 151–153
  cognitive effort; 150–151, 153, 156
  communicative intentions; 153, 160
  contextual effects; 155
  contextual premises; 153, 155
  global inferences; 153, 156
  manifest; 151
  maximal relevance; 153
  optimal relevance; 152
  principle of relevance; 152
  relevance (property); 152
  relevance theoretic comprehension protocol; 155
Russia
  imperial; 157, 159
  Soviet; 159
  Soviet Union; 161, 164, 170
Rwanga; 106

salience; 209, 287
Sartre; 22
schizophrenia,; 253, 264, 267
Série Noire; 121
Shakespeare, William; 23, 62, 72, 84, 282
Sherlock (BBC-TV series); 157, 168–169
  Cumberbatch, Benedict; 169
silence; 202, 206–207, 211
Sillitoe, Alan; 28, 255
Simpson, Paul; 84, 100, 111, 116, 132, 136, 144, 174, 242, 292
Sinclair, Upton; 51
Slovenian; 121–123, 127–132, 134–135, 140, 145–146
Speech and Thought Presentation
  direct speech; 64, 68–69, 117, 175–176, 180–184, 190, 306

Free Direct Speech; 35, 92–93, 98, 180–182
Free Direct Thought; 69, 76–77, 79–80, 82–83
Free Indirect Speech; 92–93
Free Indirect Thought; 64, 68–70, 74, 76, 82–83
narration; 67–70, 72–73, 75–76, 79–80, 83, 91–92, 94–95, 98–100, 102, 125, 236
Narrative Report of Speech Act; 68
Sperber, Dan; 288
Systemic Functional Grammar; 114
staccato; 143
stance; 28, 58, 60–61, 63, 65–66, 69, 72–74, 77, 80, 167, 177, 180–184, 237, *See also* attitude; evaluation; point of view
status
  social; 77, 79, 131, 168, 264
stereotype; 18–19, 52, 65, 81, 90, 102, 161, 164, 188, 198, 219, 225, 241
stigmatisation; 6, 18–19, 36, 220, 225, 238, 244–245
story
  detective; 59–60, 121–123, 145, 150, 159–160, 169–170
Strand, The; 157
stylistics
  multimodal; 194, 208, 210, 212
Stylistics
  Critical; 107–110, 114
subject-self relationship; 23–24, 36
syllogism
  Aristotelian; 286, 289, 297
symptoms; 241, 258, 261
Systemic Functional Grammar; 114, 218
  behavioural processes; 189
  material action
    material action intention processes; 266
  material processes; 29, 34, 80, 99, 112–113, 181–182, 189, 266, 268, 274, 324
  material intention processes; 318
  material intention processes; 318
  mental processes; 84, 132, 263, 266, 268, 270, 272, 274
  mental cognition processes; 266
  mental perception processes; 113, 140, 144, 266, 268, 273, 318
  mental reaction processes; 266, 268
  processes; 268

Tantei Jitsuroku (*Real Tales of Detection*); 157
testimonial; 174–176, 180, 184, 186–187, 189–191
text world; 138, 180, 203, 254
  architecture; 178

Index 337

empty; 180
epistemic; 180
Text World Theory; 175–176
textual-conceptual function; 109
The Loneliness of the Long Distance Runner; 28
the Self; 22–25, 36, 268, 271–272, 274
The Small Mirrors (by Sherko Bekas); 105–109, 116, 118
transformation; 115
transitivity; 79, 91, 99, 103, 112, 125, 133, 140, 144–145, 254–255, 266, 313
translation; 150–151, 154–155
  shift; 121, 134, 145
  translator; 157, 170
Tsutsumibayashi, M.; 157

value judgment. *See* evaluation
verb
  factive; 113

victim; 88–91, 94, 101–103, 111
  ideal; 90, 102–103, 113, 118
victimisation; 116, 118, 174, 180, 184, 187–188, 190–191
  indirect; 111
victims; 99
violence
  domestic; 231
  physical; 245
  structural; 245
  symbolic; 216, 220, 224, 245
voice-over; 174, 176, 179–180, 182, 184, 187–189, 191
Voltaire; 286

Watson, John (character); 158, 169
Werth, Paul; 174, 176–177
Wilson, Deirdre; 288
world-switch; 178–180, 182–183
worldview; 35, 44, 58, 60–61, 65–66, 68–69, 71, 178